The Princeton Review®

MCAT®

Elite:
Advanced Strategies for a 45

The Staff of The Princeton Review

Random House, Inc. New York

The Princeton Review, Inc.
2315 Broadway
New York, NY 10024
E-mail: editorialsupport@review.com

Terms of Service: The Princeton Review Online Companion Tools ("Online Companion Tools") for the *Cracking* book series and *MCAT Elite: Advanced Strategies for a 45* are available for the most recent edition. Online Companion Tools may be activated only once per eligible book purchased. Activation of Online Companion Tools more than once per book is in direct violation of these Terms of Service and may result in discontinuation of access to Online Companion Tools Services.

ISBN: 978-0-375-42797-8
ISSN: 2150-878X

Sr. Author: Judene Wright
Editor: Rebecca Lessem
Production Coordinator: Kim Howie
Production Editor: Meave Shelton

Printed in the United States of America on partially recycled paper

10 9 8 7 6 5 4 3 2 1

Editorial

Rob Franek, VP Test Prep Books, Publisher
Seamus Mullarkey, Editorial Director
Laura Braswell, Senior Editor
Rebecca Lessem, Senior Editor
Heather Brady, Editor
Selena Coppock, Editor

Production Services

Scott Harris, Executive Director, Production Services
Kim Howie, Senior Graphic Designer
Ryan Tozzi, Production Manager

Production Editorial

Meave Shelton, Production Editor
Jennifer Graham, Production Editor
Kristen O'Toole, Production Editor

Random House Publishing Team

Tom Russell, Publisher
Nicole Benhabib, Publishing Manager
Ellen L. Reed, Production Manager
Alison Stoltzfus, Associate Managing Editor

ACKNOWLEDGMENTS

The Princeton Review would like to acknowledge the very significant contributions of the following individuals:

Judene Wright, M.S., M.A.Ed. - Senior Author

Bethany Blackwell, M.S. – Organic Chemistry
Katherine Miller, M.S. – General Chemistry
Carolyn Shiau, M.D. – Physics
Jennifer Wooddell – Verbal Reasoning and Writing Sample

Without their unfailing dedication to this project and endless hours of work, this book, quite literally, would not have been written.

The author would also like to acknowledge the contributions of the members of the MCAT Development teams for not only some of the text of the book, but more importantly, for the writing and editing of the practice sections:

MCAT Biology:

Jessica Adams, M.S., John Bahling, M.D., Kristen Brunson, Ph.D., Josh Dilworth, M.D., Ph.D., Chris Fortenbach, B.S., Sarah Woodruff, M.S., Judene Wright, M.S., M.A.Ed.

MCAT G-Chem:

Katherine Miller, M.S., Patrick Abulencia, Ph.D., Bethany Blackwell, M.S., Bill Ewing, Ph.D.

MCAT O-Chem:

Bethany Blackwell, M.S., Kristen Brunson, Ph.D., Bill Ewing, Ph.D., Karen Salazar, Ph.D.

MCAT Physics:

Carolyn Shiau, M.D., Jon Fowler, M.A., Chris Pentzell, M.S., Teri Stewart, B.S.E.

MCAT Verbal:

Jennifer Wooddell, Alix Claps, M.A., Gina Granter, M.A.

Finally, the author would like to acknowledge the work of the Princeton Review MCAT teachers, who contributed passages and FSQs for the practice sections:

Elizabeth Aamot, Kashif Anwar, M.D., M.M.S., Farhad Aziz, B.S., Gary Bedford, Jessica Burstrem, M.A., Brian Butts, B.S., B.A., Argun Can, Phil Carpenter, Ph.D., Brian Cato, Khawar Chaudry, B.S., Nita Chauhan, H.BSc., MSc., Dan Cho, M.P.H., Cynthia Cowan, B.A., Sarah Daniel, B.S., Nathan Deal, M.D., Ian Denham, B.Sc., B.Ed., Annie Dude, Amanda Edward, H.B.Sc., H.B.Ed., Cory Eicher, B.A., Robert Fong, M.D., Ph.D., Chris Fortenbach, B.S., Kirsten Frank, Ph.D., Ben Gill, Carlos Guzman, Christopher Hinkle, Th.D., Alison Howard, B.A., James Hudson, B.S., B.A., Isabel L. Jackson, B.S., Ryan Katchky, Jason N. Kennedy, M.S., Omair Adil Khan, Erik Kildebeck, Paul Kugelmass, George Kyriazis, Ph.D., Ben Lee, Jay Lee, Brendan Lloyd, B.Sc., Travis MacKoy, Rohit Madani, B.S., Neil Maluste, B.S., Joey Mancuso, M.S., D.O., Ashley Manzoor, Ph.D., Janet Marshall, Ph.D., Evan Martow, BMSc., Mike Matera, B.A., Doug McLemore, Marion-Vincent L. Mempin, B.S., Donna Memran, Ashleigh Menhadji, B.A., B.S., Al Mercado, Brian Mikolasko, M.D., M.B.A., Katherine Miller, B.A., Abhisehk Mohapatra, B.A., Katherine Montgomery, Chris Moriates, M.D., Tenaya Newkirk, Ph.D., Jason Osman, M.S., Gina Passante, Rupal Patel, B.S., Vivek Patel, B.S., Tyler Peikes, Mary Qiu, Chris Rabbat, Ph.D., Nadia Reynolds, M.A., Jayson Sack, M.D., Will Sanderson, Jeanine Seitz-Partridge, M.S., Sina Shahbaz, B.S., Maryam Shambayati, M.S., Mark Shew, H.B.Sc., Gillian Shiau, M.D., Angela Song, Kate Speiker, Teri Stewart, B.S.E., David Stoll, Dylan Sweeney, Preston Swirnoff, Ph.D., Jonathan Swirsky, B.S., Felicia Tam, Ph.D., Rhead Uddin, Danish Vaiyani, Jia Wang, Tom Watts, B.A., David Weiskopf, M.A., Barry Weliver, Sarah Woodruff, B.S., B.A., Hesham Zakaria.

Periodic Table of the Elements

1 H 1.0																	2 He 4.0
3 Li 6.9	4 Be 9.0											5 B 10.8	6 C 12.0	7 N 14.0	8 O 16.0	9 F 19.0	10 Ne 20.2
11 Na 23.0	12 Mg 24.3											13 Al 27.0	14 Si 28.1	15 P 31.0	16 S 32.1	17 Cl 35.5	18 Ar 39.9
19 K 39.1	20 Ca 40.1	21 Sc 45.0	22 Ti 47.9	23 V 50.9	24 Cr 52.0	25 Mn 54.9	26 Fe 55.8	27 Co 58.9	28 Ni 58.7	29 Cu 63.5	30 Zn 65.4	31 Ga 69.7	32 Ge 72.6	33 As 74.9	34 Se 79.0	35 Br 79.9	36 Kr 83.8
37 Rb 85.5	38 Sr 87.6	39 Y 88.9	40 Zr 91.2	41 Nb 92.9	42 Mo 95.9	43 Tc [98]	44 Ru 101.1	45 Rh 102.9	46 Pd 106.4	47 Ag 107.9	48 Cd 112.4	49 In 114.8	50 Sn 118.7	51 Sb 121.8	52 Te 127.6	53 I 126.9	54 Xe 131.3
55 Cs 132.9	56 Ba 137.3	57 *La 138.9	72 Hf 178.5	73 Ta 180.9	74 W 183.9	75 Re 186.2	76 Os 190.2	77 Ir 192.2	78 Pt 195.1	79 Au 197.0	80 Hg 200.6	81 Tl 204.4	82 Pb 207.2	83 Bi 209.0	84 Po [209]	85 At [210]	86 Rn [222]
87 Fr [223]	88 Ra 226.0	89 †Ac 227.0	104 Rf [261]	105 Db [262]	106 Sg [266]	107 Bh [264]	108 Hs [277]	109 Mt [268]	110 DS [281]	111 Rg [272]	112 Cp [285]		114 Uuq [289]		116 Uuh [289]		

*Lanthanide Series:

58 Ce 140.1	59 Pr 140.9	60 Nd 144.2	61 Pm [145]	62 Sm 150.4	63 Eu 152.0	64 Gd 157.3	65 Tb 158.9	66 Dy 162.5	67 Ho 164.9	68 Er 167.3	69 Tm 168.9	70 Yb 173.0	71 Lu 175.0

†Actinide Series:

90 Th 232.0	91 Pa [231]	92 U 238.0	93 Np [237]	94 Pu [244]	95 Am [243]	96 Cm [247]	97 Bk [247]	98 Cr [251]	99 Es [252]	100 Fm [257]	101 Md [258]	102 No [259]	103 Lr [260]

CONTENTS

CONTENTS

Chapter 1
Welcome to *MCAT Elite*

If you're buying this book, you already have some experience with the MCAT. You've studied using your school science textbooks, perhaps even used test preparation books or took preparation courses, you have a solid grasp of science content, and you've done reasonably well on the practice tests and problems you've been given. But you're not satisfied. You want to do better than "reasonably well." You want to improve and get those last few points. You want to take your MCAT score to the next level.

Succeeding on the MCAT requires a combination of content knowledge, critical reasoning, and reading comprehension skills. Be aware that this book is not intended as content review...we assume you know your science content and verbal strategies. (However, if you need to review any of the science content areas or verbal reasoning and writing strategies, consider our other books in the *MCAT Review* series.) *MCAT Elite* is designed to help you brush up on your passage reading and analysis skills, hone your test-taking abilities, and learn how to analyze the results of your practice exams to identify your weaknesses so you can improve. By learning how to identify problem areas, you can make your MCAT preparation as efficient and effective as possible. You can bring your score up a few crucial notches and enter the realm of the MCAT Elite.

WHAT IS THE MCAT...REALLY?

Most test takers approach the MCAT as though it were a typical college science test, where they just have to regurgitate facts and knowledge in order to do well. They study for the MCAT the same way they did for their college tests, by memorizing facts and details, formulas and equations. And when they get to the MCAT they are surprised...and disappointed in their scores.

It's a myth that the MCAT is purely a test of knowledge. If medical school admission committees want to see what you know from college, all they have to do is look at your transcripts. What they really want to see, though, is how you *think*. Especially, how you think under pressure. And *that's* what your MCAT score will tell them.

The MCAT is really a test of your ability to apply basic knowledge to different, possibly new, situations. It's a test of your ability to reason out and evaluate arguments. It's a test of your ability to communicate ideas. Do you still need to know your science content? Absolutely. But not at the level that most test takers think they need to know it. Furthermore, your science knowledge won't help you on the Verbal Reasoning or Writing Sample sections, which many students forget to practice for. So how do you study for a test like this?

You study for the science sections by reviewing the basics and then applying them to MCAT practice questions. You study for the Verbal Reasoning section by learning how to adapt your existing reading and analytical skills to the nature of the test. And once you've done that, you hone your skills by reviewing your practice tests and analyzing your weaknesses to target your ongoing study to your specific needs.

The book you are holding will teach you how to review and analyze your practice tests, it includes hundreds of the most difficult MCAT questions designed to make you think about the material in a deeper way, and it includes full explanations to clarify the logical thought processes needed to get to the answer. And, since the MCAT is a computer-based test, this book also comes with online access to hundreds of additional practice questions and two full-length practice exams to further hone your skills. After all, what better way to practice for a computer-based test than with computer-based practice questions?

Chapter 2
MCAT Nuts and Bolts

OVERVIEW

The MCAT is a computer-based test (CBT) that is *not* adaptive. Adaptive tests base your next question on whether or not you've answered the current question correctly. The MCAT is *linear*, or *fixed-form*, meaning that the questions are in a predetermined order and do not change based on your answers. However, there are many versions of the test so that on a given test day, different people will see different versions (and can't cheat off the computer next to them). The following table highlights important facts about taking the MCAT exam.

Registration	Online via www.aamc.org. Begins as early as six months prior to test date; available up until week of test (subject to seat availability).
Testing Centers	Administered at small, secure, climate-controlled computer testing rooms.
Security	Photo ID with signature, electronic fingerprint, electronic signature verification, assigned seat.
Proctoring	None. Test administrator checks examinee in and assigns seat at computer. All testing instructions are given on the computer.
Frequency of Test	28 times per year distributed over January, March, April, May, June, July, August, and September.
Format	Exclusively computer-based. NOT an adaptive test.
Length of Test Day	5.5 hours.
Breaks	Optional 10-minute breaks between sections.
Number of Questions and Timing	52 Physical Sciences (PS), 70 minutes. 40 Verbal Reasoning (VR), 60 minutes. 2 Essays for the Writing Sample (WS), 30 minutes each. 52 Biological Sciences (BS), 70 minutes.
Essay Grading	Two graders, one human and one computer, with a third (human) grader if scores differ.
Scoring	Test is scaled. Several forms per administration. PS, VR, and BS receive scaled scores of 1–15, WS receives scaled score of J–T.
Allowed/Not allowed	No timers/watches. No ear plugs. Noise reduction headphones available. Scratch paper and pencils given at start of test and taken at end of test. Locker or secure area provided for personal items.
Results: Timing and Delivery	Approximately 30 days. Electronic scores only, available online through AAMC login. Examinees can print official score reports.
Maximum Number of Retakes	Can be taken a maximum of three times per year, but an examinee can be registered for only one date at a time.

REGISTRATION

You can register for the exam online at www.aamc/org/students/mcat. The AAMC opens registration for a given test date at least two months in advance of the date, often earlier. It's a good idea to register well in advance of your desired test date to make sure that you get a seat.

SECTIONS

There are four sections on the MCAT exam: Physical Sciences (PS), Verbal Reasoning (VR), Writing Sample (WS), and Biological Sciences (BS). The PS, VR, and BS sections consist of multiple-choice questions, while the WS section consists of two essays.

Section	Concepts Tested	Number of Questions and Timing
Physical Sciences	Basic concepts in physics and general chemistry, data analysis, basic non-calculus math, critical reasoning skills.	52 questions, 70 minutes, approximately 50% physics and 50% general chemistry.
Verbal Reasoning	Reading comprehension and critical thinking.	40 questions, 60 minutes.
Writing Sample	Organizational skills and written communication.	2 essay prompts, 30 minutes each.
Biological Sciences	Basic concepts in biology and organic chemistry, data analysis, critical reasoning skills.	52 questions, 70 minutes, approximately 80% biology and 20% organic chemistry.

Most questions on the MCAT (39 out of 52 on the science sections, and all 40 in the VR section) are *passage based*, and each section of the test will have a total of seven passages. A passage consists of a few paragraphs of information on which several following questions are focused. In the science sections, passages often include equations or reactions, tables, graphs, figures, and experiments to analyze. Verbal Reasoning passages come from literature in the social sciences, humanities, and natural sciences and do not test content knowledge in any way.

Some questions in the science sections are *freestanding questions* (FSQs). These questions are independent of any passage information. They appear in three groups of between 3 and 5 questions each, and are interspersed throughout the passages in each section. There are 13 freestanding questions in each of the science sections and the remaining 39 questions are passage-based.

Each section on the MCAT is separated by a 10-minute break. Here is the breakdown of how your test day will look:

Section	Time
Test Center Check-In	Variable, can take up to 40 minutes if center is busy.
Tutorial	10 minutes
Physical Sciences	70 minutes
Break	10 minutes
Verbal Reasoning	60 minutes
Break	10 minutes
Writing Sample	60 minutes
Break	10 minutes
Biological Sciences	70 minutes
Void Option	5 minutes
Survey	10 minutes

The survey includes questions about your satisfaction with the overall MCAT experience, including registration, and check-in, as well as questions about how you prepared for the test.

SCORING

The MCAT is a scaled exam, meaning that your raw score will be converted into a scaled score that takes into account the difficulty of the questions. There is no guessing penalty. The PS, VR, and BS sections are scaled from 1–15 and the WS section is scaled from J–T. Because different versions of the test have varying levels of difficulty, the scale will be different from one exam to the next. Thus, there is no "magic number" of questions to get right in order to get a particular score. Plus, some of the questions on the test are considered "experimental" and do not count toward your score; they are just there to be evaluated for possible future inclusion in a test.

To generate a score for the WS section, each essay is scored twice, and the total raw score is the sum of the four individual scores. The individual scores can range from 1–6. The total numerical score is then converted to an alphabetic score from J (lowest) to T (highest).

At the end of the test (after you complete the Biological Science section), you will be asked to choose one of the following two options: "I wish to have my MCAT exam scored" or "I wish to VOID my MCAT exam." You have five minutes to make a decision, and if you do not select one of the options in that time, the test will automatically be scored. If you choose the VOID option, your test will not be scored (you will not now, or ever, get a numerical score for this test), medical schools will not know you took the test, and no refunds will be granted. You cannot "unvoid" your scores at a later time.

Even though we can't tell you a specific number of questions to get right in order to receive a particular score, we can tell you the percentile numbers that the scores correspond with. The percentile numbers tell you what percent of examinees scored lower or higher than you. For example, if you are in the 90th percentile, then 90 percent of examinees scored lower than you did, and 10 percent scored higher.

Score	Physical Sciences Percentile*	Verbal Reasoning Percentile*	Biological Sciences Percentile*
14–15	100%	100%	100%
13	97%	99%	97%
12	91%	96%	92%
11	82%	91%	80%
10	69%	75%	64%
9	52%	53%	41%
8	37%	35%	23%
7	22%	22%	12%
6	11%	14%	7%
5	4%	7%	4%
4	2%	4%	2%
3	1%	2%	1%
2	0%	1%	0%
1	0%	0%	0%

Avg score 9.3, std dev 2.3   Avg score 9.0, std dev 2.3   Avg score 9.8, std dev 2.1

Total Score	Percentile*	Writing Sample Score	Percentile*
42–45	100	T	100
39	99	S	99
36	95	R	93
33	85	Q	81
30	66	P	60
27	43	O	49
24	25	N	35
21	13	M	25
18	6	L	6
15	3	K	2
12	1	J	0
9	0		
6	0		
3	0		

Avg score 28.1, std dev 5.6

75th percentile = Q
50th percentile = P
25th percentile = M

*Data from *The Official Guide to the MCAT Exam*, 2009 ed., © 2009 Association of American Medical Colleges

So, what's a good score? Most people would agree that since the average total score on the MCAT is around 28, you want to at least hit that number. To be competitive, you really want scores in the low 30s, and for the top-ranked medical schools, you'll want scores in the high 30s or 40s. If your GPA is on the low side, you'll need higher MCAT scores to compensate, and if you have a strong GPA, you can get away with lower MCAT scores. But the reality is that your chances of acceptance depend on a lot more than just your MCAT scores. It's a combination of your GPA, your MCAT scores, your undergraduate coursework, letters of recommendation, experience related to the medical field (such as volunteer work or research), extracurricular activities, and your personal statement. Medical schools are looking for a complete package, not just good scores and a good GPA.

PREPARATION

Academic preparation for the MCAT should include one year each of physics, general chemistry, organic chemistry, and biology. Specific topic lists for each subject can be found in their respective chapters in this book; you should peruse these lists and if you find any subject in which your knowledge is deficient, you should review that material. Note however, that this book does not include content review. We recommend The Princeton Review's *MCAT Review* series for science content review. Since the Verbal Reasoning section is not content-based, there is no specific coursework to take to prepare yourself, however any course that requires you to read high-level content can help. Again, The Princeton Review's *MCAT Verbal Reasoning & Writing Review* can provide in-depth coverage of strategies and techniques for this section.

Chapter 3
MCAT Strategies

In this chapter, we'll teach some strategies that apply to any section of the MCAT and can improve your test-taking skills in general.

PASSAGE TYPES

In the science sections of the MCAT, the passages fall into one of three main categories.

1. Information and/or Situation presentation: This type of passage either presents straightforward scientific facts or describes a particular event/occurrence. Questions associated with these passages ask you to answer basic science facts, or predict outcomes if variables are changed, etc.
2. Experiment/Research presentation: This type of passage presents the details of an experiment or some research procedure. It often includes data in the form of tables or graphs. Questions ask you to interpret data, draw conclusions, and make inferences.
3. Persuasive Reasoning: This type of passage describes a scientific phenomenon and a hypothesis to explain it. Often there may be a counter-argument presented as well. Questions ask you to evaluate the arguments.

Verbal reasoning passages also fall into three main groups, based on the content they are derived from.

1. Natural Sciences and Technology (geology, computer science, botany, etc.): These passages tend to center on factual scientific knowledge and straightforward presentation of material.
2. Humanities (art, music, literature, religion, etc.): These passages tend to focus on ideas and how they connect to one another, and may include authors' opinions.
3. Social Sciences (political science, psychology, economics, etc.): These passages often center on interpretation or implications of social science research, and can be based on studies about particular social or cultural groups. They can include complex ideas and events.

More details on passage types will be discussed in each of the subject sections.

QUESTION TYPES

In the science sections of the MCAT, the questions fall into one of three main categories:

1. Memory questions: These questions can be answered directly from prior knowledge and represent about 25 percent of the total number of questions.
2. Explicit questions: These questions are those for which the answer is explicitly stated in the passage. To answer them correctly, for example, may just require finding a definition, or reading a graph, or making a simple connection. Explicit questions represent about 35–40 percent of the total number of questions.
3. Implicit questions: These questions require you to apply knowledge to a new situation or make a more complex connection. The answer is typically implied by the information in the passage. These questions often start "if…then…" (for example, "if we modify the experiment in the passage like this, then what result would we expect?"). Implicit style questions make up about 35–40 percent of the total number of questions.

In the Verbal Reasoning section, the questions also fall into three main categories:

1. Specific questions: These questions ask you for specific information from the passage, such as a fact (Retrieval question), an inference ("which of the following is best supported by the passage?"), or a definition (Vocabulary-in-Context question).
2. General questions: These questions ask you to summarize themes (Main Idea and Primary Purpose questions) or evaluate an author's opinion (tone/attitude questions).
3. Complex questions: These are typically more difficult questions that can ask you to do a number of different things. Generally, Complex questions will ask you to do one of the following: consider how the author constructs his/her argument (Structure questions), decide how or how well the author supports his/her argument (Evaluate questions), decide which answer most supports or undermines the author's argument (Strengthen/Weaken questions), evaluate how new facts or scenarios relate to or affect the author's points (New Information questions), or apply the author's argument to a new situation (Analogy questions). These questions generally take the longest to answer.

More details on question types will be discussed in each of the subject sections.

Remember that for all sections, you should do the questions in the order you want to. In the science sections, it's wise to do all the FSQs first since they are often quick memory questions, and then tackle the passages. Start with the subject you feel the most comfortable with, and then come back to the other subject. This helps keep your brain focused on a single subject at a time, instead of jumping, for example, between biology and organic chemistry randomly. Do the passages within a section in the order that you feel most comfortable with, and within the passages themselves, tackle the easier questions and get the quick points first, leaving the most time-consuming problems for last.

In the Verbal Reasoning section, it is best to do the Specific questions within a passage first, then the General questions (after you have learned more about the passage by answering the Specific questions), and to leave the Complex questions until the end of the set. For the section as a whole, answer the questions for the easier passages in your first "pass" through the section, and then come back for a second pass, completing some of the more difficult passages.

CBT TOOLS

There are a number of tools available on the test, including highlighting, strike-outs, the Mark button, the Review button, the Exhibit button, Writing Sample tools, and of course, scratch paper. The following is a brief description of each tool.

1. Highlighting: This is done in passage text (including table entries and some equations, but excluding figures and molecular structures) by clicking and dragging the cursor over the desired text. To remove the highlighted portion, just click over the highlighted text. Note that highlights DO NOT remain once you click away from the passage.

2. Strike-outs: This is done on the various answer choices by clicking over the answer choice that you wish to eliminate. As a result, the entire set of text associated with that answer choice is crossed out. The strike-out can be removed by clicking again. Note that you cannot strike out figures or molecular structures, and strike-outs DO persist after leaving the passage.

3. Mark button: This is available for each question and allows you to flag the question as one you would like to review later if time permits. When clicked, the Mark button turns red and says "Marked."

4. Review button: This button is found near the bottom of the screen, and when clicked, brings up a new screen showing all questions and their status (either "answered," "unanswered," or "marked"). You can then choose one of three options: "review all," "review unanswered," or "review marked." You can only review questions in the section of the MCAT you are currently taking, but this button can be clicked at any time during the allotted time for that section; you do NOT have to wait until the end of the section to click it.

5. Exhibit button: Clicking this button will open a periodic table. Note that the periodic table is originally large, covering most of the screen. However, this window can be resized to see the questions and a portion of the periodic table at the same time. The table text will not decrease, but scroll bars will appear on the window so you can center the section of the table you wish to see in the window.

6. Writing Sample: Simple cutting, copying, and pasting will be allowed in this section through the use of buttons on the screen, but no keyboard shortcuts are available. There is no spell-check.

7. Scratch Paper: You will be given four pages (8 faces) of scratch paper at the start of the test. While you may ask for more at any point during the test, your first set of paper will be collected before you receive fresh paper. Scratch paper is only useful if it is kept organized; do not give in to the tendency to write on the first available open space! Good organization will be very helpful when/if you wish to review a question. Indicate the passage number in a box near the top of your scratch work, and indicate which question you are working on in a circle to the left of the notes for that question. Draw a line under your scratch work when you change passages to keep the work separate. Do not erase or scribble over any previous work. If you do not think it is correct, draw one line through the work and start again. You may have already done some useful work without realizing it.

PASSAGE MAPPING

In general, an MCAT passage should not be read like textbook material, with the intent of learning something from every sentence (science majors especially will be tempted to read this way). Passages should be read to get a feel for the type of questions that will follow and to get a general idea of the location of information within the passage. This will allow you to create a passage "map," with the most critical information summarized on your scratch paper. More details on passage mapping will be discussed in the subject sections.

Use the highlighting tool sparingly, or you will end up with a passage that is completely covered in yellow highlighter! Remember that highlighting does not persist as you move from passage to passage within the section. If you want to make more permanent notes, use your scratch paper.

1. For each paragraph, note "P1," "P2," etc. on the scratch paper and jot down a few notes about that paragraph. Try to translate the information in the paragraph into your own words using everyday language. Be sure to note down simple relationships (e.g., the relationship between two variables).
2. Lists: Whenever a list appears in paragraph form, jot down on the scratch paper the paragraph and the general topic of the list. It will make returning to the passage more efficient and help to organize your thoughts.

Again, remember that scratch paper is only useful if it is kept organized! Make sure that your notes for each passage are clearly delineated and marked with the passage number. This will allow you to easily read your notes when you come back to review a marked question.

PACING

Since the MCAT is a timed test, you must keep an eye on the timer and adjust your pacing as necessary. It would be terrible to run out of time at the end only to discover that you could have easily answered the last few questions in just a few seconds each.

If you complete every question, in the science sections you will have about one minute and twenty seconds (1:20) per question, and in the Verbal Reasoning section you will have about one minute and thirty seconds per question (1:30).

Section	# of Questions in Passage	Approximate time (minutes)
Physical Sciences and Biological Sciences	5	6.5–7 minutes
	6	8 minutes
	7	9–9.5 minutes
Verbal Reasoning	5	7.5 minutes
	6	9 minutes
	7	10.5 minutes

When starting a passage in the science sections, make note of how much time you will allot for it, and the starting time on the timer. Jot down on your scratch paper what the timer should say at the end of the passage. Then just keep an eye on it as you work through the questions. If you are near the end of the time for that passage, *guess* (there is no penalty) on any remaining questions, make some notes on your scratch paper (remember that highlighting disappears), "Mark" the questions (so you can come back later if there's time), and *move on*.

For Verbal Reasoning, most people will maximize their score by not trying to complete every question, or every passage, in the section. A good strategy for a majority of test takers is to complete six of the seven passages, randomly guessing on one passage. This allows you the time to have good accuracy on the passages you complete and to maximize your total percent correct in the section as a whole. To complete six of the passages, you should spend about 8 minutes on a five-question passage, 9 minutes on a six-question passage, and 10 minutes on a seven-question passage. That is, a total of about 3 minutes plus 1 minute for each question (# of questions + 3).

To increase your points in any section, do the questions and passages in the order you want to do them in. Skip over the more difficult questions (guess and "Mark" them), and answer the questions you feel most comfortable with first.

PROCESS OF ELIMINATION

Process of Elimination (POE) is probably the most useful technique to tackle MCAT questions. Since there is no guessing penalty, POE allows you to increase your probability of choosing the correct answer by eliminating those you are sure are wrong. If you are guessing between a couple of choices, use the CBT tools on your screen to your advantage:

1. Strike out any choices that you are sure are incorrect or do not answer the issue addressed in the question.
2. Jot down some notes on your scratch paper to help clarify your thoughts if you return to the question.
3. Use the "Mark" button to flag the question for review at a later time. (Note, however, that in the Verbal Reasoning section, you generally should not be returning to rethink questions once you have moved on to a new passage.)
4. Do not leave it blank! If you are not sure and you have already spent more than 60 seconds on that question, just pick one of the remaining choices. If you have time to review it at the end, you can always debate the remaining choices based on your previous notes.
5. Special note: if three of the four answer choices have been eliminated, the remaining choice must be the correct answer. Don't waste time pondering *why* it is correct, just click it and move on. The MCAT doesn't care if you truly understand why it's the right answer, only that you have the right answer selected.

GUESSING

Remember, there is NO guessing penalty on the MCAT. NEVER leave a question blank!

PRACTICE ON A COMPUTER

The MCAT is a computer-based test, so it makes sense to practice as much as possible on computer-based practice material. This book comes with an online companion tool that you can access at PrincetonReview.com/Cracking that includes dozens of MCAT practice passages and over a hundred freestanding questions, as well as two full-length practice tests.

A NOTE ABOUT FLASHCARDS

Contrary to popular belief, flashcards are NOT the best way to study for the MCAT. For most of the exams you've taken previously, flashcards were probably helpful. This was because those exams mostly required you to recall specific information, and flashcards are pretty good at helping you memorize facts. Remember, however, that the most challenging aspect of the MCAT is not that it requires you to memorize the fine details of content knowledge, but that it requires you to apply your basic scientific knowledge to unfamiliar situations. Flashcards won't help you do that.

There is however, one situation in which flashcards can be beneficial, and that's if your basic content knowledge is lacking in some area. For example, if you don't know the hormones and their effects in the body, flashcards can help you memorize these facts. Or, maybe you are unsure of some of the organic chemistry functional groups you need to know; flashcards can help you solidify that knowledge. You might find it useful to make flashcards to help you learn and recognize the different question types or the common types of wrong answers for the Verbal Reasoning section.

THE MCAT TEST DAY

On the day of the test, you'll want to arrive at the test center about 30 minutes prior to the starting time of your test. Examinees will be checked in the order they arrive at the center. You will be assigned a locker or secure area in which to put your personal items. Textbooks and study notes are not allowed, so there is no need to bring them with you to the test center. Nothing is allowed at the computer station except your photo identification, not even your watch. Your ID will be checked, a digital image of your fingerprint will be taken, and you will be asked to sign in. You will be given scratch paper and a couple of pencils, and the test center administrator will take you to the computer on which you will complete the test. (Note that if a white-board and erasable marker are provided, you can specifically request scratch paper at the start of the test.) You may not choose a computer; you must use the computer assigned to you.

If you choose to leave the testing room at the breaks, you will have your fingerprint checked again, and you will have to sign in and out. You are allowed to access the items in your locker except for notes and cell phones. At the end of the test, the test administrator will collect your scratch paper and shred it.

General Test-Day Tips

1. Take a practice run to the test center a day or two before your actual test date so that you can easily find the building and room on test day. This will also allow you to gauge traffic and see if you need money for parking or anything like that. Knowing this type of information ahead of time will greatly reduce your stress on the day of your test.

2. Don't do any heavy studying the day before the test. Try to get a good amount of sleep on the days leading up to the test.

3. Eat well. Try to avoid excessive caffeine and sugar. Ideally, in the weeks leading up to the actual test you should experiment a little bit with foods and practice tests to see which foods give you the most endurance. Aim for steady blood sugar levels; sports drinks, peanut-butter crackers, and trail mix make good snacks for your breaks.

4. Definitely take the breaks! Get up and walk around. It's a good way to clear your head between sections so you can focus more on the next one and get the blood (and oxygen!) flowing to your brain.

5. Ask for new scratch paper at the breaks if you use it all up.

Chapter 4
Test Analysis Overview

Every time you take an exam, you should be sure to review your results thoroughly. Most people know to review the questions they got wrong in order to learn why their answer choice was incorrect and why the correct answer was a better choice. However, it is also important to review the questions you got right to reinforce proper thought processes. This is especially important for questions you happen to have gotten right but were unsure about or guessed on. Going back will help you solidify knowledge you may be weak in. After you complete a practice passage or take a Princeton Review practice exam (either on paper or on the computer), you can perform a detailed review of your results using a number of analysis tools. If the practice passage or test happened to be an online test, you will have additional tools built into the online environment to help you analyze your results.

ONLINE REVIEW TOOLS

When you view the results of an online Princeton Review practice exam (or subject drill), there are three "views" to choose from in the drop-down menu. The default is "Test Analysis," which gives a general overview of your results by displaying the percentage right, wrong, or incomplete for each section of each exam. The "Question Analysis" view provides more detail by showing these same divisions but within individual subject categories. For instance, in the physical sciences section, your performance is not just broken down into percentages right, wrong, and incomplete in chemistry and physics, but in specific topic areas such as "Vectors and Motion," "Electricity and Magnetism," and "Acids and Bases." This type of breakdown is very helpful in identifying consistent content issues. For example, if you take a practice exam and miss four out of the six questions classified as "Acids and Bases," it's likely you are weak on this content and should review your notes on acid-base chemistry.

The third view option, "Section Analysis," is particularly good for reviewing individual questions, as it provides a list of individual questions and allows you to click directly on a number and review the question, its passage (if necessary), and its solution. The list of questions also provides information on whether your answer was correct, incorrect, or incomplete, and whether or not you marked the question. Thus, the "Section Analysis" view makes it very easy to keep track of and review the questions you were unsure of.

Even if the online exam you took was not a Princeton Review test, it should come with similar analysis tools. For example, the AAMC provides online practice exams for purchase and has score reports with comparable types of section breakdown and examination.

WORKSHEET SELF-ANALYSIS

While the online tools are useful for identifying content deficiencies in the sciences, often what holds students back from getting higher scores in these sections is not a lack of content knowledge, but instead a difficulty in dealing with certain question types. Therefore, it is important to review your test not only for content errors and weaknesses, but also to see how the questions you missed fall into the categories described below. You also need to think about what led you to the wrong answer choice. For Verbal Reasoning, an online report will likely give you a breakdown based on question type. However, that breakdown is not enough; you need to figure out why you are having trouble with certain question types as well as identify other reasons, aside from the question type, why you might be missing questions. The Question Review Worksheet on pages 21 and 22 will help you diagnose reasons for your mistakes in all three of the multiple choice sections by asking you to first categorize the question and then to decide why you got it right or wrong. Let's look in more detail at this worksheet.

OVERVIEW OF THE QUESTION REVIEW WORKSHEET

Question Type

As stated previously, in the science sections of the MCAT the questions fall into one of three main categories:

1. **Memory questions** are answered directly from prior knowledge without any use of the passage.
2. In **Explicit questions**, the correct answer is explicitly stated in the passage or requires making a simple connection between passage information and prior knowledge. To answer them correctly, for example, may just require finding a definition, or reading a graph, and connecting that to what you already know.
3. **Implicit questions** require you to apply your existing knowledge to a new situation, or require more complex connections between passage information and prior understanding. The correct answer is typically implied by the information in the passage; you need to think logically and carefully to arrive at it.

There are three main Verbal categories:

1. **Specific questions** ask you for specific information from the passage, such as a fact, an inference, or a definition.
2. **General questions** ask you to summarize the main theme or purpose of the passage, or to evaluate the author's overall attitude.
3. **Complex questions** are typically more difficult questions that can ask you to do a number of different things, such as consider how the author constructs his/her argument, evaluate how well the author supports his/her argument, evaluate answer choices in terms of whether they support or undermine the argument, evaluate new facts or scenarios in light of the author's point, or apply the argument to a new situation.

Result Code

This code helps you identify why you got a question right or wrong.

1. **Correct, easy:** You understood this. It was very clear, you have no concerns or worries, and you were absolutely sure the answer was right when you chose it.
2. **Correct, the hard way:** You read every single word of every single answer choice, pondered, debated, calculated, and struggled, but got the right answer.
3. **Correct, got it down to two:** You eliminated two answer choices as wrong, guessed between the remaining two, and got lucky.
4. **Wrong, got it down to two:** You eliminated two answer choices as wrong, guessed between the remaining two, and didn't get lucky.
5. **Wrong, eliminated the right answer:** Oops. (Kudos for trying to use Process of Elimination, though!)
6. **Guessed randomly (right or wrong):** You had no clue and guessed. Randomly. Picked the "letter of the day."

Most codes have an action associated with them; note below that the ONLY code with no action is the one for correct/easy. Again, in order to maximize your MCAT score you must review not only the incorrect answers, but the correct ones as well in order to recognize and reinforce the correct thought processes.

1. Action for Code 2: Review for shortcuts, POE strategies, deductions, etc. You got this question right, and that's great, but there may be an easier way to do it. Did you miss something in the passage? Forget to use proportionality? Miss a connection?

2. Action for Codes 3 and 4: Read the question solution and think about what led you to your answer choice. Try to follow the logic of the explanation and apply that to future similar questions.

3. Action for Code 5: Review for comprehension. In other words, did you fully understand the question before you tried to answer it? If it was a verbal question, did you ID it properly? Would it be better if you slowed down a bit and read the question/answer choices more carefully?

4. Action for Code 6: Make sure that any questions you guessed on were the super-tough ones you really had no clue on.

Notes/Subtopic

Here you can list the specific reason you got the question wrong, strategies you may want to employ next time, the subtopic of science questions, etc.

Key:

- **Test or Book/pg #:** This is the diagnostic exam you are reviewing or the passage you have completed.
- **Section:** Either PS (Physical Sciences), VR (Verbal Reasoning), or BS (Biological Sciences)
- **Q #:** Question number
- **Q type:** Question type; for the science sections this is either M (memory), E (explicit), or I (implicit). For VR this is either R, (retrieval), I (inference), V (vocabulary), MP (main idea/purpose), T (tone or attitude), S (structure), E (evaluate), SW (strengthen/weaken), NI (new information), or A (analogy).

Result Code:

Code	Question Result	Action
1	correct, easy	none
2	correct, the hard way	review for shortcuts—POE strategies, deductions, etc.
3	correct, got it down to two	review, look for WHY you picked the correct answer, compare remaining, decide why the correct answer was better, consider what you will do next time
4	wrong, got it down to two	review, look for WHY you picked the incorrect answer, compare remaining, decide why the correct answer was better, consider what you will do next time
5	wrong, eliminated the right answer	review for comprehension—did you ID the question correctly? Did you RTFQ (read the full question)? Misapply POE strategies?
6	guessed randomly (letter of the day)	review for difficulty—did you attempt the easiest questions and passages?

Test or Book/pg #	Section	Q#	Q type	Result Code	Notes/ Subtopic

Test or Book/pg #	Section	Q#	Q type	Result Code	Notes/ Subtopic

What's the Point?

Filling out the Question Review Worksheet allows you to see patterns, the types of questions you usually get right, the types of questions you usually get wrong, and why. It helps you target your future study and practice according to your specific areas of weakness. Feel free to copy the worksheet as many times as you need to review your practice passages and tests.

ANALYZING THE SCIENCE SECTIONS

If you find you are missing a lot of science Memory questions, it might indicate a content area weakness, and you should review material in that subtopic. However, MCAT students typically have more trouble with the second two science categories, Explicit and Implicit questions, because they expect that they should be able to answer the questions based purely off information they already know. This is not the case, since the MCAT is not a test of your science recall. One of the most important things to remember when taking the MCAT is that if you are unsure of how to approach a question, look to the passage for help; it is likely that you are dealing with a question that requires information from the passage in order to be answered correctly.

If you are consistently missing Explicit questions, it might be because you are relying too heavily on memory and not enough on passage retrieval. Make sure you have an effective passage map (passage mapping will be discussed in more detail in the subject sections) to help clarify where information is located in the passage. As you are doing practice problems, force yourself to actively refer to the passage more frequently for relevant information, even on questions where you think you can use memory alone. On some problems, although you may have inherent knowledge of the topic being tested, it's possible that the passage mentions a more specific or anomalous example related to the topic. Therefore, what you know may not apply, and you must retrieve the new information from the passage in order to answer the question correctly.

Implicit questions also involve a fair amount of passage retrieval; they are often based on analogous examples to those given in the passage. Of all of the question types, Implicit questions rely most heavily on critical reasoning skills. If you consistently miss Implicit questions, you should carefully consider what the question is asking, go back to the passage for relevant information, combine that with your knowledge of the topic, and formulate a possible answer in your head before reading through the answer choices. Often the process of formulating the answer in your head first helps the correct answer choice stand out when you see it. You will also have to spend time carefully reviewing the explanations for Implicit questions to make sure you understand the logic required to get to the correct answer. If you can determine where your logic failed, you won't make the same mistake in the future.

ANALYZING THE VERBAL REASONING SECTION

We will discuss Verbal Reasoning in more detail with particular Verbal question types later in the book. For now, let's go over some more general patterns to look for when analyzing a full practice test section.

Pacing

The two obvious pacing issues are: Were you going too fast? Or were you going too slowly? MCAT students who are already scoring at or above average often finish every question on the test. And if you are already doing well, it can be difficult to accept the idea of slowing down and randomly guessing on a certain number of questions. However, if you are writing a lot of comments in your Worksheet along the lines of, "I didn't read it carefully enough," "I didn't go back to the passage when I should have," or "I misunderstood what the question was asking," you may improve your score even more by:

- slowing down where you need to on harder questions,
- reading more carefully,
- using the passage text more actively, and
- randomly guessing on a full passage (or at least on a couple of questions in the last passage you get to).

If you are missing one or two questions on every passage because of careless errors, or if you often crash and burn on one passage and get most of those questions wrong, you should definitely slow down and work harder to be more accurate on the problems you attempt.

On the other hand, if you are completing five or six of the seven passages in the section and getting almost every question right, you can improve significantly only by picking up the pace. This takes a bit of timed practice. If you find yourself using Code 2 ("Correct the Hard Way") on a lot of the questions on the Worksheet, you may be overthinking the answers or not using POE enough. Go back and review those questions and ask yourself, "Where did I do more work than necessary to get this question right?" and "How could I have worked the passage and answered this question more efficiently?" For your Code 3 or 4 questions ("Correct, Got it Down to Two," "Incorrect, Got it Down to Two") ask yourself, "What difference between these two answers could I have identified in order to more quickly get it down to the correct choice?"

Question Type Categories

Look for patterns in categories of question types that you tend to miss. If you are missing a high percentage of General questions, did you have a good idea of the main point or last line of the passage? If not, it means that you need to work the passage more effectively. Or, are you consistently picking answers that are too narrow? If so, you need to keep the scope of the whole question more clearly in mind. Are you missing lots of Specific questions? If so, you most likely need to read more carefully and go back to the passage more consistently. Finally, if you are missing a lot of Complex questions, you need to translate the question more carefully to get a better understanding of what it is really asking you about the passage.

A FEW THINGS TO REMEMBER ABOUT USING THE QUESTION REVIEW WORKSHEET

- Fill it out soon after taking your practice test or drill, so that you remember your reasoning for choosing your answers. The longer you wait, the more likely you are to forget why you chose a particular answer over another.
- For full-length tests, fill out a separate Question Review Worksheet for each section, and tackle each section one at a time.
- After filling out the worksheet, go back and highlight or circle the questions you got right in green and the questions you got wrong in red. Also, for the science sections, highlight one of the two subjects in yellow (e.g., highlight G-Chem in the PS section and O-Chem in the BS section in yellow). This will help you see patterns in your answer choices.
- Expect to spend a few hours per section reviewing with the Question Review Worksheet. It takes time to look at each question and think about your reasoning for the answer. Consider it time well spent, though, since you will gain valuable insight into not only your thought processes, but your areas of weaknesses and strengths. This information will help you tailor your study sessions so that you can boost your total MCAT score to the range you want.

ANALYZING THE WRITING SAMPLE

When reviewing your essays, you need to be as objective as possible. Give yourself a day or two (or at least a few hours) between writing the essays and reviewing them to see how you could have done better. Often, even good essay writers will see in retrospect that what they meant to say, or what they thought they said, didn't come through as clearly as they expected. As you review your essays, look in particular for a few essential qualifications:

- Did you understand what the prompt was asking, and did you respond to it directly?
- Did you stick to the topic all the way through, or did you go off on a tangent?
- Did you address all three parts of the prompt clearly and distinctly?
- Did you show a clear contrast between the two sides of the question, and did your examples clearly illustrate this contrast?
- Was your essay as a whole coherent and logically consistent?

Even someone who is not an MCAT expert can give you useful feedback. Print out copies of your essay and give them to friends and family members along with a red pen, and ask them to mark it up. Did your argument make sense; could they understand what you were saying? Did you contradict yourself anywhere? Were there so many spelling or grammatical mistakes that your writing was difficult to follow? You might be embarrassed to show your writing to other people, but getting a different perspective, and even criticism, is one of the best ways to improve.

In the next chapter, we'll take a look at how Joe Bloggs used the Online Review Tools to help analyze the results of his practice exam. This is based off Practice Exam 1 in your *MCAT Elite* Online Companion[1].

---

[1] Note that this is the same exam as Practice Test 1 in the *MCAT Workout* Online Companion. *MCAT Workout* is a different Princeton Review retail book; you may have previously purchased *MCAT Workout* and completed the practice exams in that text. No worries—you can still analyze your results using the tools described above, and you have a completely new practice exam on which to hone your test-taking ability (*MCAT Elite* Practice Exam 2).

Chapter 5
Sample MCAT
Practice Test Analysis

OVERALL ANALYSIS OF PRACTICE EXAM 1

After completing Practice Exam 1, Joe viewed his Score Report in the Test Analysis View and was reasonably happy with his scores: PS 10, VR 10, and BS 10. The Test Analysis View showed that he got about 80 percent of the questions on the exam correct.

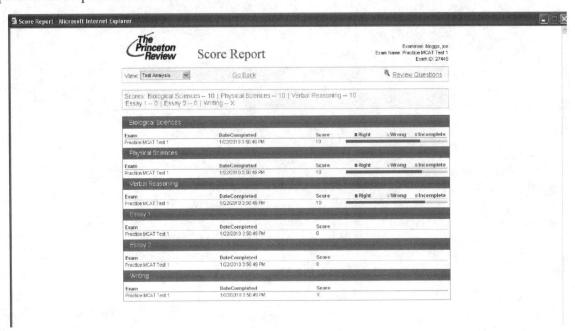

Next, Joe switched to Section Analysis View and did not notice any significant patterns in either the Physical Sciences or Biological Sciences sections. However, in the Section Analysis view for Verbal Reasoning, Joe noticed that while he got all the questions correct on the last passage, it seems that he missed at least one question on each of the other passages. Also, something clearly had gone wrong around the middle of the section, where he missed lots of questions in a row. He knew he would need to figure out exactly what was going on there and how to avoid having the same thing happen in the future.

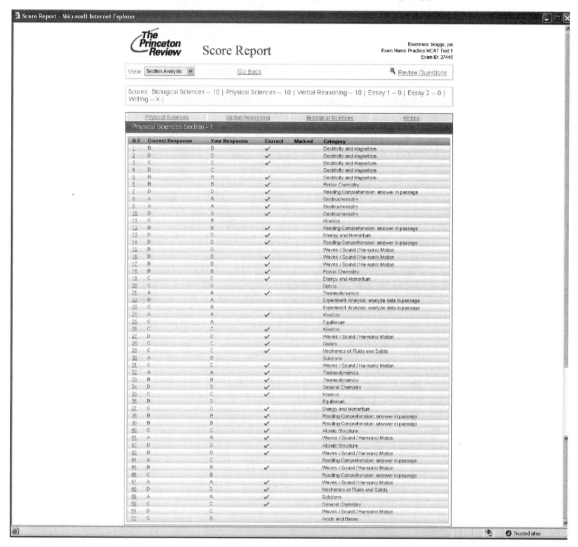

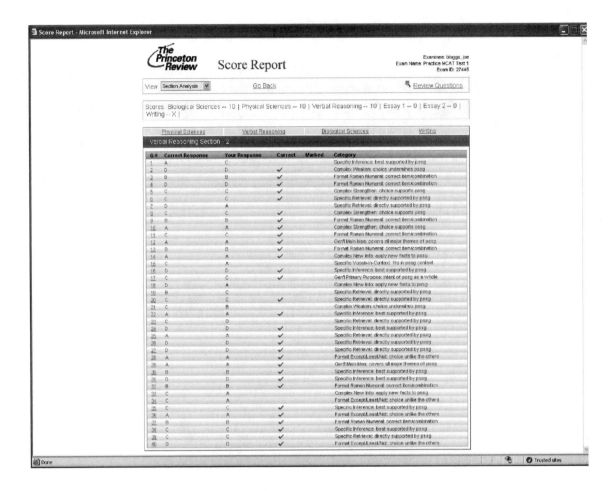

SAMPLE MCAT PRACTICE TEST ANALYSIS

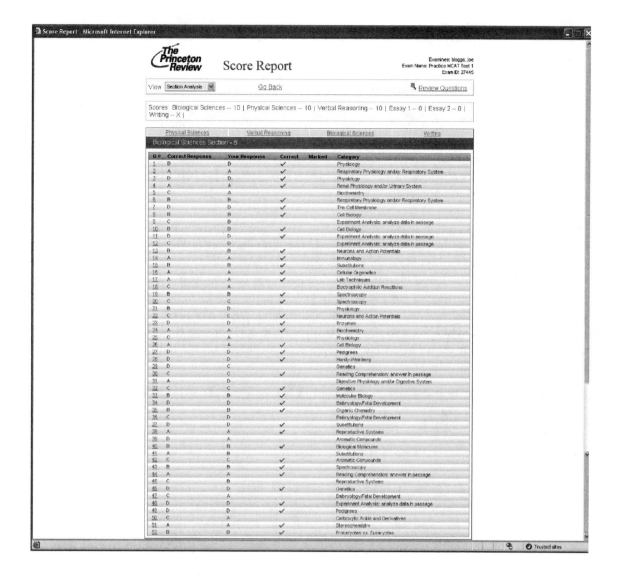

31

Although the Section Analysis View presented an overall look at each section, it was a little difficult to see any real patterns, so Joe decided to switch to Question Analysis View. He did note, however, that in the Section Analysis View, the individual question numbers were clickable and would open a new window directly to that question and its explanation.

When Joe switched to Question Analysis View, he quickly realized that this was the most useful view of the Score Report. In this view, the PS, VR, and BS sections were broken down by subtopic. For each subtopic, the total number of questions and number correct were shown, along with a handy bar graph detailing the data. It was much easier to see patterns in this view, so Joe had a better idea of which areas and subtopics he needed to improve in.

In the Physical Sciences section, Joe first compared Physics and General Chemistry to see if there was a subtopic weakness. Since he missed approximately the same number of Physics questions as G-Chem questions, he felt that his basic content knowledge was fairly balanced. He was pleased to note that he got almost all the Waves, Sound, and Harmonic Motion questions correct; he had been struggling with that topic and had put additional study time in on it. In G-Chem, it seemed like he had a good grasp of Kinetics, Thermodynamics, Electrochemistry, and Redox chemistry, but might need to brush up on Solutions, Equilibrium, and Acids-Bases. He also missed about half the questions on Reading Comprehension and Experiment Analysis, but wasn't sure what subtopic those belonged to. He figured he would sort it out when he reviewed the individual questions.

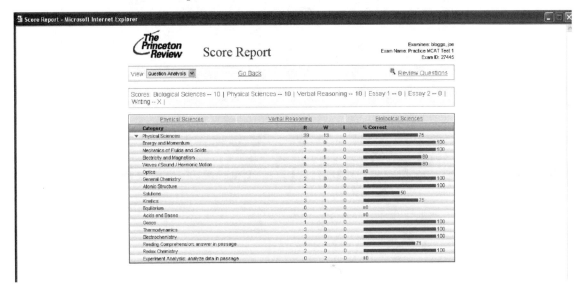

In the Verbal Reasoning section, Joe was surprised to see that he missed a lot of Specific questions. He had felt really good about the passages (in fact, he had finished this section with five minutes to spare) and had assumed that he would get all of those easier questions right. The 0% bar on Specific Vocab-in-Context looked especially scary, but then he realized that there was only one of that question type. Still, Vocab questions are usually not that difficult, so he definitely needed to see why he missed this one. He was glad to see that he got all the Roman numeral questions right. He did miss one Except/Least/Not, however, and was curious to see if he forgot the Except when he answered it. He saw that among the Complex questions listed, he did well on Strengthen, but not so much on the Weaken and New Information questions. Perhaps he needed to pay more attention to keeping track of how new information applies to the passage, and what direction the correct answer needs to take. Finally, the General questions were all good (which made him especially interested in figuring out why he missed so many Specific questions on those passages, given that he seemed to have understood the passages themselves fairly well).

In the Biological Sciences section, Joe decided to look at the results for his Biology questions first. Like the other two sections, he noted that a bar indicating 100% felt good to look at, but might be a little misleading; it was far more useful to look at the number of right and wrong answers to get a better feel for his strengths and weaknesses. For example, Joe got 100 percent of the questions on Molecular Biology correct, but there was only one question in the Molecular Biology subtopic, so the 100 percent may not be indicative of a strength in Molecular Biology. He did note that he could group some subtopics together to get a better sense of his abilities. For example, Cell Biology, Cell Membranes, and Cell Organelles all deal with cellular structures and functions. Out of five possible questions in these subtopics, Joe got four of them right, so he felt pretty good about his content knowledge and ability in Cellular Biology. Joe also noted strengths in Genetics and in Physiology, although there was one random wrong question on the digestive system, so he made a note to go back and look at that question to see where he made his mistake. However, when looking at the Reproductive Systems and Embryology subtopics, Joe noticed that out of five possible questions, he got three of them wrong, indicating a possible weakness and a need for further study and review.

Joe continued by looking at the results of the O-Chem questions. He noticed first that there were far fewer O-Chem questions than Biology questions; only 14 of the 52 questions were O-Chem. Of those 14 questions, he only missed four. With such a small sample size, Joe thought it would be better to wait until he looked at the individual questions rather than try to make any assumptions based on this view of the Score Report.

After reviewing the Online Score Report, Joe clicked "Review Questions" to see the individual questions for the test, and as he reviewed them, he filled out the Question Review Worksheet for each section. He highlighted his correct answers in green and his wrong answers in red, and in the science section, highlighted PS G-Chem questions and BS O-Chem questions in yellow. The rest of this chapter will discuss these sections and the Question Review Worksheet in more detail.

PRACTICE TEST ANALYSIS—PHYSICAL SCIENCES

After completing Practice Test 1, Joe reviewed each question in the Physical Sciences section. As he reviewed the questions, he filled out his Question Review Worksheet, highlighting appropriately. He decided to pay more attention to Physics this first time through, and then go back to review G-Chem (the questions he had highlighted in yellow) in more detail. He also noted that one of the passages (Questions 38–42) could easily have been classified as either G-Chem or Physics, so he decided to review it with G-Chem. He did not spend a lot of time thinking about any question he coded as a "1," presuming that he knew this material well enough.

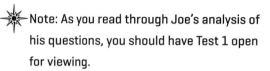

Note: As you read through Joe's analysis of his questions, you should have Test 1 open for viewing.

Physical Sciences Question Review Worksheet

Let's review the abbreviations and types of information you'll see on the worksheet.

- **Test or Book/pg #:** This is the diagnostic exam you are reviewing or the passage you have completed.
- **Section:** Either PS (Physical Sciences), VR (Verbal Reasoning), or BS (Biological Sciences)
- **Q #:** Question number
- **Q type:** Question type; for the science sections this is either M (memory), E (explicit), or I (implicit). For VR this is either R, (retrieval), I (inference), V (vocabulary), MP (main idea/purpose), T (tone or attitude), S (structure), E (evaluate), SW (strengthen/weaken), NI (new information), or A (analogy).

Result Code:

Code	Question Result	Action
1	correct, easy	none
2	correct, the hard way	review for shortcuts—POE strategies, deductions, etc.
3	correct, got it down to two	review, look for WHY you picked the correct answer, compare remaining, decide why the correct answer was better, consider what you will do next time
4	wrong, got it down to two	review, look for WHY you picked the incorrect answer, compare remaining, decide why the correct answer was better, consider what you will do next time
5	wrong, eliminated the right answer	review for comprehension—did you ID the question correctly? Did you RTFQ (read the full question)? Misapply POE strategies?
6	guessed randomly (letter of the day)	review for difficulty—did you attempt the easiest questions and passages?

Since we are unable to depict the color highlighting in this book, a circled number or letter = green = correct, a boxed number or letter = red = wrong, and grey highlighting = yellow highlighting = G-Chem. The full color version of this worksheet can be seen in your online companion.

Test or Book/pg #	Section	Q #	Q type	Result Code	Notes/Subtopic
PT 1	PS	1	Ⓜ	①	*charge on capacitor eqn*
PT 1	PS	2	Ⓔ	②	*current alarm in passage*
PT 1	PS	3	Ⓔ	①	*capacitance eqn*
PT 1	PS	4	▢M	▢6	*forgot V = Ed!*
PT 1	PS	5	Ⓜ	①	*RHR for B field by current*
PT 1	PS	6	Ⓔ	①	*reducing reagents*
PT 1	PS	7	Ⓘ	①	*battery*
PT 1	PS	8	Ⓔ	①	*voltaic cell*
PT 1	PS	9	Ⓔ	①	*galvanic cell*
PT 1	PS	10	Ⓜ	②	*caught up in too many factors, confused self…voltage was + or −*
PT 1	PS	11	▢I	▢5	*tried to use too much outside info— don't batteries go dead in cold? resistance does go down…but doesn't relate to the info*
PT 1	PS	12	Ⓜ	①	*PE for spring*
PT 1	PS	13	Ⓘ	②	*momentum, used passage eqn for v*
PT 1	PS	14	Ⓔ	②	*portions in psg eqn for v*
PT 1	PS	15	▢E	▢4	*understood concept, misinterpreted figure*
PT 1	PS	16	Ⓜ	①	*functional dependence in PE for spring*
PT 1	PS	17	Ⓘ	③	*summing spring constants: used POE for square root*
PT 1	PS	18	Ⓜ	①	*oxidation numbers*
PT 1	PS	19	Ⓜ	②	*used F_c, KE eqns*
PT 1	PS	20	▢M	▢4	*POE weird numbers (A, B); remember $\lvert f \rvert = R/2$!*
PT 1	PS	21	Ⓜ	①	*thermodynamics*
PT 1	PS	22	▢E	▢5	*didn't read carefully enough*
PT 1	PS	23	▢E	▢5	*didn't read carefully enough*
PT 1	PS	24	Ⓜ/Ⓔ	①	*kinetics*
PT 1	PS	25	▢M	▢4	*forgot that increasing temp increases all rates*

Test or Book/pg #	Section	Q #	Q type	Result Code	Notes/Subtopic
PT 1	PS	26	E	3	*might need to review kinetics a little bit*
PT 1	PS	27	M	2	*functional dependence on k/m*
PT 1	PS	28	M	1	*gases*
PT 1	PS	29	M	1	*buoyancy and s.p. eqns*
PT 1	PS	30	I	6	*no idea on this one*
PT 1	PS	31	M	1	*E = hf, also POE (A & D same, B nonphysical)*
PT 1	PS	32	I	2	*too much on trying to remember thermo equations*
PT 1	PS	33	E	1	*heat of formation*
PT 1	PS	34	M	2	*P = W/t (W = ΔH), but long calculation*
PT 1	PS	35	E	1	*kinetics*
PT 1	PS	36	M	1	*equilibrium*
PT 1	PS	37	M	2	*tough time with calculations*
PT 1	PS	38	E	2	*use given eqn, scientific notation—ugh*
PT 1	PS	39	E	2	*POE with figure OK*
PT 1	PS	40	E	1	*answer in passage*
PT 1	PS	41	E/M	1	*E = hf, f, lambda inverse proportion*
PT 1	PS	42	E/I	1	*atomic energy states*
PT 1	PS	43	E	1	*wave speed eqn*
PT 1	PS	44	I	4	*correctly interpret fig (not just functional dependence)*
PT 1	PS	45	E	2	*Doppler shift*
PT 1	PS	46	I	4	*logic wrong: read psg more carefully*
PT 1	PS	47	I	1	*POE negative speeds, d = rt*
PT 1	PS	48	M	1	*floating ratio eqn*
PT 1	PS	49	M	2	*calculations, more scientific notation*
PT 1	PS	50	M	1	*stoichiometry*
PT 1	PS	51	M	4	*stupid mistake: counted 1/2-wavelengths in my picture!*
PT 1	PS	52	M	5	*got tired, didn't read answers carefully enough*

Individual Physics Question Analysis

- Question 2: Joe got this one right, but in retrospect he spent too much time thinking about it. He had considered what it might mean that the device was in series with the battery and resistor and whether $V = IR$ could guide his answer choice. Eventually he decided that because the device was in series with the battery and resistor, it must have the same current, and should thus function as a current-measuring device (as opposed to the other options). However, when Joe reviewed the passage, he realized that it stated clearly (and more than once!) that the device measured current, so that should have led him immediately to ammeter. Joe figured that the lesson here is when the passage describes some new device or phenomenon, it will most likely define it in terms that relate to known concepts, so it's useful to look carefully at that language.

When new devices are introduced in a passage, note how they are specifically described in the text.

- Joe realized that he missed Question 4 simply because he forgot the equation $V = Ed$ for capacitors. He made a note to review that topic. One of the great advantages of taking multiple practice MCATs is that a student like Joe is more likely to discover his knowledge deficiencies and take steps to remedy them.

- Joe got Question 13 right, but relied too heavily on algebraic manipulation and not enough on a basic understanding of the problem. The question mentions total momentum transfer and gives an equation for the speed of the mass on the spring as a function of position. So Joe used $p = mv$ and the given equation for v to determine the momentum of the block after the collision, then substituted this value into $KE = \frac{1}{2}mv^2$. Joe used this approach because he allowed the language of the question to suggest an approach without thinking about the physics. Because energy is conserved in an elastic collision, the total energy of the system is a constant, thus the energy in the block after the collision is just the initial system energy minus the final energy of the oscillating mass (which must be all elastic potential—no kinetic—after it "transfers all its momentum to the block").

The MCAT will often phrase questions and answer choices to catch the unwary, so make sure you stay alert.

- Question 14: This question just took longer than it should have for Joe. The given equation for the mass's speed v shows a clear proportionality to the square root of k/m, meaning that an increase in k increases v and a decrease in m increases v. Joe tried to reason the question out from his prior knowledge instead of just extracting this proportion.

- Joe missed Question 15 because he misinterpreted the figure, believing that the mass was passing through the equilibrium point instead of at a displacement X. He knew that C could not be correct because it is never true for a mass-spring system, and he *thought* he knew that it could not be B because after the mass passes the equilibrium point, it will slow down. Joe realized that he needed to be more careful in interpreting the figures, particularly because any confusion in the figure is often addressed in the surrounding text (as in the text afterward: "undamped oscillation can be found at any distance X from rest").

Look at the surrounding text for information about figures.

- Question 17: Joe had puzzled over this question for a while. He realized that having two springs attached directly to the mass would increase the force it experienced and therefore its acceleration and maximum velocity (eliminating choice A), but he wasn't sure by what factor. Joe figured that two springs would increase the effective value of the spring constant in the given equation for v, and that an increase by a factor of 16 didn't make much sense, so he also eliminated D. Ultimately he just guessed that the spring constants added and so chose B, but he couldn't give a good argument for why this was. Had Joe considered the energy picture, he would have realized that energy must add linearly because it is a scalar. Thus, the effect of two springs attached directly to the mass must be to double the maximum potential energy and kinetic energy, leading to the answer. Joe decided that for implicit questions like this he needed to sometimes think "outside the box" of given equations and back to fundamental principles like conservation laws.

- Joe got Question 19 right, but did so inefficiently. He knew the appropriate formulas, but he forgot the rule of writing out the equations first, manipulating the algebra second, and finally substituting in values at the end. Instead, Joe first solved for the numerical value of the velocity and then substituted into the kinetic energy equation, instead of writing an expression for mv^2 and then substituting that into $KE = \frac{1}{2}mv^2$.

- Question 20: Joe forgot a crucial equation for this problem, namely that $|f| = R/2$. So he made a note to himself to include this in the list of equations to memorize for optics. He thought that choices A and B didn't make much sense numerically (he did remember $1/o + 1/i = 1/f$), but even this was something of a guess based on the values given.

- For Question 27, Joe remembered that the equation for the period of a spring-block SHO depended on the square root of m/k, but he had to spend a fair amount of time convincing himself with numerical examples that increasing the values of m and k could have any of the effects listed in choices A through C. Joe needs to remember that the change in a ratio cannot be uniquely determined merely by a simultaneous increase or decrease in the numerator and denominator.

- In Question 44, Joe again had some problems interpreting the figure correctly. He eliminated Item III (and therefore choice D) because there's nothing about the figure that would suggest any dependence on frequency (Joe knew that all frequencies of microwaves would move at speed c). However, Joe saw a functional dependence of the cosine term on both y and the range, so he thought incorrectly that both Items I and II were true. This was a careless mistake, because though the cosine is functionally dependent on y, the cosine *error* is actually *diminished* as y decreases. Joe made a note to himself to be more careful about both reading the questions (the word "increase" is crucial) and interpreting figures.

- Question 45: Joe used his knowledge of how Doppler shift works to eliminate choices A and C immediately, because a downward shift in frequency always indicates relative movement away from the source or detector. However, completing the calculation took some doing, and there was no easy way to eliminate one answer or another based on order of magnitude. There are occasionally computation problems on the MCAT that require solving to the end, and the best someone like Joe (who knows himself to be rather slow with calculations) can do is be aware of these and always look for Process of Elimination shortcuts, or guess if time is tight.

- Joe missed Question 46 (an implicit reasoning question) because he overthought the solution instead of looking for clues in the language of the passage. Joe correctly eliminated choices A and D for being nonphysical (the infrared of ladar is higher frequency than the microwaves of radar, and both devices use electromagnetic waves, not sound waves). However, he thought that because a radar gun uses a larger beamwidth than ladar, in the case of dense traffic it might confuse cars with one another and thus be less accurate. There is a key sentence in the passage that suggests the opposite is true: "Although ladar devices are more accurate, the operator must aim the device at a single target vehicle." This tells us that dense traffic conditions are more of a problem for ladar devices (because the operator would have to keep her aim at one car amidst many). That would eliminate choice B. Moreover, the passage explicitly mentions that ladar measures distance to a vehicle but makes no such mention about radar, another clue to the answer. Upon reviewing this question, Joe decided that although interpretation questions tend to require the most complex reasoning, this doesn't mean he should avoid paying attention to the text of the passage to see if the answer is implied by it.

Even if the question asks you to interpret, you should still go back to the passage to look for clues.

- By the time Joe got to Question 51, he was tired and hurried. He had done the test in order instead of doing all the FSQs first, and under those conditions made the silly mistake of counting half-wavelengths instead of full ones. Joe swore to himself that he would be more careful about the easy questions and that he would do them first while his brain was fresh. It's better to get these all right and miss a few hard ones than to put all his effort into hard questions (that he might miss anyway), and then also miss easy questions due to carelessness and time constraints.

Summary of Joe's Physics Analysis

In the Physics portion of the PS section, Joe noticed that he missed two memory questions (Q4 and Q20) because he had forgotten two simple equations related to the topics (capacitors and lenses) for which he remembered the more complex and more important equations. He made a note of those; otherwise he felt confident in his content knowledge. He was more concerned about the fact that he missed three questions (Q15, Q44, and Q51) because he had somehow misinterpreted the significance of a figure or diagram (in the latter case, a picture of a standing wave he had drawn himself). This suggested to Joe that he needed to be more careful about examining both the figures in passages and his own drawings on his scratch paper. He had to resist the urge to jump at the first answer that makes sense to him without recalling the equation or principle that explains it (e.g., that in Q44 it is the difference between the range and D that causes the cosine effect, not just any change to the right triangle). Even Q2 and Q39, which he got right, he probably could have done more quickly by looking for key words in the passage as opposed to trying to use equations or figures. Finally he noticed that he missed two questions near the end of the test (Q46 and Q51) because of silly mistakes, even though Q51 was one of the easiest questions. Joe did the test in order, and the fact that he missed these later questions (particularly the FSQ, Q51) suggested to him that he spent too much time thinking about harder passage problems instead of doing the FSQs first. He decided next time that he would tackle the FSQs right away to maximize points while his mind was fresh and not tired from difficult passage interpretations and anxious about finishing on time.

Individual G-Chem Question Analysis

After reviewing Physics, Joe jumped right into his G-Chem review.

- Question 10: Joe got caught up in trying to figure out whether the voltage of the cell was positive or negative. He spent a lot of time overthinking this point, only to realize that he knew the reverse direction was spontaneous, so the ΔG of the forward reaction must be positive. This allowed him to narrow the choices to B and D. Then, the only choices available have a cell voltage that is negative. To avoid this problem in the future, Joe decided to focus on the parts of questions he is comfortable with first, then use POE to narrow down the answer choices before getting caught up in aspects of the question that are more difficult.

  ✳ Don't forget POE!

- Question 11: Joe had heard about this phenomenon of batteries going "dead" in the cold. In fact, he had experienced it, as his cell phone battery often depleted while he was skiing. Therefore, he reasoned that there must be a logical explanation for this phenomenon, and he eliminated the "No," answer choices, C and D. From his background knowledge of physics, he was fairly sure that internal resistance decreased with temperature, so he chose B. On review, however, Joe realized there was very specific information in the passage with which to evaluate this question (the temperature coefficient for voltage loss) and he failed to use it. Although it may be true that internal resistance decreases with temperature, this does not explain the reason batteries go "dead" in the cold, and therefore is not the correct answer choice. Joe decided to be more careful about using outside knowledge to answer questions. He decided that if this situation comes up again, he would go back to the passage and use the information provided to evaluate the question. He also decided to make sure that the answer choices he selects actually answer the questions, rather than just providing true, unrelated statements.

  ✳ Be careful about using outside knowledge to answer questions.

- To determine the rate of reaction in Question 22, Joe had looked directly at Figure 1 for the rate of disappearance of reactant. However, this graph shows the rate of reaction at 25°C, while the question asks for the rate at 65°C. He realized that he missed that important point and needs to read not only the questions more carefully, but also the text just before and after figures before interpreting or analyzing data.

- Question 23: Joe had a similar problem here as on Question 22. He needed to read the text before Figure 1 more carefully in order to recognize that the reaction depicted in the figure consisted of 2 L of solution. This piece of information was key to getting this answer right, and Joe had missed it. He was a little annoyed that he made the same mistake on two questions in a row, but decided that in the future he would always read the text surrounding figures and graphs.

  ✳ Always read the text around figures.

- On Question 25, Joe knew that since the reaction was endothermic, increasing the reaction would shift the reaction toward the products. This allowed him to eliminate choices B and D. He had reasoned that since the reaction shifted toward the products, the forward reaction would be faster and the reverse reaction would be slower. This is false, however, and a common error in equilibrium questions. Increasing the temperature increases the rate of both the forward *and* reverse reactions. In the case of an endothermic reaction, it simply increases the forward reaction *more* than the reverse reaction, resulting in a shift toward the products. This mistake represented a content error in kinetics.

 When you make a content error, be sure to go back and study that subject.

- Questions 26: Based on the rate law given in the passage, Joe could see that doubling the concentration of A would double the rate of reaction. However, he was unsure whether or not this would affect the rate constant, k, and guessed between answer choices A and C. Again, this represented a content deficiency in kinetics. Since Joe had now missed two questions in this subtopic, he decided that he needed to go back and review his notes for kinetics.

- Joe had no idea how to do Question 30, so he blindly guessed. When he read the explanation, it made sense, but he had no idea how he would have gotten to the answer.

  This is a tough and somewhat unique question; it requires quite a bit of critical reasoning, despite the fact that it is not associated with a passage. A good first step would have been for Joe to think about what subtopic this question likely falls into. The question asks about solubility, which is part of equilibrium. When you are dealing with an equilibrium, it's often helpful to write the equilibrium equation:

$$BaF_2(s) \rightleftharpoons Ba^{2+}(aq) + 2F^-(aq)$$

When you know you're in over your head, just guess and move on. Don't get bogged down.

  In order to increase the solubility of BaF_2, this equation would have to be shifted toward the products side. Are any of the reagents in the answer choices directly involved in this equilibrium? How else could the barium or fluoride ions be removed from solution? By forming complexes with one of the other ions in the answer choices. The key with this type of question is to ask yourself, what would have to happen in order to cause the effect described? How do each of these answer choices play into that? Although Joe did not get this question correct, he was glad that he had just guessed rather than waste time trying to figure out something he clearly didn't understand.

- Question 32: Joe remembered from his studies of thermodynamics that enthalpy and entropy played an important role in determining the free energy of a reaction, and that temperature could balance the affect of one on the other. Unfortunately, he had blanked out on the equation he thought he needed, and spent about 30 seconds trying to remember it. Eventually, he had looked at the passage and realized that the enthalpy of the reaction was positive, eliminating choices B and D. When he looked more closely at Equation 1, he saw that there were more moles of gas in the products than in the reactants, indicating that entropy must be increasing over the course of the reaction. This led him to the correct answer, A. Although Joe got this question right, he realized that he wasted his time trying to rely too heavily on memory, and should have focused on using the information given to him in the passage. He also recognized that this was similar to the problem he had with Question 10.

- Questions 34 and 37: Both of these questions took Joe a long time. Question 34 alone took about two minutes. Joe realized that he was hesitant to do any rounding because he wanted to be careful with his arithmetic, but if he had made quick and dirty estimates to simplify the calculation ($24 \approx 20$, $198 \approx 200$), he could have narrowed down the choices more quickly. He noted also that in both of these questions, the answer choices were relatively far apart, which also indicates that estimates would have been fine. If he was pressed for time and needed to guess, he could have made a choice based on order of magnitude. Joe decided that this was something he should be more cognizant of in the future, as it will save him a significant amount of time on these types of problems.

- Question 38 was also difficult for Joe. Because he is somewhat uncomfortable with scientific notation, he spent some extra time on this question. He thought that with this and the other calculation questions, the best way to improve is to just continue to practice.

- Joe got Question 39 right, but only after first starting with the given Equation 2 and trying to substitute values for n_i and n_f. After about a minute he realized that the figure shows only one line above 600 nm (eliminating choices A and D) and no line between 500 nm and 600 nm (eliminating choice C). Again Joe realized that he needs to use information in the passage more effectively. He doesn't have to jump directly to an equation; he can also make use of the figures. This is especially true if the differences among the choices allow for process of elimination. Joe didn't need to compute the allowed transition values; he just needed to eyeball which sets of values didn't fit the figure.

- Question 49 was difficult for Joe for the same reason as Question 38; it also involves scientific notation. This strengthened Joe's resolve to practice computational questions.

- By the time he got to Question 52, Joe was tired. He knew two things were equal at the equivalence point, so he quickly skimmed the answer choices and saw B. This looked like an obvious choice, so he selected it. But had Joe read a little more carefully and used his knowledge of titrations, he would have remembered that at the equivalence point, the amount of H_3O^+ added is equal the number of moles of OH^- originally present, not the number *currently* present. Joe should have tried to concentrate and focus a little more at the end of the exam.

Summary of Joe's G-Chem Analysis

Joe realized that he has a tendency to rely too heavily on memory. He needs to refer to the passage more (Q11, Q32) and to use POE a little more aggressively (Q10). In addition, when he goes back to retrieve information, he needs to read a little more thoroughly (Q11), and watch out for extracting data directly from figures without reading the text associated with them (Q22 and 23). Since he has a content deficiency in kinetics (Q25 and 26), he decided to review that topic. He also remembered that his Question Analysis View in the score report did not show this content weakness; he decided that some of the questions labeled "Reading Comprehension" or "Experiment Analysis" must have been Kinetics questions he got wrong, so the weakness did not jump out at him when looking at that particular view. He was glad he decided to do a more in-depth review using the Question Review Worksheet. Joe also decided to practice more calculation problems to become more comfortable with estimating and scientific notation.

Remember to...

- Fill out the Question Review Worksheet soon after taking your practice test or drill.
- Fill out a separate Question Review Worksheet for each section, and tackle each section one at a time.
- Highlight or circle the questions you got right in green and the questions you got wrong in red; for the science sections, highlight one of the two subjects in yellow.
- Spend whatever time you need (usually about 2–3 hours per section) reviewing your test.

PRACTICE TEST ANALYSIS—VERBAL REASONING

As with the Physical Sciences section, Joe reviewed each question in the Verbal Reasoning section. As he reviewed the questions, he filled out his Question Review Worksheet, highlighting appropriately. Also, as before, he did not spend a lot of time thinking about, or reviewing further, any question he coded as a "1." (Note: As you read through Joe's analysis of his questions, you should have Test 1 open for viewing.)

Verbal Reasoning Question Review Worksheet

- **Test or Book/pg #**: This is the diagnostic exam you are reviewing or the passage you have completed.
- **Section**: Either PS (Physical Sciences), VR (Verbal Reasoning), or BS (Biological Sciences)
- **Q #**: Question number
- **Q type**: Question type; for the science sections this is either M (memory), E (explicit), or I (implicit). For VR this is either R, (retrieval), I (inference), V (vocabulary), MP (main idea/ purpose), T (tone or attitude), S (structure), E (evaluate), SW (strengthen/weaken), NI (new information), or A (analogy).

Result Code:

Code	Question Result	Action
1	correct, easy	none
2	correct, the hard way	review for shortcuts—POE strategies, deductions, etc.
3	correct, got it down to two	review, look for WHY you picked the correct answer, compare remaining, decide why the correct answer was better, consider what you will do next time
4	wrong, got it down to two	review, look for WHY you picked the incorrect answer, compare remaining, decide why the correct answer was better, consider what you will do next time
5	wrong, eliminated the right answer	review for comprehension—did you ID the question correctly? Did you RTFQ (read the full question)? Misapply POE strategies?
6	guessed randomly (letter of the day)	review for difficulty—did you attempt the easiest questions and passages?

Since we are unable to depict the color highlights in this book, a circled number or letter = green = correct, and a boxed number or letter = red = wrong. The full color version of this worksheet can be seen in your Online Companion.

Test or Book/pg #	Section	Q #	Q type	Result Code	Notes/Subtopic
PT 1	VR	1	[I]	[4]	Missed OPEC reference, ignored ¶ 5
PT 1	VR	2	(SW)	(1)	Kept to issue of question and passage
PT 1	VR	3	(I)	(1)	Used good POE: II clearly wrong and in 3 choices
PT 1	VR	4	(R)	(1)	Saw that III different than I & II but still supported
PT 1	VR	5	(SW)	(3)	B & C: saw "without policy change" in B
PT 1	VR	6	(R)	(1)	Kept to correct part of the passage
PT 1	VR	7	[R]	[4]	A & D: need to stick to question issue (framers)
PT 1	VR	8	(I)	(3)	B & C: Went back to beginning of ¶ 4
PT 1	VR	9	(R)	(3)	B & C: finally saw "routinely abuse" in I
PT 1	VR	10	(SW)	(2)	Look for difference: only A has effect of influence
PT 1	VR	11	(I)	(1)	Eliminated I, focused on III
PT 1	VR	12	(MP)	(1)	Had a good Bottom Line
PT 1	VR	13	(I)	(1)	Had good Bottom Line and POE
PT 1	VR	14	(NI)	(3)	A & D: didn't like A but D bad tone and too strong
PT 1	VR	15	[V]	[5]	Went with own definition rather than author's
PT 1	VR	16	(I)	(3)	C & D: saw C half right half wrong
PT 1	VR	17	(MP)	(1)	Had good Bottom Line
PT 1	VR	18	[NI]	[5]	Made up mind too fast, didn't read A carefully
PT 1	VR	19	[S]	[5]	Didn't go back to pssg, C "sounded good"
PT 1	VR	20	(R)	(1)	Easy POE
PT 1	VR	21	[SW]	[4]	B & C: lost track of exact issue of the Q
PT 1	VR	22	(I)	(1)	Translated answers A and D corrctly
PT 1	VR	23	[R]	[5]	Saw #'s in the passage, didn't read carefully
PT 1	VR	24	(I)	(1)	Used pssg, saw A–C were opposite
PT 1	VR	25	(R)	(1)	Used passage, read carefully
PT 1	VR	26	(R)	(3)	C & D: used tone to eliminate C
PT 1	VR	27	(I)	(3)	A & D: compared the two based on tone
PT 1	VR	28	(R)	(1)	Read carefully, avoided using outside knowledge

Test or Book/pg #	Section	Q #	Q type	Result Code	Notes/Subtopic
PT 1	VR	29	MP	1	*Had good bottom line*
PT 1	VR	30	I	1	*Went back to ¶ 1, read carefully, used Bottom Line*
PT 1	VR	31	I	1	*Used Bottom Line and ¶ 1*
PT 1	VR	32	A	1	*Saw similarity between I & II, difference with III*
PT 1	VR	33	NI	4	*A & C: overthought it, used outside knowledge*
PT 1	VR	34	R	5	*Forgot the Except, rushed it*
PT 1	VR	35	NI	3	*A & C: paraphrased C, saw extreme in A*
PT 1	VR	36	I	2	*Got confused, forgot the "least"*
PT 1	VR	37	I	3	*B & D: Unsure of I, but used POE based on III being wrong*
PT 1	VR	38	I	3	*B & C: went back to focus/issue of question*
PT 1	VR	39	S	3	*B & C: stuck at first b/c C mentioned "people"*
PT 1	VR	40	S	2	*Forgot the NOT at first*

Individual Verbal Reasoning Question Analysis

In looking at the questions he coded as a "1" Joe saw that his accuracy and efficiency in answering those questions was due to three things: using the Bottom Line effectively, employing good process of elimination, and reading carefully. So, he decided to take an even closer look at the questions that didn't go as well to figure out exactly what went wrong, or what he could have done better. First he looked at the questions he coded as "3: Correct, got it down to two."

- Question 5: This question from the first passage was a Strengthen question. Joe had easily eliminated choices A and D because they were out of scope. He initially kept choice B in contention because he thought that if inflation increased prices even more than a tax, the effect of the tax would be less noticeable. But his very next step was to compare the two choices and look for differences. That is when he saw "Without the policy change" in choice B, and "With the new federal tax" in choice C. When he went back to the question stem and reminded himself that it specified "if the policies outlined in the passage were followed," it became clear that choice C was the correct answer; choice B did not correspond to the issue of the question stem. Joe realized that he could have done this question even faster if he kept his focus on the issue of the question from the beginning.

- Question 8 was an Inference question from Passage 2. Joe had liked choice B at first because he thought, "If the Supreme Court had more power, it could fix the problem." However, choice C gave a different way of fixing the problem. So, one of these two choices had to be more consistent with the passage than the other. Then Joe went back to the passage looking for what the author said about the Supreme Court and saw something he hadn't really taken into account before: The author has a fairly negative tone towards the Court. For example, the first paragraph says that the Court has "continued to erode" the protection offered by the Fourth Amendment, and this idea carries through much of the rest of the passage. Furthermore, the fourth paragraph says that "it is the politicians, not the courts" who should be responsible for protecting citizens against privacy invasions by the private sector. Finally, nothing in the passage suggests that the Constitution itself should be changed; it's all about better guaranteeing existing constitutional protections. While seeing all of this eventually led Joe to pick the right answer, choice C, over B, he saw that if he had paid more attention to the author's tone in the passage, he could have made that choice more quickly.

- Question 9 was also from Passage 2, a Roman numeral/Retrieval question. Joe had narrowed the choices down to B: III only, and C: I and III only. The factor that finally led him to choose B was careful reading. He went back to paragraph 2 and saw that while police routinely set up roadblocks, it doesn't say that they routinely abuse their authority. Therefore, Item I was too strong. He saw that careful reading led him to some easy correct answers on other questions, and congratulated himself for seeing that subtle difference between the passage and the wrong answer in this case.

- Question 14: This was a New Information question from Passage 3. Here again, tone was the determining factor in choosing A over D. Choice A, like the passage, had a more positive tone and choice D was very negative. Seeing this strengthened Joe's resolve to pay more attention to tone when going through the answer choices the first time.

- Question 16 from the same passage was an Inference question. Here, as in previous "down to two" situations, careful reading led Joe to the correct choice. In his second cut through the answers, he finally saw that the second part of choice C was inconsistent with the passage. Joe reminded himself to always check each part of each answer against the passage the first time through.

- Moving on to Passage 5, Joe found two more "down to two and got it right" situations, Questions 26 and 27. And, yet again, the determining factor was tone. For Question 26, a Retrieval question, he saw that choice C had a purely positive tone towards the regulations, while both choice D and the passage referred to drawbacks. As for Question 27, an Inference question, the same issue arose. Joe was down to choices A and D. Once he went back to the passage to check what it had to say about limitations on sulfur dioxide and nitrogen oxides, he rediscovered paragraphs 7 and 8, which suggested that those limitations may have been counterproductive. Once he took another look at that part of the passage, choice D emerged as clearly better, based on tone. Joe reminded himself that for both Retrieval and Inference questions, the correct answer will be the one that is best supported by the passage, and that this includes the author's attitude.

- Joe had three more "down to two and correct" entries in his worksheet, all from Passage 7. On Question 35, a New Information question, Joe was down to choices A and C. He saw that he had done a good job translating a confusing question stem; he had recognized that this film critic must be a cultural critic and not a film reviewer. Keeping in mind the differences between the two was very useful in answering the question, he quickly eliminated choices B and D. However, the negative wording of choice C threw him off at first, and this pushed him towards choice A until he came to terms with the overly strong wording ("would refuse to write") in that answer. Once he accepted that choice A was in fact too strong, he went back to choice C, translated it more precisely, and saw that it was a fairly moderate description that matched what the author had to say about cultural critics in paragraph 4. Joe felt good about getting this Complex question correct. He also saw that he could have gotten it right even faster if he had translated choice C more carefully the first time he read it, which would have helped him avoid his momentary attraction to choice A.

- Question 38 was an Inference question from the same passage. Joe saw that he was initially down to choices B and C. As in question 35, Joe recognized up front that the contrast in the passage between film reviewers and cultural critics would be the key. It took him a moment to figure out what a "daily film analyst" was, but then he realized that according to the first paragraph, this was NOT a cultural critic. Joe had spent a moment debating between choices B and C, but once he realized that choice B was about cultural critics while choice C was about film analysts, the right choice became clear.

- Finally, in looking at Question 39, a Structure question, Joe recognized that he got it right for the same reason that he got question 5 (another Complex question) right; he reminded himself of the issue of the question once he was down to two. Choice B looked good at first, even better than choice C, because B mentioned "people" (which sounded a lot like "consumers") while choice C was about film reviewers (who were not specifically mentioned in the question stem). However, in thinking again about what the question was asking, he saw that it asked how the author supported a claim about consumers determining the success or failure of a film, and that film reviewers, according to the passage, were directly relevant to this issue. Now Joe saw that choice C, first impressions to the contrary, was in fact more relevant to the question than choice B. Joe didn't feel too bad about not seeing that distinction the first time through the answer choices; it was a tough question. However, if he wants to get his goal score of a 13–15 on this section, he'll have to be even more sensitive to the issue at the heart of complex questions so that he can choose correct answers even faster and even more consistently.

In summing up what he did right when he was down to two choices, Joe first realized that while he had been thinking that he always "got it down to two and then picked the wrong answer," he was actually right in those situations more often than he was wrong. Joe also saw that rereading and translating the question stem, comparing choices to each other, going back to the passage with that difference in mind, keeping track of the author's tone, and overall, reading carefully were the key factors in choosing the right answer. So now, with that in mind, Joe decided to analyze the questions where he was down to two but did in fact get it wrong.

Go back to the passage and look for clues once you're down to two answer choices.

- The first of these was Question 1, an Inference question, where Joe was down to choices A and C. And as he expected, Joe saw that he missed this question because he did NOT go back to the passage to find where the author discussed OPEC in the last paragraph. Also, he over-interpreted the author's tone regarding the issue of loans and credits. While debt is an issue in paragraph 2, this part of the passage is about how debt is used to scapegoat the United States. The author also mentions debt as a serious problem in the third and fourth paragraphs, but the passage is largely about how Mexico can find ways to pay off its debt; the author doesn't go so far as to suggest that no more loans should be offered.

- The next question Joe analyzed was Question 7 on Passage 2, also an Inference question. Joe saw that he missed this question because he did not go back to the question stem to remind himself that it asked about the framers of the Constitution. He was down to choices A and D, and he failed to recognize that while choice A represented the author's views, it had nothing to do with the framers' ideas.

- Joe missed two questions on Passage 4 where he had narrowed it down to two choices. The first was Question 21, a Weaken question. Joe was deciding between choices B and C. Here, Joe saw that he did not keep close enough track of the issue in the question, which was about the *function* of myth. He also did not go back to the passage effectively to see if different myths in different societies could perhaps serve the same function. Choice B, the wrong answer that Joe picked, sounded good, but when reviewing the passage (paragraph 2 in particular) he realized that the author clearly suggests that different ideas and practices can serve the same function. Joe also realized that he was treating this more as an Inference question than a Weaken question. Choice C didn't sound as good as choice B because it brought in something that sounded new and different: the effect of observation on what is being observed. But now Joe saw that one way to weaken a conclusion is to cast doubt on the evidence used to support that conclusion; this is what choice C accomplishes. Joe jotted down a note to himself to remember that Weaken questions can bring in new information as long as they are relevant to the passage.

  Remember that Weaken questions can introduce new information.

- The last of these "down to two and got it wrong" situations arose with Question 33 on Passage 6, a New Information question. Joe was down to choices A and C. He realized that he picked choice A because he failed to ask himself which of the two answer choices related most directly to not only the question stem, but also to the passage text. The new information sounded like it was describing something that the humanities try to achieve: a deeper self-understanding. However, Joe now realized that this issue never came up in the passage, whereas choice A directly relates to both the question stem and the passage.

In comparing all the questions where he narrowed it down to two, Joe saw a clear pattern, not so much in the types of questions he got right or wrong, but in the approach he took (or didn't take) to answering those questions. When he compared choices, reminded himself of the question task, went back to the right part of the passage, read carefully, and actively translated the meaning of what he was reading, he got the question right. When he failed to do one or more of these things, the results were not so good.

When you are down to two choices, do you get more right or wrong? Why?

Now Joe decided to take a look at the questions he got right but only after a struggle, to see if the same kinds of issues arose. There were three such questions.

- The first was Question 10 on Passage 2, a Strengthen question. Joe had spent a lot of time debating between all four answer choices because they all seemed to describe ways in which politicians could be influenced. But now Joe saw that if he had kept track of the specific issue of the question, and if he had remembered that Strengthen questions need strong, decisive answers, he would have seen quickly that only choices A and B mentioned campaign contributions (which was the issue of the question). Furthermore, between those two, only choice A suggested that politicians actually were influenced in their decision-making by those contributions. Here, keeping track of the question task and issue would have saved Joe a lot of time that he could have better spent answering or checking other questions.

- The last two "got it right the hard way" questions were on Passage 7. The first, Question 36, was an Except/Least/Not Inference question. At first, Joe eliminated choice A (the correct answer) because he forgot the "least" in the question stem. He somehow remembered it for the rest of the choices, and when he was down to choices C and D, both sounded inconsistent with the passage. Then Joe realized that for choice C, the author never suggested that films with artistic merit can't also be box office smashes. Similarly for choice D, the passage doesn't say that having celebrity actors *guarantees* success. So, these choices were actually very similar to each other, and wrong for the same reasons. Joe went through all the answers again, crossed them all out, and then realized he had lost track of what he was even looking for. After taking a deep breath, he took one more shot, and saw that choice A, while not literally impossible according to the passage, was the least likely of the four to occur, given the author's discussion in paragraph 3.

- Now Joe took a look at the last of the questions in this category, Question 40, which was an Except/Least/Not Structure question. He was curious to see if the same thing had happened, and yes, in fact it did. He spent way too much time getting this question right, largely because he forgot to keep track of the "NOT." Joe resolved to avoid ever again putting himself in this very frustrating situation, first, by using his scratch paper on Except/Least/Not questions to keep track of why he was eliminating each answer, and second, by reminding himself of the question task the moment he realized he had lost his way on a question.

> ✸ Don't forget to use your scratch paper to keep track of Except/Not/Least questions.

Finally, Joe went through his last category: questions he got wrong because he eliminated the right answer (Code 5).

- The first of these was Question 15 on Passage 3. He was surprised he missed this question, because he has a great vocabulary, and these Vocab-in-Context questions are usually pretty easy for him. However, he saw in looking back at the answers that he picked choice A right away because it fit with his own definition of "disclosure," and didn't even seriously consider choice C. Joe made a note to himself to always consider all four choices carefully and to go back to the passage on Vocab questions, even if an answer looks "obvious," because it is the context of the passage, not a dictionary definition, that defines the correct answer.

- The next question was Question 18 on Passage 4, a New Information question. Joe realized that he understood the question and the passage perfectly well. However, he had read choice A too quickly and didn't even notice that it referred to "living cultures," while the new information was about a text from an ancient civilization. Looking at the correct choice, D, Joe couldn't even remember why he eliminated it. He suspected that he didn't read it because he liked choice A so much.

- Looking at Question 19, a Structure question, Joe realized that something similar happened here. Choice C jumped out at him and he picked it without looking at it carefully enough to see that it was the wrong analogy; the author never says that the gods, heroes, and anthropomorphized entities themselves are analogous, but only that they play analogous roles. He saw that if he had seriously considered choice B (the correct answer), it would have led him to return to choice C, think about it more carefully, go back to the passage, and recognize what was in fact wrong with that choice.

- Question 23 on Passage 5 was a Retrieval question. Joe remembered going back to the passage on this one, so he was especially curious as to why he missed it. Now, in retrospect, he saw that the same thing jumps out at him that jumped out the first time: those numbers 74 and 49 in paragraph 8. Once he read paragraph 8 more carefully and looked back at the question, he saw that it asked about the levels of cations in the Hubbard Brook forest, but the 74 percent is in reference to the forests of Sjoangen. Further, he realized that the passage says that atmospheric cations had declined by 49 percent in the Hubbard Forest, and this is more or less stated in choice C. Joe realized that he threw away an easy question by not taking the few seconds required to read that sentence carefully. If he wants a 13, 14, or 15 in Verbal, he can't make these kinds of careless mistakes.

- Finally, Joe took a look at Question 34 on Passage 6. The minute he saw that it was an Except question, he knew (given the patterns that had already emerged) what had probably happened. As he expected, Joe found that he had rushed the question, forgot the "except," and too quickly chose a wrong answer that was the exact opposite of the one he should have been looking for.

Summary of Verbal Reasoning Analysis

After Joe finished his analysis of all of these questions, clear patterns emerged that gave him very specific things to work on.

Joe noticed that for many of the questions he missed, he either rushed and didn't go back to the passage carefully enough, or he didn't read the question or the answer choices closely enough. When looking back at those questions on the test, most of the answers seemed pretty obvious in retrospect; he knew he could have gotten most of them right if he had been a little more careful. As he thought back to what was going on in his mind as he was working the fourth passage (the one where he missed four of the six questions), he remembered that he was starting to worry a lot about time, and because he understood the passage pretty well, he zoomed through the questions without thinking them through. He was also annoyed that he missed the very first question, and decided that he needed to settle down and consciously focus himself at the very beginning of the section.

The good news was that he had a solid grasp of the Bottom Line on all the passages, and he saw that he used it well on many of the questions (even the Specific ones) to answer those questions efficiently. Furthermore, he often used good POE technique to get the right answer when he was down to two: He now needs to do that more consistently. And while he saw that he needed to slow down on some questions, he also realized that if he had approached those "Code 2" questions correctly, it would have saved him time that he could have used to work other questions more carefully.

When Joe looked at the New Information and Weaken questions that he missed, he saw that he didn't adapt well enough to the difficulty level of the question. He also didn't think through what the question was really asking and what the correct answer needed to do. He decided to work through a bunch of examples of those question types so that he can refine and improve his approach. When he compared how he answered the Roman numeral questions with how he worked the Except questions, he saw that his POE on the numerals was good. But, he forgot the Except/Least/Not on one question (Question 34) and got stuck for a long time on another question (Question 40) because he didn't keep track of the NOT all the way through. He vowed to always use his scratch paper to keep track of Except/Least/Not questions from now on.

Overall, Joe saw that he needed to:

- slow his pacing down,
- use all the time available to read more carefully,
- think about the meaning of what he is reading,
- compare choices to each other when he is down to two, and
- go back to the passage more consistently.

Most importantly, he must stop making snap decisions before he has carefully read and considered all four answer choices; this cost him several easy questions. Joe decided that he may even do better if he allows himself to randomly guess on a few questions on the last passage that he does (the hardest one that he is leaving until the end) so he has more time to read carefully.

Remember to...
- Fill out the Question Review Worksheet soon after taking your practice test or drill.
- Fill out a separate Question Review Worksheet for each section, and tackle each section one at a time.
- Highlight or circle the questions you got right in green and the questions you got wrong in red; for the science sections, highlight one of the two subjects in yellow.
- Spend whatever time you need (usually about 2–3 hours per section) reviewing your test.

WRITING SAMPLE SELF-ANALYSIS

Although Joe decided to review the multiple choice sections right after he took the practice test (so that he could remember his thought process clearly), he chose to wait until the next day to look at his essays. He wanted to be able to divorce himself from what he meant to say, and to look at what he actually said as objectively as possible.

Here is Joe's first essay:

> **In a democracy, the rights of the minority should take precedence over the desires of the majority.**
>
> Write a unified essay in which you perform the following tasks. Explain what you think the above statement means. Describe a specific situation in which the desires of the majority might take precedence over the rights of the minority. Discuss what you think determines whether the rights of the minority or the desires of the majority should take precedence.

"Majority rule." This is often the first thing that comes to mind when we think of the word "democracy." However, the idea and ideals of a democracy are much more complicated than that, and there are times when other things, such as individual or minority rights, should override what the majority wants. A democracy is founded on many basic ideals, one of the most important being the protection of individual rights and liberties from abuses of power. "Minority rights" can relate to a racial minority, but more generally it means the rights of any group or set of individuals who does not have the power of a numerical majority behind it. The desires of the majority can be expressed in a variety of ways: through votes, public statements, through basic foundational documents like the constitution that most people accept as valid, or through common cultural practices that express or embody the opinion and beliefs of not just a majority at one point of time, but of basic social tenets that we accept as members of a democratic society. One of the most difficult tests of a democracy is how it reacts to distasteful speech. If a democracy allows only speech that is widely accepted by the majority, free speech doesn't really exist. The concept of free speech requires that we accept the expression of idea by an individual or group that we may not agree with, or may even disagree violently with. It has been said that Voltaire claimed in the defense of such freedoms that "I disapprove of what you say, but I will defend to the death your right to say it." An example of this was the attempted neo-Nazi march through Skokie Illinois in the 1970's. The ACLU defended the right of the Nazi's to march through this largely Jewish neigborhood, even though public opinion was in favor of banning the march. Almost no one "desires" that Nazi ideas should be expressed or even exist. However, if this kind of hateful speech is banned (assuming that there is no physical threat involved), while it may preserve the peace in the short run, it will undermine what a democracy stands for in the long run.

However, there are circumstances in which the reverse is true, and majority desires should take precedence. Another way to look at "desires of the majority" is how it may be expressed not in votes or opinion pieces, but in social policy. The protection of the environment is a long term process with the goal of preserving the earth not only for ourselves but for future generations. In certain circumstances, this need or desire must take precedence over the rights of subsections of the population. Those subsections are often businesses or industries who wish to exploit certain natural resources, but at the potential cost to endangered species. For example, the spotted owl in the Pacific Northwest. Lumber companies have the right to use resources on land that they own, but sometimes the desire of the majority to protect species who depend on that land must take precedence. Other ways in which majority desires should take precedence would be in issues like helmet laws that mandate that motorcycle riders wear helmets. This is based on the cost of medical care for those who have accidents and sustain severe head injuries. Although we have in many cases the right to take risks, even to risk our own lives, sometimes that right must be limited if there is a potential high cost to society.

Life in a democratic society requires the recognition that we may be exposed to, and required to tolerate, things that we find disturbing or offensive. It also entails the recognition and acceptance of the fact that our own rights may be restricted for the good of others. What determines whether or not the rights of a minority or desires of the majority should take precendece is the long term good and stability of the society. Even though objectionable speech may present a short-term disruption, excessive limitations on free speech present an even greater long term risk. If these short term costs were never tolarated, slavery might still exist, women and African Americans may never have been granted the right to vote, there might be no such thing as a free press. Some of our greatest heros are those who stood up against public condemnation in order to defend those who did not have the political power to defend themselves. However, if protction of minority rights involves too high of a cost, and if the damage done, such as extinction of a species, cannot be recovered from, and especally if those rights don't go back to fundamental constitiutional issues, those rights must be limited in service of protecting the desire of the majority.

Joe's Self-Evaluation

Joe felt very good about this essay as he was writing it. He had considered many of these issues in the past, and had lots of relevant ideas and examples in mind. Upon rereading it, however, while he still thought parts of the essay were excellent, he saw that some of his ideas didn't come through as clearly as he expected.

The first paragraph started off well with an interesting hook. He brought in a core issue of the prompt: the ideals embodied with a democracy that go beyond, and may even conflict with, the will of the majority. However, he saw that his definition of "desires of the majority" was unfocused, and even created a contradiction within his argument in that first paragraph. If majority desire can be expressed through the constitution, how would we say that limitation of free speech is consistent with the desires of the majority? The transition from his delineation of ways in which desires of the majority can be expressed into his discussion of free speech and his specific example was a bit too abrupt, but the point he was trying to make came through adequately. The example of the attempted neo-Nazi march worked reasonably well, but Joe saw that he could have made it even better with another sentence or two explaining the connection between the march and "the rights of the minority" (that is, why neo-Nazis do in fact have a right to speak). The connection was implicit, but could have been made more explicitly. Joe saw a couple of typos ("idea" instead of "ideas" and "neighborhood"), but not so many that it significantly detracted from the quality of his argument in that paragraph. Overall, Joe was happy with how he responded to the first task of the essay.

However, Joe saw that he was less well organized and his ideas were less fully developed in the second paragraph. His transitions were more abrupt, especially where he moved into his spotted owl example. A few key points needed further explanation: In particular, on what basis can it be said that the *majority* desires conservation of endangered species (and not, say, a minority of environmentalists who are fighting to preserve these species, in opposition to a priority placed on economic development by the majority). The connection had seemed obvious to Joe when he was writing, but he saw that it required at least another sentence or two of explanation. Joe also saw that the second example in that paragraph, helmet laws, centered on a very different issue than his first example. He had thrown it in with the plan to explain it further, but then was running out of time and had to move on to the last paragraph. He saw that the paragraph would have worked much better as a whole if he stuck to his spotted owl example and explained its relevance in more detail. Joe also noticed that his wording became repetitious in this paragraph. For example, he said some version of "majority desires take precedence" over and over. Using different wording would not only be less annoying and distracting, but would also have helped him express and develop his ideas more fully. He was, however, happy with his idea about majority will being expressed in social policy; he thought that this was a fairly sophisticated idea that would impress the readers.

The first thing Joe noticed in the last paragraph was that his spelling became even more erratic. It distracted him, and he imagined it would distract the graders as well (Joe knows that he is neither a great typist nor a perfect speller, so he needs to be extra careful when writing quickly). He saw that this paragraph also centered too much on one form of minority rights, free speech. He decided he needs to focus more on generalizing from his specific examples in the last task. Certain other key points were left too vague. For example, how is "long-term good of society" defined? How do we weigh the value of the protection of rights against other concerns such as economic development, when the two are in conflict but both relate in some way to social good and stability? What constitutes "too high of a cost"? And, as in the second paragraph, he needed to better explain the connection to majority desires.

Overall, Joe decided that this essay would score solidly above average, but it could have been even better. He had excellent ideas; if he had focused and organized his thoughts better and further explained the relevance of his examples to the terms of the prompt (and cleaned up at least some of the spelling and typos), this could have scored a 6.

Here is Joe's second essay:

Advances in technology contribute to an increase in the standard of living.

Write a unified essay in which you perform the following tasks. Explain what you think the above statement means. Describe a specific situation in which advances in technology might not contribute to an increase in the standard of living. Discuss what you think determines whether or not advances in technology contribute to an increase in the standard of living.

The motto of modern society is "faster, better, cheaper." Our technology is geared towards achieving each of these three goals in order to improve our productivity and to make our lives better. However, while sometimes the three act in synergy with each other, at other times doing things faster or cheaper means that we don't in fact do them better. Technological innovations do in fact improve our standard of living when they allow us to do things we were not previously able to accomplish. Computer technology, for example, allows us to communicate almost instantaneously over long distances. In the past, keeping in touch with friends and family who lived far away took days, weeks, or months. Now, we can keep in touch easily and better maintain important relationships.

However, computer technology may also degrade our quality of life. This is especailly true when it is used in the workplace. The fact that we can be easily reached at home, or even work from home, has blurred the line between personal and profesional lives. Now, we are often expected to be available at any moment of any day to respond to our employer.

What determines whether or not advances in technology improves or detracts from our standard of living is the effect it has on our quality of life. If it helps us maintain important relationships, it is all for the good. However, if it significantly limits our free time, it has a negative effect.

Joe's Self-Evaluation

Joe wasn't looking forward to reviewing this second essay; he knew that it was much less successful than the first. When the second prompt appeared, he had already felt discouraged; this was not an issue he had really thought about in the past. Further, his own personal opinion was that technology always increases our standard of living, so the second task just sounded wrong to him. Also, he was tired; he felt that he had used up all his mental energy on the first essay. He spent almost ten minutes staring at the screen before he even started brainstorming on his scratch paper, and then he was rushed to come up with at least a few sentences on each of the three tasks. But he knew that there is much to be learned from (relative) failure, so he braced himself and started reading.

In reviewing his first paragraph, Joe was pleased with the first few sentences. As in the first essay, he felt that he did a good job of drawing in the reader. Also, he thought that he did a nice job of suggesting a theme for the essay as a whole: sometimes by working towards one goal, we detract from another. Once he got into his example, however, some serious problems became clear. First, he did not explain how better communication improves our standard of living. What is the connection between standard of living and maintaining relationships? That connection was never explained. In fact, Joe never did define "standard of living," and this vagueness was a problem throughout the essay. Overall, he thought that the example of communication technology could have worked well, but he would have needed to explain it, and its connection to the terms of the prompt, in much more detail.

Reading through the second paragraph, Joe realized that his example for the second task was too similar to his first example. Both examples are about communication technology, and he did not make it sufficiently clear in the second paragraph what his real contrast was (aren't professional relationships also "important relationships"?). And, again, he did not explain the connection to the terms of the prompt: How does blurring the line between our work and personal lives lessen our standard of living?

In the last paragraph, Joe saw two main flaws (aside from its excessive brevity). First, he more or less repeated what he had already said, rather than further developing his argument by responding directly to the third task. Second, in part because he never defined "standard of living," he fell into circular reasoning. Basically his argument was: if technology makes our lives better, it makes our lives better.

Overall, Joe saw that while he had some promising ideas, he did not develop them enough to create a coherent, consistent, and unified argument that directly responded to the issue and terms of the question. On the positive side, he had few spelling or typographical mistakes, but perhaps this was because there weren't that many words to be spelled in such a short essay. Joe figured that this would almost certainly score below average: although his first essay was good, this second essay would have dragged down his overall Writing Sample score. His goal is to get an S or a T, so he can't let one bad essay ruin the outcome.

Summary of Writing Sample Analysis

After evaluating both essays, Joe wrote the following "to do" list for himself.

1. Go to the AAMC Writing Sample Items list, find all the prompts about technology, and brainstorm examples and ideas.
2. Find other prompts in AAMC list that would be difficult for me, and brainstorm on them too.
3. Rewrite the second essay, in case something similar comes up on the real MCAT.
4. Practice writing two timed essays, back-to-back, to increase endurance.
5. During test, start brainstorming and outlining on scratch paper immediately—never just sit and stare at the screen.
6. Always define abstract terms, and make sure the definitions are consistent with the rest of the essay.
7. Don't use the same (or overly similar) examples for both the first and second tasks: Show a clear contrast.
8. Explain how the examples relate to and illustrate key terms and core ideas in the prompt.
9. Generalize, don't just repeat, in the third task.
10. Save at least a few minutes for proofreading.

PRACTICE TEST ANALYSIS—BIOLOGICAL SCIENCES

As with the Physical Sciences and Verbal Reasoning sections, Joe reviewed each question in the Biological Sciences section. As he reviewed the questions, he filled out his Question Review Worksheet, highlighting appropriately. He decided to pay more attention to Biology this first time through, and then go back to review the O-Chem in more detail. Also, as before, he did not spend a lot of time thinking about, or reviewing further, any question he coded as a "1." (Note: As you read through Joe's analysis of his questions, you should have Test 1 open for viewing.)

Biological Sciences Question Review Worksheet

- **Test or Book/pg #:** This is the diagnostic exam you are reviewing or the passage you have completed.
- **Section:** Either PS (Physical Sciences), VR (Verbal Reasoning), or BS (Biological Sciences)
- **Q #:** Question number
- **Q type:** Question type; for the science sections this is either M (memory), E (explicit), or I (implicit). For VR this is either R, (retrieval), I (inference), V (vocabulary), MP (main idea/purpose), T (tone or attitude), S (structure), E (evaluate), SW (strengthen/weaken), NI (new information), or A (analogy).

Result Code:

Code	Question Result	Action
1	correct, easy	none
2	correct, the hard way	review for shortcuts—POE strategies, deductions, etc.
3	correct, got it down to two	review, look for WHY you picked the correct answer, compare remaining, decide why the correct answer was better, consider what you will do next time
4	wrong, got it down to two	review, look for WHY you picked the incorrect answer, compare remaining, decide why the correct answer was better, consider what you will do next time
5	wrong, eliminated the right answer	review for comprehension—did you ID the question correctly? Did you RTFQ (read the full question)? Misapply POE strategies?
6	guessed randomly (letter of the day)	review for difficulty—did you attempt the easiest questions and passages?

Since we are unable to depict the color highlighting in this book, a circled number or letter = green = correct, a boxed number or letter = red = wrong, and grey shading = yellow highlighting = O-Chem. The full color version of this worksheet can be seen in your Online Companion.

Test or Book/pg #	Section	Q #	Q type	Result Code	Notes/Subtopic
PT 1	BS	1	(E)	(1)	*Cell structure*
PT 1	BS	2	(E)	(3)	*Resp physio, educated guess, use equ'n in passage*
PT 1	BS	3	(I)	(3)	*Circulatory syst, I II III, review content*
PT 1	BS	4	(E)	(1)	*Urine production and blood pressure*
PT 1	BS	5	[I]	[5]	*Biochemistry—missed "EXCEPT"!!!*
PT 1	BS	6	(E)	(2)	*Resp system, try to use logic and passage*
PT 1	BS	7	(E)	(1)	*Cell membrane/hormones—used POE, good*
PT 1	BS	8	(E)	(1)	*Experiment analysis*
PT 1	BS	9	[I]	[5]	*Expt analysis, missed point re pesticide effects*
PT 1	BS	10	(E)	(1)	*Graph*
PT 1	BS	11	(E)	(1)	*Experiment analysis*
PT 1	BS	12	[I]	[6]	*Expt analysis, didn't understand Q, read more carefully*
PT 1	BS	13	(M)	(1)	*FSQ; Neuron function*
PT 1	BS	14	(M)	(1)	*FSQ; Immune system*
PT 1	BS	15	(M)	(1)	*FSQ; stability (C^+ intermediates),S_N1/S_N2*
PT 1	BS	16	(M)	(1)	*FSQ; Cell organelles*
PT 1	BS	17	(M)	(3)	*lab (TLC), reduction*
PT 1	BS	18	[I]	[4]	*reaction types, stability (Roman numeral)*
PT 1	BS	19	(I)	(1)	*lab (^1H NMR)*
PT 1	BS	20	(M)	(3)	*lab (IR), rxn types, structure (Nuc^-/E^+), fnct'l groups*
PT 1	BS	21	[E]	[5]	*Eye physiology, missed the NOT!!*
PT 1	BS	22	(I)	(1)	*Neurons and action potentials*
PT 1	BS	23	(M)	(1)	*Molecular bio/enzymes*
PT 1	BS	24	(E)	(1)	*Biochem? Eye physiology?*
PT 1	BS	25	[E]	[6]	*Eye struct, Missed impt point in psg re layers*
PT 1	BS	26	(E)	(1)	*Rod cell function*
PT 1	BS	27	(E)	(2)	*Pedigree analysis, review common patterns in pedigrees*
PT 1	BS	28	(E)	(1)	*Hardy Weinberg*
PT 1	BS	29	[I]	[5]	*Genetics, missed psg info re lethal homozygous*

Test or Book/pg #	Section	Q #	Q type	Result Code	Notes/Subtopic
PT 1	BS	30	(E)	(1)	*Reading comp*
PT 1	BS	31	[E]	[5]	*GI, knew ans, read choices too quickly*
PT 1	BS	32	(I)	(1)	*Genetics*
PT 1	BS	33	(E)	(1)	*Mutations*
PT 1	BS	34	(M)	(6)	*FSQ; Guessed, got lucky—need to review embryology*
PT 1	BS	35	(M)	(2)	*FSQ; predict product (Diels-Alder), use POE better*
PT 1	BS	36	[M]	[4]	*FSQ; Fetal development, need to review content*
PT 1	BS	37	(I)	(2)	*FSQ; reaction type (S_N1/S_N2), kinetics (gchem)*
PT 1	BS	38	(M)	(1)	*FSQ; Reproductive system*
PT 1	BS	39	[I]	[4]	*structure, Nuc^-/E^+*
PT 1	BS	40	(E)	(1)	*reading comprehension*
PT 1	BS	41	[I]	[5]	*reaction types (slow down)*
PT 1	BS	42	(I)	(3)	*structure, Nuc^-/E^+, sterics (Roman numeral)*
PT 1	BS	43	(I)	(1)	*lab (^{13}C NMR)*
PT 1	BS	44	(E)	(3)	*Repro syst, review content*
PT 1	BS	45	[I]	[5]	*Repro, didn't know right ans possible, bad luck*
PT 1	BS	46	(M)	(1)	*Genetics*
PT 1	BS	47	[M]	[4]	*Embryology, need to review*
PT 1	BS	48	(I)	(2)	*Hormones, had to analyze chart*
PT 1	BS	49	(E)	(3)	*FSQ; Pedigree analysis, review common patterns*
PT 1	BS	50	[M]	[4]	*FSQ; stability/structure, COOH derivatives*
PT 1	BS	51	(M)	(1)	*FSQ; structure (chirality)*
PT 1	BS	52	(M)	(1)	*FSQ; Mol bio*

Individual Biology Question Analysis

- Joe got Question 2 right based on an educated guess. He knew that water pressure increases with depth, so it was highly unlikely that the volume of air in Mark's lungs would increase, and he eliminated choices C and D. He wasn't entirely sure that the volume would decrease, but this seemed to make more sense than the volume staying the same, so Joe chose A. He realized, though, that had he returned to the passage, he could have used Equation 1 to answer the question and would have been more sure of the answer.

- Question 3: Joe was pretty sure about Items I and II being true, so he narrowed down the answer choices to C and D, then made a lucky guess. He decided he needed to go back and review cardiovascular physiology, since this was pretty much a memory question.

- Question 5 had a pretty long question stem, so when Joe was taking the test, he skipped over this question. Then when he returned to answer it, he realized he was running out of time, so he hurried up and chose an answer. Unfortunately in his haste he missed the EXCEPT. Joe chose A because it discussed reduced O_2, which he knew to be true at higher elevations in mountains. He thought perhaps he should be a little more careful with these types of questions.

- In Question 6, Joe knew pretty quickly that choices C and D could be eliminated, since the pressure in the lungs would decrease on ascension. Plus, it was unlikely that there would be a rapid expansion of the rib cage. However, he had a hard time deciding between A and B. He ultimately chose correctly, but spent a lot of time thinking about it; on reflection, he realized that if he had gone back to the passage, Equation 1 would have helped him make a faster decision.

- Question 9: Joe was deciding between choices B and C, and he eliminated choice C because he didn't think a pesticide would cause estrogen-like effects. However, he realized that he missed a critical piece of information in the passage regarding how the pesticide led to increased transcription of mRNA, which can be the effect of a steroid hormone. Additionally, Table 2 indicates that every time the estrogen receptor is bound (red fluorescence), estrogen effects are observed, but Joe did not make that connection.

Read the passage carefully and make deductions from information in tables.

- Question 12: Joe knew that Pesticide A did not bind to the receptor's active site, and he knew that Pesticide B did. But he didn't realize that the binding of Pesticide A would prevent the binding of Pesticide B. He felt like maybe he didn't completely understand this question, plus he was tired of thinking about this experiment, so he just guessed D. If Joe had gone back to the passage, he might have realized from Table 2 that every time the estrogen receptor is bound (red fluorescence), estrogen effects are observed. This would have allowed him to eliminate choices B and D since they would both be correct, and there cannot be two correct answers.

- Joe felt that Question 21 was a very difficult question. It seemed like there were a lot of confusing things to remember, particularly the idea about rod cells being depolarized at rest. As he tried to get it all sorted out in his brain, he missed the NOT and chose the wrong answer. Joe recognized that this was the second time he missed an EXCEPT/NOT question, and he realized that these might be a problem for him.

- Joe completely guessed on Question 25 and got it wrong. He knew the answer couldn't be choice B (photoreceptors) and was pretty sure it couldn't be choice D (collagen). However, he missed the information in the passage about the middle layer being a vascular layer. He remembered being annoyed when trying to answer this question because it seemed like a Memory question that was beyond the scope of the MCAT, but he realized on review that it was actually an Explicit question. He began to think that to improve, he would have to be a little more careful about reading and mapping the passage.

- Joe got Question 27 right, but spent too much time thinking about it. He thought for a while that maybe CF could be X-linked recessive, since more men had it than women, and it seemed to be passed down from mothers. He did ultimately figure it out, but it took too long. He decided he needed to review pedigree analysis.

- Question 29: Joe knew that the probability of any child from this mating being a carrier for CF was 100%; since the mother has CF, she must be homozygous recessive and can only pass on the recessive allele to her children. He also knew that both parents in this mating were heterozygous for achondroplasia; one of each of their parents did not have the disorder and had to have passed on the recessive (normal) allele. Joe figured that in order to not be affected by achondroplasia, an individual had to be homozygous recessive, and a cross between two heterozygotes has a ¼ chance of producing a homozygous recessive (normal) child. Thus the probability of being both a carrier for CF (100%) and not affected by achondroplasia (¼) is equal to the product of the individual probabilities, or $1 \times ¼$, choice C. However, Joe realized he forgot or missed the point in the passage about how the homozygous dominant genotype for achondroplasia was lethal; thus, there are only three possible surviving outcomes, and only one of those is unaffected. Joe was angry to have missed this question and he realized again that reading and mapping the passage was crucial.

- Question 31: Joe did alright with the EXCEPT this time, but he read the choices too quickly and missed the "produced by the gallbladder" part. Also, he didn't think it was possible for CF people to have normal digestive systems, so he chose D. He reminded himself again to slow down on the EXCEPT/NOT questions.

- Joe completely guessed on Question 34 and got lucky. He did not remember the order of embryological development, and made a mental note to review that topic.

- Question 36: Joe knew that an individual without a Y chromosome would not develop male genitalia, but he was unsure about the female genitalia. He could not remember if both X chromosomes were needed for this. Thus he thought choice D would be more likely. This indicated to him (again) that he needs to review development.

- In Question 44, Joe knew that choices C and D were unlikely because the *guevedoche* do not have any internal female genitalia, thus MIF must be present. It didn't seem likely that it would be greatly elevated, however, so he selected (correctly) choice A. He was a little annoyed to realize that, again, the answer was in the passage (…all other hormones…are at relatively normal levels).

- Question 45: Joe saw how choice C could lead to the phenomenon described in the passage, but he did not think it was possible, so he talked himself into choice B. He knew choices A and D weren't right because estrogen would not be involved in masculinization. He realized with exasperation that had he pulled the point out of the passage about relatively normal hormone levels, he could have eliminated choice B.

- Question 47: Joe knew that skeletal muscle was derived from mesoderm, so Item I was true and he could eliminate choices B and D. But he wasn't sure about the kidney, so he guessed and guessed wrong. Again, he needs to review embryology.

- Joe got Question 48 right but he felt that he had to think too long and hard about hormone functions in order to eliminate choice C. He decided to review hormones.

- Question 49: Joe saw that he briefly got hung up again on the X-linked recessive pattern. He knew the disorder wasn't mitochondrial and ultimately decided it must be dominant because it was present from generation to generation, but this reinforced his original thought that he should go back and review pedigree analysis.

Summary of Biology Analysis

As he did a final review of his Question Review Worksheet for Biology, Joe noticed that he only missed three Biology Memory questions (Q34, Q36, Q47), and that they all had to do with embryology and fetal development. He felt pretty good about his content knowledge overall, and made a note that he should review those two subtopics. He recognized that in two of the questions he missed the "EXCEPT" or "NOT" part of the question (Q5 and Q21) and he needs to slow down and be more careful with those types of questions. Several of the questions he got wrong because he missed important information in the passage (Q9, Q25, Q29, Q45), and even on a few of the questions he got right, he could have answered them more quickly and confidently if he had used the passage (Q2, Q6, and Q44). Joe decided that he really needed to slow down to read and map the passage more carefully. He also decided that he would make a more diligent effort to return to the passage if a question seemed like it should be a Memory question and he didn't know the answer. One other thing that Joe noticed was that even though he got both pedigree questions correct (Q27 and Q49), he had to think too much and too hard about them, and wasn't completely clear on X-linked recessive inheritance. He decided it would be prudent to review the common inheritance patterns in pedigrees.

Individual O-Chem Question Analysis

Joe was a little tired from reviewing the Biology questions and he was glad to notice in looking over the Question Review Worksheet that there were only fourteen O-Chem questions in the entire BS section. Five of the fourteen questions Joe coded as a "1," so he did not review them further. Two of the questions were coded as a "2," getting them right, but the "hard way." Both of these questions were freestanding, but one was a Memory question while the other was an Implicit question. Joe reviewed these questions first to see if there could be a different way to approach them.

- Question 35: Joe noticed first of all that this is both a predict-the-product question and a Memory question, requiring an understanding of how the Diels-Alder reaction works. He recognized that he spent time drawing out the possible products on his scratch paper only to find that his structures were oriented in a different way from the given answer choices. Redrawing his answers to reflect the answer choice orientation took some time, but he eventually chose the correct answer, choice B. Upon reflection, however, Joe realized that by using some good test-taking strategies, he could have gotten to the answer faster and without having to choose between several potentially correct answers. The only important detail about the Diels-Alder reaction at play here is that the substituents on the dienophile (the COOH and CN groups) should maintain the same relative positions in the product as they had in the reactant. Since they are *cis* in the double bond, they are *cis* in the product ring, making choice B the only option. By using some good deductive reasoning, Joe might have chosen this answer based solely on the fact that it's the only answer that's not like the others.

- Joe then turned his attention to his other hard-won correct answer, Question 37: Joe knew that one of his content strengths is substitution reactions, but he wasn't smart about his approach to this question. He noticed that this was an Implicit question about reaction types, and the answer choices had two parts. The first part identifies the reaction mechanism, while the second part justifies the assignment. Joe saw mechanistic data and he started doing math (instead of using POE). He found that the reaction rate depended on the concentration of the electrophile; as its concentration doubled, so did the rate. This piece of information alone, however, did not allow him to select a final answer, since both S_N1 and S_N2 reactions depend on the concentration of the electrophile. Choice A does not conclusively identify the mechanism as S_N1. Joe then compared Trials 2 and 3, noting that both the nucleophile concentration and the reaction rate quadrupled (choice D is correct). Joe realized that for nucleophilic substitution studies, looking at the nucleophile trials should always be the place to start.

> ✴ When you are tempted to do math on an O-Chem problem, step back and see if there's a better way.

Joe then turned his attention to questions where he used good strategies to narrow down his answer choices to two options and correctly chose the answer.

- For Question 17, a Memory question, Joe needed two pieces of information. This question is a combination of predicting-the-product and lab technique analysis, and Joe knows he is generally stronger with lab techniques. Since Joe understands how TLC works, he was quickly able to eliminate choices B and D; R_f values can never be greater than 1, and on the MCAT it will never be the case that two compounds with different functional groups will have identical polarities and R_f values. At this point, Joe needed to know what effect $NaBH_4$ will have on an aldehyde. Based on his knowledge of functional groups, he deduced that either the terminal carbonyl would end up as a primary alcohol or a carboxylic acid, both of which are more polar than the aldehyde itself (due to their ability to hydrogen bond). In both instances, the R_f values would be lower than the starting material. Joe realized that he lucked out. He needs to review his carbonyl reactions, but relying on fundamentals worked.

- Question 42 is another Implicit question, requiring analysis of the structures given in the question stem and Figure 2. Joe understood that greater electron density makes for a good nucleophile. He also knew that electron donating groups (like amines) make the benzene ring more nucleophilic, while electron withdrawing groups (like the sulfonic acid) make the benzene ring less nucleophilic. By identifying Item I as a true statement, Joe eliminated choices B and D (and realized he could ignore Item III as a result). As this point, the question became a straight Memory question, and Joe remembered that electron withdrawing groups are meta-directors.

Joe then began to examine the questions where he got it down to two choices but chose the wrong answer.

- Question 18: This is an Implicit question requiring reference to the structure given in the passage, but no other passage information proves useful. This question asks about reaction types, and requires an understanding of resonance stability as well. Joe recognized C-1 as a good electrophile due to the polar C=O bond, so Item I is an allowed reaction. Based on the question stem (a NOT question), Joe eliminated all answers containing I (choice D). Joe knew that conjugate addition occurs in α,β-unsaturated compounds when the nucleophile attacks the β carbon, or C-3. Since the conjugate addition is defined incorrectly in Item II, this is not an allowed reaction. Joe knew to include it in the correct answer and eliminated choice B. Finally, Joe thought that electrophilic addition reactions which occur at C=C bonds could add the electrophile to either C-2 or C-3 in the given reactant. Thus, he thought Item III was an okay reaction, eliminating it from his options, and chose A incorrectly. Joe realized that his instincts about Item II should have helped him with Item III, but he didn't consider the impact that the conjugated C=O would have on the C=C bond in an electrophilic addition reaction. After sketching out some resonance structures, Joe realized that since C-3 in this reagent has a partial positive charge (making it susceptible to nucleophilic attack), it cannot make a new bond to another electrophile. Conjugate addition and electrophilic addition at C-3 are mutually exclusive here. Joe might have recognized this using his scratch paper more effectively.

- In Question 39, Joe eliminated choice B easily. Reading this option first made sense to him since it was the shortest answer choice without a justification clause for the (false) definition given. Joe then eliminated choice C since it is internally inconsistent. If an electron donating group is attached to the ring, the ring will not be electron deficient. The sneaky part Joe got stuck on is that both remaining answer choices are internally consistent, but only one of them answers the question (choice D). While the ring of the diazonium ion is more electrophilic than benzene due to the positively charged substituent, benzene does not act as the electrophile in the analogous reaction alluded to in the question stem. Joe needed to apply what he knows to a new situation. Here, both the nucleophile and electrophile have aromatic portions, so he needed to pay closer attention to the arrow pushing described to better identify the roles of each molecule. Most importantly and in general, he needs to ensure that the answer choice he picks clearly answers the question posed.

- Question 50: Knowing the relative reactivities of carboxylic acids derivatives, Joe was able to eliminate choices B and D. He knew acid chlorides were the most reactive derivatives, but got tripped up by the fact that acetic acid wasn't a derivative, but was the acid itself. Noting that HCl was also present in choice A, and remembering that mineral acids often catalyze nucleophilic addition reactions, Joe chose A incorrectly. Joe forgot that the nucleophile in this case was also basic. Under the reaction conditions suggested in choice A, the amine would be protonated by both acids to yield a non-nucleophilic ammonium ion. The nucleophilic addition reaction is therefore faster with the acid chloride derivative. Joe realized that he missed this memory based freestanding question because he again did not think about the intermediates or the mechanism. He decided he needs to use his scratch paper a bit more.

The biggest mistake Joe made was in this final question, coded with a 5, which indicates he eliminated the correct answer. This often occurs when moving too quickly or misunderstanding what the question is asking.

- Question 41: In this example, the question stem is pretty straightforward, but the reaction mechanism shown was not one Joe was familiar with. In Joe's mind, nucleophilic additions are associated with carbonyl reactions, so he quickly eliminated choice A, the correct answer. Instead of focusing on specific known examples, it's best to generalize reaction type definitions, because the MCAT is likely to ask you to apply these definitions to new reactions or situations. Joe should recognize the reaction as an addition because a π bond is broken. From there, he can recognize that the species that *adds* to the π bond is a nucleophile, hence a nucleophilic addition. From the perspective of the aromatic ring on the nucleophile, the reaction might also appear to be a substitution. However, the grouping of atoms that replaces the aromatic H is an electrophile, not a nucleophile, so choice A is the best answer.

Summary of O-Chem Analysis

Joe only missed 4 of the 14 O-Chem questions on this test (29 percent of them). He was glad to see that he got most of the easier (read: Memory) questions correct. In addition, Joe recognized the only Explicit O-Chem question in this test and found the important information in the passage. This seemed like an improvement over his passage work with the Biology questions, but he remembered that Biology passages generally contain more relevant information than O-Chem passages. Three of the four questions he missed were Implicit questions. His content strengths in the O-Chem section include lab techniques and substitution reactions, while he had mixed results with questions about structure, stability, and reaction types. Joe decided to review that material.

Remember to...
- Fill out the Question Review Worksheet soon after taking your practice test or drill.
- Fill out a separate Question Review Worksheet for each section, and tackle each section one at a time.
- Highlight or circle the questions you got right in green and the questions you got wrong in red; for the science sections, highlight one of the two subjects in yellow.
- Spend whatever time you need (usually about 2–3 hours per section) reviewing your test.

Chapter 6
Verbal Reasoning
on the MCAT

I. OVERVIEW

The Verbal Reasoning section can be intimidating for many test takers, and this is why, even though it is the second section of the test, we are addressing it before the science sections. You've been studying hard for many years, packing your brain with lots of science knowledge and refining your memorization skills. But now, as you confront the Verbal Reasoning section, all those facts and mnemonics are useless; you have to employ an entirely different approach. Even if you have taken lots of humanities and social science classes and have been speaking and reading English for many years, you may find that you aren't doing as well as you expected on Verbal. This is because you haven't yet learned to adapt to the specific nature and requirements of the MCAT.

There are many false beliefs out there regarding Verbal Reasoning, one of which is "either you get the passage or you don't." According to this myth, your Verbal score depends on luck; if you get "good" passages, all is well, but if you don't, you're in trouble. However, this is in fact completely untrue; there are ways any test taker can improve his or her Verbal score and get points on even the most difficult passages.

Many of you reading this chapter will fall into one of two categories:

1. Your science scores are high on practice tests or past real MCATs, but your Verbal Reasoning score is hovering at or below average; or,
2. Your Verbal score is above average, but now your goal is to move it even higher.

Regardless of which category you are in, you can boost your score in two ways. First, you must follow a methodical and consistent approach. Many people who are already good at Verbal rely on their existing reading comprehension skills: They just "read the passage and pick the answer that sounds right." However, no matter how good of a reader you already are, you need to employ analytical methods specific to the unique nature of this section of the test. You must also do consistent and detailed self-analysis to figure out the types of mistakes you are making and develop a strategy to avoid those mistakes in the future. While the same fundamental plan of attack works for everyone, different people think and read differently, and you have to adapt the basic tactics that we will be discussing in this chapter to your own needs.

—MCAT Verbal is very different from the reading you're used to.

Change is scary, especially if you are already doing fairly well in Verbal Reasoning. However, in order to improve, you will have to do something different. Simply taking test after test or working passage after passage won't do it; you need to refine your strategy in order to increase your score. In the rest of this chapter we'll look at the skills you need and review the basics; even high scorers can benefit from solidifying their basic approach. We will also discuss advanced methods for refining your skills and pushing your score even higher.

MCAT VERBAL REASONING SKILLS[1]
The following is a general list of the skills tested in the VR section.

Reading Comprehension Skills—you will need to:
- recognize the main theme of a passage and pinpoint the support given for a particular theme or thesis.
- recognize the background knowledge that sustains a particular interpretation of the passage.
- recognize explicit and implicit claims contained in the passage.
- identify a correct paraphrase of complex details and information.
- ascertain the meaning of "vocab-in-context"; that is, important terms used in the passage.
- recognize relationships between ideas and details in the passage.

Evaluation Skills—you will need to:
- determine how solid a particular argument or reasoning step is.
- decide on the relevance of facts or data to an argument or claim.
- decide whether a source of information is reliable or plausible.
- decide whether or not a claim is supported by the passage.
- determine if a particular assumption follows logically from information in the passage.
- evaluate the evidence for a conclusion to determine its validity.

Application of Passage Information—you will need to:
- recognize a general premise based on passage information.
- recognize the most likely reason for a specific occurrence or outcome based on passage information.
- use information from the passage to solve a particular issue or problem, and recognize the range of application of theories, reasons, and conclusions.
- predict the result of a theoretical situation based on new information as well as information in the passage.
- ascertain the implications to the real world of particular assumptions or outcomes.

Integration of New Information—you will need to:
- identify processes or outcomes that would contest theories given in the passage.
- identify reasonable competing conclusions or theories that could be drawn from passage information.
- decide on the influence of new facts and data on arguments presented in the passage.
- figure out how a conclusion from the passage can be altered to make it more consistent with new data.

---

[1]   Adapted from *The Official Guide to the MCAT Exam*, 2009 ed., 2009 Association of American Medical Colleges

BASIC PREPARATION

Before we get into the specific Verbal Reasoning Techniques, let's talk about other ways to build up your skills.

Outside Reading

Many MCAT students feel uncomfortable with the Verbal Reasoning passages because they are more used to reading science texts than material from the social sciences or humanities. If this is true for you, build up your reading comprehension and active reading skills using material similar to that which you will encounter on the test. Find a text written at a fairly high level (that is, not a simple news article) and treat it like a passage: highlight it, summarize the main point of each paragraph, define how the paragraphs relate to each other and what the author's overall argument is in each chunk of paragraphs. If you are using printed material, make a Xerox copy (never highlight a library book!). Even better, find material online and work with it on the screen rather than printing it out. Remember that you are not reading it to learn the content, but to practice your Verbal Reasoning skills, so don't get caught up in the subject; focus on analyzing the structure of the material.

Some useful sources:

- Periodicals: *The New Yorker, Atlantic Monthly, Smithsonian, Scientific American.*
- Authors: Here are some authors whose work is similar to the material you will find in Verbal passages (in fact, work by many of these authors has been used in the past by the real MCAT writers):

    René Wellek
    Austin Warren
    Joseph Campbell
    Stephen Jay Gould
    Will Durant
    Walter Jackson Bate
    Henry Giroux
    Donna Haraway
    George Lakoff
    Erwin Panofsky
- Gutenberg.org

    This is a site where you can download material that is not copyrighted or whose copyright has expired. This is a good source for MCAT-like material that you can practice reading and working on a computer. Go through their catalog and find material that looks unfamiliar and difficult to understand (just like the hardest Verbal Reasoning passages).

Build Endurance

If you are just beginning to study for MCAT Verbal, start by doing one or two passages at a time. In this initial stage, check your answers immediately after completing those passages so you can remember your thought process and see where you may have failed to apply the correct method. Gradually build up to the point where you are doing at least three passages, and ideally five to seven passages, at a stretch. At this stage, do not check your answers after every passage or two. You want to get used to working through a new passage without the reassurance of knowing how you did on the previous passage. Also, practice dealing with distraction. Do some timed work in less than ideal conditions (a library where people are moving around, a calm but not dead-silent coffee house, etc.). Practice tuning out your surroundings and keeping your energy focused on the test.

Timing

Start by doing passages untimed. Whenever you learn a new skill, you need to practice it slowly until you learn to do it right. Once you've become comfortable with the basic steps and techniques, start keeping track of the time you spend per passage or on a chunk of passages. Eventually work up to doing timed Verbal Reasoning sections and full timed practice tests. If you've been studying for a while but have never done much untimed work, this might be a good time to go back and work a series of passages without timing yourself. In particular, list the mistakes you tend to make on timed passages, and then work through a series of passages untimed, focusing on avoiding those same mistakes.

Self-Evaluation

As you saw in the Test Analysis section, self-evaluation is a necessary component of the quest to maximize your score. This is especially true of Verbal, since only your logical and analytical skills, rather than your factual knowledge, is being tested. You will see in the rest of this chapter that whenever we discuss advanced methods and ways in which to refine your skills, they will always tie back to self-evaluation.

Implementing Your Skills

Using whatever resources are available to you; take as many full timed practice tests as you can. Don't wait to start taking practice tests until a few weeks before the real exam. Taking full tests and evaluating your performance is an essential part of your preparation. Test takers may make different kinds of mistakes on timed passages than on untimed passages, on timed Verbal sections than on individual timed Verbal passages, and during full timed MCATs than during isolated timed sections.

Stress Management

Most test takers feel a certain level of stress on and before the big day. A certain level of anxiety can be useful; it motivates you, keeps you alert, and sharpens your focus. However, if you find that your stress levels get so high that they interfere with your studying or with your concentration during a test, find ways to alleviate your stress and bring it down to manageable levels. Here are some suggestions:

- **Deep breathing.** When you realize that your focus is fading or your muscles are tensing up during a test, sit back from the screen (or the book), close your eyes, and take three slow, deep breaths. It can be hard to look away from the screen during a timed test, but if those 10–15 seconds of relaxation help you concentrate and work productively for the rest of the time, it is the best investment of time that you can make.
- **Positive reinforcement.** It's easy to fall into negative thinking during moments of frustration, and this can push you into an overly self-critical mindset. It doesn't help to beat yourself up over mistakes you have made. Instead, think about (1) what you can learn from those mistakes, and (2) all the questions you got right and how you did it.
- **Reward yourself.** Studying for this test should be a high priority for you over the next few weeks or months. However, there is no point in burning yourself out physically or emotionally. If you go into the test in a state of exhaustion, you will not be able to put all that time and effort to good use. Build time for enjoyable activities into your studying schedule. This is especially important during the week leading up to the day of the real test. Taper off in your studying in those last few days, and do little if any MCAT work the day before test day (basic review at the most, but no timed practice tests or timed sections).

Now let's go through each of the steps of doing Verbal Reasoning in more detail, discussing basic approach and how to further refine your skills.

II. THE SIX STEPS

First we'll go through an outline of the Six Steps, then we'll break down each step in more detail, using a sample passage.

▬ STEP 1: RANK AND ORDER THE PASSAGES

Decide if the passage is a relatively easy "Now" passage, a more difficult "Later," or a "Killer" on which you will just randomly guess.

▬ STEP 2: PREVIEW THE QUESTIONS

Quickly read through the question stems for references to passage content. The purpose is to get an idea of what will be important in the passage and to help you annotate the passage text more effectively.

▬ STEP 3: WORK THE PASSAGE

Read through the passage relatively quickly, but with enough attention that you can track its logical structure and the main points of each paragraph. Highlight key words and phrases within the passage text, and use your scratch paper to take notes as needed.

■ STEP 4: DEFINE THE BOTTOM LINE

Define the main point, purpose, and tone of the entire passage.

■ STEP 5: ATTACK THE QUESTIONS

Translate and define the question task. When the question gives you a reference to the passage, go back to the passage text first, read above and below that reference, and generate an answer in your own words. Go through the choices using Process of Elimination (POE); look for what is wrong with each answer and eliminate down to the "least wrong" choice.

■ STEP 6: INSPECT THE SECTION

Use the Review screen to make sure that you haven't left anything blank (including random guesses). Note that we won't discuss step 6 in any further detail.

STEP 1: RANKING AND ORDERING THE PASSAGES

In the Verbal Reasoning section, some passages will be significantly harder than others. However, you don't get any more credit for correctly answering the hardest question in the section than for correctly answering the easiest question. And the passages are rarely presented in order of difficulty from easiest to hardest (that would be too easy). Often, the most difficult passage or passages are buried in the middle of the section. Therefore, if you just plug away at the passages from first to last, you will likely spend lots of time struggling with the hardest passage in the section, perhaps getting a high percentage of those questions wrong and spending a lot of time doing it. Or, you will run out of time and have to randomly guess on, or rush through, one of the easier passages, missing questions that you could have gotten right. Maximizing your Verbal score is all about taking control over the section, and one way to do this is to attack the passages in the order that works best for you. You need to make well-founded decisions about which passages to complete and when.

 Do the passages out of order and find the easy ones first!

Ranking

Two factors play into how difficult a passage is: the comprehensibility of the passage text and the difficulty level of the questions. Here's how to predict the overall difficulty level of a passage:

- Skim the first two or three sentences of a paragraph. Try to paraphrase what you have just read. If you can paraphrase easily, the passage is likely to be fairly easy to read and understand. If all you can do is repeat the words you have just read because the meaning is difficult to extract, the passage text is likely to be difficult as a whole.

- Scroll through the questions—don't read each question carefully, but rather, get a sense of the distribution of different question types and the average length of the question stems and answer choices. If there are lots of difficult question types, or lots of lengthy questions and answer choices, the set of questions may be quite challenging to complete. Also, all other things being equal, it is better to do a passage with more questions. However, don't make this your primary consideration; it's better to do an easy five-question passage than a killer seven-question passage.

- Based on a combination of the difficulty level of the passage text and of the set of questions, give each passage a ranking of NOW (passages you will complete early on in the section), LATER (passages you will come back to and complete after the easier ones) or KILLER (passages on which you will randomly guess).

So, let's look at each of these two factors in a little more detail.

Evaluating the Passage Text

Read through each of the following paragraphs quickly, and write a paraphrase in the space provided below.

1. In his consideration of the meaning of the evolution of forms of punishment and imprisonment in different societies over time, Foucault shows that the way in which punishment is inscribed upon the body, or rather, the way in which it may be sequestered from public view and carried out behind the walls of institutional constructs, indicates the meaning of crime within that society and the ramifications of trespassing against accepted modes of behavior within different cultural nets of significance. Ontological considerations necessarily follow from identification of different disciplinary modes: Meaning is fluid.

    _____

    _____

    _____

2. Prison overcrowding is a serious problem in modern society. When prisons are filled beyond their capacity, it is difficult or impossible to carry out necessary rehabilitation programs. This failing contributes to recidivism and future crime rates.

    _____

    _____

    _____

Did you find the first paragraph to be much more of a challenge? If so, why? Beyond having vocabulary that may have been unfamiliar, it is highly abstract. The complicated sentence structure adds insult to injury; when sentences are constructed out of several parts cobbled together with commas and colons and semicolons, you will have to put a lot of effort into untangling them in order to get any understanding of the author's meaning. The second paragraph, while on the same overall topic (prisons and punishment), is concrete, descriptive, and written in a straightforward manner. The rest of the passage is likely to continue along the same lines. If these were two passages on a real exam, you'd want to do the second first and the first later (or never).

Evaluating the Questions

Questions that ask you to extract information from the passage, or to summarize the main theme of the passage as a whole, tend to be faster and easier to answer. On the other hand, complex questions that ask you to apply new information to the passage text, or to describe or evaluate the author's reasoning, will tend to be more difficult. And all other things being equal, longer questions and answer choices tend to be harder to manage than shorter question stems and choices.

Take a look at the following questions and decide if they are likely to be easy or hard to answer. Circle your choice (Easy or Hard) for each of the five, and then read through the explanations below.

1. Which of the following statements, if true, most *undermines* the author's contention regarding the debate between Reynolds and Adams?
    Easy or Hard?

2. Which of the following statements regarding Impressionism is best supported by the passage?
    Easy or Hard?

3. Assume that it was shown that the political goals of the Surrealists were in direct conflict with their artistic mission. What impact would this have on the author's argument regarding Louis Aragon, as that argument is presented in the passage?
    Easy or Hard?

4. By "recidivism," the author most likely means:
    Easy or Hard?

5. Which of the following statements best captures an accurate evaluation of the strength of the author's argument regarding the impact of the growth of coffee sales on Central American economies in the absence of a stable infrastructure?
    Easy or Hard?

Evaluation

Question 1: Hard. This question asks you to take new information in the answer choices and apply it to the passage. It also requires you to pick an answer that goes against the author's argument, making it easy to get turned around.

Question 2: Easy. This question essentially asks you to locate what the author says about Impressionism, and to find the choice that is best supported by that part of the passage.

Question 3: Hard. This question gives you new information in the question stem, and requires you to decide how it would apply to the author's argument.

Question 4: Easy. Questions that ask for definitions tend not to be that challenging, especially if the passage text is reasonably comprehensible. Even if you are unfamiliar with the word being defined, if you can understand that part of the passage you will get the question right.

Question 5: Hard. To answer this question, you will not only have to understand what the author has to say on this issue, but to take another step and decide whether or not it is well founded or well supported.

Summary of Ranking

Even the easiest passage can have a few difficult question stems, and the hardest passage may have some easy-looking questions. However, if the majority of questions appear to be logically difficult and/or unusually lengthy, take this into account in your ranking decisions. This may, for example, change what would have been a NOW passage (based only on the passage text) into a LATER passage.

Overall, you should be spending about two minutes, spread out throughout the 60 minutes you have on the section, making your ranking decisions.

 Spend 2 minutes looking at all passages and questions and ranking them.

Ordering the Passages Based on Ranking

The ordering system that works best for most test takers is the Two-Pass System.

First Pass

If a passage is a NOW, go ahead and complete it. If it is a LATER or KILLER, skip over it in your first pass. (You might wait until you have done all the Now passages to make the final distinction between LATER and KILLER passages.) If you are skipping over a passage, write down the number of the passage on your scratch paper: Keep an area on the top of your Verbal scratch paper dedicated to this list. Also, go ahead and fill in random guesses on all the questions. If you decide never to come back to them, you will have already made your guesses, and there will be no risk of leaving questions blank. If you decide to return and do it as a LATER passage, it takes little or no time to change your answers as you work through the questions. You can also use the Mark function so that these questions will be listed as "marked" in the Review screen. (Note: Since you should rarely, if ever, come back to rework Verbal questions once you have finished a passage and moved on, this is most likely the only time you will be marking questions within the Verbal Reasoning section.)

 Mark passages you are skipping and fill in guesses just in case you don't have time to come back.

Second Pass

Once you have completed the easier passages, come back through the section a second time, completing the LATER passages. At or by the 5-minutes-left mark, check the Review screen to make sure that you haven't left anything blank.

Advanced Ranking and Ordering: Refining Your Skills

Improving your score by working on these skills requires taking your current pacing into account (how many questions and passages you are completing). Take a look at the following two categories. If your pacing changes in the future, you may move into a new category; at that time, reconsider your ordering strategy.

Finishing All Seven Passages

If you are currently working at this pace and scoring a 10 or above, passage choice is still important. (If you are completing all seven and not yet scoring in the double digits, you may need to slow down your pace to six passages, at least for now.) Many who are planning to finish all the passages feel that there is no need to rank them, since they will be working them all at some point. However, getting stuck on a hard passage early on in the section can throw off the rest of your timing, causing you to become frustrated and lose your cool, rush through other easier passages and make unnecessary mistakes, and lose concentration and work less efficiently.

As you work through the passages, when you come across one that looks more difficult than the others (in particular, if the passage text is highly abstract and difficult to understand), skip over it in your first pass. This way, you can make sure that if you do run short on time and have to guess on a few questions, it will be on the hardest passage. And you don't risk hitting a bump early on that throws you off your game for the rest of the section. If you are going to lose your form, better that it happens in the last 10 minutes than in the first half of your time, when you could be scoring easy points.

Finishing Six or Fewer Passages

If the pacing that is currently working best for you is randomly guessing on one or more passages, skip over at least two or three LATER/KILLER passages during your first pass. Since you will not be completing all the passages, it is important that you make well-considered choices and avoid wasting your time on the hardest one. You want to be able to compare several passages with each other toward the end and make the best choice.

You may even find that effective passage ordering helps you speed up and get to more questions in the end, especially if you usually tend to waste time struggling with one hard passage.

READING AND MAPPING THE PASSAGE (STEPS 2, 3, AND 4)

Students who are already scoring above average in Verbal Reasoning often get blasé about how they are working the passage. They tend to rely on their natural reading skills without thinking very much about how they are working through the passage text. It certainly all comes down to the questions in the end, but to answer the questions as accurately and efficiently as possible, you need to have an appropriate foundation in the passage. If you aren't working the passage to the best of your abilities, you will not get the highest possible score. So let's review the basic process of passage reading and mapping. There are three phases in this process: Previewing the Questions, Working the Passage, and Defining the Bottom Line. Let's take a look at each, using the fourth passage from online Practice Test 1. (Note: If you have not yet completed this test, you may wish to take it as a full timed practice test before reading through the following material.) After we get through the basics, we will discuss ways in which you can refine your skills within that stage.

STEP 2: PREVIEWING THE QUESTIONS

Why preview the question stems before reading the passage text? After all, you will be reading them again to answer the questions. There are several advantages to this step. First, there are no line references in the questions (and only a rare few paragraph references) to help you locate the information in the passage that you need. Test takers who don't preview the questions often find themselves on long meandering searches through the passage trying to find specific topics. This eats up a lot of your precious time. If you know the question topics ahead of time, you can locate and highlight them as you read, setting up a map for yourself to follow once you hit the questions.

Second, not everything in the passage is important for answering the questions. If you know what at least some of the key issues are ahead of time, you can maximize your efficiency in working the passage, paying attention to what is most important and reading more quickly through what is less crucial.

Third, reading a passage without previewing is like jumping into the middle of a discussion and trying to figure out what's going on with no context to guide you. Knowing something about the overall passage topic before you begin to read gives you a base to which you can connect all the new information; it helps you make sense of the passage more quickly. It also improves your focus. If you have found yourself realizing halfway through a passage that you have no idea what you are reading, previewing can go a long way toward helping you keep your concentration.

After a bit of practice, previewing the questions should take you 15–30 seconds. This is generally *not* a time to use your scratch paper; don't take notes as you preview, but rather focus your mind on each issue as it arises. Think about how the different topics you are discovering might relate to each other. If your mind is staying active and engaged, you will naturally find yourself generating questions about those relationships. This also helps you maintain focus and interest in the passage text.

To see how this works in practice, let's take a look at the questions from your online Practice Test 1.

Below are the questions attached to Passage IV. In the Preview stage you should *not* be looking at the answer choices, so only the question stems are provided for now (with the original numbering). You cannot highlight the text of the question stems on the CBT, so do not make any marks on the page as you read. Preview them for about 20 seconds, looking only for references to passage content and not worrying at this stage about the question type. Then, for the purposes of this drill, answer the Preview Question that follows the list of questions before reading through the explanation.

Practice Test 1: Question Stems

17. The author's primary purpose in the passage is to:

18. Suppose an original poetic text from the first century B.C. celebrating the heroic deeds of the god Apollo were discovered in an archeological dig. How would this discovery affect the author's claim that we in modern society find it difficult to comprehend the meaning of myth in ancient societies?

19. In the passage, the author draws an analogy between:

20. According to the passage, anthropologists can still gain understanding of the meaning and function of early human myth by:

21. Which of the following statements, if true, would most *weaken* the author's argument that Malinowski's work in the Trobriands does justice to the true function of myth in that culture?

22. The author implies that the need ancient peoples had for myth's clarity and reassurance arose mainly from:

Preview Question: What will be important in the passage text? _____

_____

_____

_____

_____

_____

_____

_____

Before answering that question together, let's see what you could have gotten out of each question stem.

- Question 17 is a generic Main Point/Primary Purpose question. You will quickly learn to recognize these generic questions and to immediately move on to the next question. You are always defining the Bottom Line of the passage (main point, purpose, and tone of the passage as a whole), regardless of whether or not there is a General question attached to it.
- Question 18 contains new information. Once you recognize this in the preview, it is reasonable to move on; it may take too much time to separate the new information from the passage reference. However, you might have seen that this question refers to an ancient text and to the author's argument about what myths meant to ancient societies.
- Question 19 asks about an analogy used by the author. Now you know to be on the lookout for where this kind of logic appears in the passage.
- Question 20 asks about the meaning of early myths; at this point you may be wondering if the analogy will have something to do with this meaning. This also appears to relate closely to what you saw in question 18: understanding the meaning of ancient myths.
- From Question 21, you know that you need to find and understand what the author has to say about Malinowski's work as it relates to the function of myth.
- Finally, Question 22 alerts you to the fact that the author will be discussing why ancient people needed clarity and reassurance from myths.

On a test, this summary is best done in your head instead of writing it down on your scratch paper.

Based on all this, you might have answered the Preview Question as follows:

The importance and function of myth in ancient societies and how we might understand it, especially through Malinowski's work.

Advanced Previewing: Refining Your Skills
Ask yourself if you are getting what you need out of this step. If not, here are some things to consider.

- Do you find that once you start reading the passage, you can't remember anything that you previewed? If so, you may be previewing too quickly. If you are simply running your eyes over the questions without pulling out the content, you probably aren't getting enough of a sense of the passage, or remembering enough of the question topics, to make it worthwhile. In this situation, try spending an extra 10–15 seconds, and see if they stick better. Or, it may be an issue of focus rather than time. Imagine that you are imprinting each topic on your brain as you read. With a half-second pause after each question, the topics are more likely to make it into your memory bank and to stick around for the passage.

- Are you spending too much time previewing (more than a minute)? If so, you are likely reading for too much detail, including the question type (which is irrelevant at this stage). Practice running your eyes over the question stem until you hit true content, and only then slowing down to read more carefully. Familiarizing yourself further with the common ways in which question tasks are worded will help you focus on the passage content in the question stem (or to recognize and skip over a generic question) and to tighten up the process as a whole.

- Do you become distracted by your memory of the question topics, to the extent that you find yourself just searching for certain words in the passage rather than understanding the author's main points? If so, think of the question topics as clues, not the whole story. You are a detective gathering those clues, and once you read the passage, you are building the story around them. Also, once you improve your skills in working the passage, previewing will contribute to, rather than detract from, your understanding of the key themes in the passage text.

STEP 3: WORKING THE PASSAGE

There are two tasks to accomplish as you work through each paragraph of the passage: highlight the important parts of the passage text, and summarize the main point of each paragraph or chunk. Let's talk about each in turn.

Highlighting

Passages are made up of parts that work together to communicate the author's argument. Some of these parts are more critical than others, however. Obviously, anything related to the question topics will be important to understand. However, to get the correct answers to the questions as efficiently as possible, you also need to have an understanding of the logic of the passage. Highlighting allows you to both maintain your focus on those logical aspects and to leave a trail of breadcrumbs behind so that you can follow it back to the information you need when answering the questions. If you think of yourself as a "good reader," meaning that you read relatively quickly with good comprehension, you may feel that you don't need to highlight at all. However, unless you have a photographic memory and can remember every detail and the major themes with perfect accuracy after a 2–4 minute reading of the passage, you will do better if you use some highlighting.

As you read, highlight key words and phrases that (1) relate to question topics you saw in your preview and (2) tell you about the logical structure of the passage. Authors use words to communicate clearly. Take advantage of this by noticing and highlighting these "indicator words."

The key to effective highlighting is the Goldilocks approach: not too much or too little, but just right. On one hand, highlighting everything that "sounds important" will cause you to highlight a large portion of the text. This does not help you focus on, or understand, the major themes as you read, and it doesn't provide you with a useful map to rely on as you answer the questions. On the other hand, if you do little or no highlighting, you are wasting a handy tool kindly provided to you by the test makers. While some people will legitimately highlight less or more than others, there are basic categories of things that should always be highlighted.

1. **Question topics.** You will not only have to find these references again as you answer the questions, but you will need at least a basic understanding of the surrounding text. Highlight a few key words as a marker, not multiple sentences.
2. **Author's opinion.** Knowing the author's tone is crucial; many wrong answers are wrong because they misrepresent the author's opinion. If the author says good or bad things about anything, highlight the words that indicate attitude. Make sure to separate the author's opinion from the opinions of others cited by the author, and to define whether or not the author expresses agreement or disagreement with those other opinions.

3. **Transitions.**
   - **Pivotal words:** Words like "however," "but," and "although" tell you something very important about the logical structure of the author's point. Tricky wrong answers often *appear* to be supported by the text, but once you take a logical pivot or shift into account, end up being the opposite of what the author is really trying to say. By highlighting these words (or phrases), you plant a signal for yourself to pay attention to that shift.
   - **Continuations:** Authors use words such as "furthermore," "additionally," and "also" to show that two or more ideas are connected to each other, and that the latter idea is some kind of extension of the first. As with pivotal words, the test writers will give you wrong answers that look good if you haven't taken those connections into account.
4. **Conclusion indicators.** Authors use words like "therefore" or "thus" to tell you, "Here's what everything I just told you was leading up to," or, "Here is the most important thing to get out of all of this information." Conclusions are inherently important to the logic of the author's argument, and by marking them and focusing on them, you will much more easily distinguish the details from the main points.
5. **Comparisons and contrasts.** A common passage structure is one that discusses similarities and/or distinctions between different things. Use your highlighting to delineate what is being compared or contrasted and how. As you highlight the indicator words, ask yourself what the *purpose* of the comparison or contrast is: What role does it play within the author's argument? Wrong answers will often mix up the two, suggesting that things compared are instead contrasted, or vice versa, or that two or more things mentioned in the passage are compared/contrasted when in fact they are not.
6. **Different points of view.** When an author quotes or cites someone else, highlight the name or marker for the other point of view. Also ask yourself as you read *why* the author is citing someone else's ideas. Is it to agree? To disagree? To add support to the author's own claims? To contrast different points of view?
7. **Emphasis words.** When an author says something like "most importantly," "primarily," or "key," take him or her at their word. The point that follows is more or less guaranteed to be important to the author, and is often "crucial" to answering the questions as well.

These first seven categories are important for understanding the big picture: the author's main point, tone, and purpose. In addition, there are a few other categories of words and phrases that should be highlighted for location purposes. That is, highlight them so that you can find them again if and when you need to as you answer the questions, but don't spend a lot of time mulling them over, memorizing them, or trying to gain some deep understanding of the details in that section of the passage.

8. **Example indicators.** When you see "for example," "in illustration," or "in this instance," your main focus should be on figuring out what this is an example of (that is, the larger claim being supported) rather than on the details of the example itself. However, by highlighting the indicator words, you leave yourself a sign to guide you back to the details of the example if you need them to answer a question.
9. **Lists.** If you see a list strung together with words like "first," "second," and "third," as with examples (and lists are often lists of examples), ask yourself what this is a list of and what purpose it serves within the passage. However, highlight just the list markers to help you locate any of those items on the list if they become important to the questions.

10. **Names.** It is very annoying to spend large amounts of time hunting down a name to answer a question when you can't remember where it showed up. If you find that by skimming through a text, you easily locate names (which, like numbers, tend to stand out from the surrounding text), you might decide not to highlight them. However, if this is not the case, highlight names wherever they appear. If you do this consistently, you have a guarantee that by skimming through your highlights you will quickly locate them when needed.

This may seem like a lot to keep track of. However, once you practice highlighting for a while you will find yourself doing it automatically; it becomes a natural part of how you read. Furthermore, elements from all the categories of indicator words will not appear within a single paragraph. Even if you highlight all these things consistently, it will only add up to a relatively small percentage of the text.

Advanced Highlighting: Refining Your Skills

Developing your highlighting skills, like all other things Verbal, requires careful self-evaluation. As you review completed passages, ask yourself: "Did I highlight too much? Too little? Did I fail to highlight parts of the text that would have helped me answer the questions more accurately or efficiently? Did I neglect to use my highlighting at times when it would have led me to the correct answer? Did I highlight so much that I couldn't sort through it all?"

- **Highlighting too much and/or highlighting the wrong things:** This often occurs when students treat a passage like a science textbook. When you are studying for a class, you are often most focused on the details and facts, and your highlighting reflects this. In the Verbal Reasoning section, however, the details are least important during your first reading of the passage. Save your highlighting for select words and phrases: those clusters of words that tell you something about the main theme of the paragraph and of the passage as a whole. Think of it as signposting; you don't need in most cases to highlight entire sentences or blocks of text, but rather just the signposts that tell you what important things happen within those blocks of text. Additionally, given the challenge of doing large amounts of reading on a computer screen, sometimes students overhighlight just to keep their eyes moving and to track their progress through the passage. However, while this may seem useful at the time, it does you little or no good once you are answering the questions. Practice questioning why you are about to highlight something. If there is no defined reason, leave it clean. After a while, you will find yourself highlighting less, and only those things that serve a logical or location purpose.

- **Highlighting too little:** Ironically, the cause of highlighting too little can be the same as a cause of highlighting too much: thinking of the passage as an undifferentiated series of facts to be learned and memorized, rather than as an argument made up of different parts to be mapped and analyzed. Or, you may feel that there just isn't enough time to highlight effectively. However, highlighting is one of those small investments of time that pays off in the long run. If you tend to highlight too little, review the list in the previous section. Then do some practice passages untimed, consciously looking for and highlighting the indicator words. As you answer the questions, pay attention to how useful those highlighted chunks are in finding the correct choice and in defining what is wrong with the bad choices. Once you train yourself to highlight as a natural part of reading, and once you can see how it contributes to your speed and accuracy, it gets easier and easier to do it effectively and quickly under timed conditions.

- **Not using your highlighting:** One of the more frustrating experiences is to look back at a question that you have missed, or a question that took you too long to get right, and see that you had the relevant part of the passage highlighted but never looked at it as you were answering the question. This usually happens partway through the learning curve: You are now highlighting well, but working the questions as if you hadn't highlighted at all. It seems simple, but all you need to do in this situation is remind yourself to look at your highlighting. You may even want to write "Look at highlighting!!!" on the top of your scratch paper. A basic reminder may be all it takes for you to remember to take advantage of that effort you put into mapping the passage.

Don't let your good highlighting go to waste—use it!

Summarizing the Main Point of Each Paragraph

Paragraphs (or different chunks within long paragraphs) are generally made up of claims and evidence: There is some central claim being made, and evidence is provided in support of that claim. Or an entire paragraph may consist of evidence intended to support a claim made elsewhere in the passage. Either way, your goal is to separate the claims from the evidence and to keep your focus on the author's central points (and to skim over the details that may or may not be needed to answer the questions). Sometimes an author will do the work for you by giving you a topic sentence at the beginning or end of the paragraph. At other times the burden is placed on you to imagine what that topic sentence would be, given the information presented in the paragraph. Regardless, after you read each paragraph, pause and ask yourself, What is the one central idea to which this chunk of information relates? Why did the author write this paragraph in the first place? What function does it serve within the passage as a whole?

Knowing the main point of each paragraph or chunk not only keeps you focused on the main themes of the passage, it also gives you a label for that chunk that you can use to locate information later on as you answer the questions. This is the main use to which you will put your scratch paper in the Verbal section: writing down a very brief summary (say, 5–10 words) of each main point as you read. Some test takers will write more or less than others (you may find, for example, that you only need to physically write down the main points during more challenging passages), but every student will benefit from using his or her scratch paper actively (to some extent). Whenever you use your scratch paper, do so in an organized fashion: Write down the passage number on the top of the space you are using for that passage and label each paragraph as you go.

Aside from helping you analyze the author's logic and locate information for the questions, defining the main points serves an even more basic function: It keeps you awake. If you are passively reading through 600–700 words of (often not so fascinating) text, it can be a challenge to keep your mind engaged. However, if you give yourself this task to perform after each paragraph, it keeps you alert and focused.

Advanced Summarization: Refining Your Skills

- **Getting the main point wrong:** If you find that you often misidentify the main point, ask yourself if you focused too much on one part of the paragraph to the exclusion of the rest. In particular, did one subsidiary detail stand out and stick in your mind, distracting you from the larger purpose of the paragraph? Also, while topic sentences often come at the beginning or end of a paragraph, there is no guarantee that the first or last sentence will in fact sum up the purpose of the paragraph as a whole. Did you miss some key indicator words (for example, a conclusion indicator or a pivotal word) that would have pointed you towards the true central theme of the paragraph?

  If any of this sounds familiar, put yourself through a series of main point drills: Do a set of passages untimed, requiring yourself to write down the main point of each paragraph on scratch paper. While doing this, concentrate on the highlighting skills we discussed above, paying close attention to indicator words, especially conclusions, pivotal words, and expressions of the author's opinion. Even if this entails more writing than you think you will need to do for the actual test, the act of putting it into words and writing it down (for each and every paragraph) will force you to engage with the logic of the material. This is the way to learn how to avoid mistaking the author's real argument, or to keep yourself from passively identifying things that "sound important" in the paragraph as the main point. You may find that writing more doesn't actually take up too much of your time and that it contributes significantly to your accuracy. Or, you might go back to only using your scratch paper for harder paragraphs or harder passages, but with an improved ability to mentally articulate the major themes.

- **Writing too much:** If you find yourself essentially rewriting each paragraph on your scratch paper, you may be writing an outline of that chunk of passage rather than distilling the information down to one central theme. Keep your focus on the overall purpose of the paragraph rather than on all the facts and details within it. Limit yourself to eight words at most, and think of the main point as a label rather than as an outline. Sometimes writing too much comes from thinking too little; it is easier (but more time consuming and less useful) to regurgitate every detail of the paragraph than to stop and ask: What theme do all those details relate back to? If this sounds familiar, take a distinct pause after you finish each paragraph to ask yourself what that overall theme is before you take the next step of jotting down the main point.

✳ Keep your main points short and sweet.

STEP 4: DEFINING THE BOTTOM LINE

The Bottom Line of the passage is the main point, purpose, and tone of the passage as a whole. While you don't necessarily need to define each of those three aspects separately, thinking of them as facets of the Bottom Line can help you put it into words. If you have worked the passage effectively as we have discussed above, defining the Bottom Line should come fairly easily. Essentially, it is the connecting thread that ties all the paragraphs together. And nicely enough, the Bottom Line is one of the most powerful tools you have in hand when answering the questions. Many answers even on Specific questions are wrong because they violate or are inconsistent in some way with the Bottom Line, and recognizing this is often the fastest way to eliminate those choices. You may find it useful to jot down a concise expression of the Bottom Line on your scratch paper for every passage or at least for the most difficult passages. Make sure that you have a clear idea of the point and purpose of the passage before you start on the questions.

Advanced Bottom Lining: Refining Your Skills

As we suggested above, problems defining the Bottom Line often track back to troubles with mapping the passage. If you find that you often just flat out get it wrong, ask yourself if you paid enough attention to key indicator words as you were reading the passage. If, for example, you thought the Bottom Line was the opposite of what it really was, did you miss an opinion/tone indicator? Did you overlook a pivotal word or phrase that sent the passage in a different direction from where it first appeared to be going? If you find that your Bottom Line was too narrow (and you got General questions wrong because of this), did you focus too much on one paragraph to the exclusion of the others? In particular, did you incorrectly assume that the main point of the last (or the first) paragraph was the main point of the whole passage? Sometimes the first or last paragraph will sum it all up for you, but not always. Think of the passage as a puzzle, with the paragraphs as the pieces. The Bottom Line is the picture made by fitting all the pieces together.

Putting it All Together

Let's practice your passage mapping and Bottom Line skills on a passage. Here is the text of the fourth passage from Practice Test 1 (for which you already previewed the questions). We will use this same passage later in our discussion of question types and strategies; for now, however, we are just focusing on working the passage itself. First, go back to the discussion of previewing the questions and remind yourself of the topics that appeared in the question stems. Then read and highlight the passage below, and jot down the main point of each paragraph in the spaces provided. (Even if you have already taken that test, rework the passage for the purpose of this drill.) Finally, define the Bottom Line and write it down as well. Then read through the explanations that follow and see if you worked the passage effectively, and how you could have worked it even better. These explanations, in addition to providing a statement of the main points and the Bottom Line, will walk you through an analysis of the thought process you want to follow as you work the passage yourself.

Whenever you are working a passage on paper, use a highlighting pen to map the passage.

For the purposes of this drill there are spaces provided under each paragraph for notes. When doing passages on your own, however, use scratch paper, just as you will when taking a test on a computer.

Practice Test 1: Passage IV

In our contemporary world so obsessed and controlled by science and technology, the idea of myth has fallen into disrepute. For most people, if one were to ask them, "myth" amounts to little more than superstition, wives' tales, illusion, fantasy, or false conception. But the great ancient civilizations from which our own society evolved cherished fabulous tales of gods and heroes.

Main Point of paragraph 1: _____

_____

For the civilizations that produced them, myth occupied a place and served a function within the social fabric reserved today for medicine, astrophysics, and cybernetics. Myth blazed like a beacon of clarity and reassurance in an uncertain and terrifying universe. Myth gave people a finite idea of their place in the scheme of things, taught them how to see themselves in relation to forces beyond their control and how to survive and relate within a human society built on hierarchical power and often ruthless savagery.

Main Point of paragraph 2: _____

_____

The chasm of experience and time separating our lives at the third millennium from those who created the classical myths in antiquity makes it difficult for us to comprehend the feelings of those to whom myth represented a living reality. We lack the testimony of the committed believers, who knew Athena's power as we know the atom's, who consulted the Delphic oracle as we do the Hubble telescope, who deciphered the Muses' secret whispers as we decode the chromosomal helices. (For that matter, even the texts that have come down to us across the epochs are suspect, rescripted along the way by thousands of oral poets, censors, translators, and politically correct intelligentsia of every stripe.)

Main Point of paragraph 3: _____

_____

Nevertheless, in certain far-flung corners of the globe, more or less impervious to the glitter, flash, and buzz of this Early Electronic Age, communities of humans who maintain their people's ancient knowledge still practice the traditional rituals, still follow the folkloric customs. Anthropologists willing to shed their cosmetics of doctrine and costumes of theory might thus still gain a firsthand understanding of essential myth. For just as astronomers study astroradial photographs of exploding supernovas to learn about the evolution of planets and the origins of organic life, so might we study modern aborigines to discover the strategies and insights of human consciousness in its primal attempts to process perceptual reality into cultural rules.

Main Point of paragraph 4: _____

_____

Prior to the work of Sir James Frazer, mythologists for the most part lined themselves up in one of two opposing camps. On one side were the naturalists, who believed that aboriginal peoples limited themselves to an elegiac worship of cosmology, investing the sun, moon, stars, and climate with anthropomorphic identities. On the other side, the historicists argued that aboriginal myth amounted to nothing more than historical chronicle, a fact-based record of past events. Yet neither of these approaches does adequate justice to the fundamental power and function of myth in aboriginal societies.

Main Point of paragraph 5: _____

_____

By venturing into the field to live within aboriginal society, however, Bronislaw Malinowski, one of Frazer's disciples, penetrated the core of the matter. His pioneering work in the Trobriand Islands led him to a comprehensive view of myth as a "vital ingredient of human civilization; not an idle tale, but a hard-worked active force; not an intellectual explanation or an artistic imagery, but a pragmatic charter of faith and moral wisdom."

Main Point of paragraph 6: _____

_____

Bottom Line of the passage as a whole:_____

_____

Sample Highlighting and Analysis

In our contemporary world so obsessed and controlled by science and technology, the idea of myth has fallen into disrepute. For most people, if one were to ask them, "myth" amounts to little more than superstition, wives' tales, illusion, fantasy, or false conception. But the great ancient civilizations from which our own society evolved cherished fabulous tales of gods and heroes.

Analysis: The first appearance of the word "myth" is highlighted. As long as the passage continues to discuss myth, you don't need to highlight every recurrence of the word. The pivotal word "But" marks a contrast between how most people today think of myth and the importance it had for ancient civilizations. When you come across phrases like "for most people," or "many people claim," or "in the past it was believed," look out for the pivotal word that often follows to suggest a contrast or some other kind of shift.

Main Point of paragraph 1:   Unlike today, myth important in past.

For the civilizations that produced them, myth occupied a place and served a function within the social fabric reserved today for medicine, astrophysics, and cybernetics. Myth blazed like a beacon of clarity and reassurance in an uncertain and terrifying universe. Myth gave people a finite idea of their place in the scheme of things, taught them how to see themselves in relation to forces beyond their control and how to survive and relate within a human society built on hierarchical power and often ruthless savagery.

Analysis: "Function" and "clarity and reassurance" showed up in our preview of the questions. Both the word "function" and the phrase "reserved today" relate to the continuation of the contrast the author began to draw in the first paragraph: the difference between ancient and modern societies in relationship to myth. This part of the passage tells us that myth served the same function for ancient societies that medicine and science serve for us today, and describes that function in more detail. This analogy is something we were on the lookout for, based on our preview of the questions.

Main Point of paragraph 2:   Myth in past same function as science today.

The chasm of experience and time separating our lives at the third millennium from those who created the classical myths in antiquity makes it difficult for us to comprehend the feelings of those to whom myth represented a living reality. We lack the testimony of the committed believers, who knew Athena's power as we know the atom's, who consulted the Delphic oracle as we do the Hubble telescope, who deciphered the Muses' secret whispers as we decode the chromosomal helices. (For that matter, even the texts that have come down to us across the epochs are suspect, rescripted along the way by thousands of oral poets, censors, translators, and politically correct intelligentsia of every stripe.)

Analysis: Most of the highlighting in this paragraph relates to both the continuation of the author's contrast between past and present ("chasm of experience and time"), and a series of comparisons between how knowledge was gained in the past versus in the present. Notice that a new idea has been introduced: the difference between ancient and modern society and the lack of reliable evidence makes it difficult for us to understand the true meaning of myth for those who lived in the distant past. The word "suspect" relates to this problem of evidence and carries a negative tone.

Main Point of paragraph 3: Understanding of ancient meaning of myth limited by lack of evidence.

Nevertheless, in certain far-flung corners of the globe, more or less impervious to the glitter, flash, and buzz of this Early Electronic Age, communities of humans who maintain their people's ancient knowledge still practice the traditional rituals, still follow the folkloric customs. Anthropologists willing to shed their cosmetics of doctrine and costumes of theory might thus still gain a firsthand understanding of essential myth. For just as astronomers study astroradial photographs of exploding supernovas to learn about the evolution of planets and the origins of organic life, so might we study modern aborigines to discover the strategies and insights of human consciousness in its primal attempts to process perceptual reality into cultural rules.

Analysis: The pivotal word "Nevertheless" sends the passage off in a different direction at this point. However, this is not entirely unexpected; we saw a question about ways in which we may be able to gain an understanding of the meaning and function of early myths. The phrase "thus still gain a firsthand understanding" continues this shift into a discussion of how we may in fact be able to gain firsthand evidence of the ancient or essential role of myth. This phrase is highlighted because it performs a variety of roles: It relates to a question topic, it introduces a conclusion, and it presents a contrast with the theme of the previous paragraph. In the second half of the paragraph, the author introduces another analogy, indicated by the words "just as" and "so might."

Main Point of paragraph 4: Might study aboriginal myths to understand ancient myths.

Prior to the work of Sir James Frazer, mythologists for the most part lined themselves up in one of two opposing camps. On one side were the naturalists, who believed that aboriginal peoples limited themselves to an elegiac worship of cosmology, investing the sun, moon, stars, and climate with anthropomorphic identities. On the other side, the historicists argued that aboriginal myth amounted to nothing more than historical chronicle, a fact-based record of past events. Yet neither of these approaches does adequate justice to the fundamental power and function of myth in aboriginal societies.

Analysis: This paragraph has a fairly complicated structure. The word "Prior" at the beginning of the paragraph introduces a new contrast: mythologists before and after Frazer. Within this contrast is embedded a further distinction, that between the naturalists and the historicists. Then, the phrase "Yet neither of these approaches does adequate justice" indicates the author's negative opinion about both of these schools of thought. At this point you would want to be on the lookout for the other side of the suggested contrast in time. This was true of mythologists before Frazer, so what was different about those that came after?

⟡ If there is a "before," look for what the "after" might be.

Main Point of paragraph 5: Two types of mythologists before Frazer—both inadequate.

> By venturing into the field to live within aboriginal society, however, Bronislaw Malinowski, one of Frazer's disciples, penetrated the core of the matter. His pioneering work in the Trobriand Islands led him to a comprehensive view of myth as a "vital ingredient of human civilization; not an idle tale, but a hard-worked active force; not an intellectual explanation or an artistic imagery, but a pragmatic charter of faith and moral wisdom."

Analysis: This paragraph answers the question we just posed, beginning with the word "however." Malinowski, in following Frazer, was "pioneering" and came up with a "comprehensive view." Both of these phrases indicate a contrast between Malinowski and the mythologists mentioned in the previous paragraph; both also have a positive tone within the context of the author's discussion. The repeated pairing of "not" and "but" in the rest of the paragraph continues the contrast between the naturalists and historicists on one hand, and Malinowski on the other. Note that this paragraph is also a continuation of the idea introduced in paragraph 4, where the author indicates how we may actually be able to find evidence to help us understand the essential function of myth.

Main Point of paragraph 6: Malinowski, studying aboriginal people, able to develop better understanding of myth.

Bottom Line of the Passage: Myth played an important role in ancient society, and we may come to better understand it through studying aboriginal societies today.

STEP 5: ATTACKING THE QUESTIONS

Now it comes down to the heart of your Verbal score: answering the questions as quickly and accurately as possible. A common reason even high-scoring students miss questions is that they approach them too "intuitively." That is, they quickly read the question, go though the answer choices, and look for something that seems like a reasonable answer. If something jumps out at them, they pick it and move on. If not, they reluctantly go back to the passage looking for something that appears to support one of the answer choices. If you are already scoring at or above average, this process is often leading you quickly to the right answer. However, unless you are already getting the score you want, sometimes it isn't. So, let's go though the basic approach to answering the questions, the different question types and strategies, and ways in which to refine your skills.

Basic Approach

1. **Read the question stem word for word.**

   You will have already skimmed through the question stems during the previewing process. However, if you previewed effectively, you were not paying attention to the question type at that stage. Now, every word in that question is potentially important. If you misread the question at this point in the process, it is difficult to recover.

2. **Identify the question type and format, and translate the question task.**

   Ask yourself, "What is this question asking me to do?" This defines your strategy from that point on.

3. **Go back to the passage to find the relevant information.**

   This applies to all questions that include some reference to a defined area of the passage. (If the question is asking about an issue that appears in multiple paragraphs, or if it has no reference to particular passage content, go directly to the answer choices.) Read at least five lines above and below the reference in the passage; pay attention to indicator words that may tell you that you need to read even more of the text. Paraphrase what the author had to say.

4. **Generate an answer in your own words.**

   Based on the question task and your paraphrase of the passage text, come up with a guide to what the correct answer needs to do or say.

5. **Use Process of Elimination (POE) to choose an answer.**

   Read all four answer choices word for word. Paraphrase complicated wording to make sure that you understand the meaning of each choice. Strike out choices that are clearly wrong; don't, however, select an answer until you have read all four carefully and thoughtfully. Often, you will need to take two passes or "cuts" through the choices before you make a final selection. Even though you may have a good idea of what the answer should be, don't just look for the closest match. Instead, approach the choices negatively: Look for what is *wrong* with each choice, and eliminate down to the "least wrong" answer.

   Even test takers who have followed good form up to this point (both in how they worked the passage and interpreted the question) can still get the question wrong if they don't use good POE. The test writers purposefully construct certain wrong answers to be "Attractors." That is, they are written to sound even better than the credited response, and to distract you away from it. Those writers may even take into account what someone who has understood the passage and the question task will be looking for, in order to tempt that person into picking the Attractor without reading the rest of the choices carefully (or at all). Stay on your toes: often the answer that looks good at first glance turns out to have something wrong with it. However, don't fall into paranoia, striking out an answer just because it looks too obvious.

   Answering in your own words before looking at answer choices makes you less likely to fall for attractors.

   POE is so fundamental to improving your score that it is worth further discussion here, before we get into the details of the different question types and formats. Let's go through the different types of tricky wrong answers that most commonly appear in the Verbal Reasoning section and discuss ways to identify and avoid them.

Advanced POE: Attractor Types

- **Out of scope:** These are choices that bring in issues not discussed in the passage. They are often the most clearly wrong answers and therefore usually the easiest ones to eliminate. Do be careful, however, not to overuse this rationale: just because something isn't directly stated by the author doesn't necessarily mean that it is irrelevant to what the author does have to say.

- **Too extreme/too absolute:** This is a common Attractor for questions that ask you in some form what the author or the passage would support. These answers take information from the passage but take it too far beyond what the question is asking and what the author is claiming. They may include strong words like "all," "none," "most," "rarely," "should," or "must." However, a statement doesn't have to explicitly include these words in order to be too strong to be supported by the passage; the test writers know that students often have learned to look out for these words. Think about the meaning of the statement, not just the individual words that it includes. Also keep in mind that a strongly worded passage can support a strongly worded answer choice. This is why you should think of this Attractor not as "extreme" or "absolute" but "*too* extreme" and "*too* absolute." That is, *too* strong for what the question is asking and for what the passage will support.

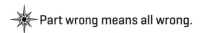 Pay attention not only to the content of the answer choice but also to the strength of its language and of its claim.

- **Half right/half wrong:** These choices are partially but not fully supported by the passage; even one word is enough to make an answer wrong. In fact, the "good" part of this Attractor may sound even better than the whole of the correct answer. The test writers dangle the good part in front of you like a lure, testing to see if you can look past it to discern that there is something else in that statement that invalidates the whole choice.

Part wrong means all wrong.

  To avoid this trap, always read the answer choices word for word the first time through the choices, and take every word into account. It can be tempting to try to rehabilitate these choices by talking yourself into ignoring the bad parts (and to take up a lot of time doing so); remind yourself instead that part wrong means *all* wrong.

- **Words out of context:** These are traps set for students who are not going back to the passage, or not going back carefully enough. They have words or phrases lifted directly from the passage text, but the meaning of the statement is not supported by the passage.

  To avoid this trap, use the passage actively rather than relying on your memory. Also, don't choose answers based on "word matching"; that is, don't choose an answer only because it includes a certain number of words that match back to the passage. Instead, paraphrase the answer choices to see their true meaning. It is the meaning, not the words themselves, that must match. However, don't get paranoid and eliminate an answer only because it reproduces wording from the passage; it might just be an easy question (such things do in fact exist!).

- **Outside knowledge:** These are statements that are either true in the real world or consist of claims with which any reasonable person would agree. However, they are not supported by the passage text. If you are working too quickly and carelessly, these will seem like super-easy questions; the answer looks so obvious that you feel like it would only be wasting time to go back to the passage. However, the Verbal section never tests outside knowledge (and the correct answer doesn't have to correspond to common sense). It's all about whether or not the answer is supported by the passage in some form.

  To avoid this trap, use the passage more actively. Go back to the passage before reading the choices whenever possible; if you already have found what the author actually had to say on the issue, you will be much less tempted by these Attractors.

- **Opposites:** These choices state the exact opposite of what the passage says, or of what the question requires. The test writers may accomplish this by using a negation. That is, they take what would be a correct answer and drop a negative word like "not" into it (or, take out a negative word that should be included). Don't feel stupid if you discover that you have fallen for this trap; sometimes everything in them is good except for that one word that switches the direction. However, people often fall for this because they are not reading carefully enough, or because they are looking for an answer that sounds most like what they think it should say, rather than using careful POE.

  To avoid this trap, read word for word but also pay close attention to: 1) the direction in which the right answer needs to go, and 2) the direction in which each choice actually goes.

- **Right answer/wrong question:** Unlike the previous Attractors, these choices *are* in fact supported by the passage text. However, they don't address the question. These are traps intended for students who fail to pay sufficient attention to the question itself, or who lose track of it as they get caught up in evaluating the choices.

  To avoid this trap, read the question word for word and translate it before you look at any of the choices. If you have narrowed it down to two answers, reread the question before making your final decision.

Summary: Refining your POE skills

These are not the only ways in which choices can be wrong, and we will discuss some more Attractors in the next section that are specific to certain question types. However, if you find that you often waste all the good work you put into working the passage by falling for a trap answer at the last minute, learn these common types and use that knowledge actively to ask questions of the choices (especially when you are down to two). That is, ask questions such as: "Are you too extreme? Do you have one word that makes you wrong? Are you the exact opposite of what you should say?" Asking these questions keeps your mind focused on POE and often alerts you to a problem that you may have overlooked the first time through the answers.

Read the question and answers carefully and remember to go back to the passage.

QUESTION TYPES AND STRATEGIES

Question stems fall into ten different types and three different formats. The ten types can also be grouped into three categories: **Specific** questions that ask about a particular issue within the passage, **General** questions that ask about the passage as a whole, and **Complex** questions that require you to identify or evaluate the reasoning used by the author, or to apply new information to the passage text. Here are the ten types by category.

Specific Questions

1. Retrieval
2. Inference
3. Vocabulary in Context

General Questions

4. Main Idea/Primary Purpose
5. Overall Tone/Attitude

Complex Questions

6. Structure
7. Evaluate
8. Strengthen/Weaken
9. New Information
10. Analogy

These ten types appear in three different formats:

1. Standard
2. Except/Least/Not
3. Roman numeral

These labels will make much more sense if we examine what the questions look like in action. Let's go over each type and format using the passage from Practice Test 1 that we have already highlighted. When a certain question type shows up in that passage, we'll use it as an example and walk through the ideal logical process you should take. If there was no example of a particular type already attached to the passage, we'll look at a sample question to see how you would answer it if it did in fact appear with that passage. As we go through the steps for each question type and format, we'll group steps 1 and 2 under "Reading and translating the question task," steps three and four under "Going back to the passage and generating an answer," and then go through POE.

Below is the highlighted text of the passage. Our notes about the main point of each paragraph and the Bottom Line are underneath the passage (as you should have them written down on your scratch paper).

Practice Test 1: Passage IV

In our contemporary world so obsessed and controlled by science and technology, the idea of myth has fallen into disrepute. For most people, if one were to ask them, "myth" amounts to little more than superstition, wives' tales, illusion, fantasy, or false conception. But the great ancient civilizations from which our own society evolved cherished fabulous tales of gods and heroes.

For the civilizations that produced them, myth occupied a place and served a function within the social fabric reserved today for medicine, astrophysics, and cybernetics. Myth blazed like a beacon of clarity and reassurance in an uncertain and terrifying universe. Myth gave people a finite idea of their place in the scheme of things, taught them how to see themselves in relation to forces beyond their control and how to survive and relate within a human society built on hierarchical power and often ruthless savagery.

The chasm of experience and time separating our lives at the third millennium from those who created the classical myths in antiquity makes it difficult for us to comprehend the feelings of those to whom myth represented a living reality. We lack the testimony of the committed believers, who knew Athena's power as we know the atom's, who consulted the Delphic oracle as we do the Hubble telescope, who deciphered the Muses' secret whispers as we decode the chromosomal helices. (For that matter, even the texts that have come down to us across the epochs are suspect, rescripted along the way by thousands of oral poets, censors, translators, and politically correct intelligentsia of every stripe.)

Nevertheless, in certain far-flung corners of the globe, more or less impervious to the glitter, flash, and buzz of this Early Electronic Age, communities of humans who maintain their people's ancient knowledge still practice the traditional rituals, still follow the folkloric customs. Anthropologists willing to shed their cosmetics of doctrine and costumes of theory might thus still gain a firsthand understanding of essential myth. For just as astronomers study astroradial photographs of exploding supernovas to learn about the evolution of planets and the origins of organic life, so might we study modern aborigines to discover the strategies and insights of human consciousness in its primal attempts to process perceptual reality into cultural rules.

Prior to the work of Sir James Frazer, mythologists for the most part lined themselves up in one of two opposing camps. On one side were the naturalists, who believed that aboriginal peoples limited themselves to an elegiac worship of cosmology, investing the sun, moon, stars, and climate with anthropomorphic identities. On the other side, the historicists argued that aboriginal myth amounted to nothing more than historical chronicle, a fact-based record of past events. Yet neither of these approaches does adequate justice to the fundamental power and function of myth in aboriginal societies.

By venturing into the field to live within aboriginal society, however, Bronislaw Malinowski, one of Frazer's disciples, penetrated the core of the matter. His pioneering work in the Trobriand Islands led him to a comprehensive view of myth as a "vital ingredient of human civilization; not an idle tale, but a hard-worked active force; not an intellectual explanation or an artistic imagery, but a pragmatic charter of faith and moral wisdom."

Scratch Paper Notes

1: *Unlike today, myth important in past.*
2: *Myth in past same function as science today.*
3: *Understanding of ancient meaning of myth limited by lack of evidence.*
4: *Might study aboriginal myths to understand ancient myths.*
5: *Two types of mythologists before Frazer—both inadequate.*
6: *Malinowski, studying aboriginal people, able to develop better understanding of myth.*

Bottom Line of the Passage: Myth played an important role in ancient society, and we may come to better understand it through studying aboriginal societies today.

Question Types

1. Retrieval Questions

Reading and Translating the Question Task These questions are usually phrased "According to the passage..." or "As stated by the author..." They will also usually give you some fairly specific reference to the passage. These are essentially "go fetch" questions; they usually give you a specific issue and send you back to the passage to find what the author says about it.

Taking a look at Practice Test 1, passage 4, you will see that Question 20 falls into this category. The question asks:

> According to the passage, anthropologists can still gain understanding of the meaning and function of early human myth by:

Going Back to the Passage and Generating an Answer Once you have read the question word for word and identified the question type, the next step is to go back to the passage and find where the author discusses the cited issue. Our main point of paragraph 4 is, "Might study aboriginal myths to understand ancient myths." This sends us back to that paragraph for the answer. The author states (with our original highlighting):

> Anthropologists willing to shed their cosmetics of doctrine and costumes of theory might thus still gain a firsthand understanding of essential myth. For just as astronomers study astroradial photographs of exploding supernovas to learn about the evolution of planets and the origins of organic life, so might we study modern aborigines to discover the strategies and insights of human consciousness in its primal attempts to process perceptual reality into cultural rules.

So, your answer in your own words might be: "studying modern aborigines." Once you have an answer in your own words, take it into the answer choices. Remember, however, that you are still using POE, looking for what is wrong with each choice.

POE Here are the answers that go along with question 20:

A) developing computer models based on modern aboriginal communities.
B) applying contemporary theories and doctrines to interpret aboriginal social structures.
C) learning about the role played by myth in the lives of aborigines today.
D) adopting aboriginal traditions and truths as guiding moral precepts and analytical tools.

Taking each choice in turn, choice A is half right, half wrong: The author never discusses computer models. This is an excellent reason to strike it out. Choice B is going in the opposite direction. The author suggests that we should get a "firsthand understanding of essential myth" by observing it in as pure a state as possible in aboriginal cultures, not that we should apply our own modern ideas to aboriginal social structure. So, choice B is out. Choice C is more or less exactly what we had in mind, so we will keep it in. Choice D goes too far. The author states that we should study aboriginal myths and traditions, but not that we should follow them ourselves. This leaves you with choice C as correct.

Advanced "Retrieval": Refining Your Skills Retrieval questions tend to be the easiest ones, so if you are missing a significant percentage of them, you definitely need to figure out why, and to make corrections in your approach. When high-scoring students miss these questions, it is often due to overthinking. Answers that are more or less straight from the passage can seem too obvious, leading you to think that there must be something wrong with them. This in turn leads you to talk yourself into some other answer. Keep it simple: You want the answer that is closest to what the passage says (and relevant to the question).

High-scoring students (or even those who are not yet high-scoring) may also miss these questions because they rely too heavily on memory, or on a cursory glance back at the passage. If you commonly fall for the "words out of context" Attractor for this question type, this is a clear sign that you need to use the passage more consistently and carefully.

2. Inference Questions

Reading and Translating the Question Task   Inference questions can be worded in a variety of ways, such as, "It can be inferred that…," The author implies/suggest/assumes that…," "With which of the following statements would the author be most likely to agree?" or "Which of the following statements is best supported by the passage?" Question 22 on passage 4 is an Inference question:

> The author implies that the need ancient peoples had for myth's
> clarity and reassurance came mainly from:

Going Back to the Passage and Generating an Answer   These questions may or may not give you a specific reference to the passage within the question stem. If it does, approach it in the same way as a Retrieval question by going back to the passage and locating the relevant information. For Question 22, we had already highlighted the key words in the second paragraph based on our preview of the questions. The second paragraph states:

> Myth blazed like a beacon of clarity and reassurance in an
> uncertain and terrifying universe. Myth gave people a finite
> idea of their place in the scheme of things, taught them how
> to see themselves in relation to forces beyond their control
> and how to survive and relate within a human society built on
> hierarchical power and often ruthless savagery.

Your answer in your own words therefore might be, "People's sense of insecurity and lack of control."

POE   As you use POE, ask yourself which choice is best supported by the passage. Although Inference answers tend to be less directly stated in the passage than Retrieval answers, your logical process on both types is essentially the same.

Now let's take a look at the choices:

> A)   feelings of powerlessness and vulnerability.
> B)   an unstable social fabric.
> C)   ineffective medical techniques.
> D)   a finite sense of themselves.

Choice A appears to be closely related to, and consistent with, the author's description of myth helping people to deal with the existence of "forces beyond their control" and with the challenges of survival in a sometimes "savage" society. Choice A is also a close paraphrase of our own answer. But since we haven't read all the choices yet, we will just keep it in contention for now. Choice B sounds good at first glance because the author does mention an "uncertain" universe. However, the passage does not describe the "social fabric" itself as uncertain or unstable. This is a "Words Out of Context" trap, and we can strike out choice B.

Choice C is out of scope; you might also think of it as words (or word) out of context. The author does mention that today's medicine performs the same function that myth did in the past. However, there is no mention or suggestion of medicine being ineffective in the past. Also be careful not to use outside knowledge or to overthink it. Medicine may well have been relatively ineffective in the ancient past, and we might be tempted to speculate that this would make people feel powerless, which for all we know might have caused them to turn to myths for reassurance or guidance. However, none of this would be supported by the passage, and thinking this way would be a big waste of your time.

Finally, choice D is an example of a combination of two different Attractors: "Opposite" and "Right Answer/Wrong Question." Looking back at the passage, the author says that "Myth gave people a finite sense of themselves," not that myths were *created because* of people's finite sense of themselves. Choice D would be a great answer for a question that asked what myth provided or resulted in, rather than for this question, which asks where it came from. This answer would also be perfect if it said the opposite of what it actually says: that is, "the *lack* of a finite sense of themselves."

In the end, therefore, we are left with choice A as the credited response.

Advanced "Inference": Refining Your Skills

It is important to keep in mind that this is not a test of your real inferring skills. People sometimes get into trouble with Inference questions because they overinterpret or misunderstand what these questions are really asking. In the real world, "inference" is most often used to indicate "conclusion" or "deduction." However, while some answer choices in the Verbal section will fit this definition, others will not. Defining it this way can lead you to overlook the easiest Inference answers: those that closely paraphrase the passage. On the other hand, we also sometimes think of inferences (or suggestions or implications) as insinuations or speculation. This can cause you to pick incorrect answers that "might be true" or "could be true," rather than relying only on what is already stated in the passage.

What it all comes down to is: an inference (or assumption, or suggestion, or implication, or what the author would most likely agree is true) is defined as "the answer choice that is *best supported* by the passage, compared to the other three." Correct inferences appear in a variety of guises. They may be more or less restatements of passage information or directly supported by a particular paragraph within the passage. Additionally, an Inference question stem that includes a reference to something within one paragraph may require you to take evidence from two or more paragraphs into account in order to locate the correct answer. The correct answer is always the one that is closer to the passage and better supported than the other three choices. As you can see, comparing choices to each other is an especially important part of your Inference strategy.

Now we are back to self-evaluation. You will probably discover that a high proportion of the questions you miss are Inference questions; this may be in part because Inference questions are one of the most common question types. Ask yourself if you tend to eliminate choices that seem too obvious. If so, you may be taking the definition too narrowly, as a deduction and not potentially as a paraphrase. Or, do you only look for choices that are in fact essentially stated in the passage? If so, remind yourself that an answer can be directly supported by the passage without being directly stated in the text. Do you miss correct answers because they required combining information from two or more paragraphs or chunks of the passage? If so, remember to look at all areas where the issue of the question appears in the passage. Finally, do you pick incorrect answers because you add in too much of your own information or speculation? If so, remind yourself to stick as closely as possible to the passage text. If you hear yourself thinking, "Well, if X were also true, and if Y and Z also happened, then this would be a pretty good answer," you are probably straying too far afield.

3. Vocabulary-in-Context

Reading and Translating the Question Task
These questions ask what the author means by a certain word or phrase. Some ways in which these questions might be phrased are, "By *X*, the author most likely means…" or "The author most likely used *X* in the sense of…" There is no Vocabulary-in-Context question for passage 4, so let's take a look at a sample question of this type. A Vocabulary-in-Context question attached to this passage might ask:

> By *suspect* (paragraph 3) the author most likely means:

Going Back to the Passage and Generating an Answer
The correct answer has to make sense if inserted in place of the existing word in the passage. Therefore, you need to take into account the context of the sentence, the paragraph, and of the passage as a whole. Reading above and below the word *suspect*, we see the following:

> We lack the testimony of the committed believers, who knew Athena's power as we know the atom's, who consulted the Delphic oracle as we do the Hubble telescope, who deciphered the Muses' secret whispers as we decode the chromosomal helices. (For that matter, even the texts that have come down to us across the epochs are suspect, rescripted along the way by thousands of oral poets, censors, translators, and politically correct intelligentsia of every stripe.)

Even though this sample question was not part of our original preview, we had initially highlighted the word "suspect" because of its negative tone.

Going back to our scratch paper notes, the main point of that paragraph was "Understanding of ancient meaning of myth limited by lack of evidence." There was clearly a negative tone to this chunk of the passage.

So, to answer in our own words, we might say "untrustworthy."

POE
Here is a set of answer choices to go along with our new sample question:

A) believe.
B) pioneering.
C) criminal.
D) dubious.

Choice A is the classic Attractor for this question type: a common definition that doesn't fit into the context of the passage. Choice B sounds familiar because it appears in paragraph 6. It isn't relevant to this question, however, and "pioneering" has a positive rather than a negative tone. Choice C has a similar problem to choice A: The word "suspect" might be used in a different context to indicate "criminal," but there is no logical connection to the passage. Finally, choice D does in fact fit. If we replaced "suspect" with "dubious" ("…even the texts that have come down to us across the epochs are dubious, rescripted along the way…"), it preserves the meaning of the sentence as well as the paragraph. This leaves us with D as the correct answer.

Advanced "Vocabulary-in-Context": Refining Your Skills   Often on these questions you will be down to one answer after only a single pass through the choices, having eliminated based on the main point of that chunk of the passage and your own answer to the question. If not, however, replace the word or phrase in the passage with each of the remaining choices, and read the sentence "out loud" in your head. If you listen to each sentence, the one that best fits the meaning of the passage will emerge.

When going over your self-evaluation, look to see if you fall for the common trap of a wrong answer that gives you a more obvious or common definition, but one that does not fit with the author's meaning. If you have a good vocabulary yourself, you have to be extra careful not to answer these questions based on your own definition rather than the author's.

4. Main Point/Primary Purpose

Reading and Translating the Question Task   These questions ask you for a summary of the central point or purpose of the passage. They are most commonly phrased like this: "The main idea/central thesis of the passage is…" or "The author's primary purpose is…" The first question on passage 4, Question 17, is a Primary Purpose question. It asks:

> The author's primary purpose in the passage is to:

Although the wording of these two subtypes is different, they are really asking for the same thing: The Main Point is the central claim or overall theme of the passage, while the Primary Purpose is what the author does in order to communicate that claim or theme.

Going Back to the Passage and Generating an Answer   To answer these questions, you generally will not need to go back to the passage before you start evaluating the answer choices. You have already answered in your own words when you defined the Bottom Line. Our Bottom Line for this passage was, "Myth played an important role in ancient society, and we may come to better understand it through studying aboriginal societies today."

POE   As you go through the answer choices, make sure that you keep the scope of the question (the entire passage) and the tone of the passage in mind. Here are the answers for Question 17:

A)   demonstrate the impossibility of understanding the function of myth in ancient society.

B)   criticize the naturalist and historicist schools of thought for presenting inadequate visions of the place and power of myth.

C)   explain the role of myth in ancient society and suggest ways of overcoming the problems involved in understanding that role.

D)   explain why, given advances in science and technology, we no longer need myths to represent the roles we play in society and nature.

Choice A is too strong. While the author says that it is difficult to understand, the last paragraph tells us that Malinowski was able to express "a comprehensive view of myth." Be on the lookout for choices that take a theme or idea expressed in the passage too far. Choice B represents one theme in the passage (from paragraph 5), but it is only one part of the author's overall argument. This is an Attractor specific to General questions: answers that are too narrow for the scope of the question task. Choice C is similar to our own Bottom Line and doesn't appear to have anything wrong with it, so we will keep it in contention. Choice D is something the author suggests to be true in the second paragraph. However, while D could be a correct answer for an Inference question, it is too narrow to be the primary purpose of the passage as a whole. This leaves us with C as the correct choice.

Advanced Main Point/Primary Purpose: Refining Your Skills   The most important thing to keep in mind when answering these questions is scope. An answer that captures the main point of a paragraph, or even of multiple paragraphs, will be incorrect if it leaves out some major theme in the passage. On the other hand, an answer that is too broad in scope is incorrect as well. The Goldilocks approach that we discussed for highlighting applies here as well: not too big or too small, but just right.

If you consistently miss Main Point or Primary Purpose questions, ask yourself if it may be due to problems you are having working the passage in the first place. Are you explicitly defining the Bottom Line before you attack the questions? If not, the "too narrow" choices that are only the main point of a paragraph or two will be especially tempting. In particular, look to see if you have picked wrong answers that are the main point of the last paragraph but not of the passage as a whole. Also check to see if you are missing these questions because you got the tone of the passage wrong. If this is the case, focus on looking for attitude and opinion indicators as you work the passage the first time through. Overall, a low level of accuracy with this question type may be a symptom of a larger problem, and an indication that you would benefit from refining your strategy in the passage-working phase.

5. Overall Tone/Attitude

Reading and Translating the Question Task   In their General form, these questions will be phrased fairly simply: "Which of the following statements best describes the author's tone in the passage…" or "The author's attitude can best be described as…" (Be on the lookout for the occasional Specific Tone/Attitude questions, which asks for the author's attitude towards a particular issue within the passage, rather than about the passage as a whole.) There is no Tone/Attitude question attached to passage 4, so let's work through a sample question:

In this passage, the author's tone is one of:

Going Back to the Passage and Generating an Answer   As with Main Point/Primary Purpose questions, there is usually no need to go back to the passage before you start on the answer choices. Tone and attitude are parts of the Bottom Line, and you have already defined this once you finished working the passage. Here, given our Bottom Line, we could answer in our own words: "admiration for the function of myth in ancient society, and for Malinowski's work."

POE   As you go through the choices, look out for two basic things: answers with the wrong tone (e.g., positive when it should be negative), and answers that are too extreme (e.g., "dismay" when it should be "disappointment"). Here is a set of choices for our sample question:

  A) disappointment.
  B) dismay.
  C) appreciation.
  D) excitement.

Although the author does express some level of disappointment with the naturalists and historicists in paragraph 5, this does not capture the overall tone of the passage, which leads up to a positive evaluation by the end. Dismay goes even further in the wrong direction. So, choices A and B are out. Choice C goes in a positive direction, which is promising, and it could apply to both the role of myth and Malinowski's work. So, we keep it in. Finally, "excitement." It's tempting because it also has a positive tone, and because perhaps we can imagine the author being excited when he heard of Malinowski's work, or speaking in an excited way when discussing the role of myth. However, that's too much from our imagination, with not enough direct support from the passage. This leaves us with C as the correct choice.

Advanced "Tone/Attitude": Refining Your Skills   The first thing to keep in mind when answering these questions is the scope of the question task. If it is a General question, you need a general answer that captures the author's tone in the passage as a whole, not just in one part of the passage to the exclusion of others. Be on the lookout for choices that are too narrow.

 Make sure the scope of the answer matches the scope of the question and passage.

As you are doing these questions, it can help to visualize the tone of the passage and the tone of the choices you are considering. Imagine a spectrum, from totally negative on the left (say, "severe condemnation") to strongly positive on the right (such as "joyful advocacy") and with "neutral description" in the middle.

(−)_____neutral_____(+)

When you are answering tone questions in your own words, visualize where along this line the passage would fall. As you go through the choices, do the same (especially if you are down to two). For our question above, we might have visualized something like this:

B   A   C   D
(−)_____ passage _____(+)

If you are down to two on opposite sides of the spectrum, or between "neutral description/analysis" and something with an either positive or negative tone, you need to go back to the passage and look for more evidence. However, if you are down to two answers on the same side of the spectrum, the answer is usually the more moderate of the two.

Also be suspicious of descriptors that suggest uncertainty, such as "ambivalent" or "reluctant." Authors may express both positive and negative evaluations within a passage, but they are usually pretty firm and decisive about those opinions. Finally, correct answers are rarely emotional or personal. In the question above, "excitement" would be a bit strange to see in a passage; the kind of writing you usually find on the MCAT is not the kind of writing that usually expresses excitement, or fear, or sadness, or joy. Don't eliminate these choices thoughtlessly (sometimes things outside of the norm do show up), but if you are stuck between two, it is safest to go with the more "normal" choice.

If you tend to miss Tone/Attitude questions, or if you often miss other question types because you mistook the author's tone, you need to consider how you are working the passage in the first place. Are you consciously looking out for words that indicate attitude? If so, are you consistently highlighting them? Are you taking them into account when you define the Bottom Line (and are you defining the Bottom Line in the first place)? Issues with tone are usually a symptom of larger problems with how you are working the passage, problems that will affect other question types as well.

6. Structure

Reading and Translating the Question Task
Structure questions ask you to describe, in some form, the logical structure of the passage. This often involves describing the relationship between different parts of the passage. The most common phrasing uses the words "in order to," as in, "The author mentions Frazer in order to…" For our passage, Question 19 is a less obvious form of a structure question. It asks:

> In the passage, the author draws an analogy between:

The correct answer will describe or match a part of the passage where the author compares two things in this way.

Going Back to the Passage and Generating an Answer
We have a few possibilities already highlighted in the passage, based on our preview of the questions. In paragraph 2 we saw:

> For the civilizations that produced them, myth occupied a place and served a function within the social fabric reserved today for medicine, astrophysics, and cybernetics.

In paragraph 4, we saw another analogy:

> For just as astronomers study astroradial photographs of exploding supernovas to learn about the evolution of planets and the origins of organic life, so might we study modern aborigines to discover the strategies and insights of human consciousness in its primal attempts to process perceptual reality into cultural rules.

If we hadn't already found and highlighted these analogies based on either our preview or on the fact that they are comparisons, we would skip this step and go directly to the choices. Keeping these two analogies in mind, let's take a look at the choices.

POE   Here are the answer choices for Question 19:

A)   naturalist and historicist approaches to understanding the role of myth in aboriginal society.

B)   the role of science in the modern world and the place of myth in antiquity.

C)   ancient gods and heroes and anthropomorphized cosmological entities in today's aboriginal cultures.

D)   science and anthropology.

Looking at choice A, and going back to paragraph 5, we see that this is the opposite. These two schools of thought are contrasted, while analogies are based on similarities. Choice B is the first of the two analogies we already pulled out of the passage, so we'll hang on to it. Choice C is tempting because these things were in fact mentioned in the passage (paragraph 1 and paragraph 5), and it seems reasonable that they might play analogous roles in myth. So, let's say we hold on to choice C for now. Choice D is half right, half wrong. The analogy is between science and myth, not science and anthropology.

Now that we are down to two, it's time to go back to the exact wording of the question stem. It asks what the *author* draws an analogy between, not what *we* might see as analogous. This takes it down to choice B as the correct answer.

Advanced "Structure": Refining Your Skills   When answering these questions, make sure that you take indicator words into account. If the phrase "for example" appears in front of something, you know that thing is an example of a larger point made previously in the passage. If the word "therefore" shows up, it indicates that what follows is a conclusion based on evidence or an explanation that most likely immediately preceded it.

Sometimes Structure questions ask you to see the connection between things that sit in different parts of the passage. Don't assume that everything you need to take into account for a single Structure question will be within a single paragraph.

If you consistently struggle with these questions, it may be because you are not paying enough attention to the logical structure of the author's argument when you work the passage. If this is the case, review the list of indicator words given earlier in this chapter, and practice your highlighting.

7. Evaluate

Reading and Translating the Question Task   Evaluate questions come in two different forms. The most common (and generally easier to answer) form asks *whether or not* a claim is supported in the passage. For example, it might be phrased: "Which of the following claims made in the passage is supported by evidence or an example?"

The less common (and more difficult to answer) form will ask *how well* a claim made in the passage is supported. For example, the question might be phrased:

> The author's assertion that science plays the same role today as myth played in ancient societies is supported:

The answer choices then might be variations on "strongly" and "weakly" with explanations why. Given that there is no Evaluate question already attached to the passage, let's use this second variation as our sample question.

Going Back to the Passage and Generating an Answer   This question sends us back

to paragraph 2, where the author writes:

> For the civilizations that produced them, myth occupied a place and served a function within the social fabric reserved today for medicine, astrophysics, and cybernetics. Myth blazed like a beacon of clarity and reassurance in an uncertain and terrifying universe. Myth gave people a finite idea of their place in the scheme of things, taught them how to see themselves in relation to forces beyond their control and how to survive and relate within a human society built on hierarchical power and often ruthless savagery.

Looking back at this paragraph, we see that the role of myth is explained in a fair amount of detail. However, although the author claims that science (that is, medicine, astrophysics, and cybernetics) plays the same role today, there is no evidence given for that claim. How do we know that science provides clarity and reassurance? The author appears to assume that we will agree with this statement, and so no evidence is given. Thus, our answer is "weakly, because of the lack of evidence or examples."

POE   Here is a set of choices to go with our sample question:

A) strongly: The analogy between astroradial photographs and the study of modern aborigines supports the claim.

B) strongly: Evidence is provided of the role science plays to reassure us of our finite place in the world.

C) weakly: This claim contradicts the author's statement that it is difficult to understand the role of myth in ancient society.

D) weakly: No description or evidence of the role of science today is provided.

Choice A heads off in the wrong direction from the first word, "strongly." However, you should always read every word of every answer. In this case, though, choice A just gets worse. Yes, there is such an analogy made in paragraph 4, but on a different issue (how studying current evidence can teach us about the past). Choice A is out. Choice B also begins with the opposite word "strongly," and the description that follows is inaccurate. There is in fact no such evidence provided. Choice C is more promising, but the second half of it is wrong. The author claims in paragraph 3 that it is difficult to understand the feelings of those for whom myth played an essential role, not that we have little understanding of the function that myth served. Finally, both parts of Choice D match up. The claim is weakly supported, and the explanation of why is accurate. Choice D therefore is correct.

Advanced "Evaluate": Refining Your Skills   Just as for Structure questions, Evaluate

questions require you to take into account the logical structure of the passage: how the author constructs his or her argument, and additionally how good a job he or she does. Use your highlighting actively as you attack these questions, especially indicator words that mark conclusions, examples, and pivotal words.

If you are down to two choices that are opposites of each other (e.g., "strongly" vs. "weakly"), there is likely to be something important about the passage that you haven't understood. Go back to the relevant paragraph or paragraphs and re-read carefully. If you are down to two choices on the same side of the fence (e.g., both "strongly" or "weakly"), it is likely that the description that follows one or the other doesn't match the logic of the passage. Compare the two choices to each other, look for differences in the descriptions, and go back to the passage to find out which one does not fully match up.

If you tend to miss the first variation of this question type (those that ask whether or not a claim is supported), this often comes out of careless reading and/or not going back to the passage. If you tend to miss the second variation (those that ask how well a claim is supported), this may mean that you are not reading critically enough. Normally you take the passage as true (except for Weaken questions), and only treat the answer choices skeptically. For these questions, however, you need to shift gears and approach the passage skeptically as well, looking for flaws in logic. The most common flaw you will see is lack of examples or evidence supporting a claim. Again, this goes back to highlighting effectively and using your highlighting actively while answering the questions.

8. Strengthen/Weaken

Reading and Translating the Question Task   Strengthen and Weaken questions give you new information in the answer choices, and ask you to find the statement that does what it needs to do to the passage. Weaken questions might be phrased, "Which of the following statements, if true, would most *undermine* the author's claims?" or "Which of the following, if proven, would go farthest to call the author's argument into question?" A Strengthen question can be worded, "Which of the following claims, if valid, would most strengthen the author's argument in the passage?" or "Which of the following, if true, would most support the author's conclusion in the last paragraph?" Generally, the words that indicate "weaken" are italicized within the question stem, while words that indicate "strengthen" are not. For passage 4, Question 21 is a Weaken question:

> Which of the following statements, if true, would most *weaken* the author's argument that Malinowski's work in the Trobriands does justice to the true function of myth in that culture?

Going Back to the Passage and Generating an Answer   To answer Strengthen/Weaken questions, first find the relevant part of the passage, if you are being asked to strengthen or weaken a particular part of it. Paraphrase what the author has to say on that issue. You can't literally answer these questions in your own words, because the answers will bring in new information that wasn't in the passage. Your goal at this stage, then, is to come up with a guide to the correct answer: What does it need to do or say to accomplish the task of weakening or strengthening? If it's a strengthen question, you need to find something that goes along with the passage. To weaken, you need something that contradicts the passage as much as possible; put the opposite of the author's argument into your own words as a guide to the choices. If the question stem doesn't specify a particular issue within the passage, use the Bottom Line (or the opposite of it) as your guide.

For Question 21, the relevant part of the passage is the last paragraph, where the author writes:

> His pioneering work in the Trobriand Islands led him to a
> comprehensive view of myth as a "vital ingredient of human
> civilization; not an idle tale, but a hard-worked active force;
> not an intellectual explanation or an artistic imagery, but a
> pragmatic charter of faith and moral wisdom.

Therefore, we need an answer choice that indicates a reason why Malinowski's work in the Trobriands may NOT provide an accurate picture of the real function of myth in that culture.

POE   Here are the choices for Question 21:

A)   Sir James Frazer had as a primary goal the reconciliation of the naturalist and historicist schools.

B)   The specific myths that define Trobriand society contain some images and themes found in no other ancient or modern cultures.

C)   The presence of outside anthropological observers significantly changes the speech and behaviors of the members of the culture being observed.

D)   Many well-respected anthropologists have rejected Malinowski's conclusions.

Choice A is out of scope for two different reasons. First, the question is about Malinowski; even though Malinowski was Frazer's disciple, we don't know that what was true of Frazer was necessarily true of Malinowski. Second, there is no reason to think that an attempt to reconcile the two schools of thought would inherently fail to capture the true function of myth; even if this were true of Malinowski as well as of Frazer, it would not by itself weaken the author's argument. Therefore we can strike out choice A. To evaluate choice B, we need to check back to the passage: does the author ever suggest that Malinowski's conclusions were based on an assumption that the Trobriand myths themselves were identical to myths in other cultures? Looking back at paragraphs 3–6, we can see that it is the function of myth that the author claims to be the same, not the specific myths themselves. Therefore, choice B does not weaken the passage.

Choice C, at first glance, looks irrelevant. The author never talked about the effect of observers on the observed. However, since the right answer will bring in new information, we can't eliminate it on that basis alone. And, if the presence of an outsider would change how people act, it is possible that Malinowski did not in fact get a true picture of how myth functioned in Trobriand society; his data or observations may have been inaccurate. So, we will keep choice C in for now. Choice D is momentarily attractive because it sounds like a negative judgment of Malinowski. However, the question we need to ask of this choice is, "Is the opinion of some anthropologists, no matter how well-respected, enough to cast significant doubt on Malinowski's claims?" The answer is no. By whom are they well-respected? For all we know, they could be naturalists respected by other naturalists, or historicists respected by other historicists; both schools would be predisposed to reject Malinowski's conclusions. Also, how many is "many"? If the choice said "most" or "all," it would have a little more weight, but we have no indication of how truly widespread this opinion might be. So, we see that D is a classic type of Attractor for Strengthen/Weaken questions; it isn't strong enough to have a significant impact on the author's argument. This leaves us with choice C as the correct answer.

Advanced "Strengthen/Weaken": Refining Your Skills

In general, a correct Weaken answer will provide empirical evidence against the claim being weakened. It may also suggest an alternate cause or explanation, or question the methodology used to support the claim. Often a correct Strengthen answer will give empirical evidence in support of the claim. It may also fill in a logical gap in the argument, state that an assumption made in the passage is in fact true, or rule out possible objections to, or problems with, the claim being strengthened.

There are a couple of things about Strengthen and Weaken questions that distinguish them from other question types. First, the correct answer will have new information in it that you must apply to the passage. If you treat these too much like Inference questions (especially easy to slip into on the Strengthen version), you will eliminate the correct answer, thinking that it is out of scope. In fact, the wording of some Strengthen questions sounds a lot like Inference questions. If the question asks "what is supported by the passage," this is an Inference. If it asks "what supports the passage," it is a Strengthen. If you tend to miss Strengthen questions, use your Question Review Worksheet and self-evaluation to figure out if you are mistaking them for Inference questions.

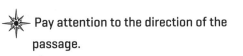 Pay attention to the direction of the passage.

The second aspect of Strengthen and Weaken questions to keep in mind is that you want a strong answer rather than a wishy-washy one. If you are doing any other question type (except for Except questions), strong language is suspicious, and choices are often wrong because they are too extreme or absolute. However, for a Strengthen or Weaken question, the stronger the language is in the answer choice, the better that choice is, all other things being equal. If you tend to eliminate the right answer the first time through the choices, look to see if you eliminated it because you thought it was too strong.

A third aspect, this time of Weaken questions in particular, is that they require keeping close track of the direction of the passage, the direction required by the question task, and the direction of each answer choice. Given that you are more used to picking answers that go along with the passage than choices that go against it, it can be a challenge to keep your wits about you and keep headed in the right direction on Weaken questions. If you find that you tend to get turned around and pick an answer that is the opposite of what it should be, or that you waste a lot of time having to backtrack and start all over because you get confused, this is a good time to use your scratch paper. Write down a paraphrase of the argument from the passage that you are weakening, jot down a guide to the correct answer (the opposite of what the passage said), and refer to that guide as you make your way through the choices.

9. New Information

Reading and Translating the Question Task

All New Information questions have one thing in common: They give you a new fact or scenario in the question stem and ask you to apply it in some form to the passage. New Information questions have become quite common in the Verbal Reasoning section, to the extent that they now rival Inference questions as one of the most commonly seen question types.

There are two types of these questions: New Information/Inference and New Information/Strengthen/Weaken. New Information/Inference might be phrased something like: "If X were shown to be true, what, based on information in the passage, would also be true?" For these, you take the new information, combine it with existing passage information, and find the answer choice that is best supported by that combination. New Information/Strengthen/Weaken questions ask you what effect the new information in the question stem would have on the author's argument in the passage. For example, the question might ask, "Which of the following claims made in the passage would be most weakened by data showing X?" or "Suppose X were proven to be true. This finding would offer the most support to the author's claim that…"

Regardless of which type it is, the key to answering these questions is to paraphrase the new information in the question stem (treat it like a chunk of passage and figure out its theme or main point), and then decide on its relationship to information provided in the passage.

Question 18 for passage 4 is a New Information/Strengthen/Weaken question:

> Suppose an original poetic text from the first century B.C. celebrating the heroic deeds of the god Apollo were discovered in an archeological dig. How would this discovery affect the author's claim that we in modern society find it difficult to comprehend the meaning of myth in ancient societies?

The theme of this scenario is, "We found new primary evidence of an ancient myth."

Going Back to the Passage and Generating an Answer

The relationship of this evidence to the passage is, "This appears to be less 'suspect' than the evidence discussed in paragraph 3. However, it doesn't seem to be enough to represent a 'living reality.' So, it doesn't appear to either significantly weaken or strengthen the author's argument."

POE

Here are the choices for Question 18:

A) It would refute the claim by indicating that data from living cultures can give us some insight into the role and power of myth.
B) It would support the claim, because rescripted texts are inadequate indicators of what myth meant to the people of that time.
C) It would be irrelevant to the claim, which is about mythological stories, not poetry.
D) It would not fully refute the claim, because even an original text does not recreate the living reality essential to cultural meaning.

Choice A is, first of all, too strong. As we already decided, the new evidence is not enough to significantly undermine the passage. If we weren't sure about it on that basis, there is something else wrong with this choice: This is an ancient text, not one from a "living culture." Choice B also begins in a dubious manner; the new information doesn't directly support the author's claim. And, as in choice A, choice B makes another mistake: There is no indication that this is a "rescripted" (rather than original) text. Choice C isn't clearly wrong from the very beginning. Having no significant impact could perhaps be described as "irrelevant." However, the author's argument is not limited to *nonpoetic* mythological stories. Therefore this choice is incorrect. Finally, choice D matches our own answer and does not misrepresent either the passage information or the new information in the question stem. This leaves us with choice D as the correct answer.

Advanced "New Information": Refining Your Skills   For both types of New Information questions, if you are down to two answers, compare them on the basis of the following: Which one of the two is most relevant to both the question stem and the passage information? If one of them relates to both the passage and the question, while the other is supported by the passage but has no direct connection to the new information, the first of the two is a more likely choice.

For New Information/Inference questions (just as on Specific Inference questions), beware of choices that are too extreme to be supported by the passage and/or the new information. Beware of choices that go in the opposite direction or that focus on the wrong issue in the passage. Additionally, extreme language can in fact be a problem for New Information/Strengthen/Weaken questions (unlike for regular Strengthen/Weaken), if the language of the answer goes too far past the actual impact of the new information on the passage.

10. Analogy

Reading and Translating the Question Task   These questions ask you to take something described in the passage, logically abstract it, and then compare that abstracted logic to new situations in the choices, looking for the best match. Like Strengthen and Weaken questions, the new information will be in the answer choices. Unlike those questions, however, the answer choice will match the logic of what is stated in the passage, rather than make it better or worse. There wasn't an Analogy question attached to passage 4, so let's use the following sample question:

> Which of the following would be most analogous to the relationship between the role of myth in ancient societies and the role of medicine and astrophysics today, as those roles are described in the passage?

Going Back to the Passage and Generating an Answer   In paragraph 2, the author states:

> For the civilizations that produced them, myth occupied a place and served a function within the social fabric reserved today for medicine, astrophysics, and cybernetics. Myth blazed like a beacon of clarity and reassurance in an uncertain and terrifying universe. Myth gave people a finite idea of their place in the scheme of things, taught them how to see themselves in relation to forces beyond their control and how to survive and relate within a human society built on hierarchical power and often ruthless savagery.

The relationship between myth on one hand, and medicine and astrophysics on the other, is that they perform the same function ("clarity and reassurance") in different societies. So, in the choices we are looking for something like different things, same function.

POE   Here are the choices for our Analogy question:

A)   Eyes and ears
B)   Teeth and fur
C)   Wings and fins
D)   Teeth and tongue

Choice A gives us two different structures with different functions (seeing and hearing), which eliminates A. Choice B has a similar problem: perhaps teeth and fur both perform a protective function, but we need a tighter analogy. Choice C is the best so far: Wings and fins are both forms of locomotion (and are generally used by, or attached to, different kinds of animals). Choice D doesn't match the relationship in the passage in a different way than A and B fail to match. Teeth and tongue usually work together in the mouth. So, while they may perform the same (or a related) function, it isn't in two different contexts. This leaves us with choice C as the best match.

Advanced "Analogy": Refining Your Skills   Don't panic! While the answer choices may all seem out of scope at first glance, this is because you need to match the logic, not the content, of the passage. Expect to take two passes through the choices for most of these questions. On your second pass, compare the pieces of the remaining choices to each other (within the choice and between different choices) in order to eliminate "Half right/half wrong answers. Also beware of wrong answers that match or connect to the content in the passage, but not the logic of it.

Question Formats

Before we wrap up our discussion of question strategies, let's take a look at the three formats in which these ten question types can appear.

1.   **Standard**
     This essentially means not Roman numeral and not Except/Least/Not. That is, you have one of the ten question types in its pure form.
2.   **Roman numeral**
     These questions give you three statements labeled with numerals, and the choices present you with different combinations of those numerals. An example of how one of these questions might be structured is:

With which of the following statements would the author be likely to agree?

I.   blah blah blah
II.   blah blah blah
III.   blah blah blah

A)   I only
B)   III only
C)   I and II only
D)   I, II, and III

The most efficient strategy in approaching these questions is to work with the combinations in the choices as you evaluate the statements in the numerals, and to eliminate choices as you go. You can't strike out numerals on the screen, only the lettered choices, so this is also a good time to use your scratch paper. Let's say you were unsure of I and II, but you have a solid reason to eliminate III. Cross off III on your scratch paper, and strike out answer choices B and D on the screen, since they include III. Now compare what you have left, choices A and C. You see that I is in both of the possible answers. Now, you don't have to worry about I anymore: It all comes down to whether or not II is sufficiently supported.

3. **Except/Least/Not**

These questions try to confuse you by asking, for example, what is NOT supported by the passage rather than what IS supported. Or, what LEAST Weakens rather than what most Weakens. The key to these questions is to not let yourself get turned around. Use your scratch paper to keep track of POE. Quickly jot down A–D vertically on your paper. As you strike out each choice on the screen, jot down a note next to the letter on your scratch paper indicating WHY you crossed it off. For example, if it is a Strengthen Except question, write an "S" next to each choice that you eliminate because it does in fact Strengthen. This will keep you focused on eliminating answers for the right reasons and will alert you to what has gone wrong if you get confused.

The most challenging Except/Least/Not questions tend to come in combination with Strengthen and Weaken questions. Do not translate "Weaken Except" as "Strengthen" or "Least Strengthen" as "Weaken." A choice that does go to the opposite extreme (for example, it weakens on a "Strengthen Except") may in fact be the right answer, but the right answer doesn't *have* to go to the opposite extreme. It may instead have no impact on the passage. For example, if three of the choices do significantly strengthen the passage, and one of them does nothing (or strengthens less than the other three), that "does nothing" or "barely strengthens" answer is the correct choice. As you can see, keeping track of your direction and comparing remaining choices to each other is crucial for doing these questions as quickly and accurately as possible. It can help keep your focus on what you are eliminating rather than on what you are choosing. For example, if you have a "Weaken Except" question, write down on your scratch paper "cross off what weakens" and keep track of POE accordingly.

III. SELF-EVALUATION

We've been discussing the specifics of self-evaluation throughout this chapter and the previous one as well. Here, then, let's summarize the big categories in which to look for additional room for improvement.

Overall Pacing

The first step is to diagnose if you are going too fast or too slow, and then to decide the best way to adjust.

Too Fast

- You are completing 6 or 7 passages but missing on average three or more per passage, or you tend to crash and burn on one passage that you are rushing through at the end of the hour.
- You often miss easy questions.
- You are completing all 7 passage and not scoring a 12 or above.

Strategy Adjustments

- Slow down from 7 to 6, or from 6 to 5 passages, and work on improving your accuracy. If your accuracy improves, you may then be able to bring the pace back up. If you are scoring in the double digits and completing all 7, try randomly guessing on 1–3 questions and saving that time for getting the rest of the questions right.
- Read the question stems and answer choices more carefully the first time through.
- Go back to the passage more carefully and consistently.

Too Slow

- You consistently get all or most of the questions that you answer correct, but you are completing 5 or fewer passages.
- You spend a disproportionate amount of time on one passage, or on one or two questions within a passage.
- You spend 6 or more minutes reading the passage the first time through.

Strategy Adjustments

- Force yourself to spend less time on your first read-through of the passage. Remember that you don't have to memorize it, or even fully understand every aspect of it, on your first reading; you can always go back to find what you need.
- If you often have to read the question stem or choices multiple times, read it more slowly and translate/paraphrase it the first time. Better to read it once well than to get stuck reading it five times over.
- Use aggressive POE. You don't always have to know exactly why the right answer is right as long as you know why the other three are wrong. Compare choices to each other when you are down to two, keeping the focus on finding what is more wrong with one of them.
- Pick your passages more carefully, especially if you tend to waste a high percentage of your time bogged down in a Killer passage.

Working the Passage and Bottom Line

Do your mistakes in the questions tend to track back to mistakes you made when reading the passage the first time through? If so, focus on:

- Mapping and highlighting for logical structure and tone,
- Defining the main point of each paragraph based on that structure: jot it down on your scratch paper,
- And defining the Bottom Line as a distinct step before you attack the questions. Ask yourself, Does my Bottom Line include all the major themes of the passage? Does it take into account any major shifts in the passage? Does it match the author's tone?

Attacking the Questions

Do you find that you had a beautifully mapped and understood passage, and yet something went wrong in the questions? If so, diagnose exactly where you strayed from the path leading towards the correct choice, and come up with a strategy to stay on that path next time. Ask yourself:

- Did you misread or misidentify the question? If so, read word for word and paraphrase the question task. Also, review the ten question types in the previous section.
- Did you understand the question, but misunderstand the relevant part of the passage? If so, read the passage text closely at this stage, read farther above and below, and pay attention to indicator words. Make yourself paraphrase the author's argument before taking the next step.
- Did you understand the question task and the relevant part of the passage, but got turned around in the answer choices? If so, focus on answering in your own words, keeping both the question task and passage information in mind.
- Did all of that go great, up to and including having a perfect answer in your own words, and yet you still picked the wrong answer? If so, focus on reading each choice word for word the first time through, looking for what's wrong rather than for what "sounds right." Review the types of Attractors discussed earlier in this chapter, and look for patterns in the types of Attractors that you tend to fall for.
- Did you in fact select the right answer, and then changed it to a wrong answer? If so, live by the following rule: Never change an answer unless you can define exactly what was wrong with your first choice. If the other answer just "sounds better," leave it be.

Final Note

To improve your score, you have to do something different, even something radically different, perhaps even something you would never had done on your own unless someone had (strongly) suggested it. As we have discussed, simply doing test after test or passage after passage will get you nowhere. Don't be afraid to experiment in order to find what works best for you. Nothing is set in stone until test day (or perhaps a few days before). You may be surprised at the good results you get once you step out of your strategy comfort zone and try something new!

Chapter 7
Verbal Reasoning
Practice Section

Practice Passage 1

"One Journalism" defines good journalism as the kind of journalism produced at the top of corporate pyramids—the networks and the major national and regional newspapers. This means that journalists address the particular problems and needs of a community in an artificial journalistic context, created and driven from other places. But people practice democratic government in specific locations, in the municipalities and states where they seek to answer the question, "What shall we do?" through deliberation. That process requires shared information and some common values—above all the value of democratic deliberation is the best way to express and experience public life, and that all citizens have a personal responsibility to take part in that process.

The reflexive, value-neutral techniques of One Journalism do not promote democratic deliberation. Rather, their skewed definitions of sources and issues systematically exclude people from democratic deliberation and generate much irrelevant information that does not advance that essential deliberation. One Journalism determines, for instance, that we define "balance" as "both sides" when in fact most issues have multiple sides. It insures the high value we put on conflict as the ultimate illuminator of political discussion. It makes it inevitable that the world we present one day seems disconnected from the world we present the next day. Meanwhile, the culture of detachment denies any journalistic concern or responsibility for what happens, if anything. When citizens see reflected in newspapers and broadcasts a politics of polar extremes that excludes them, when the machinations of experts and absolutists seem beyond their reach, they withdraw into private concerns. They abandon public life. This is a direct threat to journalism, for if people are not involved in public life, they have no need for journalists.

Journalism's authority—its right to be attended to—is disappearing in a cloud of cynicism and loss of credibility brought on by the routine and detached way we go about business. But public journalism offers a solution to this problem. At its core, public journalism suggests a close examination of the alleged overriding value of detachment and seeks to develop more useful journalistic reflexes. Its objective is to find ways for journalism to serve a purpose beyond—but not in place of—telling the news: the purpose of reinvigorating public life by re-engaging people in it. This requires both a change in the perspective of journalists and a change in what they do. It means learning to report and write about public life beyond traditional politics; to write about political issues in ways that reflect the true array of choices; to report the very important news of civic life—including civic successes—that now occurs outside our pinched definition of news. This can only be done if journalists think of the people by their efforts not as an audience to be entertained or as spectators at an event, but as citizens capable of action.

This response to the decline in public life and journalism

conflicts sharply with One Journalism's guiding axiom of detachment. A key tenet of public journalism is that the "line" of detachment defined by One Journalism is a false construct. Traditional journalists speak of "crossing the line" as if three questionable things were true: that a single line defines all possible points of moral, ethical and professional concerns; that every journalist understands precisely where that line lies; and that anything on one side of the line is "good journalism" and everything on the other side is something else.

Think of the line not as a boundary, but as a continuum that runs between two points. One point defines total detachment or non-involvement in what we cover. The other defines total involvement. Journalists exploring public journalism accept the construct of a continuum and seek to operate somewhere beyond total involvement. Precisely where their activity falls is determined by their consciences, their judgment and the needs of their communities. Public journalism is the antithesis of One Journalism.

Public journalism is openly based on broad values as: This should be a better place to live, and people should determine what that means by taking responsibility for what goes on around them. Public life, according to the values of public journalism, requires shared information and shared deliberation; people participate in answering democracy's fundamental question of "What shall we do?" Public journalism opens the possibility that journalists can serve their communities in truly useful ways that go beyond telling the news. It also offers us a chance to regain our lost credibility.

Adapted from D. Merritt, "Public Journalism—Defining a Democratic Art," *Media Studies Journal: Media and Democracy.* ©1995

1. What is the most direct threat to journalism, according to the author?

A) When the exclusion of citizens' private concerns is reflected in newspapers and broadcasts.
B) Presenting a disconnected worldview from day to day.
C) Traditional journalists "crossing the line."
D) When people forsake their community lives for their private lives.

2. According to the author, what is the purpose of public journalism?

A) To serve as the only solution to the overt problem of One Journalism plaguing society.
B) To challenge the commonly held belief that rather than a boundary, there is a continuum between detachment and total involvement.
C) To promote civic involvement and foster democratic deliberation.
D) To directly influence traditional journalists to become more open-minded about the capacity of their audience.

3. In order to transition to public journalism, the author argues that the responsibility to change lies with:

   I.   journalists.
   II. the public.
   III. media conglomerates.

A) I only
B) II only
C) I and II only
D) I and III only

4. Which of the following hypothetical examples most closely represents the objective of public journalism, as it is described in the passage?

A) A documentary illuminating the traditional values of detachment and neutrality in the news, detailing how certain local news stations are trying to change this traditional approach to reporting.
B) A magazine article about small town life, written by a national news reporter in New York City.
C) An expose on the subversive involvement of corporations in democracy.
D) A local newspaper article about a successful community service initiative to clean the town lake.

5. The passage suggests that journalists seeking to explore public journalism will determine their desired level of involvement by all of the following EXCEPT:

A) their personal principles.
B) their opinions and individual conclusions.
C) the needs of the communities that they serve.
D) their acceptance of the line between detachment and total involvement as a continuum instead of a dichotomy.

6. Elsewhere, the author states, "it means: understanding that framing issues at the extreme excludes most people, challenging the assumption that conflict is the most interesting narrative device, having an interest in whether problems are solved through democratic deliberation." Based on information provided in the passage, the "it" that the author is referring to is most likely:

A) the key concerns of One Journalism.
B) the core values of public journalism.
C) the primary needs of the civic audience.
D) the traditional problems inherent to journalism, in general.

7. All of the following are fundamental differences between One Journalism and public journalism, EXCEPT that:

A) one is value-neutral and detached while the other seeks community involvement.
B) while one sees two sides to any given news story, the other recognizes the multisidedness of events.
C) where one attempts to avoid responsibility, the other seeks to initiate change.
D) where one is primarily concerned with reporting news, the other hopes to encourage democratic deliberation above all else.

Practice Passage 2

The notion that memory can be "distorted" assumes that there is a standard by which we can judge or measure what a veridical memory must be. If this is difficult with individual memory, it is even more complex with collective memory, where the past event or experience remembered was truly a different event or experience for its different participants. Moreover, whereas we can accept with little question that biography or the lifetime is the appropriate or "natural" frame for individual memory, there is no such evident frame for cultural memories. Neither national boundaries nor linguistic ones are as self-evidently the right containers for collective memory as the person is for individual memory.

I take the view that, in an important sense, there is no such thing as individual memory, and it is well for me to make this plain at the outset. Memory is social. It is social, first of all, because it is located in institutions rather than in individual human minds in the form of rules, laws, standardized procedures, and records, a whole set of cultural practices through which people recognize a debt to the past (including the notion of "debt" itself) or through which they express moral continuity with the past (tradition, identity, career, curriculum). These cultural forms store and transmit information that individuals make use of without themselves "memorizing" it. The individual's capacity to make use of the past piggybacks on the social and cultural practices of memory. I can move over great distances at a speed of 600 miles per hour without knowing the first thing about what keeps an airplane aloft. I benefit from a cultural storehouse of knowledge, very little of which I am obliged to have in my own head. Cultural memory, available for the use of an individual, is distributed across social institutions and cultural artifacts.

As soon as you recognize how collective memory, and even individual memory, is inextricable from social and historical processes, the notion of "distortion" becomes problematic. As the British historian Peter Burke writes, "Remembering the past and writing about it no longer seem the innocent activities they were once taken to be. Neither memories nor histories seem objective any longer. In both cases, this selection, interpretation and distortion is socially conditioned. It is not the work of individuals alone." Distortion is inevitable. Memory is distortion since memory is invariably and inevitably selective. A way of seeing is a way of not seeing, a way of remembering is a way of forgetting, too. If memory were only a kind of registration, a "true" memory might be possible. But memory is a process of encoding information, storing information, and strategically retrieving information, and there are social, psychological, and historical influences at each point.

Contest, conflict, controversy—these are the hallmark of studies of collective memory, rather than the concept of distortion. Discovering the attitudes and interests of the present becomes of much greater concern than the legitimate claims of the past upon them. Still, a focus on distortion makes sense in studies of collective or cultural memory. Even the most ardently relativist scholars among us shiver with revulsion at certain versions of the past that cry out "distortion." The most famous example is the flourishing fringe group of Holocaust revisionists who deny that there was ever a plan to exterminate the Jews or that such a plan was ever set in place. The question of what content of the past is not or cannot or should not be subject to latter-day reinterpretation haunts the papers at a 1990 conference at U.C.L.A. on "Nazism and the 'Final Solution': Probing the Limits of Representation" (Friedlander, 1992). The fascination with conflicting versions of the past and the excitement over legitimately revisionist interpretations of once settled and consensual accounts come precisely from the fact that even trained historians (or perhaps especially trained historians) retain strong beliefs in a veritable past. If interpretation were free-floating, entirely manipulable to serve present interests, altogether unanchored by a bedrock body of unshakable evidence, controversies over the past would ultimately be uninteresting. But in fact they are interesting. They are compelling. And they are gripping because people trust that a past we can to some extent know and can to some extent come to agreement about really happened.

Adapted from M. Schudson, "Dynamics in Distortion of Collective Memory," in *Memory Distortion: How Minds, Brains, and Societies Reconstruct the Past.* © Harvard University Press, 1995

1. With which of the following statements would the author most likely agree regarding the nature of individual memory?

A) It is a fiction created to explain collective memory.
B) It causes conceptual problems when considering approaches to understanding distortion.
C) It is entwined with and dependent on social institutions that perpetuate it.
D) It is distinct from collective memory in several important ways.

2. In the last lines of the final paragraph the author notes that controversies over the past are in fact interesting. How is this claim related to the author's argument in this paragraph?

A) It is an interesting side note used to conclude the discussion, but has little relevance to the argument as a whole.

B) It is of historical importance regarding the underpinnings of distortions that periodically occur.

C) It supports the overall argument by implication, as the contrary notion would undermine it.

D) It is an exception noted to anticipate arguments to the contrary.

3. In the first paragraph the author says that "there's no such evident frame for cultural memories." This most likely means that:

A) the fact that the human race has no natural lifespan implies a continuity of institutional memories for the race as a whole.

B) cultural memories are a property of a group and are thus not shared with other groups.

C) cultural memories are not directly accessible to individuals, whose memories have natural frames.

D) national or linguistic boundaries do not adequately define the nature of collective memories.

4. The author's claims regarding the nature of individual memory would be most *undermined* if which of the following were to become evident?

A) The relationship of seemingly persistent cultural memories to any particular individual can change over time without the knowledge of the individual.

B) Individuals can demonstrably memorize information in a standard memory task.

C) Cultural forms are exceptionally consistent within certain linguistic realms.

D) Small, isolated populations carry little institutional memory, yet thrive within their environments.

5. The author argues that memory is inevitably distortion. Which of the following, if true, would most support this point of view?

A) We selectively choose the memories we report to others.

B) The majority of participants in memory tests are able to successfully recall most items in a list.

C) Numerous mental faculties have been shown to be integral to the process of memory storage and retrieval.

D) Studies show that human attention is limited and that little sensory information is retrievable later.

6. The author says toward the end of the passage that "people trust that a past we can to some extent know and can to some extent come to agreement about really happened," while stating elsewhere in the passage that there is no such thing as individual memory. These claims are:

A) not inconsistent, because they refer to discussions of different aspects of memory.

B) consistent, because the claim regarding the possibility of agreement supports the claim regarding individual memory.

C) somewhat contradictory, because it is difficult to justify the notion that controversies over the past are gripping, given the absence of individual memories.

D) strongly at odds, because the claim regarding the non-existence of individual memory undermines the claim regarding coming to agreement about the past.

7. Suppose a psychological study were performed in which participants in a group setting were asked to come to a consensus regarding the value of recording certain (real or hypothetical) historical facts and ignoring others. If in the study it was observed that certain dominant individuals had a much greater influence on the process of selecting the salient facts to report (e.g., one or a few were able to alter the views of the majority on many issues), what effect would this have on the author's claim in the first sentence of the third paragraph?

A) It would have little bearing on the issue, as dominant individuals have always had inordinate influence on documented facts.

B) It would tend to support the author's claim, as it would show a particular mechanism via which distortions of collective memory might proceed.

C) It would tend to weaken the author's claim, as it would show that distortion of memories is a fairly ordinary event in social settings.

D) It would tend to weaken the author's claim, as it would explain the ultimate origin of most distortions of collective memory.

Practice Passage 3

Satori obtains when eternity cuts into time or impinges upon time, or, which is the same thing after all, when time emerges itself into eternity. Time means *shabetsu*, differentiation and determination, while eternity is *byodo*, all that is not *shabetsu*. Eternity impinging upon time will then mean that *byodo* and *shabetsu* interpenetrate each other, or to use Kegon terminology, the interfusion of *ri* (the universal) and *ji* (the individual). But as Zen is not interested so much in conceptualization as in "existential thinking" so-called, satori is said to take place when consciousness realizes a state of "one thought". "One thought," *ichinen* in Japanese, is the shortest possible unit of time. Just as English-speaking people say "quick as thought," thought, i.e., *nen*, represents an instant, i.e., time reduced to an absolute point with no durability whatever. The Sanskrit *kshana* means both thought and instant. When time is reduced to a point with no durability, it is "absolute present" or "eternal now." From the point of view of existential thinking, this "absolute present" is no abstraction, no logical nothingness; it is, on the contrary, alive with creative vitality.

Satori is the experience of this fact. Buddhist scholars often define *ichinen*, "one thought," as a point of time which has neither the past nor the future, that is to say, *ichinen* is where eternity cuts into time, and when this momentous event takes place it is known as satori.

It now goes without saying that satori is not stopping the flow of consciousness, as is sometimes erroneously contended. This error comes from taking *samadhi* as preliminary to the experience of satori and then confusing *samadhi* with the suspension of thoughts—a psychological state of utter blankness, which is another word for death. Eternity has a death-aspect, too, as long as it remains in itself, that is, as long as it remains an abstraction like other generalized ideas.

Eternity to be alive must come down into the order of time where it can work out all its possibilities, whereas time left to itself has no field of operation. Time must be merged into eternity, when it gains its meaning. Time by itself is non-existent very much in the way that eternity is impotent without time. It is in our actual living of eternity that the notion of time is possible. Each moment of living marks the steps of eternity. To take hold of eternity, therefore, consciousness must be awakened just at the very moment when eternity lifts its feet to step into time. This moment is what is known as the "absolute present" or "eternal now." It is an absolute point of time where there is no past left behind, no future waiting ahead. Satori stands at this point, where potentialities are about to actualize themselves. Satori does not come out of death; it is at the very moment of actualization. It is in fact the moment itself, which means that it is life as it lives itself.

The bifurcation of reality is the work of the intellect; indeed it is the way in which we try to understand it in order to make use of it in our practical life. But this is not the way to understand reality to the satisfaction of our hearts. The bifurcation helps us to handle reality, to make it work for our physical and intellectual needs, but in truth it never appeals to our inmost needs. For the latter purpose reality must be taken hold of as we immediately experience it. To set it up, for instance, in space and time, murders it. This is the fundamental mistake we have committed in the understanding of reality. At the beginning of the intellectual awakening we thought we achieved a grand feat in arranging reality within the frame of time and space. We never thought this was really preparing for a spiritual tragedy.

Adapted from D.T. Suzuki, *Living by Zen*. © Samuel Weiser, 1972.

1. The statement by the author in the third paragraph that "it now goes without saying that satori is not stopping the flow of consciousness" is:

A) supported by references to the nature of satori as a state of one thought.
B) supported by the distinction between "absolute present" and "eternal now."
C) supported by the discussion of our inmost needs.
D) not supported by any information in the passage.

2. With which of the following statements would the author most likely agree regarding the nature of satori?

   I.   It is not facilitated by the suspension of thought.
   II. It is not merely conceptual.
   III. It consists of the experience of eternity.

A) I only
B) II only
C) I and II only
D) II and III only

3. Which of the following, if true, would most *undermine* the author's argument in the concluding lines of the last paragraph?

A) One can use one's intellect and still achieve satori.

B) Many canonical Zen texts refer to the pursuit of rational thought as a means of attaining enlightenment (satori).

C) The division of reality into pieces of time tends to obscure the experience of each moment.

D) Certain Zen teachers consider the ingestion of psychedelic drugs to represent a false enlightenment (satori).

4. Which of the following would the author most likely agree with regarding what he terms the "bifurcation of reality?"

A) It is necessary for certain practical pursuits.

B) It rests on a fundamental mistake regarding practical needs.

C) It leads to spiritual tragedy because of the intellectual effort it requires.

D) It is needed to make spiritual progress.

5. Suppose a brain researcher were engaged in brain scan studies of experienced meditators, who were asked to focus all of their attention on one thing. The researcher discovered in the course of the studies that several different parts of the brains of the majority of subjects were involved in generating this unitary focus. What effect would this have on the author's argument in the last paragraph?

A) It would be of little or no relevance to the argument in question.

B) It would support the idea discussed elsewhere in the passage that intellect tends to divide up reality into moments.

C) It would tend to support the idea that satori is necessary to counter the temptation to bifurcate reality.

D) It would tend to weaken a point of the underlying support for the argument in question, stated in the third paragraph, that eternity also has a death aspect.

6. Which of the following would the author be LEAST likely to agree is part of the "best way to understand reality to the satisfaction of our hearts?"

A) Attaining a perception of reality, such as it is.

B) Experiencing the one moment in which time interpenetrates eternity.

C) Attention to the differentiation of moments as experienced in the "absolute present" or "eternal now."

D) Awakening consciousness to the instant of time as it is experienced.

Practice Passage 4

There are two musics (at least so I have always thought): the music one listens to, the music one plays. These two musics are two totally different arts, each with its own history, its own sociology, its own aesthetics, its own erotic; the same composer can be minor if you listen to him, tremendous if you play him (even badly)—such is Schumann.

The music one plays comes from an activity that is very little auditory, being above all manual (and thus in a way much more sensual). It is the music which you or I can play, alone or among friends, with no other audience than its participants (that is, with all risk of theatre, all temptation of hysteria removed); a muscular music in which the part taken by the sense of hearing is one only of ratification, as though the body were hearing—and not 'the soul'; a music which is not played 'by heart': seated at the keyboard or the music stand, the body controls, conducts, co-ordinates, having itself to transcribe what it reads, making sound and meaning, the body as inscriber and not just transmitter, simple receiver.

This music has disappeared; initially the province of the idle (aristocratic) class, it lapsed into an insipid social rite with the coming of the democracy of the bourgeoisie (the piano, the young lady, the drawing room, the nocturne) and then faded out altogether (who plays the piano today?). To find practical music in the West, one has now to look to another public, another repertoire, another instrument (the young generation, vocal music, the guitar). Concurrently, passive, receptive music, sound music, is become the music (that of concert, festival, record, radio): playing has ceased to exist; musical activity is no longer manual, muscular, kneadingly physical, but merely liquid, effusive, 'lubrificating', to take up a word from Balzac.

So too has the performer changed. The amateur, a role defined much more by a style than by a technical imperfection, is no longer anywhere to be found; the professionals, pure specialists whose training remains entirely esoteric for the public (who is there who is still acquainted with the problems of musical education?), never offer that style of the perfect amateur the great value of which could still be recognized in a Lipati or a Panzera, touching off in us not satisfaction but desire, the desire to *make* that music. In short, there was first the actor of music, then the interpreter (the grand Romantic voice), then finally the technician, who relieves the listener of all activity, even by procuration, and abolishes in the sphere of music the very notion of *doing*.

The work of Beethoven seems to me bound up with this historical problem.... [T]he amateur is unable to master Beethoven's music, not so much by reason of the technical difficulties as by the very breakdown of the code of the former *musica practica*. According to this code, the fantasmatic (that is to say corporal) image which guided the performer was that of a song ('spun out' inwardly); with Beethoven, the mimetic impulse (does not musical fantasy consist in giving oneself a place, as subject, in the scenario of the performance?) becomes orchestral, thus escaping from the fetishism of a single element (voice or rhythm). The body strives to be total, and so the idea of an intimist or familial activity is destroyed: *to want* to play Beethoven is to see oneself as the conductor of an orchestra.... Beethoven's work forsakes the amateur and seems, in an initial moment, to call on the new Romantic deity, the interpreter. Yet here again we are disappointed: who (what soloist, what pianist?) can play Beethoven well?...

What is the use of composing if it is to confine the product within the precinct of the concert or the solitude of listening to the radio? To compose, at least by propensity, is *to give to do*, not to give to hear but to give to write. The modern location for music is not the concert hall, but the stage on which the musicians pass, in what is often a dazzling display, from one source of sound to another. It is we who are playing, though still it is true by proxy; but one can imagine the concert—later on?—as exclusively a workshop, from which nothing spills over—no dream, no imaginary, in short, no 'soul' and where all the musical art is absorbed in a praxis with *no remainder*....

Adapted from R. Barthes, "Musica Practica," *Image-Music-Text*. © Hill, 1977.

1. The author describes the two musics as different in that:

A) one is sociological while the other is erotic.
B) one is German while the other is Romantic
C) one is listened to while the other is played.
D) one is vocal while the other is orchestral.

2. The author does NOT suggest which of the following about Beethoven?

A) His music did not follow past musical traditions.
B) Many amateur musicians have trouble playing his works.
C) He often did not rely on one particular theme.
D) His work can be understood as Romantic interpretation.

3. Suppose that statistics showed that attendance at the symphony and the number of listeners to classical radio stations is higher when Beethoven's piano concertos are played than when the works of Schumann are played. How would this information affect the author's argument about the two musics?

A) The argument would be strengthened because Beethoven's music is passive rather than muscular.
B) The argument would be strengthened because Beethoven's works are superior to those of Schumann.
C) The argument would be weakened because professionals can perform Beethoven's music as well as Schumann's music.
D) The argument would be weakened because the guitar has not become more popular than the piano.

4. The most reasonable inference from the passage discussion of amateur pianists is that they:

A) ceased to exist in Beethoven's time because his music was too difficult for an amateur to master.
B) possessed a certain degree of muscular strength due to the physical demands of playing piano.
C) aspired to play with the technical perfection demonstrated by professional musicians.
D) played music with a physicality that is not evident when one listens to music in the concert hall.

5. Concerning Beethoven and his music, the author appears to be perplexed as to why:

A) Beethoven wrote piano concertos even though they cannot be played well.
B) Beethoven's music rejects *musica practica* in favor of Romantic interpretation.
C) Beethoven wrote music that could be enjoyed only in the concert hall.
D) Beethoven's music is so difficult for an amateur to play well.

Practice Passage 5

The nineteenth century, which prided itself upon the invention of steam and evolution, might have derived a more legitimate title to fame from the discovery of pure mathematics. This science, like most others, was baptized long before it was born; and thus we find writers before the nineteenth century alluding to what they called pure mathematics. But if they had been asked what this subject was, they would only have been able to say that it consisted of Arithmetic, Algebra, Geometry, and so on. As to what these studies had in common, and as to what distinguished them from applied mathematics, our ancestors were completely in the dark.

Pure mathematics was discovered by Boole, in a work which he called the *Laws of Thought* (1854). This work abounds in asseverations that it is not mathematical, the fact being that Boole was too modest to suppose his book the first ever written on mathematics. He was also mistaken in supposing that he was dealing with the laws of thought: the question how people actually think was quite irrelevant to him, and if his book had really contained the laws of thought, it was curious that no one should ever have thought in such a way before. His book was in fact concerned with formal logic, and this is the same thing as mathematics.

Pure mathematics consists entirely of assertions to the effect that, if such and such a proposition is true of *anything*, then such and such another proposition is true of that thing. It is essential not to discuss whether the first proposition is really true, and not to mention what the anything is, of which it is supposed to be true. Both these points would belong to applied mathematics. We start, in pure mathematics, from certain rules of inference, by which we can infer that if one proposition is true, then so is some other proposition. These rules of inference constitute the major part of the principles of formal logic. We then take any hypothesis that seems amusing, and deduce its consequences. If our hypothesis is about *anything*, and not about some one or more particular things, then our deductions constitute mathematics. Thus mathematics may be defined as the subject in which we never know what we are talking about, nor whether what we are saying is true. People who have been puzzled by the beginnings of mathematics will, I hope, find comfort in this definition, and will probably agree that it is accurate.

It is not easy for the lay mind to realize the importance of symbolism in discussing the foundations of mathematics, and the explanation may perhaps seem strangely paradoxical. The fact is that symbolism is useful because it makes things difficult. (This is not true of the advanced parts of mathematics, but only of the beginnings.) What we wish to know is, what can be deduced from what. Now, in the beginnings, everything is self-evident; and it is very hard to see whether one self-evident proposition follows from another or not. Obviousness is always the enemy to correctness. Hence we invent some new and difficult symbolism, in which nothing seems obvious. Then we set up certain rules for operating on the symbols, and the whole thing becomes mechanical. In this way we find out what must be taken as premise and what can be demonstrated or defined. For instance, the whole of Arithmetic and Algebra has been shown to require three indefinable notions and five indemonstrable propositions. But without a symbolism it would have been very hard to find this out. It is so obvious that two and two are four, that we can hardly make ourselves sufficiently skeptical to doubt whether it can be proved. And the same holds in other cases where self-evident things are to be proved.

But the proof of self-evident propositions may seem, to the uninitiated, a somewhat frivolous occupation. To this we might reply that it is often by no means self-evident that one obvious proposition follows from another obvious proposition; so that we are really discovering new truths when we prove what is evident by a method which is not evident. But a more interesting retort is, that since people have tried to prove obvious propositions, they have found that many of them are false.

Self-evidence is often a mere will-o'-the-wisp, which is sure to lead us astray if we take it as our guide. For instance, nothing is plainer than that a whole always has more terms than a part, or that a number is increased by adding one to it. But these propositions are now known to be usually false. Most numbers are infinite, and if a number is infinite you may add ones to it as long as you like without disturbing it in the least. One of the merits of a proof is that it instills a certain doubt as to the result proved; and when what is obvious can be proved in some cases, but not in others, it becomes possible to suppose that in these other cases it is false.

Adapted from B. Russell, *Mysticism and Logic and Other Essays.* © Longmans, Green 1918

1. Which of the following descriptions best corresponds to the author's attitude towards symbolism with respect to mathematical foundations?

A) Obscure but provable
B) Increasingly important in modern mathematics
C) Crucial for pedagogical purposes
D) Invaluable without being obvious

2. Which of the following is illustrated with an explicit example in the passage?

A) A pre-nineteenth-century mathematician.
B) A seemingly self-evident proposition that is in fact inaccurate.
C) An infinite number that does not increase when another number is added to it.
D) An important mathematical symbol.

3. According to the information in the passage, which of the following can properly be inferred concerning Boole?

A) If asked for a definition of mathematics, Boole's definition would differ from that given by the author of the passage.
B) In his writings Boole made inaccurate claims about how the majority of people actually think.
C) Boole's writings corrected some of the mathematical errors of previous authors.
D) Boole underestimated the influence of his writings on later mathematicians.

4. What is the meaning of "baptized" in the context of its usage within the passage (paragraph 1)?

A) Originated
B) Treated reverently
C) Named publicly
D) Cleansed

5. Which of the following statements would best be encompassed within the author's description of pure mathematical content?

A) $2 + 2 = 4$
B) If Henry is currently twice as old as Bobby, and six years ago Henry was three times as old as Bobby, then how old will Bobby be when Henry is 60?
C) For any x, if x is divisible by 3 and by 4, then x is also divisible by 12.
D) Let S be a set consisting of all positive integers divisible by 10.

6. Based on the information in the passage, each of the following may be properly inferred EXCEPT that:

A) in certain exceptional cases, a whole may have fewer terms than does one of its parts.
B) a fact that has been proven can still be doubted.
C) investigating the relationship between two assertions may itself constitute a worthwhile intellectual pursuit.
D) it is possible to add together an infinite and a finite number.

7. Which of the following best describes the organization of the reasoning in the passage above?

A) A field of study is defined; certain errors in the historical development of that field are discussed; a new proposal for eliminating further errors is developed; and consequences of pursuing the new proposal are described.
B) Two different perspectives concerning a particular field of study are compared and contrasted; the more symbolic of the two is described by the author as superior; a potential objection to the author's position is addressed; and particular benefits of the field of study are again affirmed.
C) The chronological development of one academic field is outlined; the contemporary form the field has taken is defined; the most distinctive methodological innovation of the field is defended against several potential objections; and two interesting developments within the field are referenced.
D) Certain aspects of the early development of a specialized field are described; the proper range of content for that field is defined; one confusion concerning a key facet of that field is addressed; and the importance and benefit of certain foundational projects within the field are again affirmed.

Practice Passage 6

The disappearance of public executions marks the decline of the spectacle; but it also marks a slackening of the hold on the body. In 1787 Benjamin Rush remarked: "I can only hope that the time is not far away when gallows, pillory, scaffold, flogging and wheel will, in the history of punishment, be regarded as the marks of the barbarity of centuries and of countries and as proofs of the feeble influence of reason and religion over the human mind." Branding had been abolished in England (1834) and in France (1832); in 1820, England no longer dared to apply the full punishment reserved for traitors. Only flogging still remained in a number of penal systems (Russia, England, Prussia). But, generally speaking, punitive practices had become more reticent. One no longer touched the body, or at least as little as possible, and then only to reach something other than the body itself. From being an art of unbearable sensations punishment has become an economy of suspended rights.

At the beginning of the nineteenth century, then, the great spectacle of physical punishment disappeared; the tortured body was avoided; the theatrical representation of pain was excluded from punishment. The age of sobriety in punishment had begun. Of course, this generalization requires some qualification. To begin with, the changes did not come about at once or as part of single process. There were delays. Paradoxically, England was one of the countries most loath to see the disappearance of public execution: perhaps because of the role of model that the institution of the jury, public hearings and respect of habeus corpus had given to her criminal law; above all, no doubt, because she did not wish to diminish the rigor of her penal laws during the great social disturbances of the years 1780–1820.

The reduction in the use of torture was a tendency that was rooted in the great transformations of the years 1760–1840, but it did not end there; it can be said that the practice of the public execution haunted our penal system for a long time and still haunts it today. In France, the guillotine, that machine for the production of rapid and discreet deaths, represented a new ethic of legal death. But the Revolution had immediately endowed it with a great theatrical ritual. For years it provided a spectacle. [Yet eventually] the open cart was replaced by a closed carriage; the condemned man was hustled from the vehicle straight to the scaffold; hasty executions were organized at unexpected times. In the end, the guillotine had to be placed inside prison walls and made inaccessible to the public by blocking the streets leading to the prison in which the scaffold was hidden, and in which the execution would take place in secret. Witnesses who described the scene could even be prosecuted, thereby ensuring that the execution should cease to be a spectacle and remain a strange secret between the law and those it condemns. [Yet] one has only to point out so many precautions to realize that capital punishment remains fundamentally, even today, a spectacle that must actually be forbidden.

Similarly, the hold on the body did not entirely disappear in the mid-nineteenth century. Punishment had no doubt ceased to be centered on torture as a technique of pain; it assumed as its principle object loss of wealth or rights. But a punishment like forced labor or even imprisonment—mere loss of liberty—has never functioned without a certain additional element of punishment that certainly concerns the body itself: rationing of food, sexual deprivation, corporal punishment, solitary confinement. Are these the unintentional, but inevitable, consequences of imprisonment? In fact, in its most explicit practices, imprisonment has always involved a certain degree of physical pain. The criticism that was often leveled at the penitentiary system in the early nineteenth century (imprisonment is not a sufficient punishment: prisoners are less hungry, less cold, less deprived in general than many poor people or even workers) suggests a postulate that was never explicitly denied: it is just that a condemned man should suffer physically more than other men.

There remains, therefore, a trace of 'torture' in the modern mechanisms of criminal justice—a trace that has not been entirely overcome, but which is enveloped, increasingly, by the non-corporal nature of the penal system.

Adapted from M. Foucault, *Discipline and Punish: The Birth of the Prison*, trans. Alan Sheridan. © Vintage, 1977.

1. It is the practice in many contemporary prisons to employ only very minimal anesthetic for required dental procedures. This fact would:

A) support the author's argument concerning the need to improve the treatment of prisoners.
B) undermine the author's claim that a trace of torture still exists in modern mechanisms of punishment.
C) suggest the impossibility of completely eliminating the bodily component of punishment.
D) support the author's contention that inflicting physical pain remains a component of the modern penal system.

2. Which of the following does not appear in the passage as an example of either the "decline of spectacle" or a "slackening hold on the body"?

A) The introduction in France of the guillotine as the principal mode of execution
B) Restrictions concerning certain forms of communication
C) The complete elimination of some techniques of punishment
D) Changes in the location of certain apparatus for execution

3. Which of the following, according to the passage, might the author expect to be correlated with an increase in the frequency or visibility of public executions?

A) A strong influence of religious beliefs on social practices
B) Political revolution or unrest
C) New technological innovations
D) A struggling national economy

4. The author describes in paragraph 4 a criticism raised against the nineteenth-century penal system in order to:

A) highlight the deplorable conditions still present in modern prisons.
B) underscore an ongoing association between imprisonment and pain.
C) emphasize alterations in the treatment of prisoners since the nineteenth century.
D) compare the plight of prisoners to that of other poor or persecuted segments of society.

5. Based on the passage, which of the following may be inferred about nineteenth-century England?

A) England was, in general, slower than other countries to adopt penal reforms.
B) England experienced more social disturbances than did its European neighbors.
C) The English legal system was seen, in certain capacities, as superior to those of some other nations.
D) There was a decrease in the frequency of prosecution of treason.

6. Which of the following most closely corresponds to the usage of the term "sobriety" in the passage (paragraph 2)?

A) Restraint
B) Responsibility
C) Clearheadedness
D) Justice

7. With which of the following statements would the author be most likely to agree?

A) It is still true today that prisoners sometimes receive better accommodations than do poor workers.
B) Shock over the excesses of torture and punishment in the eighteenth century contributed to a general shift away from corporal punishment to the loss of various rights and privileges.
C) In modern times, many civilized nations forbid the practice of capital punishment.
D) The reduction in the practice of torture constitutes part of a broader shift in emphasis away from the body as the appropriate object of punishment.

Practice Passage 7

In 1986, Osherson, Smith and Shafir described numerous modes of induction, three of which are best related to categorization. The first mode is the similarity mode of induction. This mode claims that an inductive argument is regarded as strong if the objects and relations declared in the premise are similar to the ones declared in the conclusion. The conclusion will contain the usual properties of mentioned objects and relations. Thus if the objects that are in the premise and the conclusion have similar properties, they can be considered to be in the same category. For example, a bird that is flying, perching, and singing (the premise) has similar properties to the typical bird (the conclusion). Since the premise and conclusion are similar the argument can be considered strong and the bird can be categorized as a bird.

The next mode of induction that Osherson and his colleagues considered was forward deduction (originally called enthymeme). This mode claims that an inductive argument is strong when a belief that is thought to be true can be added to the premise, making it a deductive argument (an argument that has a conclusion that can not be false if the premises are true). Going back to the bird, if the belief, *if an animal flies, sings, and perches it is probably a bird*, is added to premise, then the conclusion of probable birdhood follows deductively. Finally, the third mode is reverse deduction. This mode claims that an inductive argument is strong when a belief can be added to the conclusion making it possible to deduce the premise. In the bird example, the belief, *if the animal is a bird, it will fly, sing, and perch*, could be added to the conclusion to make the argument strong.

The similarity mode of induction lacks the ability to become deductive and for that reason [often] fails to be useful in categorization. A study conducted by Rips in 1989 proves this. Participants were told that an animal that was originally born with the usual bird characteristics suffered an accident that changed its characteristics to ones similar to insects. The participants go on to learn that after the accident the animal eventually mates with a normal female of the same species, who produced normal offspring. The majority of participants agreed that the animal was most likely a bird rather than an insect, but most similar to an insect rather than a bird. A participant using only the similarity mode of induction would have concluded that the animal was an insect. It can be assumed that the participants used a deduction-type mode of induction to conclude that the animal was a bird.

When using forward or reverse deduction, it may be necessary to add in more than one belief to the premise or conclusion. This can be illustrated by Murphy and Medin's "drunk" example. They concluded that if a man jumps into a swimming pool clothed (at a party), the man is probably drunk. Using forward deduction, the beliefs, *jumping into water clothed is an instance of erratic behavior* and *anyone who behaves erratically (at a party) is probably drunk*, can be added to the premise. Using both new premises alongside the original one of a man jumps into a swimming pool clothed, it can be deduced that the man was drunk. Even though the final conclusion that the man is drunk can be drawn, the relative strength of this conclusion seems weaker than one where only one belief is needed.

When people are faced with a categorization problem, it is reasonable to assume people can go beyond similarity and use a deduction-type mode involving the addition of beliefs. However, it is not known which part of the problem causes individuals to switch from similarity to deduction-type modes. Nor is the variability of the added beliefs known. This variability is particularly important because many philosophers maintain that the practicality of developing a theory of categorization is dependent on the limitations put on the beliefs added.

Adapted from E.E. Smith, "Concepts and induction," *The Foundation of Cognitive Science*, ed. Michael Posner. © MIT University Press, 1989.

1. Which of the following beliefs would most likely have been added to the premises by a participant using forward deduction in the Rips study?

A) Forward deduction cannot have been used during this study, therefore no belief was added.

B) If an animal produces normal offspring with a female of that animal's same species, then the animal is probably of that species.

C) If an animal is a bird, it originally had bird properties and produces normal offspring with a normal mate of the same species.

D) If an animal is an insect, it cannot be born with bird properties.

2. Which of the following statements, if true, would most *undermine* the author's claim that the similarity mode of induction often fails to be useful in categorization?

A) A normal bird's characteristics are found to be gliding, sitting, and humming.
B) Most observers used the similarity mode to correctly conclude that an animal that flies, perches, and sings is a bird.
C) Most people usually use similarity modes over deductive-type modes of induction.
D) The similarity mode is simpler than the deductive modes.

3. Which of the following modes of induction is NOT illustrated by an example in the passage?

A) Similarity
B) Forward deduction using one additional belief
C) Enthymeme using two additional beliefs
D) Reverse deduction using two additional beliefs

4. With which of the following statements would the author be most likely to agree?

A) The diversity of added beliefs is neither known nor important.
B) Switching from similarity to a deductive-type mode of induction is something that only people familiar with different modes of logic can accomplish.
C) Induction can only be accomplished through deduction.
D) There are more than three modes of induction related to categorization.

5. Which of the following definitions of "categorization" (paragraph 1) would be most consistent with the implied meaning of the word as it is used in the passage?

A. The grouping of similar objects and relations together using observations
B) The disproving of similarity between objects and relations
C) The ability to classify objects based on opinions about the object
D) The addition of beliefs in order to group similar objects together

Practice Passage 8

All our attitudes, moral, practical, or emotional, as well as religious, are due to the "objects" of our consciousness, the things which we believe to exist, whether really or ideally, along with ourselves. Such objects may be present to our senses, or they may be present only to our thought. In either case they elicit from us a reaction; and the reaction due to things of thought is notoriously in many cases as strong as that due to sensible presences. It may be even stronger. The memory of an insult may make us angrier than the insult did when we received it. We are frequently more ashamed of our blunders afterwards than we were at the moment of making them; and in general our whole higher prudential and moral life is based on the fact that material sensations actually present may have a weaker influence on our action than ideas of remoter facts.

The absence of definite sensible images is positively insisted on by the mystical authorities in all religions as the sine qua non of a successful orison, or contemplation of the higher divine truths. Such contemplations are expected (and abundantly verify the expectation) to influence the believer's subsequent attitude very powerfully for good.

Immanuel Kant held a curious doctrine about such objects of belief as God, the design of creation, the soul, its freedom, and the life hereafter. These things, he said, are properly not objects of knowledge at all. Our conceptions always require a sense-content to work with, and as the words "soul," "God," "immortality," cover no distinctive sense-content whatever, it follows that theoretically speaking they are words devoid of any significance. Yet strangely enough they have a definite meaning for our practice. We can act as if there were a God; feel as if we were free; consider Nature as if she were full of special designs; lay plans as if we were to be immortal; and we find then that these words do make a genuine difference in our moral life. Our faith that these unintelligible objects actually exist proves thus to be a full equivalent from the point of view of our action, for a knowledge of what they might be, in case we were permitted positively to conceive them. So we have the strange phenomenon, as Kant assures us, of a mind believing with all its strength in the real presence of a set of things of no one of which it can form any notion whatsoever.

My object in thus recalling Kant's doctrine to your mind is not to express any opinion as to the accuracy of this particularly uncouth part of his philosophy, but only to illustrate the characteristic of human nature which we are considering, by an example so classical in its exaggeration. The sentiment of reality can indeed attach itself so strongly to our object of belief that our whole life is polarized through and through, so to speak, by its sense of the existence of the thing believed in, and yet that thing, for purpose of definite description, can hardly be said to be present to our mind at all. It is as if a bar of iron, without touch or sight, with no representative faculty whatever, might nevertheless be strongly endowed with an inner capacity for magnetic feeling; and as if, through the various arousals of its magnetism by magnets coming and going in its neighborhood, it might be consciously determined to different attitudes and tendencies. Such a bar of iron could never give you an outward description of the agencies that had the power of stirring it so strongly; yet of their presence, and of their significance for its life, it would be intensely aware through every fiber of its being.

It is not only the Ideas of pure Reason as Kant styled them, that have this power of making us vitally feel presences that we are impotent articulately to describe. All sorts of higher abstractions bring with them the same kind of impalpable appeal.

This absolute determinability of our mind by abstractions is one of the cardinal facts in our human constitution. Polarizing and magnetizing us as they do, we turn towards them and from them, we seek them, hold them, hate them, bless them, just as if they were so many concrete beings. And beings they are, beings as real in the realm which they inhabit as the changing things of sense are in the realm of spaces.

1. The "objects of our consciousness" referred to in the first paragraph could best be described as:

   A) external phenomena of dubious reality.
   B) potentially fictitious objects.
   C) beliefs regarding the workings of our consciousness.
   D) illusions of the supernatural.

2. With which of the following statements would the author be most likely to agree?

A) Tangible objects are less real to us than mental objects.

B) The mind can strongly believe in things of which it can have no knowledge.

C) The mind is prone to distort reality.

D) One's emotional reaction to an event may be amplified during recollection.

3. The passage suggests that Kant would most likely hold which of the following statements to be most valid?

A) We behave as if certain things are true and they become so.

B) We attempt to live up to an ideal that requires patience and persistence.

C) We behave as if certain things were true and this belief affects the course of our future judgments or actions.

D) We feel as if we might understand what is inconceivable if we behave as if we had a notion of its form.

4. The author's conclusions in the last paragraph are most directly supported by which of the following statements made elsewhere in the passage?

A) "All sorts of higher abstractions bring with them the same kind of impalpable appeal."

B) "Such a bar of iron could never give you an outward description of the agencies that had the power of stirring it so strongly."

C) "… the absence of definite sensible images is positively insisted on by the mystical authorities."

D) "In either case, they elicit from us a reaction; and the reaction due to things of thought is notoriously in many cases as strong as that due to sensible presences."

5. Which one of the following statements is most *inconsistent* with information given in the passage?

A) Objects of subjective awareness are as real as objects of objective awareness.

B) Certain things that cannot be objectively perceived are believed by some to contain valuable information.

C) Kant viewed religious beliefs as being as real as any object of sensible perception.

D) Things that affect our lives may nonetheless be absent from our minds.

Practice Passage 9

Should there be a single norm of human functioning for men and women? One might grant that human capabilities cross cultures while still maintaining that in each culture a division of labor should be arranged along gender lines. One such position, position A, assigns to both males and females the same general list of functions but suggests that males and females should exercise these functions in different spheres of life: men in the public sphere, for example, and women in the home. The second, position B, insists that the list of functions should be different: for men, citizenship and rational autonomy, for women, family love and care.

Position A is compatible with a serious interest in equality and in gender justice. For what it says, after all, is that males and females have the same basic needs and should get what they need.... It simply holds that this can (and perhaps should) be done in separate spheres. Is this any more problematic than to say that human functioning in India can, and even should, take a different concrete form from functioning in England? Or that some people can realize musical capacities by singing; others by playing the violin?

The trouble comes when we notice that Position A usually ends up endorsing a division of duties that is associated with traditional forms of hierarchy. Even Mill, who made so many fine arguments against women's subordination, did not sufficiently ask how the very perpetuation of separate spheres of responsibility might reinforce subordination.... It is likely that women's subordination will not be adequately addressed as long as women are confined to a sphere traditionally devalued, linked with a low "perceived well-being contribution." The *Human Development Report's* Gender Empowerment Measure rightly focuses, therefore, on the ability of women to win entry into the traditional male spheres of politics and administration.

I turn, then, to Position B, which has been influentially defended by many philosophers, including Rousseau and some of his followers in today's world. Insofar as B relies on the claim that there are two different sets of basic innate capacities, we should insist, with John Stuart Mill, that this claim has not been borne out by any responsible scientific evidence. Experiments that allegedly show strong gender divisions in basic (untrained) abilities have been shown to contain major scientific flaws; these flaws removed, the case for such differences is altogether inconclusive.... It is therefore impossible at present to separate "nature" from "culture."

But we can also criticize Position B in a different way, arguing that the differentiated conceptions of male and female functioning put forward by B are internally inadequate.... What do we usually find in the versions of B that our philosophical tradition bequeaths us? (Rousseau's view is an instructive

example.) We have, on the one hand, males who are capable of practical reasoning, independent and self-sufficient. These males are brought up not to develop strong emotions of love and feelings of deep need that are associated with the awareness of one's own lack of self-sufficiency. For this reason they are not equipped to care for the needs of their family members or, perhaps, even to notice those needs. On the other hand, we have females such as Rousseau's Sophie, brought up to lack autonomy and self-respect, ill equipped to rely on her own practical reasoning, dependent on males, focused on pleasing others, and good at caring for others. Is either of these viable as a complete life for a human being?

Women belong to cultures. But they do not choose to be born into any particular culture, and they do not really choose to endorse its norms as good for themselves, unless they do so in possession of further options and opportunities—including the opportunity to form communities of affiliation and empowerment with other women. Women in much of the world lack support for the most central human functions, and this denial of support is frequently caused by their being women. But women, unlike rocks and plants and even horses, have the potential to become capable of these human functions, given sufficient nutrition, education, and other support. That is why their unequal failure in capability is a problem of justice.

Adapted from M. Nussbaum, *Sex and Social Justice.* © Oxford University Press, 1999.

1. The organization of the passage most nearly corresponds to which of the following?

A) Two different answers to a question are considered; the first answer is soundly rejected; the second answer is criticized, although a positive consequence is recognized; a new problem is addressed.

B) Two different positions in support of a perspective are presented; the first position is implicitly defended, although a shortcoming is recognized; the second position is rejected; the first position is reaffirmed.

C) Two different answers to a question are considered; the first answer is implicitly defended, although a shortcoming is recognized; the second answer is determined to be unjustified; a further analogy is developed.

D) Two different positions in support of a perspective are presented; the first position is criticized; the second position is rejected as unsupported and unfruitful; an alternative perspective is advocated.

2. On the basis of the information in the passage, it may be inferred that the author would agree with which of the following statements concerning women?

A) They lack the capabilities necessary for complete life as a human being.

B) In certain contexts, they demonstrate less capability than do men.

C) It has been scientifically proven that they have the same capabilities as men.

D) Their innate capabilities in certain spheres of life are superior to those of men.

3. Based on the author's description, Rousseau and John Stuart Mill would be expected to disagree over:

A) the abolition of the assignment to women and men of distinct spheres of responsibility.

B) the degree to which differences between men and women should be understood as resulting from nature or from culture.

C) the appropriateness of the subordination of women.

D) whether science is an appropriate tool to employ in determining the proper social relations of men and women.

4. Which of the following would constitute evidence against position B, as that position is described in the passage?

   I. A cross-cultural study of children ages two to four showing no difference between the capacity for practical reason in boys and that in girls.

   II. A series of sociological surveys documenting a correlation between belief in innate differences between the sexes and approval of the assignment of men and women to distinct social spheres.

   III. A report based on in-home observation demonstrating that fathers of young children were far less likely than mothers to notice either that the children were hungry or ill and so were less likely to provide appropriate food or medical attention.

A) III only

B) I and II only

C) I and III only

D) I, II, and III

5. In the context of the passage, the figure Sophie is used to illustrate:

A) the inherent deficiency of a particular account of the respective capabilities of men and women.

B) the extent to which Rousseau's writings encouraged a hierarchy of men over women.

C) the fact that some female philosophers agree with Rousseau that women's innate capacities differ from those of men.

D) the unhappiness that results from the subordination of women and the stunting of women's capabilities.

6. The author of the passage suggests each of the following to be true of Position A EXCEPT:

A) many proponents of this position would discourage women from taking political office.

B) certain proponents of this position may advocate for women's equal rights.

C) in practice, if not in theory, the position upholds a prioritization of men's activities over women's activities.

D) the position holds that innate differences between male and female basic capacities can (and perhaps should) be lived out in disparate spheres.

7. Which of the following is most analogous to the relationship between men and women implicitly endorsed by the author in the passage?

A) Religion and philosophy both seek to answer life's basic questions and are of equal importance. The latter principally functions in the public square, including the universities, the former in the home or in the church.

B) The essential function of philosophy is the development and application of formal reason unmixed with emotion. The nature of religion, by contrast, is the practice of a non-empirical faith.

C) Religion, like philosophy, should be governed by norms of rationality, evidence, and full engagement with various intellectual traditions and spheres of thought. To do less is to limit religion to a partial and inferior modality.

D) There can be no single answer to the question of the relationship between religion and philosophy. Rather, the relationship must always be addressed and enacted within a particular culture, and only from within that particular culture can an adequate solution be reached.

Chapter 8
Verbal Reasoning
Practice Section
Solutions

SOLUTIONS TO PRACTICE PASSAGE 1

1. **D** This is a Retrieval question.

   A: No. While the exclusion of citizens' concerns causes the direct threat, is in not itself the direct threat: "When citizens see reflected in newspapers and broadcasts a politics of polar extremes that excludes them…they withdraw into private concerns. They abandon public life. This is a direct threat to journalism" (see end of paragraph 2).

   B: No. While this is one of the many concerning aspects of One Journalism that leads to the alienation of citizens (see middle of paragraph 2), it is also not the most direct threat to journalism.

   C: No. This refers to the question of One Journalism's axiom of detachment, as described in paragraph 4. This is not described as posing a direct threat to journalism. If anything, the author thinks that this line should be crossed.

   D: **Yes. This is directly stated in the last three sentences of paragraph 2: "…they withdraw into private concerns. They abandon public life. This is a direct threat to journalism, for if people are not involved in public life, they have no need for journalists." The language used in this answer choice is synonymous with what is stated in the passage: to forsake is to abandon, and civic means public.**

2. **C** This is a Retrieval question.

   A: No. This answer choice is too extreme ("the *only* solution") and does not agree with the tone and implications of the passage. While the author does contend that "public journalism offers a solution to this problem" (paragraph 3), the author does not imply that One Journalism is necessarily an "overt problem" (obvious or explicit) "plaguing society."

   B: No. While public journalism embraces the continuum concept (paragraph 5 states, "Journalists exploring public journalism accept the construct of a continuum") there is no implication that the purpose of public journalism is to challenge this belief. That is, public journalists do not accept the idea of a boundary, but they also don't see it as their role as journalists to challenge the belief in a boundary. Rather, the author contends that the purpose of public journalism is to foster community and get people involved.

   C: **Yes. This answer is most directly supported in paragraph 3, "[Public journalism's] objective is to find ways for journalism to serve a purpose beyond—but not in place of—telling the news: the purpose of reinvigorating public life by re-engaging people in it." It is further supported by the author's comments about the value of democratic deliberation in paragraph 1 and the author's closing comments about the values of public journalism in paragraph 6.**

   D: No. The passage states that this is a *requirement to fulfill* the primary objective (or purpose) of public journalism, not the purpose itself: "[Public journalism's] objective is to find ways for journalism to serve a purpose beyond—but not in place of—telling the news: the purpose of reinvigorating public life by re-engaging people in it…. This can only be done if journalists think of the people by their efforts not as an audience to be entertained or as spectators at an event, but as citizens capable of action" (paragraph 3).

3. **A** This is an Inference/Roman numeral question.

   I: **True. "This requires both a change in the perspective of journalists and a change in what they do" (paragraph 3) directly supports that the author believes journalists are responsible for the change.**

   II: False. The author never mention's the public's role in transitioning to public journalism.

III: False. The author blames large media conglomerates for One Journalism, but never argues that they have a responsibility to change.

4. **D**   This is an Analogy question.

A: No. The objective of public journalism is to "reinvigorat[e] public life by re-engaging people in it" (paragraph 3), so while this choice demonstrates how local media might be transitioning away from One Journalism, it does not answer the question because it does not touch on re-engaging people in public life.

B: No. The author clearly states that one of the problems with One Journalism is that "Journalists address the particular problems and needs of a community in an artificial journalistic context, created and driven from *other places,*" (paragraph 1) and that this does NOT reflect the true issues of a local community, and does NOT re-engage people in public life. Therefore, while this is an article about small-town life, the fact that it is written by a national news reporter puts this choice out of the realm of public journalism.

C: No. This answer jumbles together a few concepts from the passage, but does not appropriately compare the link between corporations (paragraph 1: "One Journalism defines good journalism as the kind of journalism produced at the top of corporate pyramids") and democracy (paragraph 1: "above all the value of democratic deliberation is the best way to express and experience public life"). There is no suggestion that this kind of expose would reinvigorate public life.

D: **Yes. Paragraph 3 states, "[public journalism's] objective is to find ways for journalism to serve a purpose beyond—but not in place of—telling the news: the purpose of reinvigorating public life by re-engaging people in it…to report the very important news of civic life—including civic successes—that now occurs outside our pinched definition of news." This answer choice demonstrates a "civic success" that might not be considered "newsworthy" by One Journalism. Furthermore, this answer indicates that the coverage of the event was by a local newspaper, not corporate media, which the author clearly considers inappropriate or fake (paragraph 1 states, "Journalists address the particular problems and needs of a community in an artificial journalistic context, created and driven from other places.").**

5. **D**   This is an Inference/Except question.

A: No. Paragraph 5 states that this IS one of the factors that will determine their desired level of involvement: "Journalists exploring public journalism accept the construct of a continuum and seek to operate somewhere beyond total involvement. Precisely where their activity falls is determined by *their consciences,* their judgment and the needs of their communities." A personal principle is synonymous with conscience.

B: No. Paragraph 5 also states that this IS one of the factors that will determine their desired level of involvement: "Journalists exploring public journalism accept the construct of a continuum and seek to operate somewhere beyond total involvement. Precisely where their activity falls is determined by their consciences, *their judgment* and the needs of their communities." "Opinions and individual conclusions" is a definition of the word judgment.

C: No. Paragraph 5 also states that this IS one of the factors that will determine their desired level of involvement: "Journalists exploring public journalism accept the construct of a continuum and seek to operate somewhere beyond total involvement. Precisely where their activity falls is determined by their consciences, their judgment and *the needs of their communities.*"

D: Yes. Paragraph 5 states that the acceptance of the line between detachment and involvement is *already* accepted by journalists exploring public journalism: "journalists exploring public journalism accept the construct of a continuum…" Therefore, it is not one of the factors in determining their desired level of involvement.

6. **B**   This is a New Information question.

A: No. The quote doesn't only list many key concerns about One Journalism, but also frames them in a problem-solving light, i.e.: "It means: *understanding* that framing issues at the extreme excludes most people, *challenging the assumption that* conflict is the most interesting narrative device, *having an interest in* whether problems are solved through democratic deliberation." Therefore, the "it" in this quote is referring to the *solution to* the problems of One Journalism.

B: Yes. The author claims that "Public journalism is the antithesis of One Journalism" (paragraph 5) and "Journalism's authority—its right to be attended to—is disappearing in a cloud of cynicism and loss of credibility brought on by the routine and detached way we go about business. But public journalism offers a solution to this problem" (paragraph 3). Therefore, given the way in which this quote lists many of the problems of One Journalism (excluding the public, end of paragraph 2; high value put on conflict, middle of paragraph 2) and the ultimate goal at the core of public journalism (solving problems through democratic deliberation (paragraph 1 & 6), you can conclude that this quote is ultimately describing the core values of public journalism.

C: No. Because this quote refers to what journalists need to do to change One Journalism, the "it" is not referring to the public's needs.

D: No. Similar to answer choice A, this answer is incorrect for the same reasons: the quote is phrasing these concepts in a problem-solving way; therefore the "it" is referring to the only thing that we know, based on the passage, can solve these issues (public journalism).

7. **D**   This is an Inference/Except question.

A: No. This IS a key difference between the two: "value-neutral techniques of One Journalism" (paragraph 2) vs. "Public life, according to the values of public journalism, requires shared information and shared deliberation; people participate in answering democracy's fundamental question[s]" (paragraph 6).

B: No. This IS a key difference and is directly supported by paragraph 2: "One Journalism determines, for instance, that we define 'balance' as 'both sides' when in fact most issues have multiple sides."

C: No. This IS a key difference between the two: "Meanwhile, the culture of detachment denies any journalistic concern or responsibility for what happens, if anything" (paragraph 2) vs. "[public journalism's] objective is to find ways for journalism to serve a purpose beyond—but not in place of—telling the news: the purpose of reinvigorating public life by re-engaging people in it" (paragraph 3).

D: Yes. Because this answer states that public journalism "hopes to encourage democratic deliberation *above all else*," it is implying that reporting of news would be secondary to fostering democratic deliberation, something the passage clearly does not support: "[public journalism's] objective is to find ways for journalism to serve a purpose beyond—but not in place of—telling the news…" (paragraph 3). Therefore, this answer is not a fundamental difference between the two, since both One Journalism and public journalism are primarily concerned with reporting news.

SOLUTIONS TO PRACTICE PASSAGE 2

1. **C** This is an Inference question.
   A: No. This is too extreme. The author suggests that in some important sense there is no such thing as individual memory, but he is stressing the interdependence of individual and collective memory, not the complete absence of the former.
   B: No. This answer may be tempting for those who don't check back to the passage, as the author says that there is no such thing as individual memory, and that the concept of distortion becomes problematic once one dispels the notion that individual memory is independent of collective memory. However, we don't know, based on the text, that the nature of individual memory itself *causes* problems in considering distortion. That is, the concept of individual memory may be problematic, but the author does not suggest that individual memory causes conceptual problems.
   C: **Yes. The author makes this point in a number of places in the second paragraph, especially in the last line when he notes that "Cultural memory...is distributed across social institutions."**
   D: No. The author stresses the dependence of individual memory on collective institutions. That is, individual memory doesn't really exist because "memory is social" (paragraph 2). The author's point is not that they are two different things, but rather that they are one and the same thing.

2. **C** This is a Structure question.
   A: No. The statement in question does have a bearing on the overall argument. If the controversies did not exist, it would suggest that collective memories might be entirely unstable and not therefore of use in judging how much we might come to agreement about what really happened.
   B: No. The statement is not in itself of historical importance, as far as we know. That statement is, rather, about some aspect of history.
   C: **Yes. This statement, when examined along with the prior sentence, is used by the author to point out that memory is not so entirely open to interpretation that it is matter of pure fiction. The passage states: "If interpretation were free-floating, entirely manipulable to serve present interests, altogether unanchored by a bedrock body of unshakable evidence, controversies over the past would ultimately be uninteresting. But in fact they are interesting. They are compelling. And they are gripping because people trust that a past we can to some extent know and can to some extent come to agreement about really happened." If controversies were uninteresting, it would suggest that there is no foundation at all for agreement, which would be inconsistent with the author's argument in this paragraph.**
   D: No. It is not an exception, but does stand in contrast to the statement in the prior sentence, which is a bit of a trap for those who don't return to the passage to check on the claim in this answer.

3. **A** This is an Inference question.
   A: **Yes. This is a rather oblique way of referring to something the author says nearby in the first paragraph, that "the biography of a lifetime is the appropriate "natural" frame for individual memory." Given this fact and the statement mentioned in the question stem, we can conclude that the fact that "there's no...evident frame" means that the ongoing "lifespan" of the human race, still around, obviates any snapshot of race memory as representative of the whole.**

B: No. The author never suggests that there is no sharing of experience or memory between different cultures.

C: No. This contradicts the passage, as individuals certainly have access to common cultural memories and in fact depend on this access to survive (see paragraph 2).

D: No. While this is true according to the passage, it's not a translation of what the author is saying in the sentence quoted in the question stem. That is, the fact that these boundaries fail to define collective memory is not the reason why there is no such evident frame such as the person (biography or lifespan) for collective memories. This answer choice is the right answer to the wrong question.

4. **A** This is a Weaken question.

A: **Yes. The author's main view of individual memory is that it's partly illusory, since it reflects so many aspects of cultural knowledge carried over from generation to generation and vested in various institutions. This choice would weaken this claim, as it would indicate that social memories are changeable and do not necessarily persist outside the individual. This sounds like a bit of science fiction, but it's important to remember that weaken and strengthen questions ask you to evaluate the effect of a piece of information that is assumed to be true, not to evaluate the plausibility of the information in the answer.**

B: No. The fact that people can memorize information is not inconsistent with the author's argument about the nature of memory. By saying that memory is inherently social, the author is not literally arguing that individuals cannot remember things.

C: No. This would strengthen the argument, if anything, as it would support the notion that memories reside chiefly in institutions rather than individuals.

D: No. While this choice is not entirely consistent with the author's claim that institutional memory is advantageous (paragraph 2), it doesn't significantly weaken the author's argument as a whole, especially as compared to choice A. It relates only to a small and probably non-representative sample, rather than to individual and institutional memory as it functions more generally.

5. **D** This is a Strengthen question.

A: No. The author says that the choice of what we recall and the consequent distortion is "socially conditioned" (third paragraph), implying that it's unconscious. If we were to purposefully and consciously choose to withhold certain information and report other information, it wouldn't affect the underlying issue of what was available for the recollection of the individual.

B: No. This would have no effect on the author's claim, as it would show a capability on a particular task, but would not affect the unconscious biases in storage and retrieval the author is interested in.

C: No. This might support the failure of the mental hardware to store or retrieve certain items of memory, but it wouldn't have much effect on the issue of socially conditioned memory distortions.

D: **Yes. The author's point is that memory is inherently distorted, as it involves selecting what to pay attention to and what to ignore. If the brain is inherently limited in its ability to notice and store memories, then the individual must inevitably choose what to notice and what to ignore, as is the author's point.**

6. **A**   This is an Evaluate question.

   A: **Yes. The statement regarding agreement about the past is a statement about what may be derived from collective memory, institutions, and the like. The statement about individual memories is generally unrelated to the idea of coming to some agreement about what has actually happened in the past. An argument might be made that the statement about individual memories gives some support for the statement about coming to agreement, but this would not suggest that the two are inconsistent in any case.**

   B: No. While the statements are consistent it is not because the second claim in the question stem supports the first. An argument might be made that the first claim supports the second, if weakly, but not the other way around.

   C: No. Difficulties in judging whether controversies over the past are gripping or not are irrelevant, as we are told directly by the passage that they are gripping, and saying that individual memories are absent is an overstatement, in any case.

   D: No. The relationship stated in this answer choice is not true. The idea that individual memories are inextricably linked to cultural memories doesn't undermine the idea that we can come to some agreement about what's occurred in our collective past and may support it slightly.

7. **B**   This is a New Information question.

   A: No. The fact that dominant individuals have inordinate influence would go directly to the heart of issue of why certain cultural memories are emphasized and others are downplayed.

   B: **Yes. If dominant individuals can influence large groups to change their opinions about what is most relevant and what is less so, then their influence would have a direct bearing on "social and historical processes" and therefore on the notion of distortion being problematic.**

   C: No. That distortions are fairly ordinary would tend to strengthen rather than weaken the author's claim.

   D: No. This answer is too extreme in its second half ("explain the ultimate origin"). It also incorrectly states that the situation described would weaken the author's claim, when in fact it would support it.

SOLUTIONS TO PRACTICE PASSAGE 3

This is an example of the hardest type of passage you would ever see on the MCAT: an uber-killer, so to speak. When confronting a passage like this (which you would only need to do if you were doing all seven passages and going for a 12–15), make sure not to get bogged down in the abstraction of the text. Read for logical structure, basic contrasts and transitions, etc., rather than for deep understanding. Also, use aggressive POE on the questions; remember that you don't need to know exactly why the right answer is right as long as you know that the other three are wrong.

1. **A**   This is an Evaluate question.

   A: **Yes. The author seeks to correct a misconception and does so by contrasting the notion that satori is a cessation of thought with the idea that it is "one thought" of a certain kind.**

   B: No. The absolute present and the eternal now are treated as synonyms, or at least two ways of looking at the same idea: "When time is reduced to a point with no durability, it is "absolute present" or "eternal now." From the point of view of existential thinking, this "absolute present" is no abstraction, no logical nothingness; it is, on the contrary, alive with creative vitality" (paragraph 1). The author doesn't treat these as separate things, so there is no distinction between them to be used in supporting anything else.

C: No. The discussion of inmost needs, which comes in paragraph 5, is not relevant to correcting the misconception the author addresses in the third paragraph. Instead, it is part of the author's discussion of how the division or reality serves practical needs but not our spiritual needs.

D: No. The statement in the question stem is supported by information in the passage, as discussed regarding choice A.

2. **C** This is an Inference/Roman numeral question.

I: **True. Item I is supported by the statement that "It goes without saying that satori is not the stopping of the flow of consciousness" (that is, the suspension of thought) in paragraph 3.**

II: **True. This is supported by the discussion toward the end of the first paragraph, in which the author says the "absolute present is no abstraction." To recognize that "abstract" and "conceptual" mean the same thing in this context, it helps to take into account the author's comment in paragraph 1 that "Zen is not interested so much in conceptualization as in 'existential thinking.'"**

III: False. The author indicates that satori is the experience of one thought and the intersection of time with eternity rather than the experience of the whole of eternity. Also, it is overly strong to say satori "consists of" eternity, which suggests that there is nothing else to it, which would contradict the statements made about satori being the intersection of time and eternity.

Note: Be sure to use the combinations of numerals in the choices actively. You might have struggled with making a decision on Item III. However, it never appears in combination with Item I, which is the most clearly supported of the three options.

3. **B** This is a Weaken question.

A: No. The author's concluding statements are concerned with the fact that certain intellectual processes are useful for practical things, but that use of the intellect will not itself contribute to satori, and may in fact detract from it. However, the author never suggests that to achieve satori one must divorce oneself from *all* practical concerns. Thus, this statement does not significantly undermine the author's argument.

B: **Yes. This answer would directly counter the author's argument that "setting (reality) up in space and time murders it," as the use of rational thought as a means of attaining satori would suggest that this arrangement of reality is not as destructive as the author suggests, and that the task of approaching satori might be accomplished through other means than taking hold of reality as we immediately experience it. Note the difference between choices A and B: Choice A says that the intellect and satori can coexist, while B suggests that the intellect can contribute to satori.**

C: No. This would tend to strengthen the author's argument, as it is very nearly a restatement of some of the author's support for the statements cited in the question stem, particularly those regarding "the bifurcation of reality" toward the beginning of the last paragraph.

D: No. This is not relevant to the statements in question. The author's discussion is about an obstacle to satori, whereas this answer is about something that might produce a false satori.

4. **A** This is an Inference question.

   A: **Yes. This is supported by the first sentence of the last paragraph: "The bifurcation of reality is the work of the intellect; indeed it is the way in which we try to understand it in order to make use of it in our practical life."**

   B: No. This is half right, half wrong. The author indicates that the bifurcation is a fundamental mistake, but he is referring to things required for spiritual attainment rather than for practical needs.

   C: No. It leads to a spiritual tragedy, but not due to the intellectual effort required in order to bifurcate reality (which would suggest that the problem is that it is detracting from intellectual effort needed to achieve satori, which is the opposite of what the author argues). Rather, it is due to the nature of the intellectual error itself.

   D: No. This contradicts the last paragraph where the author states: "The bifurcation helps us to handle reality, to make it work for our physical and intellectual needs, but in truth it never appeals to our inmost needs. For the latter purpose reality must be taken hold of as we immediately experience it."

5. **A** This is a New Information question.

   A: **Yes. The author's argument is concerned with the way we perceive reality, dividing it into fragments of time and missing the reality of the instant, not with the way in which such perceptions might arise in the brain. Note that there is no discussion of biological factors in the passage.**

   B: No. This is a right answer to the wrong question. It is likely to be true, given what we know from the passage, but doesn't answer the question. It does not bear directly on the author's argument in the last paragraph that this mistake in one's mode of attention obstructs the experience of the reality of the moment.

   C: No. This answer is not supported by the passage, as we don't know that satori is the only and *necessary* antidote for the division of reality.

   D: No. The information in the study would tell us little about a concept as abstract as eternity having a death aspect (the death aspect being the idea that the concept of eternity is barren without time to give it a structure our minds can relate to).

6. **C** This is an Inference/Except question.

   A: No. The author's argument is generally concerned with attaining a certain perception of reality, that of the present moment, so he would likely agree with this statement.

   B: No. This is a paraphrase of statements in the first paragraph: "Satori obtains when eternity cuts into time or impinges upon time, or, which is the same thing after all, when time emerges itself into eternity…. Eternity impinging upon time will then mean that *byodo* and *shabetsu* interpenetrate each other."

   C: **Yes. The author argues the opposite in paragraphs 1 and 5. For example, in paragraph 5 he claims that the differentiation or bifurcation of reality "never appeals to our inmost needs. For the latter purpose reality must be taken hold of as we immediately experience it."**

   D: No. This is well supported by statements toward the end of the fourth paragraph: "To take hold of eternity, therefore, consciousness must be awakened just at the very moment when eternity lifts its feet to step into time. This moment is what is known as the 'absolute present' or 'eternal now.' …Satori does not come out of death; it is at the very moment of actualization. It is in fact the moment itself, which means that it is life as it lives itself."

SOLUTIONS TO PRACTICE PASSAGE 4

1. **C**   This is a Retrieval question.

   A: No. The passage states that each of the two musics has its own sociology and erotic, not that one is sociological and the other is erotic (paragraph 1).

   B: No. The author never identifies the nationality of the composers discussed, so "German" is out of scope.

   C: **Yes. The author defines the musics in the first sentence: "the music one listens to, the music one plays."**

   D: No. This choice is half right, half wrong. The author does connect music that "becomes orchestral" (paragraph 5) to one of the two types of musics, "the music one listens to" (paragraph 1). However, the other of the two musics, "the music one plays" (paragraph 1) is not described as specifically vocal music. Although the author mentions that the player of practical music is guided by the image of a song (paragraph 5), the author does not mean this literally to mean vocal music. Note also that the author mentions keyboards (paragraph 2) and the guitar (paragraph 3) in the context of practical music.

2. **D**   This is an Inference/NOT question.

   A: No. The author tells us that Beethoven did not write music around a song (musica practica) but around orchestral themes. The author's description of this as "the very breakdown of the code of the former musica practica" (paragraph 5), in combination with earlier parts of the passage that describe a move away from "the music one plays" or practical music to the music one listens to (like Beethoven's work), indicates that practical music is a "past musical tradition."

   B: No. The author states that an amateur "is unable to master" Beethoven's work and that the work "forsakes" the amateur. "Who can play Beethoven well," the author asks rhetorically (paragraph 5).

   C: No. The author indicates that the impetus for Beethoven's work was orchestral, rather than the "single element (voice or rhythm)" or "song" that defined practical music (paragraph 5).

   D: **Yes. We are told that Beethoven's work seems appropriate for an interpreter with Romantic vision, not that the work itself is a Romantic interpretation (paragraph 5). This answer choice takes words out of context, and therefore is the correct answer to a NOT question.**

3. **A**   This is a New Information question.

   A: **Yes. The author describes music that is meant to be played as "muscular," while music meant to be listened to is "passive" (paragraph 3). Schumann is identified with the former (paragraph 1) and Beethoven with the latter (paragraph 5). If more people enjoyed listening to Beethoven than to Schumann, it would support the author's argument about the distinction between the two musics (paragraph 1).**

   B: No. First, the fact that more people listen to Beethoven does not prove that his works were superior; this claim cannot be inferred from the new information in the question. Second, even if it could be, it would not be relevant to or supportive of the author's argument. Although the author says that Schumann can be "minor if listened to," he can be "tremendous if you play him" (paragraph 1). The author does not claim that Beethoven is better, just that he is a different kind of composer, of a different kind of music.

   C: No. The author does not compare the ability of professionals (but rather amateurs) to perform Beethoven and Schumann. Furthermore, this choice has no direct connection to the new information, or to its relevance to the passage.

D: No. Although the author did mention that the guitar is a more common mode of music delivery today than is the piano, this has no direct relevance to the issue of the question stem.

4. **D** This is an Inference question.
   A: No. Although the author tells us that amateur pianists no longer exist and that they were unable to master Beethoven's music, the author did not connect these two facts. The answer is therefore only half right, which makes it wrong.
   B: No. This answer choice takes words out of context. The author describes the act of playing piano as a physical and even muscular experience, but he does not state that piano players must be muscular in order to play.
   C: No. The author tells us that the amateur is "defined much more by a style than by a technical imperfection," (paragraph 4), meaning that amateurs are not necessarily less technically proficient than professionals. Furthermore, we are not told whether or not the amateur strives for perfection, let alone with reference to professional musicians.
   D: **Yes. In the second and third paragraphs, the author describes his view that amateur piano playing is physical, muscular and sensual, whereas passive listening is not.**

5. **C** This is an Inference question.
   A: No. Although the author discusses the inability of amateur pianists to play Beethoven's music well, he does not say that professional musicians cannot play the music well. Moreover, the author does not mention piano concertos at all.
   B: No. As in question 2, choice D, this answer choice takes the words 'Romantic" and "interpreter" out of context. While we are told that Beethoven did not follow the *musica practica* that came before him, the author did not tell us that Beethoven himself instead followed a Romantic interpretation. This would be a misinterpretation of the author's statement in paragraph 5 that "Beethoven forsakes the amateur and seems, in an initial moment, to call on the new Romantic deity, the interpreter." Here, the author is not speaking of a Romantic interpretation, but rather continuing his discussion of how Beethoven's music is more to be listened to than played.
   C: **Yes. After explaining that amateur musicians cannot play Beethoven's music well, he asks in the final paragraph: "What is the use of composing if it is to confine the product within the precinct of the concert or the solitude of listening to the radio?" The author does not, and appears unable to, answer this rhetorical question.**
   D: No. The author explains that the nature of the music itself does not allow for mastery by an amateur. He understands why amateurs cannot master the music, but not why Beethoven would write such music.

SOLUTIONS TO PRACTICE PASSAGE 5

1. **D** This is a Specific Attitude question.
   A: No. While we might call it obscure because it isn't obvious, the author does not say that symbolism itself is provable, only that it can be used to prove other things (paragraph 4).
   B: No. This choice suggests a change over time that is not supported by the passage. The author does state in paragraph 4 that "The fact is that symbolism is useful because it makes things difficult. (This is not true of the advanced parts of mathematics, but only of the beginnings.)" However, this is not about the usefulness of symbolization changing over time, but rather

about how it makes early mathematics, but not later mathematics, difficult. If usefulness did equate with difficulty, this choice would be the opposite of what the passage suggests.

C: No. While this may seem to be true in our own experience, pedagogy or teaching is not discussed in the passage.

D: **Yes. The author states in the fourth paragraph that symbolism is important (invaluable) but that this may be difficult to see (that is, it isn't obvious).**

2. **B** This is a Structure question.

A: No. No mathematician other than Boole (who is 19th century) is mentioned.

B: **Yes. The sixth paragraph gives two examples of propositions that seem to be obviously true but that are in fact usually false: The whole always has more terms than a part, and a number is increased by adding one to it.**

C: No. While this statement is made, there is no example given of an infinite number.

D: No. There is no example given of a specific mathematical symbol.

3. **A** This is an Inference question.

A: **Yes. Boole claims that his book deals with the laws of thought but not mathematics, whereas the author states that formal logic (which is what Boole was really discussing) is in fact mathematics (paragraph 2).**

B: No. According to the author "the question of how people really think" (paragraph 2) was irrelevant to Boole; we know of no explicit claims Boole has made, accurate or otherwise, about this question. What the author labels as inaccurate were Boole's claims that his book was not about mathematics and that it dealt with the laws of thought (paragraph 2).

C: No. The passage includes no reference to actual mathematical errors of previous authors, only to confusion about the nature of pure mathematics.

D: No. The passage contains no information about what Boole thought to be his influence on later mathematicians. We cannot infer that because he claimed his work was not mathematical that he believed that he would have little influence; this would be going too far outside the scope of the passage.

4. **C** This is a Vocabulary-in-Context question.

A: No. The author's point is that mathematics had not yet been originated: "This science, like most others, was baptized long before it was born; and thus we find writers before the nineteenth century alluding to what they called pure mathematics."

B: No. There is no suggestion in the passage that pure mathematics was treated with reverence or devotion.

C: **Yes. The last part of the sentence in which the word "baptized" appears states that writers were "alluding" to it before it actually existed, which is to say employing the term in their writings (paragraph 1).**

D: No. While baptism often carries with it the image of cleansing (washing away of sins) in other contexts, it does not have that meaning or connotation as it is used in the passage. Beware of using outside knowledge to choose an answer.

5. **C** This is an Analogy question.

A: No. The author states that "Pure mathematics consists entirely of assertions to the effect that, if such and such a proposition is true of *anything*, then such and such another proposition is true of that thing. It is essential not to discuss whether the first proposition is really true, and not to mention what the anything is, of which it is supposed to be true. Both these points would belong to applied mathematics." The statement in choice A is too specific; it mentions what the "anything" is (2 + 2).

B: No. Aside from being a question rather than a statement, this choice has the same problem as choice A; it is too specific.

C: **Yes. Paragraph 3 states that true pure mathematical propositions should always be of the form: "If such and such a proposition is true of *anything*, then such and such another proposition is true of that thing." This is the only answer choice that matches that format.**

D: No. This statement only has one part to it; it doesn't fit the format given in the passage of a pure mathematical "if/then" statement.

6. **A** This is an Inference/Except question.

A: **Yes. The author states in the last paragraph that the whole may not have more terms than a part; however, he does not suggest that the whole may have *fewer* terms.**

B: No. In paragraph 6, the author states: "One of the merits of a proof is that it instills a certain doubt as to the result proved." Therefore the statement in this choice can be inferred.

C: No. This statement is a paraphrase of the author's argument in paragraph 5 that the relationship between self-evident propositions is not a frivolous occupation: "But the proof of self-evident propositions may seem, to the uninitiated, a somewhat frivolous occupation. To this we might reply that it is often by no means self-evident that one obvious proposition follows from another obvious proposition; so that we are really discovering new truths when we prove what is evident by a method which is not evident."

D: No. This statement is supported in the final paragraph, where the author describes the outcome of adding a finite number (one) to an infinite number.

7. **D** This is a general Structure question.

A: No. This answer mistakenly puts the definition first. Furthermore, there are no errors in the field discussed, nor is there a proposal for eliminating further errors.

B: No. This choice suggests a comparison between two different perspectives on pure mathematics that is not present in the passage.

C: No. This choice refers to a chronological outline that is not offered in the passage, and as well to a "most distinctive innovation," which does not appear in the passage.

D: **Yes. Paragraphs 1 and 2 concern early development of pure mathematics; paragraph 3 defines it; paragraph 4 addresses confusion concerning the value of symbolism; and paragraphs 5 and 6 address the importance of foundational proofs concerning self-evident propositions.**

SOLUTIONS TO PRACTICE PASSAGE 6

1. **D** This is a New Information question.

A: No. The author makes no argument concerning how prisoners *should* be treated. The tone of the passage is primarily descriptive. Be careful not to use your own opinion or common sense to answer questions.

B: No. This would strengthen rather than undermine the author's argument in paragraph 5. In paragraph 4 (which leads logically up to the conclusion in paragraph 5), the author discusses how physical pain is still a component of modern punishment, and the new information in this question would support that claim.

C: No. Providing only minimal anesthetic is not something inherent in punishment, but rather a conscious decision made by those in charge. Therefore, the new information would not suggest that the bodily component (here, physical pain) *cannot* be eliminated.

D: Yes. The main point of the fourth paragraph is that modern imprisonment tends to incorporate a certain amount of physical discomfort and deprivation. The new information in the question would be one example of this (here, inflicting pain by only providing minimal pain relief for a required procedure).

2.   **A**   This is a Structure/Not question.

Note: The reference at the end of paragraph 3 can be confusing. The author states: "[Yet] one has only to point out so many precautions to realize that capital punishment remains fundamentally, even today, a spectacle that must actually be forbidden." By this the author means that the spectacle aspect of capital punishment must be actively suppressed to be avoided. The author is not saying by this that the measures described in the middle of the paragraph (including prosecution of witnesses and changing the location of the execution) are aspects themselves of spectacle. Instead, they are in fact attempts to suppress or forbid the public spectacle of execution.

A: Yes. Note that this choice says "the introduction...of the guillotine." The guillotine initially is greatly involved with "theatrical ritual" (paragraph 3).

B: No. The third paragraph states that witnesses to an execution who described the event could be prosecuted for doing so. This is given in the context of the discussion of eventual attempts to "forbid" the creation of a spectacle by trying to hide the execution from public view.

C: No. The first paragraph lists several examples of forms of physical punishment that were eliminated, including branding. This list comes after, and illustrates, the claim that there is a reduced "hold on the body" that coexists with the decline in spectacle marked by the end of public executions.

D: No. The third paragraph describes the removal of the guillotine to a less visible environment ("inside prison walls") as a move away from presenting executions as a public spectacle.

3.   **B**   This is an Inference question.

A: No. The reference to religion in the first paragraph associates torture with the weak, not strong, influence of religion. Rush is essentially saying that he hopes that someday we will see use of these punishments as evidence of *insufficient* influence of reason and religion.

B: Yes. The second paragraph suggests "great social disturbances" as the principal reason for England not seeing an immediate decline in public executions.

C: No. Although a new technology (the guillotine) is mentioned, there is no link between inventions or innovations on the whole and the frequency of executions. Furthermore, it is not suggested that the invention of the guillotine itself led to an increased total number of executions, only that it allowed them to be performed faster.

D: No. No association is suggested between economic problems and public executions. It would be going too far outside the scope of the passage to link a struggling economy with social unrest.

4.   **B**   This is a Structure question.

A: No. The author does not suggest that the conditions in prisons are overly harsh; the strong negative tone of the word "deplorable" is not supported by the passage. Furthermore, although the author implies in this paragraph that there is still an aspect of physical pain included in modern imprisonment, the criticism is not cited in order to draw a contrast between kind conditions (according to the critics) in the past and harsh conditions now.

B: Yes. The main point of the fourth paragraph is that physical pain as an aspect of punishment has not been eliminated. The criticism is referenced to illustrate the belief that it is just or fair for prisoners to physically suffer more than others.

C: No. There is no contrast provided between nineteenth century prisoners and prisoners in later times.

D: No. The question asks *why* the author describes this criticism. That is, what logical role does it play in the passage? Although the criticism itself makes such a comparison, the *author's* purpose is to reveal ongoing attitudes about the suffering of prisoners.

5. **C** This is an Inference question.

A: No. The passage suggests with the term "paradoxically" (paragraph 2) that England was in general perhaps more progressive than its neighbors. Regardless, there is no evidence that England lagged behind in adopting penal reforms in general.

B: No. While we know that social disturbances existed in England (paragraph 2), there is no discussion of whether or not, or of how frequently, such disturbances might have occurred in other countries.

C: Yes. The second paragraph describes "the role of model" played by the English legal system with the introduction of juries and public hearings. This suggests that England was a role model for other nations with less advanced, or with in some way inferior, legal systems.

D: No. The "full punishment" for traitors was not employed in England during or after 1820 (paragraph 2), but there is no information concerning the *frequency* of prosecution.

6. **A** This is a Vocabulary-in-Context question.
Note: Be careful not to use your own opinion about what is described in this part of the passage (the move away from physical torture and public punishment). The tone of the passage is neutral and descriptive.

A: Yes. The previous sentences refer to the disappearance, avoidance, and exclusion of certain forms of punishment. This suggests principled inhibition in penal practices.

B: No. The passage contrasts sobriety with spectacle. The author does not claim that the new practices were more responsible. This choice implies an attitude on the part of the author (that torture and public spectacle are irresponsible) that is not expressed in the passage.

C: No. As in choice B, this choice implies a critical attitude of the author towards torture that is not supported by the passage. Furthermore, the author does not suggest that the use of torture arose out of confusion of muddled thinking.

D: No. As in choices B and C, this answer implies that the author actively approves of the move away from torture and spectacle (in this case, that this would be a move towards justice). This attitude, however, is not supported by the passage text.

7. **D** This is an Inference question.

A: No. The author does not endorse (or reject) the criticism of prisons found in the fourth paragraph, nor does he apply it to contemporary prisons.

B: No. The second half of the answer choice is accurate (paragraph 1), but the passage does not refer to shock or excess as contributing to the shift.

C: No. The passage does refer in the third paragraph to forbidding the spectacles of capital punishment, but not to forbidding capital punishment itself.

D: Yes. The first sentence suggests a "slackening hold" on the body and the shift is confirmed in the first paragraph, as the goal of punishment becomes to reach something other than the body.

SOLUTIONS TO PRACTICE PASSAGE 7

1. **B** This is an Inference question.

   A: No. There is no way to say for sure, based on the passage, that forward deduction can not be used.

   B: Yes. This is the only answer choice that provides a belief that can be added to the premise (which is the definition of forward deduction in paragraph 2). It also has a similar format to the example given in paragraph 2 for forward deduction ("If an animal flies, sings, and perches it is probably a bird" to support the conclusion of probable birdhood).

   C: No. This would be an example of reverse deduction. This belief is one that is formatted to be added to the conclusion ("if an animal is a bird," with the conclusion being that the animal is in fact a bird) rather than to the premises. The format for this answer choice is similar to the one given in the bird example in paragraph 2 for reverse deduction.

   D: No. As in choice C, this is an example of reverse deduction, and is similar to the example given of that mode in the second half of paragraph 2. This belief is phrased to be added to the conclusion (that the animal is an insect) rather than to the premises.

2. **B** This is a Weaken question.

   A: No. This statement doesn't tell us anything about the similarity mode itself; we are not told in the answer choice how this statement was used to reach a conclusion.

   B: Yes. The author states that the similarity mode often fails because it isn't deductive. If most people could use it to reach a valid conclusion (unlike in the example in paragraph 3), it would undermine the author's claim. While it doesn't definitively disprove the claim, this is the only one of the four choices that both focuses on the correct issue and is inconsistent with the author's argument.

   C: No. The author makes no claims about which mode is used more than the other. The fact that people *can* switch from similarity to deductive modes (paragraph 5) doesn't tell us how often that occurs.

   D: No. The author does not claim that the similarity mode is more complex. Therefore, the statement that the similarity mode is simpler has no impact on the author's argument in the passage.

3. **D** This is a Structure/Not question.

   A: No. In paragraph 1 the similarity mode is illustrated by the bird example.

   B: No. In paragraph 2 the forward deduction mode is illustrated by the bird example.

   C: No. Enthymeme is forward deduction (paragraph 2), and forward deduction using two beliefs is illustrated by the example of the drunken man in paragraph 4.

   D: Yes. There is no example that supports this mode. While reverse deduction using one belief is illustrated in paragraph 2, there is no example given of reverse deduction using two beliefs (see paragraph 4).

4. **D** This is an Inference question.

   A: No. The first half of this question is correct, as the author states that the variety or variability of the added beliefs is not known (paragraph 5). However, the second half is incorrect because paragraph 5 says that this variety is "particularly important."

   B: No. Although switching from the similarity mode to the deductive-type modes is possible (paragraph 5), the passage does not say who can or can not do it. There is no suggestion in the passage that a person following a certain type of logic would have to know what mode of logic he or she was using (that is, I could reason deductively without being aware of it).

C: No. The similarity mode of induction can be accomplished without deduction according to the first sentence of paragraph 3.

D: **Yes. The first sentence of the passage states that "Smith and Shafir described numerous modes of induction, three of which are best related to categorization." From this wording you can infer that there are other modes of induction as well, including those not related to categorization.**

5. **A** This Is a Vocabulary-In-Context question.

A: **Yes. Throughout the passage, it is shown that the three modes of induction are used to categorize objects. The way in which this is done is to compare the objects to see if they are similar (adding beliefs when necessary). Then if they are similar, they can be categorized together. The way to see if two objects are similar is to observe them (a bird's characteristics, how the drunken man behaves, etc.).**

B: No. The actual term *categorization* does not imply disproving anything; it implies the grouping or classifying of objects based on their similarities. While the *process* of categorization could in fact involve identifying differences (or disproving similarity), that is not what the word itself is used to suggest in the passage.

C: No. The second part of the answer about being based on opinions is incorrect. The passage implies that the objects are grouped based on similarities and that those similarities are observable (as shown by the examples in paragraphs 1–4).

D: No. This is the right answer to the wrong question. This definition is limited to one form of categorization: deductive-type modes of induction (see paragraphs 2 and 4). Therefore, it doesn't capture the full meaning of the word itself as it is used in the passage.

SOLUTIONS TO PRACTICE PASSAGE 8

1. **B** This is an Inference question.

A: No. The author describes these "objects" of our consciousness as "the things which we believe to exist, whether really or ideally, along with ourselves." Because these objects of consciousness may be things that do not really exist they are not necessarily "external phenomena." Furthermore, because they may in fact exist, they are not necessarily of "dubious reality."

B: **Yes. These are objects exist in consciousness because we behave as if they do, whether real or imagined. Note the words "*potentially* fictitious" in this choice, compared to choice A. The fact that this choice allows for the objects to be real as well makes it the better answer.**

C: No. First, we have beliefs about these "objects"; the objects are not themselves beliefs. Second, the beliefs we have are about the objects themselves, not about our own consciousness of them.

D: No. These objects are neither necessarily illusory nor always supernatural.

2. **D** This is an Inference question.

A: No. This answer is too strongly worded, as we don't know that tangible objects are less real, only that they may be less evocative.

B: No. This is Kant's belief (paragraph 3), not the author's. Note that the author in paragraph 4 calls this idea "uncouth" (crude or uncivilized) and an "exaggeration," and discusses it in order to illustrate a point, not to present it as true.

C: No. We have no basis in the passage for judging the nature, or level of distortion, of reality; i.e., one's perceptions may be considered as much a matter of reality as things externally perceived.

D: Yes. The passage points out in the first paragraph, for example, that "We are frequently more ashamed of our blunders afterwards…"

3. **C** This is an Inference question.

A: No. This is not supported. Our morality changes, according to Kant, but this doesn't alter the facts (what's objectively real).

B: No. There is no discussion in the relevant part of the passage of living up to an ideal, or what is required in order to do so.

C: Yes. According to Kant, The "as if" does make a difference in our moral life: "We can act as if there were a God; feel as if we were free… and we find then that these words do make a genuine difference in our moral life" (paragraph 3).

D: No. This choice may be tempting because it scrambles some key words and phrases together. However, there's no evidence in the passage to support the notion that Kant believed we might come to understand something that is in fact unknowable if we act in a certain way.

4. **D** This is a Structure question.

Two conclusions are stated in the final paragraph. First, "The absolute determinability of our mind by abstractions is one of the cardinal facts in our human constitution" and second, that these abstractions have the character of beings "as real in the realm which they inhabit as the changing things of sense are real in the realm of spaces" (that is, mental objects are as real within the mind as physical objects are in the physical world.)

A: No. The purpose of this sentence from paragraph 5 is to generalize from Kant's "Ideas of pure Reason" to all abstractions. This is a related yet different issue than the theme of the "reality" of abstractions and their effect on us in the last paragraph.

B: No. While the analogy of the bar of iron is intended to show the effect objects of belief have on us, the particular sentence in this choice has as its issue that the bar, (or human beings) *cannot describe* the things that are affecting it so strongly. As with choice A, this is a related but distinct issue.

C: No. This sentence from paragraph 2 relates to the beliefs of "mystical authorities" about what is necessary for "contemplation of higher truths." This is not directly relevant to either conclusion presented in the last paragraph.

D: Yes. This sentence from paragraph 1 states that the objects of our beliefs have a strong impact on us. This directly supports the notion that "determinability of the mind by abstractions is one of the cardinal facts in our human constitution."

5. **C** This is a variation on a Weaken question.

A: No. This is consistent with the last lines in the last paragraph.

B: No. Support for this answer can be found in the second paragraph in the reference to what's valued by the "mystical authorities."

C: Yes. This is the author's view, not Kant's, and contradicts Kant's view that religious concepts are "devoid of significance" (paragraph 3).

D: No. This is consistent with information in the fourth paragraph: "The sentiment of reality can indeed attach itself so strongly to our object of belief that our whole life is polarized through and through, so to speak, by its sense of the existence of the thing believed in, and yet that thing, for purpose of definite description, can hardly be said to be present to our mind at all."

SOLUTIONS TO PRACTICE PASSAGE 9

1. **D** This is a general Structure question.
   - A: No. No positive consequence to the second position is acknowledged and the final paragraph does not represent a new problem.
   - B: No. The author ultimately rejects the first position, which advocates separate spheres, and does not reaffirm it in the last paragraph.
   - C: No. The first position is not defended; the author ultimately rejects it. Furthermore, although there is an analogy in the last paragraph, the point of the paragraph is not to develop that analogy.
   - **D: Yes. The author addresses two possible positions supporting the idea that there should be a division of labor along gender lines. Both Position A and Position B are rejected, and instead the author suggests in the last paragraph that women should be supported in all facets of human functioning.**

2. **B** This is an Inference question.
   - A: No. This contradicts the author's second criticism of Position B's characterization of women (paragraph 5). The author would reject this statement.
   - **B: Yes. In the final paragraph the author refers to the present "unequal failure of capability" of women as a problem that should be addressed. Note that this answer does not suggest that the author believes women are *inherently* incapable.**
   - C: No. The author states that there is no compelling scientific evidence of gender differences, but does not go so far as to say that it has been proven that there are none. The lack of scientific evidence for a claim does not constitute scientific evidence against it.
   - D: No. While Positions A and B might endorse this, the author does not express agreement; nor does she make her own claim for female superiority over men in any realm.

3. **B** This is an Inference question.
   - A: No. Neither Mill nor Rousseau advocates the abolition of distinct spheres. They would agree on this issue.
   - **B: Yes. The fourth paragraph suggests a disagreement between Rousseau and Mill concerning whether differences between men and women are innate or not. The passage says: "I turn, then, to Position B, which has been influentially defended by many philosophers, including Rousseau and some of his followers in today's world. Insofar as B relies on the claim that there are two different sets of basic innate capacities, we should insist, *with John Stuart Mill*, that this claim has not been borne out by any responsible scientific evidence." This issue is the principal difference between Position A and Position B.**
   - C: No. Neither clearly advocates the subordination of women.
   - D: No. Although there may be some disagreement over scientific evidence, there is no suggestion of either man questioning whether science is an appropriate tool.

4. **C** This is a Weaken/Roman numeral question.
   - **I: True. Position B presumes that there are innate gender differences, one of which, as evidenced in paragraph 5, involves the exercise of practical reason. This study would provide evidence that this is not true.**
   - II: False. This statement does not, in itself, constitute evidence that there are not essential gender differences and is in fact compatible with Position B.

III: **True. This study provides confirmation of the author's second criticism of Position B (paragraph 5); that is, that it would create incomplete and non-viable men and women (in this case, men who could not perform a basic human function).** You may have found Item III the most difficult to evaluate; it takes some thought to see that this is consistent with the author's critique in paragraph 5, rather than something an advocate of Position B would affirm as valid or appropriate. However, note that the combinations of numerals do the work for you. Once you have eliminated anything that doesn't include Item I, and crossed out anything that does include Item II, you are left with choice C.

5.   **A**   This is a Structure question.

   A: **Yes. The figure Sophie is presented as an incomplete, nonviable person, an illustration of the author's second criticism of Position B (paragraph 5).**

   B: No. The passage provides no evidence that Rousseau advocated a hierarchy.

   C: No. As far as we know from the passage, Sophie is not a philosopher. Furthermore, the point of the example is to criticize Position B, not to show support for it.

   D: No. There is no implication that Sophie is unhappy.

6.   **D**   This is an Inference /Except question.

   A: No. The passage states that politics (the "public sphere") has, as a consequence of Position A, been a traditionally male sphere (paragraph 1).

   B: No. The first sentence of the second paragraph affirms that Position A is compatible with the pursuit of justice for women.

   C: No. Paragraph 3 states that the separate spheres advocated by Position A tend to lead to a hierarchy of men over women.

   D: **Yes. The idea of innate differences between men and women belongs to Position B, not to Position A. According to Position A, the genders share identical basic needs (paragraph 2).**

7.   **C**   This is an Analogy question.

   A: No. In suggesting separate spheres, this parallels Position A, which the author rejects.

   B: No. In suggesting different essential functions, this parallels Position B, which the author rejects.

   C: **Yes. The author argues throughout the passage against essential differences and suggests in the final paragraph that the lack of support women receive leaves them with undeveloped capabilities.**

   D: No. Although recognizing cultural differences, the author does not argue for culturally specific gender relations and, in the last paragraph, she suggests that women often need to challenge the expectations of particular cultures.

Chapter 9
The Writing Sample

I. OVERVIEW

Purpose of the Writing Sample

The MCAT Writing Sample is designed to test your ability to analyze a non-technical topic and to express your ideas in a coherent, consistent, and well-organized fashion. The multiple choice sections of the MCAT test how well you can understand, analyze, and respond to information that is presented to you (or, for some of the questions in the science sections, your ability to apply your existing knowledge to new situations). The Writing Sample, on the other hand, tests your ability to communicate your knowledge and ideas to others (certainly a valuable skill for a doctor to have).

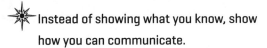 Instead of showing what you know, show how you can communicate.

While your essays may be read by admissions committees, they are not admissions essays. Therefore, this is not the time to show off your dedication to medicine or your extensive science knowledge (you have other opportunities to do that during the MCAT and in your application). Instead, this is a chance to display your capacity to think and write analytically about serious cultural, political, and social issues. While the Writing Sample score is considered by many schools to be the least important of the four sub-scores, this does not mean that it is irrelevant. To maximize your chances of acceptance, you need to make sure that you have a solid Writing Sample score. A low score can only raise problems in an admissions committee's deliberations, and you don't want to have any weak points in your application, or any reason for them to discount you early on.

Scoring

The Writing Sample is scored on a J–T scale. Each essay will be scored by at least two different graders (one human and one computer program). Each grader will give an essay a numerical score from 1–6, at 0.5 increments. If the two scores for an individual essay differ by more than a point, it goes to a third (human) grader. In the end, your numerical scores from both essays are averaged together into a single letter, which is your score for the Writing Sample section of the test. Here is how the numerical average is translated into the letter score:

1	1.5	2	2.5	3	3.5	4	4.5	5	5.5	6
J	K	L	M	N	O	P	Q	R	S	T

The average score is an "O." Later in this chapter we will go into more detail as to what kinds of essays receive what kinds of scores.

The Topics

The Writing Sample questions cover a wide range of issues within twelve general categories:

- Government/Politics
- Citizenship/Democracy
- War/International Relations
- Law/Justice
- Business
- Education
- History
- Media/Advertising
- Technology
- Science/Research
- Individual Rights
- Morality/Ethics

Basic Preparation

The list of general topics can be quite intimidating. After all, how can you be expected to know everything about all those subjects? However, it isn't actually necessary to know all of history, every aspect of international relations, or all things political. Your goal in preparing for the Writing Sample is to come up with a set of examples and core issues that you can intelligently discuss within each area. Your basic preparation should include the following:

- Familiarize yourself with the prompts. The AAMC provides a list of questions or "prompts" at www.aamc.org/students/mcat/preparing/writingsampleitems.htm. The AAMC states that questions on future tests will be either directly from this list, or similar to items on the list. This list is not organized by categories, so take the categories listed above and go through the list, picking out several items that fall within each one. Think through the issues involved with each item, how you would respond to each of the three tasks, and identify subjects that would be relevant to a variety of items within the same (or similar) categories. You do not need to write or outline an essay for all of the hundreds of prompts, but you do want to be prepared to address any type of prompt that they might give you.
- Create a list of examples. The best essays will use concrete, real-world examples to illustrate the argument being made. Generate a set of four examples within each of the twelve categories. Some of these examples might be applicable to more than one category. For example, the constitutional right to free speech might apply to a prompt about law, about citizenship, or about government and politics. Make sure you can talk about some of the details about each example and why it's important.
- Pay attention to current events. Spend at least a few hours every week reading, watching, or listening to some news source. Keep a notebook where you take notes on ongoing events, listing the issues involved and the details you could use to explain the example and its relevance to the question you are answering. If you do this consistently, you will find that within a few weeks you have a bank of serious, well-developed examples to draw upon. Historical events are equally valid examples. If a news story reminds you of an event in history, do a little research (wikipedia.org, issues of exact accuracy aside, is a good source for basic research) to fill in the details as necessary, and add it to your bank.

- Write practice essays on a variety of prompts. The more times you sit down and write a 30 minute essay, the more comfortable you will be with the timing and structure of the essay on test day. You will find, if you haven't already, that mulling over a topic at your leisure and expressing yourself coherently in 30 minutes are two different experiences. Pick items from the AAMC list at random and give yourself 30 minutes from the time you start reading the question to write an essay (always type it on your computer to mimic the real test conditions). Or pick a prompt that you know you would struggle with and do the same.

Advanced Preparation

Once you have basic familiarity with the structure and categories of the topics and have written a range of practice essays, your attention should turn to how you can make your essays even better in order to push your score up to a 5 or 6.

- **Rewrites:** If your essay turns out badly (you couldn't come up with good examples, or your organization was poor, or you didn't address all three tasks, etc.), identify the flaws in your response and then rewrite the essay in 30 minutes. If that prompt or something like it shows up on the test, you will be glad that you did, since you will have a fully formed and thought-out response ready to go.
- **Evaluation:** Self-evaluation is extremely useful; once you are familiar with the grading criteria and the structure of the essay, you can usually tell whether or not you did a good job. However, since you know what you meant to say, it can be difficult at times to see where your ideas might not have come through clearly enough. Give copies of your essays to friends, family, or teachers and ask them to critique them. A reader doesn't have to be an expert in MCAT essays to tell you if you directly answered the question, if they could follow your logic, or if there were so many grammatical or spelling mistakes that it made comprehension difficult.
- **Core principles:** Develop a list of core thesis/antithesis principles that correspond to the different categories. Examples are the bones of an essay, but your discussion of the key principles, ideals, and or values involved in the question give it heart and soul. This depth is required to score in the 5–6 range. Since you will always have to consider two sides of any question, think of the principles in pairs. For example:
    - "The role of a democratic state is to protect national security/The role of a democratic state is to preserve individual liberties."
    - "The mission of a business is to maximize profit/Businesses have social responsibilities that compete with profit maximization."
    - "One should never compromise one's ethics/Ethical compromise may be required for the good of others."
    - "Education should serve the individual needs of students/Education should serve the good of society."
    - "Technology makes life easier/Technology makes life more difficult."

II. ESSAY-WRITING TIME TABLE

Don't waste all of your preparation by neglecting some important component of the question under pressure on test day. Here is a guideline for how you should spend your precious 30 minutes:

1. Read the entire question word for word (1 minute)

If you misread the question, including the specific tasks, or miss some important aspect of the wording of the question, you risk writing an incomplete or off-topic response. No matter how good what you write is, if you don't fully and directly address the question, you will get a low score. Note all the tasks within the question and make sure you address each one.

2. Prewriting (5–10 minutes)

Brainstorm ideas and examples, using your scratch paper to take notes. Identify at least one core issue involved in the prompt statement, and think through how you will define key terms. Choose your examples, and define the contrast between them. Define your synthesis rule or principle. Write a brief outline of all three tasks.

3. Writing (5–7 minutes per task)

Make sure not to spend too much time on one task to the detriment of the others. If you fail to fully address one or more of the tasks, your score will suffer. Even if you have more to say on an early task, force yourself to move on when time for that task is running out.

4. Proofreading (3–5 minutes)

While your score is not largely based on spelling, grammar, and sentence structure, if poor mechanics make it difficult to understand what you are saying, you will not get full credit for your good ideas. The human graders spend around 3 minutes reading and evaluating each essay. If your writing is unclear, they will not spend extra time trying to decipher it. While you do not need to strive for perfection in your mechanics or typing (the graders expect and allow for a few such mistakes even in high scoring essays), do a basic proofreading to clean it up as much as possible.

III. THE PROMPT AND THE THREE TASKS

While the issues included in the full list of Writing Sample items cover a very broad range, the structure of the question itself is always the same. Let's take a look at a sample question, and break it down piece by piece.

> **The role of education in a democracy is to ensure social stability.**
>
> Write a unified essay in which you perform the following tasks. Explain what you think the above statement means. Describe a specific situation in which the role of education in a democracy should be to do something other than ensure social stability. Discuss what you think determines whether or not the role of education in a democracy should be to ensure social stability.

The theme or topic of the question is set out in the **boldfaced** prompt statement.

The first sentence of the paragraph underneath is always the same: "Write a unified essay in which you perform the following tasks." Although this might sound like a throw-away line, there are two important pieces of information here. First, your essay will be judged on how well you address *each* of the three tasks. Therefore, never plan or write your essay based only on the prompt statement, without reading and taking into account the exact wording and nature of the tasks. Second, the essay as a whole must be "unified." You are not writing three separate essays, one per task; all three parts must work together as a coherent whole.

The second sentence sets out the first task, and will also always be worded in the same way: "Explain what you think the above statement means." We will call this the **thesis** task. It sounds quite vague, but what it is really asking you is: *when and why would this statement be true?*

The third sentence sets out the second task, which we will call the **antithesis**. While it always begins, "Describe a specific situation," the rest of the sentence will depend on the wording of the original prompt. In this case, it asks you to "Describe a specific situation in which the role of education in a democracy should be to do something other than ensure social stability." Unlike the thesis task, the antithesis task appears to be asking you to simply give an example in which the opposite of the prompt is true. It is in fact asking you to provide an example, but this is not ALL it's really asking. Take this task to mean: *explain when and why the prompt statement is false.*

The last sentence of the paragraph assigns you the third task which we will call the **synthesis**. It always asks you to *"discuss what you think determines"* when the prompt statement would be either true or false.

The best way to organize your essay is in three paragraphs, following this "Thesis-Antithesis-Synthesis" structure of the question. This is not a standard five-paragraph essay; a formal introduction and conclusion are not required. This is not to say that you can't write an introduction or conclusion if they add substance to your argument, but don't waste time adding them in simply for the five-paragraph structure. Given the limited amount of time that you have, it's easiest to keep it simple with three paragraphs, one per task.

Now that the basic structure is clear, let's break down each task further into its specific components. We'll illustrate what these components look like in action by going through a possible response to each task.

Thesis Paragraph: Outline

There are six basic components to a strong thesis response:

1. **Start with a hook.** While not absolutely required, a catchy first sentence or two will draw the (human) reader's attention. Given that the graders are reading hundreds of essays on the same question, it can't hurt to wake them up a bit in the beginning of your essay.

2. **Paraphrase the prompt statement.** Make it clear from the outset that you are addressing the topic they gave you, and set up the context for the rest of the paragraph.

3. **Define key terms if necessary.** If the prompt includes abstract or vague language, explain what these terms mean in the context of your response. You can define terms however you like. However, choose relatively intuitive or common definitions; the more you have to explain and defend your definitions, the less time you will have to address the real issues at the heart of the question.

4. **Explain the core thesis principle.** Think about why the test writers thought this was an important issue for people to discuss. What social, political, cultural, or ethical principles and practices does this question relate to?

5. **Give a concrete example of when the prompt statement would be true.** Provide enough detail to make the example understandable. Remember, however, that the point of the example is to illustrate your thesis argument, not to provide the reader with a lesson in current events or history, so you don't need to go overboard on factual details.

6. **Explain the relevance of your example.** Write at least a sentence or two to wrap up the paragraph by emphasizing how the example relates to the terms of the prompt.

Although a hook, by definition, starts off the paragraph, the rest of the six components don't have to come in this exact order, as long as there is a clear organization and logical flow to the paragraph as a whole.

Here is a possible response to the thesis that includes each of these elements. The notes in the margins label the different components of the paragraph (don't include these labels in your own essays).

As a reminder, here again is the prompt statement:

The role of education in a democracy is to ensure social stability.

Sample Thesis Paragraph

The historian Will Durant once said: "Education is the transmission of civilization." A democracy is a system fundamentally based on both political participation and respect for differences, and in a democracy, we consider ourselves to be civilized when we adhere to basic principles such as cooperation, acknowledgement of the rights and beliefs of others, and productive participation in the social and political system. In many ways, our educational system plays a fundamental role in transmitting these values and guaranteeing the continued stable functioning of our democratic system by socializing children to respect these principles

hook

definition

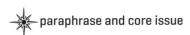

and values. John Dewey, a philosopher and educator, argued that early education should have as its central mission the instillation of core democratic principles and the formation of a "social consciousness." Given that this consciousness entails working towards long term rather than short term goals, and requires at times putting the needs and rights of others above one's own individual desires, Dewey argued that children will not acquire this "social intelligence" unless it is incorporated into the procedures and pedagogy of early education. In very early childhood, the essence of these principles is communicated through an emphasis on sharing, on settling disputes peacefully, and through group classroom and physical activities that require cooperation and coordination. Later on, the incorporation of actual political procedures continues the lesson. When a primary school class votes for a class president, for example, the point is not to actually give children a role in running the school. Rather, it is to teach them about democratic values and institutions. Children learn to debate and discuss their ideas with others, to make political decisions through voting, to abide by majority rule even if they are unhappy with the results, and to act in the interests of others if elected to a leadership position. In this way, early education teaches children the ideals, procedures, and institutions that are necessary for a stable and well functioning democracy.

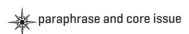

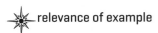

Antithesis Paragraph: Outline

1. **Make the transition.** Signal to the reader that you are moving on to the second task. If the prompt is phrased in absolute terms, paraphrase it in more moderate terms to avoid contradicting your thesis argument.

2. **Continue your definition of key terms (if necessary).** Definitions should stay consistent throughout the essay; generally you should not be providing a competing or alternate definition in the antithesis. However, if there is another aspect or facet of your definition of key terms that you will be focusing on in this task, make that clear.

3. **State and explain the antithesis principle.** Just as you should have a core idea at the heart of your thesis, the antithesis should also focus on a central theme or value. Keep in mind that the thesis/antithesis relationship should not be like pro and con positions in a debate. By the nature of the question, the prompt statement is sometimes true and at other times false. You might argue that it is true half the time and false half the time, or that it is almost always true but that there are exceptions. In any case, make sure that your antithesis principle and argument does not contradict or invalidate your thesis argument.

4. **Give an example of when the prompt statement would not be true.** This example should be comparable to your thesis example, but clearly contrasting; the contrast is the core of the essay as a whole, and it lays the groundwork for your synthesis.

5. **Explain the relevance of the example to the terms of the antithesis.** Write a sentence or two explaining why and how the example illustrates the antithesis statement and principle.

Sample Antithesis Paragraph

However, while cooperation and social stability are placed at a high level in our value system, so are other characteristics like innovation and non-conformity, and at times educational institutions must be concerned with transmitting those values as well. Sometimes this is needed even at the short-term cost of a certain level of instability. Democratic principles are founded on an acceptance of change. In contrast to aristocratic or totalitarian rule, government "by the people" must allow for and even foster change in political institutions and social and economic systems, or else a society will stagnate and a democracy may fall into a system of rule by the powerful rather than rule by the people. At the heart of the American self-image is the image of the pioneer, the innovator, the entrepreneur, the person who follows his or her own ideas even in opposition to what others believe is right or even possible. Later education, in high school and even more so in college, should be structured in a way that allows and encourages students to challenge accepted wisdom. This is why college classes in social science and humanities are and should often be structured as seminars rather than lectures. The goal is to foster debate about the reading or the professor's lectures, rather than simply encouraging memorization and regurgitation. In the sciences, lab work can be used not only to teach factual knowledge and accepted procedures, but to give students the tools they need to do independent work later on, or at least to see for themselves scientific principles in action, rather than simply learning and accepting them in the abstract. The interesting thing about intellectual independence and innovation is that at its highest level, it can cause social transformation and disruption. The invention of the internet, for example, going back to the creation of the ARPAnet in the 1960's, has radically changed society by giving people unprecedented access to information and means of communication. The transformative power of the internet can be seen in part through the fact that many non-democratic societies, China for example, limit what can exist on the internet in the service of maintaining the exiting political power structure. If educational institutions only work to maintain social stability at the cost of teaching independence of thought, society as a whole, especially a democratic society, suffers in the long run. While we want young students to learn and accept certain core principles, in later years we need to teach them to be independent thinking citizens so they can contribute to the continued vibrancy and evolution of a democratic society.

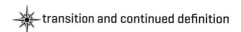 transition and continued definition

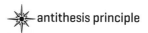 antithesis principle

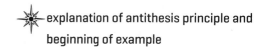 explanation of antithesis principle and beginning of example

 specific example

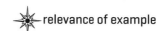 relevance of example

Synthesis Paragraph: Outline

1. **Make the transition.** Let the reader know that you are moving on to the last task. This can be a simple paraphrase of the synthesis task, and may be part of your statement of the synthesis rule (coming up next).

2. **State a general synthesis rule or principle.** This rule is closely based on the contrast you have already set out and illustrated in the first two tasks; it puts the contrast in the form of a rule or set of criteria. Make sure that it is applicable, but not limited, to both of your examples.

3. **Explain the relevance of your synthesis rule to your examples.** An easy way to explain your synthesis is to refer back to the essential characteristics of your examples that caused you to place them on either side of the prompt statement. However, this should be a continuation and extension, not a repetition, of points you have already made.

4. **Explain, refine, and extend the principle.** Go back to the core principles you raised in the first two tasks, and explain how they relate to your rule. You can bring in additional examples here, but only if they are clearly similar to and logically consistent with the examples you have already provided, and only if you have time to explain their relevance. Don't end the essay with a new specific example that raises an entirely new issue.

5. **Conclude.** Wrap up the essay with a final sentence or two. This is not the most important part of the essay, but it's best not to leave the reader hanging with an abrupt ending that reads as if you ran out of time in the middle of a sentence.

Sample Synthesis Paragraph

transition and statement of synthesis rule

relevance of synthesis rule

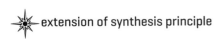
extension of synthesis principle

Therefore, what determines whether or not the function of education is to ensure social stability is the age of the students. Young children have neither the experience nor the wisdom to set their own boundaries. The image of Golding's Lord of the Flies can be seen as a cautionary tale of what can happen if children who are not fully socialized are set loose without adult guidance. While extreme, this tale is an expression of our legitimate fears of what can happen if educational and other social institutions don't or can't do their job. And if this socialization process does not come early enough to not only teach rules but to shape and form a child's perceptions and way of thinking, that child will never grow up to be a true citizen who can participate in a meaningful way in democratic institutions. Without widespread participation, and responsible and responsive leadership, a democracy can stagnate or even devolve into totalitarianism. However, once those values have been instilled in early childhood, and the "democratic personality" has been formed, the role of education should shift to foster the capacity for independent thought and action. In fact, if children are taught those unchanging core values of democracy early on, they are prepared to work for social change later in life, when changes in society are needed in order to better represent and enact those core values. No democracy is perfect; our own nation has a history of not always living up to its own ideals. Without brave people like Frederick Douglass and the abolitionists, slavery might still exist. Without women like Lucretia Mott and the suffragettes, women might never have been granted the right to vote. And without leaders like Marin Luther King Jr., Jim Crow laws might still exist. Innovation comes not only through new technologies that transform society, but also through new political and social ideas that force us to evolve into a more truly democratic state. In a democracy, there is always a tension between stability and innovation. The role of education should be to prepare citizens to manage that delicate balance, so that society can change for the better while not losing its core values in the process.

—conclusion

IV. SELF-EVALUATION: REFINING YOUR SKILLS

We've discussed the kind of prep work you can do to improve the quality of your essays. Prep work involves looking at the Writing Sample task from the outside in: how you can structure your preparation process to develop the knowledge and skills that you need. Now that we have gone through the basic components of a good essay, let's turn the discussion to how to improve your essay, looking at it from the inside: In other words, what you should do during your 30 minutes in order to write the best possible essay. This will change depending on your own self-evaluation. Diagnose the weak points of essays you have completed, and use the list below to strategize how to avoid those mistakes in the future.

1. **Pre-writing**
    - First of all, do it. Time pressure may push you to jump right in and start writing the minute you finish reading the last word of the paragraph (or even worse, immediately after you read the prompt, skipping the step of reading the three tasks). However, if you have a good plan and a basic idea of what you want to say in each task, it won't take you long to write a substantive response. So, don't let stress or time pressure keep you from doing some solid pre-writing.
    - Brainstorm. If you have ever had the most brilliant idea or perfect example pop into your head 5 minutes (or 5 hours) after you finished writing a timed essay, use that as motivation to do some true brainstorming before you start to write. This means using your scratch paper to write down every and any idea about the essay that comes into your head. Don't censor yourself at this stage; nothing yet is set in stone. If you pour out all of your thoughts, those great ideas lurking in the back of your brain have a chance to make it out on to the page and eventually on to the screen. Once your brainstorming is done, you can pick and choose the best ideas and examples to incorporate into your essay.
    - Look for the word "should" anywhere in the prompt or tasks, and make sure that you respond to it. A question that asks when governments might limit individual rights (e.g., a totalitarian nation) will require a different approach and example than one that asks when a government *should* limit individual rights.
    - Outline all three tasks. If you find that often your thesis goes well, but you run out of ideas or energy in the second or especially the third task, make sure that you are giving each one equal attention in the pre-writing stage. In particular, have an idea of what your basic synthesis rule will be. Don't leave it to the last 5 minutes with the clock ticking down when it is very difficult to come up with a new idea.

2. **Thesis task**
   - Stick to the terms of the question. If you have ever found that you have wandered off-topic later in the essay, look to see if that digression began in the first paragraph.
   - Define terms clearly, keeping in mind the direction of your antithesis. You should always keep the logic of your argument as a whole in mind as you write each task. Avoid setting out definitions that will contradict your later argument. If that happens, you will be left with a logical contradiction within your essay and you will have to go back and waste time rewriting.
   - Set up your synthesis by suggesting the point of contrast within the description of your example and its relevance to the prompt.
   - Ask yourself why your example illustrates the prompt statement, and make sure you've answered that question within the first paragraph. Doing so will lead you into a discussion of core issues, and further set up the contrast. It will also alert you to problems that need to be fixed early on.
   - Use your discussion of core principles to provide a unifying theme for the rest of the essay (for example, what a democracy needs to survive and thrive).

3. **Antithesis task**
   - Write a clear transition. If you have ever found that you inadvertently contradicted yourself in the first and second tasks, it may have been because of the lack of a transition.
   - Choose a clearly contrasting example. One of the most common mistakes students make is to choose an antithesis example that is too similar to their thesis. Never use the same example for both sides of the question, even if you think that you can explain some subtle difference within it.
   - As you explain your example, emphasize the aspects that demonstrate the contrast with your thesis case. Your synthesis shouldn't be a huge surprise to the reader once they get to the third task; you should be building up to it as you go.
   - If you are stuck because you think the thesis is always true, play devil's advocate with yourself. What would a reasonable person, one who believed in the antithesis just as much as you believe in the thesis, say? How might someone object to your thesis argument? The nature of these questions is that there is always a reasonable argument to be made on either side. Remember that you don't ultimately have to agree with the antithesis.
   - Keep core definitions consistent. If your contrast turns on a change in definition, all you will have to say in the synthesis is: "it depends on how you define it."

4. **Synthesis task**
   - Avoid the vague "it depends on the person" or "it depends on the situation" rule. On what characteristics of a person or situation does it depend? What specific factors will push it to one side or the other?
   - Avoid circular reasoning. Circular reasoning is saying something that is true by definition. For example: "French wine is the best wine in the world, because no country makes a better wine than France." True, but why? It is the why that gives your synthesis substance and weight. For our sample essay above, an example of circular reasoning would be, "The role of education in a democracy should be to ensure stability when a democracy needs to be stable." Instead, discuss when and/or *why* a democracy needs stability, and *how* education contributes to it.

- Use dichotomies. Your synthesis rule is founded on the basic thesis/antithesis contrast embodied in the structure of the essay question itself. You can think of this contrast as a dichotomy, and it often helpful to think of your central dichotomy in the prewriting stage, even before you start to write the essay itself. There are many dichotomies that can apply to a variety of prompts, but here are some of the most widely applicable ones:
  - Short term/long term: This dichotomy is particularly useful for prompts that ask when the government can limit basic rights, such as freedom of speech.
  - Wartime/peacetime: useful for prompts about government and politicians.
  - Large scale/small scale: Some things are acceptable when they are limited in scope (e.g., small amounts of industrial pollution), perhaps as a necessary evil, but unacceptable on a large scale (e.g., massive deforestation that contributes to global warming).
  - Voluntary/involuntary: Whenever a prompt relates to the need for individuals to pay certain costs or take on certain risks, this can be a useful contrast. Things that are illegitimate when imposed involuntarily (e.g., safety risks in the workplace) may be ethically acceptable if accepted voluntarily.
  - Children/adults: Many prompts are potentially relevant to level of maturity, in particular prompts that have to do with education, the effect of technology, or the effects of media and advertising. You might argue that education should have different goals, or use different methods, depending on the age of the students. Or, that technology and media have different impacts on immature or mature people.

V. SCORING GUIDELINES AND SAMPLE ESSAYS

AAMC guidelines

The AAMC has published a description of "typical characteristics of essays" that receive each different whole number score. We've paraphrased them below:

An essay with a score of 6 will show:
- obvious facility with language.
- substantial development of major ideas.
- coherent, focused treatment of the assignment.
- obvious evidence of clarity, depth, and complexity of thought.

An essay with a score of 5 will show:
- strong control of language.
- well-developed major ideas.
- a generally coherent and focused argument.
- clarity of thought, with some depth or complexity.

An essay with a score of 4 will show:
- adequate control of language.
- adequate development of major ideas.
- writing is generally coherent and shows some focus.
- clarity of thought, may have evidence of complexity or depth.

An essay with a score of 3 will show:
- some control of language, but may include grammar and spelling errors.
- some development of major ideas.
- writing is coherent, but may not be focused.
- some clarity of thought, but lack complexity.

An essay with a score of 2 will show:
- poor control of language, numerous errors in grammar, spelling, and sentence structure.
- ideas are underdeveloped.
- writing lacks integration and/or coherence.
- problems with clarity and complexity.

An essay with a score of 1 will show:
- very poor control of language, such that the writer's ideas are hard to follow.
- ideas may not be developed at all.
- major problems with organization.
- a complete lack of understanding of the assignment.

To sum it up, the more of the following characteristics an essay has, the higher score it will receive.

- On topic
- Addresses all three tasks
- Well-organized and focused
- Ideas are well developed and explained
- Logically clear and consistent
- Shows sophistication and complexity of thought
- Clearly and elegantly written

Notice that length is not one of the criteria. The AAMC states that it does not explicitly consider the length of the essay; what matters is the content and development of the argument. However, a very short essay is unlikely to have gone into enough depth and detail to get a high score (while a long essay that gets its length from repetition or rambling will get a low score). There are no page breaks on the test, but a good goal for your practice essays is to write at least two double-spaced pages.

In the next section, we'll go through a set of six essays, each one representing a reference score on the 1–6 scale. They are all on the same prompt so that you can more easily compare them with each other. Each essay is followed by an Analysis that discusses its strong and weak points. You will see that both high and low scoring essays may use similar ideas and examples. This shows that it is not only the content of your ideas that matter, but how you explain and express them, and how your ideas work together within the unified whole of the three tasks.

Prompt:

Politicians should be expected to set an example for their constituents.

Write a unified essay in which you perform the following tasks. Explain what the above statement means. Describe a specific situation in which politicians should not be expected to set an example for their constituents. Discuss what you think determines when politicians should be expected to set an example for their constituents and when they should not.

Reference Score: 1

Politicians are bad examples for our children They lie, cheat and steal in order to get elected and stay in power. They are bad examples for society as a whole, and care only about making money or getting more power. This is a problem because they have a lot of power and use it to bad ends, getting us into wars where we should just stay out and mind our own business. Constituents shouldn't vote for politicians who abuse their power. If more people voted, maybe politicians would behave better, but no one holds them accountable. Sometimes they are prosecuted. But more often are let off with a slap on the wrist, and then can go into the private sector and make even more money there. Politicians who act in shameful ways give us a bad reputation in the world because people think all mericans act and think like them. It is important that the country has a good image in the world, to better trade and negotiate with other countries. If politicians act badly and show disrespect to other world leaders, it makes this harder and hurts our economy.

Analysis

The essay as a whole reads as a diatribe against political leaders rather than a response to the question. While wording from the prompt appears in the text, it doesn't answer the question of when politicians should and should not be expected to set an example. The essay does not directly address any of the tasks, there is no real development of ideas or complexity of thought, and the language is difficult to follow. Overall, this author has strong opinions and has clearly thought about some related issues. However, he or she doesn't appear to have understood the assignment at hand.

Reference Score: 2

We elect politicians to lead state or federal governments in determining many aspects of our public and private lives. Why would we vote for a person who could or could not be moral and trustworthy and therefore a good role model or example for constituents? There is no time when a politician is excused from setting a good example in his or public or private life. When a politician chooses to run and possibly be choosen for office she or she knows that his or her life will be scrutinized and any salacious or stupid bits be on Youtube with hours. The aspect of role model is given a part of the job. Politicians are always visible and we need them to be examples for young people and to convince them to go into public life. Politicians are role models for other politicians. They need to be strong in character to resist the influence of lobbyists and other corrupting forces.

There are those that think that politicians need think that being a role model is situational. There may be times when they need to take bribes to go relected and when their actions may appear to be illegal or immoral or reprehensible but claimed to be necessary for national security or for the safety of constituents.

Politicians should always be on guard when in the public eye or when interacting with other governments. President Kennedy was popular a much liked President but would not perhaps be as respected in these times because all of his illicit activities would be revealed. His illnesses would be of great concern to voters.

When dealing with foreign countries politicians run into different ideas of good role models. This may put a politician in conflict or difficulty if they need to work out a compromise and still adhere to our moral system and being a role model to very young people (AKA children) is not always the same as being a role model for adults.

Analysis

There are a few promising ideas buried within this essay, but as written it fails to address two of the three tasks or to coherently address the issue of the prompt. While the author shows some flashes of a good vocabulary ("salacious" and "illicit"), the confusing use of language and mistakes in grammar and sentence structure also make it quite difficult to decipher what the author is trying to communicate. The first two sentences are promising; the issue of why we vote for and elect candidates is certainly relevant. However, the next sentence indicates that the prompt statement is always (rather than sometimes or usually) true, which sets up a potential conflict with the antithesis. This conflict never actually appears, however, because the essay doesn't address the antithesis or synthesis tasks; the entire essay appears to be defending the thesis. It is possible that the author intended the second paragraph to be the antithesis. However, without discussion of why politicians not only do but *should* take bribes, etc., in order to be elected, it reads more as a negative example (what politicians shouldn't do because they should set a good example) and so a continuation of the thesis. Kennedy, who appears in the third paragraph, is potentially a valid example, but it isn't clear what his illicit activities were, how his illness relates, or how the need to be on guard in public ties into to whether or not politicians should be expected to set an example. Finally, the last paragraph again hints at potentially relevant ideas without explaining them: the potential for conflicting ideas about what constitutes a good role model, and the effect on children. Overall, because there are couple of promising and relevant ideas, this essay stays, barely, out of the "1" scoring range.

Reference Score: 3

Politicians should be expected to set an example for their constituents. This is true of high level politicians like presidents, who represent the nation as a whole. Because they aren't involved in the everyday aspects of our lives, they play more of a symbolic function than an actual practical one. They are symbols of the nation, and let us know what ideals we as citizens should be living up to. Because of this, they are also examples for other nations, who aren't really constituents but it has the same effect. But politicians who serve on a local level don't have to be examples for us to follow. We care about what they can do to make our lives better, not what they symbolize on a larger scale. A mayor, or a city councilman, for example, should not worry about how their actions are seen by others, but about the practical impact of their policies. Do they fix the roads, or create parks, or keep the infrastructure functioning, is what we really care about. These politicians are also invisible on the world stage, so we don't care about the example they might set for other nations.

So, what determines whether or not politicians should be expected to set an example for their constituents is whether they are local or national level. National level politicians should be role models for us to follow in terms of how they appear in the media, and what they say in their speeches that will be broadcast across the nation and the world. However, local politicians, who are much more directly involved in the everyday lives of constituents, are only expected to make the lives of the people in their city or state better, rather than playing some kind of symbolic function as a role model.

Analysis

This essay has some promising ideas, but doesn't follow through in expressing them fully or clearly enough to score a 4 or above. First, by restating the prompt rather than paraphrasing it, the author sets up an internal contradiction in his or her argument. The essay states in the first sentence that politicians should always act as examples, but then goes on, in addressing the antithesis task, to say the opposite. The point of contrast comes through eventually, but the reader has to overcome this apparent contradiction to follow it. The discussion of the symbolic function of a president is an unexpectedly thoughtful idea, but it isn't fully explained. Why should we believe that presidents have little or no impact on our lives? Don't they set or affect policy (war, taxation, education, etc.) that does in fact affect us directly? To be convincing, this argument must be explicitly made, rather than assumed, with a concrete example given. While still

 Make your connections clear; spell it out!

addressing the thesis task, the author brings in the international role of a president. Since it isn't explained how we can see other nations in some way as "constituents," this point is off topic. Next, the author moves on to the antithesis task within the same paragraph, which makes it difficult for the reader to see that the author has in fact addressed both tasks (rather than just contradicting him or herself within the thesis). The argument about the duties of a local politician is a good one, and while the examples are overly vague, they do make the point reasonably clear. The international issue arises again, and while it is intriguing, it still isn't made directly relevant to the issue of the prompt. Finally, the synthesis (which does get its own paragraph) is on point and addresses the task, but much too briefly. There is another interesting issue hinted at here: that national level politicians set an example through speeches and appearance, but there is no development of this idea; it is left up to the reader to make the connection. In sum, this is an essay that, if rethought and more fully developed, could become a high scoring essay. As it is, however, it barely does its job of addressing all three tasks in a coherent and unified manner.

Reference Score: 4

In many cases, politicians should be expected to act as examples of good behavior for their constituents. Politicians are like celebrities in that they are always in the public eye, and because we are always hearing about their activities, we cannot help but take their actions as a model for expected behavior. This is especially true of any actions that relate to their jobs as politicians. We believe that political leaders at all levels of government should act in the interests of the public. When they live up to this duty, we praise them for setting an excellent example of putting the good of others ahead of their own careers. When presidents Eisenhower and Kennedy championed civil rights, it was at some personal risk, since it involved alienating in particular Southern voters. Yet when they fail to live up to their duties, we condemn them for setting a bad example, especially for impressionable children who are the most likely to model their own behavior on what they see public figures doing. For instance, Randy "Duke" Cunningham, the member of the House of Representatives, took bribes for awarding defense contracts, and he violated his duty as a political representative to act in the service of national security, not his own private interest in increasing his own wealth. When children hear about this, it might make them think that if a powerful politician can betray the people that they more or less work for this way, it is OK for them to do so also. These children might grow up to steal from their employer, or, cheat on their taxes, thinking that it is OK to hurt other people if it makes them better off. When politicians betray their duty to act in the best interests of the public, that is, when they betray the very ideals they were elected to represent, it sets up a conflicting message in people's minds and can set a bad example for people to follow.

However, not everything a politician does should be seen as an example for others to follow, or be judged in that way. President Clinton cheated on his wife with Monica Lewinsky, and still was an effective president. Because his public presence was as a president, and not so much as a husband, his behavior was not seen as a model to follow, but as a personal failure to be condemned.

What matters is whether or not a politician is acting in accordance with the reasons we elected them in the first place. If their actions are in the context of their public role, they should act as examples of the highest ideals, especially of self-sacrifice for the good of the nation. However, if they are acting as private citizens, with no connection to performance of their public duties, while we would hope that they like anyone would live up to high standards, we don't expect them, any more than we would any else, to set a good example. This is because there is no mixed message in these cases.

Analysis

This essay stays on topic, addresses all three tasks, and uses relevant examples to draw a clear contrast. The first paragraph is the strongest section because this is where the author's ideas are most fully developed. The use of both a positive and negative example in that paragraph does a good job of illustrating the point about expecting politicians to serve the public and to act as examples in that regard. The discussion of sending a conflicting message, especially to children, gets at a core issue and sets up a contrast on which the author will draw later in the essay. The second paragraph does its job of stating an antithesis example, but is much less fully developed. Further discussion of why Clinton's behavior would not be seen by people, especially children, as an example to follow is needed (given that in the first paragraph, the author emphasized that everything politicians do is seen by the public). The last paragraph, similarly to the second, adequately addresses the issue, but requires further elaboration. It repeats, but doesn't explain, the point about sending mixed messages. That point is a good one, and shows some sophisticated thought on the issue, but as stated it isn't fully convincing. Overall, the author shows reasonable command of language (it is often awkward, but clear), and the essay is well organized, following the three part structure of the question. Compare this essay to the next one, which uses similar ideas and examples but does a better job of explaining them in the context of incorporating discussion of core ideas.

> Make sure your last paragraph is backed up as well as your first is.

Reference Score: 5

We often equate the word "politician" with "public servant," and both of those words, "public" and "servant," say something important about the role and duties of a politician. They are public in the sense that their actions take place in the public eye. Especially given the pervasive, even invasive, role of the media in modern society, few actions taken by politicians escape scrutiny. Furthermore, politicians are expected to serve the public by acting in the public's best interests. Given the combination of these aspects of a politician's job, they are often legitimately expected to serve as examples for their constituents. Politicians are in a position of power and authority, and in the performance of their public duties they are expected to hold to high ideals of honesty and propriety. When politicians fail to act as public role models, it can have a pernicious effect not only on their own reputations, but on the opinion citizens have of the political system as a whole. For example, in the Watergate scandal, Nixon and the Committee to Re-elect the President carried out a variety of nefarious activities including ordering a break in to the Democratic Party headquarters in an attempt to gather information to be used against the opposing candidate, George McGovern. The reporters Woodward and Bernstein uncovered evidence of these actions and made it public, leading to public outcry. Nixon eventually resigned to avid impeachment, and was later pardoned by the next president, Ford, although many of the conspirators did serve jail time. While the illegality of the actions was certainly a key issue, even more important was the fact that Nixon abused his public office in the service of personal goals. This incident is often seen as a watershed moment in American politics in that it soiled the image not only of Nixon, but of the presidency itself. If a president could act in this way, what did that say about the legitimacy and morality of the political system as a whole? If the person sitting at the pinnacle of public power can't be expected to live up to ideals of honesty and public service, how can we expect a private citizen to do so? This negative example, of failure to live up to the standard of setting a good example for the public, shows how important it is for politicians to live up to certain ideals in the performance of their public duties.

However, when we think of political scandals, often other kind of incidents come to mind, incidents of a more "personal" nature. Given the scrutiny of the press and the hunger of the public for the details of so called "private" misbehavior, when politicians cheat on their spouses or commit similar "immoral" actions, it becomes a subject of public discussion and outrage. And yet, the question becomes, can we legitimately expect politicians to set a good example in all aspects of their lives? One could argue that the answer is no. An example of a politician unfairly held up to excessively high standards is Gary Hart, the senator from Colorado who ran for president in 1984 and 1988. During the 1988 campaign, stories hit the press that Hart was having an extramarital affair with a woman named Donna Rice: photos were circulated of the two embracing on a yacht. (Ironically, Hart had dared the press to follow and investigate him before these photos were made public). Hart was forced to withdraw from the race because of the public scandal. And yet, his service to the nation as a senator before the scandal, and his public service afterwards (he served on a variety of commissions dealing with national security in his capacity as a lawyer) suggests that his public indiscretions had little to do with his capacity to serve the nation as a president. If politicians are expected to act as moral exemplars in all aspects of their lives, this expectation may rob us of leaders who may in fact be able and willing to act in all important ways in the best interests of their constituents. The fact that it has become known that John F. Kennedy had numerous affairs in office, and is still seen as one of our most beloved presidents, is another indication that personal misbehavior should be evaluated by a different standard than a failure to perform the public duties that attach to the role of public servant. The difference was that the press operated in a very different way in the 1960's than it does now; the private lives of politicians were truly seen as private, that is, not legitimate source of public scrutiny.

Therefore, what determines whether or not a politician should be expected to serve as an example for their constituents is whether or not their behavior relates to the performance of their public duties. By "public servant", we should mean "one who serves the public" not, "one whose every action is open to public scrutiny." If this disctinction is not made, we may in fact lose out on the services of dedicated public servants who could do good for the nation if allowed to serve.

Analysis

This essay is well organized, on topic, and covers all three tasks. However, while the author's responses to the first two tasks are fully developed, the synthesis is much too brief (it appears that the writer was running out of time). The point made in that paragraph, the distinction between public duties and private life, is an excellent one, but without a deeper treatment of that task this essay cannot score a 6. The essay begins nicely with a definition and analysis of "public servant," and this idea carries through and unifies the rest of the essay. The writer clearly has a good control of language. Although the wording is at times overly repetitious (for example, the overuse of the word "public"), the writer employs his or her vocabulary, and the technique of using rhetorical questions to make a point, to good effect. Concrete and relevant examples are given for the thesis and antithesis, and their relevance is well-explained. There is a little too much extraneous detail given within those examples, however. Some of these facts (for example, the conviction of Nixon's co-conspirators) should have either been left out, or, tied in more closely to the author's central argument.

Reference Score: 6

Politicians today are not held in the highest repute. In fact, Machiavelli's words, "Politics have no relation to morals" appear to resonate through a news media dominated by stories of corruption and adultery on the part of our political leaders. We feel such outrage when politicians fall from grace in part because we have such high expectations of our political leaders, expectations that that are to a great extent valid. Just as "the polis" or city-state was considered by the ancient Greeks to be the State in ideal form, the word "politician" carries with it the suggestion of an ideal: the perfect representative of the people's will and well-being. To "represent" in this context is not just to enact policy, but in a more abstract way to act as an example or role model to the public. In many ways, because of their unique position in a democratic society, we should and do expect politicians to act as role models of behavior for the people who elected them and who are represented by them. These expectations help explain the sense of betrayal many people felt when it was discovered that Thomas Jefferson had an affair and a child with his slave, Sally Hemmings. This feeing of disappointment was generated not so much because Jefferson betrayed his marriage vows; we have more or less come to expect and often overlook that kind of behavior. Rather, it came from the fact that this relationship appeared to be an abuse of power, an abuse especially contemptible because of Jefferson's role and image of a founding father of a democracy fundamentally based on ideals of personal liberty and resistance to tyranny. It was a reminder that despite his high ideals (ideals that can still be appreciated and celebrated), Jefferson was in fact a slave-owner, something perhaps we all know, but don't like to think about. The slave-master relationship is, obviously, inherently coercive, and to have a sexual relationship within that conetx appears especially immoral. The expectation that politicians act as ethical examples in this way is not limited to this kind of "personal" behavior. Politicians are expected, at times required, to put certain of their financial assests into a blind trust, in part to ensure that they make policy based on what is good for their constituents rather than on what is good for their personal fortunes. This expectation is not unique to politicians; we expect the CEO of a company to act for the good of the company, a teacher to act for the good of the class, and a parent to act for the good of the family. That is, we expect people to sometimes put aside their personal desires and act in accordance with their role of caretaker. In sum, when a politician's behavior has some analogy to the expectations we have for anyone, that is, to live up to their duties and to act in a way that is consistent with their professed ideals, we expect politicians to set an example for us all.

However, looking at Machiavelli's words from a different perspective, we can divine a different meaning: politicians are not bound by the same moral rules as the average citizen in all aspects of the performance of their duties. Machiavelli meant that politicians should do whatever they must do in order to retain power, and that power is used to strengthen the polity and to protect the state. While we may not accept that politicians should do whatever is necessary to retain personal power, we do as a whole believe in the necessity of retaining national power. In this way, politicians on the national level have a duty that does not have parallels in the lives of more ordinary citizens; to use force when necessary to protect the state and people within it. The use of military force in the legitimate service of national security is required when the nation is threatened or at war. And, the use of military force inherently involves the death of innocents, be they members of our own military, or, civilian casualties of our military actions. While private citizens have a right to self-defense, we generally believe that there must first be an actual attack on our person, and that our response must be proportionate, in that we only use violence against the attacker, not against innocent bystanders. We can't kill a crowd of people just to get at one person within that crowd who presents a personal threat. In this arena, the use of deadly force, we do not and should not expect politicians to set an example for their constituents to follow. For example, the use of the atomic bomb against Hiroshima and Nagasaki is considered by many "just war" scholars to be an ethical moral action, despite the huge loss of life and suffering it caused among Japanese civilians. The rationale is that the bombing imposed such a huge cost that it motivated an end to the war, saving both the lives of Allied soldiers who would have died otherwise, and the lives of Japanese civilians and soldiers who would have died in the course of a land invasion. What has come to be known as the "Bush Doctrine" follows the same logic: preemptive strikes or even preemptive war can be taken in the service of national security, even if we are not yet under direct attack. This was the rationale behind the war in Afghanistan, by many accounts. This kind of preemption can be seen as ethically legitimate in the hands of a politician tasked with the duty to prevent, or to end and win, a war; it would never be seen as legitimate for a private citizen to act in a similar way. For example, while we expect a CEO to compete within the marketplace against other companies, we would not see it as acceptable for that CEO to take to take non-economic actions to destroy the competition in order to prevail. Therefore, in the realm of the use of violence, we do not expect politicians to act as role models for the rest of us.

What determines whether or not we should expect politicians to act as models for those they represent is whether or not their behavior has parallels in the lives of private citizens. We expect everyone to live up to the ideals they profess. Therefore, a politician like Jimmy Carter who gives service to society through his work with Habitat for Humanity is seen as a shining example of a true public servant, an example of self-sacrifice we should all emulate. On the other hand, a leader like Jefferson who in his private life did not live up to his own public critique of tyranny and the abuse of power is seen as a disappointment. A politician who touts family values and then cheats on his wife is legitimately criticized more harshly than either a private citizen who did the same, or, another politician who did not base his or her career on the "defense of family." However, when a politician, in the performance of his or her public duties, must undertake actions that do not have a counterpart in constituents' lives, we expect them not to act as examples, but to act in accordance with their special role and duties. This is most often the case in the arena of international relations and the use of military force. If a politician acted as we expect a private citizen to act, it would put the nation as a whole in great danger. Both of these expectations, acting as an example in some ways and carrying out unique responsibilities in others, carry great burdens. Politicians must live exemplary private lives, and at the same time make public decisions that involve great risks, and which can carry high costs for which they are held responsible. However, politics is, or should be, a calling or profession (in the true sense of the word), not just a job. Given that this calling is taken on with full knowledge of the expectations that go along with it, it is legimimate to expect politicians to live up to these very high standards, representing what is the best of us, while at the same time taking actions and making decisions that no ordinary person would want to make.

Analysis

This essay addresses all three tasks in an organized way, and directly responds to the issue of the prompt. Clear examples that illustrate the thesis-antithesis relationship are given and their relevance is explained. The additional examples in the synthesis are consistent with the previous examples, and well-integrated into the logical flow of the essay. Beyond that, the response deals with larger core issues involved with the prompt: the special role of politicians, and the at times demanding expectations that come along with that role. The use of the Machiavelli quote in both the thesis and antithesis helps unify the essay, and the author's analysis of the quote adds depth, showing a sophisticated level of thought. Despite the occasional misspelling, the author shows a command of language. The essay is not perfect (for example, the transition between the two thesis examples is a bit abrupt, and the logical link between them is not immediately clear; the sentence structure is at times overly complicated), but in the context of the nature of the Writing Sample task, it would get a top score.

Now do a few practice essays online (or look at previous ones you've done) and see what score you would have received and where you can improve.

Chapter 10
Science Sections
Overview

There are two science sections on the MCAT: the Physical Sciences section and the Biological Sciences section.

The Physical Sciences (PS) section is the first section on the test. It includes content-based questions from physics and general chemistry, in roughly a 50:50 ratio (for details on the topics that can appear in the PS section, see Chapters 11 and 14 in this book; Physics and General Chemistry, respectively). A solid grasp of math fundamentals is required (arithmetic, algebra, graphs, trigonometry, vectors, proportions, and logarithms), and there are no calculus-based questions.

The Biological Sciences (BS) section is the final section on the test. It includes content-based questions from biology and organic chemistry, usually in about a 75:25 ratio. However, this ratio can vary from test to test; some tests may include significantly more O-Chem (up to 40%), and some may include less (15–20%). The details on topics that can appear in the BS section can be found in Chapters 17 and 20 of this book; Biology and Organic Chemistry, respectively. Math calculations are generally not required on this section of the test.

Most of the questions in the science sections (39 out of 52) are passage-based, and each section will have a total of seven passages. Passages consist of a few paragraphs of information and will likely include equations, reactions, graphs, figures, tables, experiments, and data. Five to seven questions will be associated with each passage.

The remaining questions (13 out of 52) are freestanding questions (FSQs). These questions appear in three groups interspersed between the passages. Each group contains three to five questions.

70 minutes are allotted to each of the science sections. This breaks down to approximately one minute and 20 seconds per question.

PASSAGE TYPES
The passages in the science sections fall into one of three main categories: Information and/or Situation Presentation, Experiment/Research Presentation, or Persuasive Reasoning.

Information and/or Situation Presentation
These passages either present straightforward scientific information or they describe a particular event or occurrence. Generally, questions associated with these passages test basic science facts or ask you to predict outcomes given new variables or new information. Here is an example of an Information/Situation Presentation passage:

Figure 1 shows a portion of the inner mechanism of a typical home smoke detector. It consists of a pair of capacitor plates which are charged by a 9-volt battery (not shown). The capacitor plates (electrodes) are connected to a sensor device, D; the resistor R denotes the internal resistance of the sensor. Normally, air acts as an insulator and no current would flow in the circuit shown. However, inside the smoke detector is a small sample of an artificially produced radioactive element, americium-241, which decays primarily by emitting alpha particles, with a half-life of approximately 430 years. The daughter nucleus of the decay has a half-life in excess of two million years and therefore poses virtually no biohazard.

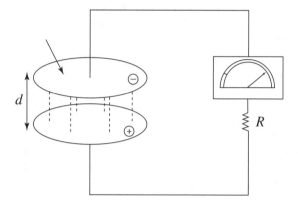

Figure 1   Smoke detector mechanism

The decay products (alpha particles and gamma rays) from the ^{241}Am sample ionize air molecules between the plates and thus provide a conducting pathway which allows current to flow in the circuit shown in Figure 1. A steady-state current is quickly established and remains as long as the battery continues to maintain a 9-volt potential difference between its terminals. However, if smoke particles enter the space between the capacitor plates and thereby interrupt the flow, the current is reduced, and the sensor responds to this change by triggering the alarm. (Furthermore, as the battery starts to "die out," the resulting drop in current is also detected to alert the homeowner to replace the battery.)

$$C = \varepsilon_0 \frac{A}{d}$$

Equation 1

where ε_0 is the universal permittivity constant, equal to 8.85 $\times 10^{-12}$ C²/(N·m²). Since the area A of each capacitor plate in the smoke detector is 20 cm² and the plates are separated by a distance d of 5 mm, the capacitance is 3.5×10^{-12} F = 3.5 pF.

Experiment/Research Presentation

These passages present the details of experiments and research procedures. They often include data tables and graphs. Generally, questions associated with these passages ask you to interpret data, draw conclusions, and make inferences. Here is an example of an Experiment/Research Presentation passage:

The development of sexual characteristics depends upon various factors, the most important of which are hormonal control, environmental stimuli, and the genetic makeup of the individual. The hormones that contribute to the development include the steroid hormones estrogen, progesterone, and testosterone, as well as the pituitary hormones FSH (follicle-stimulating hormone) and LH (luteinizing hormone).

To study the mechanism by which estrogen exerts its effects, a researcher performed the following experiments using cell culture assays.

Experiment 1:

Human embryonic placental mesenchyme (HEPM) cells were grown for 48 hours in Dulbecco's Modified Eagle Medium (DMEM), with media change every 12 hours. Upon confluent growth, cells were exposed to a 10 mg per mL solution of green fluorescent-labeled estrogen for 1 hour. Cells were rinsed with DMEM and observed under confocal fluorescent microscopy.

Experiment 2:

HEPM cells were grown to confluence as in Experiment 1. Cells were exposed to Pesticide A for 1 hour, followed by the 10 mg/mL solution of labeled estrogen, rinsed as in Experiment 1, and observed under confocal fluorescent microscopy.

Experiment 3:

Experiment 1 was repeated with Chinese Hamster Ovary (CHO) cells instead of HEPM cells.

Experiment 4:

CHO cells injected with cytoplasmic extracts of HEPM cells were grown to confluence, exposed to the 10 mg/mL solution of labeled estrogen for 1 hour, and observed under confocal fluorescent microscopy.

The results of these experiments are given in Table 1.

Table 1 Detection of Estrogen (+ indicates presence of Estrogen)

Experiment	Media	Cytoplasm	Nucleus
1	+	+	+
2	+	+	+
3	+	+	+
4	+	+	+

After observing the cells in each experiment, the researcher bathed the cells in a solution containing 10 mg per mL of a red fluorescent probe that binds specifically to the estrogen receptor only when its active site is occupied. After 1 hour, the cells were rinsed with DMEM and observed under confocal fluorescent microscopy. The results are presented in Table 2.

The researcher also repeated Experiment 2 using Pesticide B, an estrogen analog, instead of Pesticide A. Results from other researchers had shown that Pesticide B binds to the active site of the cytosolic estrogen receptor (with an affinity 10,000 times greater than that of estrogen) and causes increased transcription of mRNA.

Table 2 Observed Fluorescence and Estrogen Effects (G = green, R = red)

Experiment	Media	Cytoplasm	Nucleus	Estrogen effects observed?
1	G only	G and R	G and R	Yes
2	G only	G only	G only	No
3	G only	G only	G only	No
4	G only	G and R	G and R	Yes

Based on these results, the researcher determined that estrogen had no effect when not bound to a cytosolic, estrogen-specific receptor.

Persuasive Reasoning

These passages typically present a scientific phenomenon along with a hypothesis that explains the phenomenon, and may include counter-arguments as well. Questions associated with these passages ask you to evaluate the hypothesis or arguments. Persuasive Reasoning passages in the science sections of the MCAT tend to be less common than Information Presentation or Experiment-based passages. Here is an example of a Persuasive Reasoning passage:

Two theoretical chemists attempted to explain the observed trends of acidity by applying two interpretations of molecular orbital theory. Consider the pK_a's of some common acids listed along with each acids conjugate base:

acid	pK_a	conjugate base
H_2SO_4	< 0	HSO_4^-
H_2CrO_4	5.0	$HCrO_4^-$
H_2PO_4	2.1	$H_2PO_4^-$
HF	3.9	F^-
HOCl	7.8	ClO^-
HCN	9.5	CN^-
HIO_3	1.2	IO_3^-

Recall that acids with a $pK_a < 0$ are called strong acids, and those with a $pK_a > 0$ are called weak acids. The arguments of the chemists are given below.

Chemist #1:

"The acidity of a compound is proportional to the polarization of the H—X bond, where X is some nonmetal element. Complex acids, such as H_2SO_4, $HClO_4$, and HNO_3 are strong acids because the H—O bonding electrons are strongly drawn towards the oxygen. It is generally true that a covalent bond weakens as its polarization increases. Therefore, one can conclude that the strength of an acid is proportional to the number of electronegative atoms in that acid."

Chemist #2:

"The acidity of a compound is proportional to the number of stable resonance structures of that acid's conjugate base. H_2SO_4, $HClO_4$, and HNO_3 are all strong acids because their respective conjugate bases exhibit a high degree of resonance stabilization."

MAPPING OUT A PASSAGE

"Mapping a passage" refers to the combination of on-screen highlighting and scratch paper notes that you take while working through a passage. Typically, good things to highlight include the overall topic of a paragraph, familiar terms, unusual terms, numerical values, hypothesis, and results. Scratch paper notes can be used to summarize the paragraphs and to jot down important facts and connections that are made when reading the passage. Remember that highlighting disappears once you leave the passage, so a good set of scratch paper notes can be extremely useful if you have to return to the passage. More details on passage mapping will be presented in the individual science subject chapters.

QUESTION TYPES

Question in the science sections are generally one of three main types: Memory, Explicit, or Implicit.

Memory Questions

These questions can be answered directly from prior knowledge, with no need to reference the passage or question text. Memory questions represent approximately 25 percent of the science questions on the MCAT. Usually, Memory questions are found as FSQs, but they can also be tucked into a passage. Here's an example of a Memory question:

Which of the following acetylating conditions will convert diethylamine into an amide at the fastest rate?

A) Acetic acid / HCl
B) Acetic anhydride
C) Acetyl chloride
D) Ethyl acetate

Explicit Questions

Explicit questions can be answered primarily with information from the passage, along with prior knowledge. They may require data retrieval, graph analysis, or making a simple connection. Explicit questions make up approximately 35–40 percent of the science questions on the MCAT; here's an example (taken from the Information/Situation Presentation passage above):

> The sensor device D shown in Figure 1 performs its
> function by acting as:
>
> A) an ohmmeter.
> B) a voltmeter.
> C) a potentiometer.
> D) an ammeter.

Implicit Questions

These questions require you to take information from the passage, combine it with your prior knowledge, apply it to a new situation, and come to some logical conclusion. They typically require more complex connections than do Explicit questions, and may also require data retrieval, graph analysis, etc. Implicit questions usually require a solid understanding of the passage information. They make up approximately 35–40 percent of the science questions on the MCAT; here's an example (taken from the Experiment/Research Presentation passage above):

> If Experiment 2 were repeated, but this time exposing
> the cells first to Pesticide A and then to Pesticide B
> before exposing them to the green fluorescent-labeled
> estrogen and the red fluorescent probe, which of the
> following statements will most likely be true?
>
> A) Pesticide A and Pesticide B bind to the same site on the
>   estrogen receptor.
> B) Estrogen effects would be observed.
> C) Only green fluorescence would be observed.
> D) Both green and red fluorescence would be observed.

ATTACKING THE QUESTIONS

More detail on question attack will be presented in the individual science subject chapters, but here's a brief overview of the most useful techniques:

- Using Process of Elimination (POE) is the best way to attack any MCAT question. Every answer choice that you eliminate increases your probability of choosing the correct answer. Roman numeral questions are particularly good to answer using POE.
- Do the questions within a section in the order that you want; easiest questions first, harder questions later. You don't get any more points for a hard question than you do for an easy one, so skip around.
- Make sure the answer you choose actually answers the question and isn't just a true statement.
- Don't get tripped up in the LEAST/EXCEPT/NOT questions. These questions ask you to pick the incorrect or false statement.
- Remember that there cannot be two correct choices, thus if two answers say the same thing, they can both be eliminated.
- For calculations, use approximations whenever possible, and make sure you take units into consideration.
- Don't leave any question blank; there is no guessing penalty on the MCAT.

A FINAL THOUGHT

The next few chapters will address each science subject on the MCAT, presenting some of the nuances for that particular subject. However, the fact that you are using this book indicates that you are already scoring fairly well, which means that you are probably already mapping your passages and know how to tackle the questions effectively. We don't want to insult you by presenting information that is too basic, thus the chapters are intended primarily to give you an overview, not a great amount of detail.

Following each subject's overview chapter are FSQs and practice passages; most at a high level of difficulty. We know you want to hone your skills on the toughest material out there. Don't forget there are many more FSQs and practice passages in the Online Companion to this book found at www.PrincetonReview. com/Cracking, and don't forget to analyze your results using the skills you learned in Chapters 4 and 5.

Chapter 11
Physics on the MCAT

Of all the science sections on the MCAT, Physics relies the least on information recall and the most on problem-solving and reading comprehension skills. This is in part because the subject matter lends itself to these kinds of problems. Perhaps more importantly, though, the subject content in Physics pertains less to the material you will ultimately study in medical school, whereas the critical thinking that physics demands fits with what you will encounter (particularly during your clinical years). In many ways, your ability to formulate an "approach" to a tough problem is one of the most useful skills you can develop along the pathway to medicine.

TACKLING A PASSAGE

Passage Types as they apply to Physics

Information/Situation Presentation

These passages tend to fall into two types for Physics. The first type consists of straightforward descriptions of phenomena you should already understand well; for example, a passage about DC circuits with a battery, a couple of switches, and a few resistors in parallel and series combinations. Common question types include solving unknown variables using common formulas, true-or-false questions of physics laws, and comparisons of the "real" to the "ideal."

The second type of passage consists of technical elaborations of phenomena you know something about, but without the detail provided by the passage; for example, a passage about an AC circuit with a capacitor and an inductor (a circuit element like a solenoid) that provides equations for the time-dependent voltage across each element and the circuit's resonant frequency. Such technical passages are often marked by several new equations and possibly graphs, followed by paragraphs defining the variables and constants. Common question types for technical passages include algebraic manipulation questions, functional dependence or proportionality questions, and graph generation or interpretation questions.

Experiment or Research Presentation

These passages often include data tables; if there's a table, the passage probably covers an experiment or multiple experiments. The subject matter in experimental passages is typically familiar, though the concepts might be extended somewhat beyond basic knowledge, for example, measuring the viscosity in a fluid or the resistance of a conducting wire as a function of temperature. These passages tend *not* to push your understanding of content as much as the technical passages or heavily conceptual passages. Rather, the implicit questions found in experiment presentation passages are usually of the form, "If another trial were conducted changing [some set of parameters], then the resulting value of [another parameter] would be…." Such questions require you to read numbers from the tables and determine their functional dependence on the altered parameters. In other words, you need to write down an equation for the value of the parameter, and to check for whether the altered variables affect that value and how.

Persuasive Reasoning

Persuasive reasoning passages on the Physics portion of the MCAT are largely conceptual: They describe some particular phenomenon about which you most likely have no prior knowledge, and they do so almost entirely with words (as opposed to using figures, equations, and numbers). These are generally the hardest passages for most people, as they rely heavily on reading comprehension as well as the ability to recall and synthesize physics concepts and equations from different topics (e.g., atomic structure, magnetism, and standing waves). You can expect questions in which both the question text and the answer choices are themselves entirely in words. This means you must be comfortable translating sentences into proportions, ratios, or equations, and then translating back into sentences. Moreover, it may not be enough to be a careful reader with a good memory for formulas: Conceptual passages will test whether you know the conditions under which equations apply (such as the conditions for an ideal fluid or when to hold Q or V constant in $Q = CV$). An upcoming portion of the physics section in this book is designed to help you recognize these conceptual passages, to map them effectively, and to anticipate common pitfalls among answer choices.

Reading a Physics Passage

Don't let our heading here deceive you; "reading" in the sense we commonly use the word is seldom the best way to use physics passages effectively. A kind of "informed skimming" is usually the best strategy. A quick holistic scan of the passage, including reading its first sentence, should be enough to tell you its topic and type; this will help you decide whether to do it now or postpone it until you've tackled easier passages (for example, if you dislike circuits, or if a lot of reading comprehension slows you down, by all means leave those passages until later!). Once you decide to do a passage, use the following techniques to find what you need to know quickly.

1. Read the first sentence again carefully. It will probably define the main idea in the passage and might inform your answer to one of the questions directly. Similarly, if the passage describes a set of experimental procedures, read the first sentences in each subsection so you understand precisely what is being done and why.
2. Look for the familiar Physics terms within the passage and highlight them. Remember that the questions on the MCAT can be directly from the AAMC topics list, or they can come from a reading-comprehension topic in a passage. And in fact, many Physics passages may not seem to be about a particular Physics topic at first glance. For example, a passage about earthquakes may be about waves, or sound, or conservation of energy, or all of those topics at the same time! If you can identify the relevant physics within the passage text, you can focus in on that text and topic rather than getting stuck on the paragraph about, say, the historical perspective of how we measure earthquakes.
3. Look for any new terms. These are often italicized but not always, so scan for long unfamiliar phrases (things like "aeroelastic flutter" stick out in a paragraph even in plain type). Highlight them along with their definitions.
4. Find the equations and figures. The text immediately before or after them tends to define terms or provide numerical values (measures in a diagram or values of constants in an equation, say). If the diagrams are basically complete or the equation make sense to you, *skip this text*: There's no good reason to read a paragraph describing a ball rolling down an inclined plane if the picture already tells the whole story.

5. Look for numbers. These are sometimes worth jotting down on your scratch paper and they are easy to find (however, if a passage gives you a whole pile of values, just highlight them so you can find those you need for the questions). There are a couple of key things to remember about numbers:
    a. Numbers on the MCAT are always accompanied by their units, either immediately following the number, or in the heading of the table where the numbers appear. If there are no units, the number must be unitless.
    b. Highlighting can be done with a left-click and drag, but keep in mind that numbers in figures, and occasionally the numbers in tables, may not be in a format that allows for highlighting. In these cases, use scrap paper to note numbers.
6. Finally, if the passage is conceptual, apply the above rules but also read the passage more carefully. The fact that this will take longer is another reason to leave conceptual passages for last.

Mapping a Physics Passage

Physics work should be done on paper; there are very few answers on the test that can be found without writing something down. Thus, your scratch paper is your primary tool, whether solving FSQs or mapping a passage. As suggested above, there are a few specific reasons to use the highlighting tool, but apart from that you want to rely on your scratch paper. "Mapping" involves jotting down a schematic of the passage that will help you to answer the questions efficiently without having to fish for information. Here are some mapping strategies:

1. Label your scratch paper with the passage number. Staying organized saves time and avoids errors.
2. Write down any given equations with space below to work on them. The chances that you will *not* end up using some equation given to you in a passage are low, so it's worth the time to prepare for the algebra and estimation the questions will require.
3. If there are any simple diagrams, copy them down and label any values (some will be given in the text around the diagram and not labeled directly in the version on your screen). Again, you might resist this as a potential waste of time, but it is important to be able to manipulate the figures to answer the questions. For example, in a passage where forces are important (e.g., for most of mechanics, buoyancy in fluids, charges interacting with electric or magnetic fields, or simple harmonic oscillators), you should put the forces on your diagram *before* you do the questions. By doing so, you will probably anticipate the answers to one or more questions even before they are asked. Overall, this should both save you time and increase your percentage of right answers.
4. If the passage is conceptual or has conceptual parts to it, translate any mathematical statements written as sentences into symbols, and treat those as you would equations given in a more technical passage. For example, if you were reading a passage on Kepler's laws of planetary motion and came across the sentence, "Kepler found that the square of the orbital periods of the elliptically orbiting planets was directly proportional to the cube of semi-major axes of their orbital paths around the sun," you would jot down $T^2 \propto a^3$.
5. Especially for passages that don't include many diagrams or equations, write down the equations and basic ideas you recall about the passage topic. This will give you something tangible with which to tackle the equations. For example, a passage might describe a perfectly inelastic collision between two masses, and you might write down $p = mv$, $\mathbf{p}_i = \mathbf{p}_f$, and "momentum conserved, *KE* not."

Practice all of these strategies with the passages in this book to see which work best for you; then make those strategies a part of your standard repertoire. Give yourself about 90 seconds to map a passage before you look at the questions. Many passage maps will take less time than this, a few might take longer. Don't worry that you're spending time not answering questions; practice will make you more efficient.

Another, more advanced study technique you might use once you feel more comfortable about your passage mapping is to map a couple of passages, put those maps aside for an hour or so while you do something else (practice FSQs, say), then go back to the passages, cover up their text, and try to do the questions with just your map. You shouldn't necessarily be able to answer all the questions without referring to the passage, but if you find that you're unable to answer any but those that rely on memory of basic concepts, then you need to improve your mapping technique. Below is an example of these strategies applied to a passage from Practice Test 1.

Both radar and ladar technologies are available to police departments to measure the speeds of vehicles. Police radar (radio detection and ranging) uses microwaves available in a variety of FCC-approved frequency bands, while ladar (laser detection and ranging) uses a laser beam in the upper-infrared frequency range.

Police radar devices use one of three different narrow bands of microwave radiation: the X band, centered at a frequency of 10.525 GHz; the K band, centered at 24.15 GHz; or the Ka band, centered at 34.7 GHz, where 1 GHz = 109 Hz. Ladar devices commonly employ a laser beam whose wavelength is 904 nm. Although ladar devices are more accurate, the operator must aim the device at a single target vehicle. By contrast, radar devices have a larger beamwidth and can cover a wider area and several vehicles. Also, while most radar transmitters can be used in either stationary or moving modes (depending on whether the device is used in a stationary or moving police car), ladar transmitters are typically designed for stationary mode use only.

Police radar uses the Doppler effect to determine the speed of a vehicle. The device emits pulses of microwave radiation at its operating frequency, f; this incident radiation reflects off a moving vehicle, and the frequency of the reflected waves, detected by the detector, f_r, is recorded. If the radar detector is used in stationary mode and is pointed directly at a target vehicle along its direction of travel, then the speed v_t of the target vehicle is given by the formula

$$v_t = \pm \, vf \,/\, 2f$$

Equation 1

where $\Delta f = f_r - f$ and v is the speed of the transmitted and reflected waves.

If the incident microwave beam makes an angle α with the direction of the target vehicle's velocity $\mathbf{v}_t$ (see Figure 1), then the device will measure the speed as $v_t \cos \alpha$; this is known as the *cosine effect*.

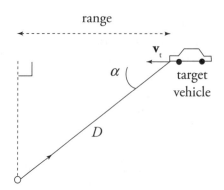

Figure 1 Radar model

The radar device uses a different principle to determine the speed of a target vehicle. After it emits each brief pulse of light, the device measures the time required for the pulse to return after reflecting off the target. This alone determines the distance between the ladar device and the target vehicle. However, in a fraction of a second, the device sends out approximately one hundred pulses and can thus determine the change in distance to—and consequently the speed of—the target vehicle.

Sample Passage Analysis and Mapping

Highlight the key terms, radar and ladar. Note that this passage is mostly words, is not heavily laden with equations (one), has several potentially unfamiliar terms, and has no tabular data. This is best characterized as a conceptual Persuasive Reasoning passage, not as obscure as some but still challenging.

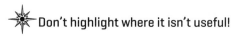
Don't highlight where it isn't useful!

The pile of numbers in paragraph 2 is both obvious and extensive, so rather than clutter the passage with highlighting, it might be best simply to leave it alone, as finding these values will be easy. Alternatively, you could include the values in a small table that you should make for the two devices anyway, summarizing their basic information (see below for map).

The Doppler shift has been mentioned twice in the passage and should be fairly obvious as the means of measurement (given the equation), so there's no need to highlight the first sentence of the third paragraph. The definitions of the given variables are worth highlighting in case you encounter a question that uses the words without the algebraic symbols. You should copy the two given equations (counting the Δf equation) on your scratch paper, noting mentally the difference between this Doppler shift formula and the one you know from memory. Remember, a new equation in a passage is always more important than a memorized equation for any questions that deal explicitly with the phenomenon described in the passage. At this point it would also be worthwhile to write down the wave speed equation ($v = f\lambda$). You should have committed to memory the rules for its use (namely v depends on wave type and medium, and f is constant between media).

A simple diagram like Figure 1 should be copied with the annotation "measured speed = $v_t \cos\alpha$" next to the "radar" label, just in case you are asked to do any trig or otherwise interpret its significance.

This last paragraph presents perhaps the greatest mapping challenge for this passage. You might be tempted to highlight the entire paragraph because it describes an unfamiliar phenomenon. However, highlighting is not the same as comprehension; further, none of the terminology here is specialized. Thus, it's better to jot down some quick notes under the heading "ladar" that simplify the processes described, and to translate sentences into formulas. Note the second and third sentences: they describe a light pulse being emitted, reflected, and received again (thus travelling twice the distance to the car). Because you know that light has constant speed in air, you could write "$2d = ct$." In the next sentence the numbers are vague (a "fraction of a second" could be a hundredth or 8/10), but the idea that subsequent pulses measure different distances and this yields a speed indicates that, for a duration between pulses of Δt, the car has moved a distance Δd. This gives us "$\Delta d/\Delta t = v$" so that too should be jotted down on the scratch paper.

 Take notes and copy down equations.

Your scratch paper map should thus look something like this:

radar	ladar
Larger beam width, more area covered	Accurate, single vehicle
Stationary or moving	Stationary only
X = 10.5 GHz K = 24 GHz Ka = 35 GHz	λ = 900 nm

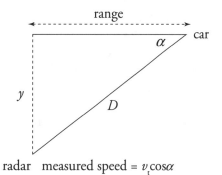

radar   measured speed = $v_t \cos\alpha$

$$v_t = \pm\, v\Delta f\,/\,2f$$

$$\Delta f = f_r - f$$

$$v = f\lambda$$

ladar

$$2d = ct$$

$$\Delta d/\Delta t = v$$

PHYSICS QUESTION TYPES

As stated previously in the General Strategies, the questions on the physics section of the MCAT fall into one of three main categories:

1. **Memory questions:** Answered directly from information you know walking into the test.
2. **Explicit questions:** Answered from information stated explicitly in the passage. To answer them correctly may require finding a definition, reading a graph, or making a calculation.
3. **Implicit questions:** Answered by applying knowledge to a new situation or making more complex connections. Often the answer is implied by the information in the passage.

Note that the way you categorize questions on the MCAT will depend on how much knowledge you bring to the test in the first place. The more confident you are about the basic material outlined in the list of Physics topics, the less you will have to rely on the passage and question text to answer questions. This will ultimately save you those few precious seconds that can be better used for answering the tougher questions. For example, a passage may explicitly state the formula for the relationship of potential difference to the electric field and physical parameters of a parallel plate capacitor (i.e., $V = Ed$), but if you already know this formula, you will not need your map of the passage to find it when you need it to answer a question. That changes the type of question for you from Explicit to Memory.

Memory Questions

These questions are often the easiest to answer. They follow a format that is more familiar for most students; typical physics course work requires the memorization of formulas, facts, and their application. Since Memory questions do not rely on information from the passage, they are similar to the freestanding questions on the MCAT.

Consider a passage about a capacitor connected in a circuit from Practice Test 1. Here is an example of a Memory question.

> If the capacitor plates were fully charged by the 9 V battery, what is the charge on the positive plate?
>
> A) 15.8 pC
> B) 31.5 pC
> C) 47.3 pC
> D) 63.0 pC

The equation to solve this question ($Q = CV$) is not included in the passage. The passage is needed only for the value of the capacitance of the capacitor.

Another example of a Memory question from the same passage is Question 5, which asks for a description of the shape and direction of the magnetic field created by the current carrying wire. Again, the information needed to answer this question (use the right hand rule to find the direction of the magnetic field) is not included in the passage. The passage is not even needed to determine the direction of the current, since all the answer choices show current in the same direction.

Explicit Questions

You need information directly from the passage in order to answer Explicit questions. It is critical to have a solid passage map so that information from the passage is easy to find and use. Even when you have inherent knowledge about the topic, it is important to read for information more specific to the precise situation in question.

Consider Passage 3 from Practice Test 1. An example of an Explicit question is Question 14.

> Which of the following changes to the system would produce the greatest increase in the block's speed at a given displacement from the resting position?
>
> A) Increasing the mass of the block and the spring constant of the spring
> B) Decreasing the mass of the block and the spring constant of the spring
> C) Increasing the mass of the block and decreasing the spring constant of the spring
> D) Decreasing the mass of the block and increasing the spring constant of the spring

The equation needed to answer this question is given in the passage (Equation 1) and should be one that you recorded in your map. Note that you will always have to include information from the passage for an Explicit question.

Sometimes Explicit questions blend with Memory questions, creating a sort of Implicit question. In order to get the correct answer, you need to merge information from the passage with information you already know. For example, the passage gives an equation for a familiar variable in a new situation, and that must be blended with an equation from memory to solve for a separate value. These questions can appear straightforward but can be deceptively difficult.

An example of an Implicit question using the blend of explicit passage information and prior knowledge from memory would be Question 13:

> If the mass, while moving to the left at a distance X to the left of the rest position, collided elastically with a block and transferred all of its momentum to the block, how much kinetic energy would the block have?
>
> A) $1/2\ kX^2$
> B) $kD^2 - kX^2$
> C) kX^2
> D) $1/2\ kD^2 - 1/2\ kX^2$

This asks about the kinetic energy transferred from the block to a second block during an elastic collision. This requires memory for information about elastic collisions and kinetic energy, but also requires using the equation from the passage to substitute for velocity in the final form of the equation.

Implicit Questions

This is the most difficult question type. Implicit questions often require information from memory, combined with information from the passage, and all applied to a new situation. They rely most heavily on critical reasoning skills, but also require a solid map, since information from the passage is usually needed. Most often, the answer choices for these questions contain a lot of words, but they can also sometimes be algebraic expressions or graphs. Note also that for many of these questions, you might be able to devise sound explanations that are not among the answer choices. However, there is always only *one* answer choice that *best* answers the question of all the options.

On Information and/or Situation passages, Implicit questions are often of the form "Which of the following best describes how the [real world parameter described in the passage] would change [another, likely familiar, parameter not mentioned in the passage] from its ideal value?" The answers are verbal descriptions of increasing and decreasing values. Consider, for example, an Information passage describing the drag force on an object travelling through air. An example of an Implicit question would be:

> Which one of the following diagrams best illustrates the actual trajectory of a real golf ball through the air (solid curve) as compared to the ideal parabolic trajectory (dashed curve), assuming that both were hit with the same initial velocity and launch angle?

The correct graph would be selected by using the passage information describing drag and applying it to the memorized information about ideal projectile motion.

On Experiment/Research passages, Implicit questions are often of the form "Which of the following changes to the experiment would result in a change to [an experimental parameter]?" and are followed by verbal descriptions of changes to the apparatus, process, or mechanism of the experiment described in the passage. Consider again the passage that gives the equation for the velocity at any point for a block attached to a spring (Passage 3 from Practice Test 1). An example of an implicit question is Question 17.

> The mass is now placed between two identical springs, each attached to a wall at the other end, such that the total energy of the system is 0 when the mass is midway between the walls. Now, if the mass were displaced a distance D from the rest position and released, by what factor would its maximum velocity from the original setup be multiplied?
>
> A) 1
> B) $\sqrt{2}$
> C) 2
> D) 4

This question requires the use of memorized equations for kinetic and potential energy, applied to a new situation with multiple springs that is a variation on the passage experiment.

On Persuasive Reasoning passages, Implicit questions are often of the form "Which of the following phenomena best exemplifies the [physics concept]?" and are followed by verbal descriptions of physics phenomena. More than one of these may be true, but only one is an example of the concept named. Consider a Persuasive Reasoning passage that gives information about both radar and ladar technologies (Passage 7 from Practice Test 1). An example of an Implicit question is Question 46.

> Comparing radar and ladar transmitters, which one of the following is most likely true?
>
> A) The ladar device has a greater accuracy since it transmits waves of a longer wavelength.
> B) The radar transmitter is more prone to error in denser traffic conditions.
> C) The radar device does not measure the distance to the target vehicle.
> D) The ladar transmitter is more accurate since it emits light waves while the radar transmitter emits sound waves.

This question requires reading and evaluating each answer choice to determine if it is true or false.

The physics question types discussed so far categorize questions based on where to find the information for the answer. There is another way to categorize questions based on *how* you achieve the answer.

Algebraic Manipulation questions:
These require use of one or several equation(s) to solve algebraically for a variable. Typically they have either numeric answer choices (e.g., "5 Newtons") or algebraic equations for answer choices (i.e. "$F_c = F_G + F_N$"). Another twist on algebraic manipulation questions would be a question that asks for the units of an unfamiliar term (e.g., "What are the units for viscosity?") followed by answer choices with a variety of units of measure.

Functional Dependence/Proportionality questions:
These require the use of one or more equations, graphs, or data tables to calculate proportions and changes in variables or values. These can have numeric answer choices, algebraic answer choices (e.g., "$a_{car} = -2a_{truck}$"), or verbal answer choices (e.g., "the radius doubles" or "The range increases from launch angle of 0° to launch angle of 45°, then decreases from launch angle of 45° to launch angle of 90°.").

Graph Generation questions:
These require use of one or more equations, graphs, or data tables to create a graph of two variables.

Interpretation questions:
These require you to evaluate a situation (often an unfamiliar situation) and apply additional knowledge (either from memory or the passage), to identify the correct statement about the situation. Typically these have verbal answer choices (e.g., "The force of the book on the table and the force of gravity on the book are equal and opposite forces but do not form an action-reaction pair," or "The high altitude rocket will experience lower gravitation force and lower drag force than the low altitude rocket.").

BEST APPROACH TO ANSWERING

As with all the science sections, when tackling the Physical Sciences section of the MCAT, do the easy questions first; typically, the freestanding questions are easier Memory questions. Then tackle the passages, one subject at a time, saving the hardest passage for last. Within each passage, again, do the easy questions first, and make sure to fill in answers for ALL the questions before moving to the next passage. If you are running out of time for the harder questions at the end of the passage, make your best guess and be sure to click the "Mark" button so that you can review the question later.

Since you will be jumping around within the test, it is important to keep your scratch paper organized. Clearly indicate the passage and question number beside the work that you do for that question. If you think you've made an error in calculation, do not waste time erasing, just draw a line through your work and start again.

Notes

After reading the text of the question, you may need to draw a quick sketch or diagram. This step is particularly useful for freestanding questions. Don't waste time or space on ornate drawings; just sketch enough to record the basic vectors and the positive direction, and make sure that your drawing is big enough for you to add vectors or numbers to it.

Draw a simple picture.

Try to predict the physics formula you'll need to answer the question before looking at the answer choices. This will either be an equation from memory or from the passage. Write this formula (or formulas) on your scratch paper by the label for the question. This will help when you want to review a question for review. Instead of having to search for the information all over again, you have an indicator on your scratch paper of where to start.

Avoid Confusion

When analyzing a question, remember that the situation will be ideal only when stated. Most of the concepts and equations you have memorized are for the ideal world. If the question asks for an approximation, the ideal world formulas are valid. If the question asks you to take the real world into consideration, look for a new formula or description in the passage that addresses the issue.

Remember to use the correct units! All calculations should be done with the "m.k.s." unit system (meters, kilograms, seconds) unless otherwise specified. If you can't remember the formula, a unit analysis can help you regenerate or confirm the correct formula (for example, if you are solving a uniform circular motion question and you can't remember if velocity or radius is squared in the centripetal force equa-

Don't forget your units!

tion, a quick unit analysis will show that velocity must be squared and the radius must *not* be squared in order to get an answer in Newtons). Also, evaluating units may help you to quickly eliminate choices that have the wrong units. Finally, don't forget the "powers of 10": you may calculate the correct answer in meters, but if the answer choices are in millimeters, you will need to convert your results.

It can be helpful to form your own idea of the answer before looking at the choices. The MCAT tries to offer you similar-sounding answer choices that can muddle your thinking. Knowing what you are looking for before you read the answer choices keeps your POE focused.

Process of Elimination

Process of Elimination (POE) is paramount! Use the strikeout tool to indicate answer choices you have eliminated. Aggressively use process of elimination to improve your chances of guessing a correct answer even if you are not able to narrow it down to one choice. Remember each of the following POE strategies:

1. Eliminate answer choices that are clearly false or that do not answer the question.
2. If you think an answer choice is correct, double-check the remaining choices to confirm that they are incorrect. There may be two true statements in the answer choices, but only one best answers the question; make sure the answer you choose addresses the issue in the question.
3. Remember that if two answer choices are essentially the same, neither can be correct, and both can be eliminated immediately. This is commonly used in physics problems.
4. Work backwards, trying each answer choice to see if it correctly answers the question. This is particularly useful for questions such as "An increase in which of the following results in an increase in [some parameter] except...." Track these on your scratch paper so you can see the work done for each answer choice tried.
5. If you have eliminated three answer choices, the fourth choice must be correct choice. Don't waste time pondering why it is correct.

Solving Math

As you work through the equations, do not substitute values into the equations until you are at the end of the algebra. It's easier to correct a mistake if you leave all the variables intact, and often many of the variables will cancel, making the math easier. Once the algebra is done, it is a matter of arithmetic to complete the calculation. Sometimes detailed arithmetic is not even necessary because the final equation eliminates all but one answer choice. For example, if the equation for the tension in a string is $T = 15 - 1.5(10/6)$ then $T < 15$ and if only one answer choice is less than 15, then no further calculation is needed.

Simplify the math by using estimates of actual numbers. Unlike in the physics classes you have taken in school, on the MCAT you do not need to calculate precise answers; you only need to be close enough to select from the given answer choices. Make sure to take into consideration whether your original estimate was greater or less than the actual value. For example, 15 divided by π is 15 divided by a little more than 3, so the answer should be a little less than 5. To evaluate square roots and logarithms, decide on an upper bound and a lower bound for the actual values. For example, the square root of 11 is somewhere between the square root of 9 and the square root of 16, therefore it is between 3 and 4.

EXAMPLES OF STRATEGY IN USE

Below is an example of these strategies applied to the radar/ladar passage we mapped earlier.

> The frequency of the waves emitted by the ladar transmitter is most nearly:
>
> A) 2.7×10^{13} Hz
> B) 3.3×10^{14} Hz
> C) 2.7×10^{15} Hz
> D) 3.3×10^{16} Hz

This question is an explicit algebraic manipulation question requiring the memorized equation for light (wavelength $\times$ frequency = speed) manipulated to solve for frequency ($f = v/\lambda$). When mapping the passage, you noted all the values and information at the beginning of the second paragraph, so you refer to that location now to find the type of waves (laser, so the speed is $c = 3 \times 10^8$ m/s) and the wavelength (904 nm or 0.904×10^{-6} m). Before plugging in the numbers, you notice that your answer choices differ by a power of 10, so the arithmetic answer for the division is not necessary, only enough detail to count the correct number of zeros. Thus, $10^8/10^{-6} = 10^{14}$ which gives answer choice B.

> When using a radar device in stationary mode, which of the following would tend to increase the error due to the cosine effect?
>
> I. Measuring the target vehicle's speed at a closer range
> II. Positioning the radar transmitter closer to the road
> III. Using the Ka band rather than the X or K band
>
> A) I only
> B) II only
> C) I and II only
> D) II and III only

This question is an implicit interpretation question requiring information from the passage (speed measured by radar is $v_t \cos \alpha$ with error increasing if $\cos \alpha$ is reduced, meaning α is increased). This, together with close evaluation of the diagram in your map (α is increased with smaller range or increased y) gives the correct answer. Since Item II translates to "smaller y", it would result in less error, making Item II false. Thus, we can eliminate all of the answer choices that contain "II", which eliminates B, C, and D, leaving us with the correct answer choice A.

> A traffic officer is using a radar employing the X band in stationary mode, pointing the device directly at a target vehicle along its direction of travel. If the calculated value of Δf is –2800 Hz, then the target vehicle is:
>
> A) approaching the officer at a speed of 40 m/s.
> B) receding from the officer at a speed of 40 m/s.
> C) approaching the officer at a speed of 50 m/s.
> D) receding from the officer at a speed of 50 m/s.

This question is an Explicit algebraic manipulation question requiring use of both equations in the passage (both of which should be already written in your map). First, use the $\Delta f = f_r - f$ equation and memorized facts about the Doppler effect to determine if the target vehicle is approaching or receding. Since Δf is negative, we know that f_r must be less than f, so the vehicle must be receding, eliminating choices A and C. Then, using Equation 1 together with the fact that $v = c$ and $f \approx 10.5$ GHz, we have that $v_t = -c\Delta f/(2f)$ $\approx -(3 \times 10^8 \text{ m/s})(-2800 \text{ Hz}) / (2)(10.5 \times 10^9 \text{ Hz}) = 40$ m/s. This eliminates choice D, leaving choice B as the correct answer.

> Comparing radar and ladar transmitters, which one of the following is most likely true?
>
> A) The ladar device has a greater accuracy since it transmits waves of a longer wavelength.
> B) The radar transmitter is more prone to error in denser traffic conditions.
> C) The radar device does not measure the distance to the target vehicle.
> D) The ladar transmitter is more accurate since it emits light waves while the radar transmitter emits sound waves.

This question is an implicit interpretation question requiring reading and evaluating each answer choice to determine if it is true or false. Choice A requires the passage information from the first paragraph that states radar uses microwaves and ladar uses infrared, coupled together with the prior knowledge that infrared waves have shorter wavelength than microwaves, making choice A false. From the same information, we find that radar and ladar both emit electromagnetic waves, not sound waves, making choice D false. Choice B requires information from paragraph 2 that states ladar is aimed at a single vehicle whereas radar can cover a wider area. Thus, ladar would be more prone to error in denser traffic conditions, making choice B false. This leaves choice C as the correct answer.

> Suppose a ladar device emits light at an average rate of 500 pulses per second at an approaching target vehicle. The device measures the time interval between emission and reception of one of the pulses to be T_1 sec, and the time interval for the next pulse as T_2 sec. If c is the speed of light, which one of the following expressions gives the speed of the target vehicle?
>
> A) $250(T_1 - T_2)c$
> B) $250(T_2 - T_1)c$
> C) $500(T_1 - T_2)c$
> D) $500(T_2 - T_1)c$

This question is an Implicit algebraic manipulation question requiring a mathematic interpretation of the information provided in the passage. While it is certainly possible to derive this equation using distance = rate × time, a more efficient approach to this question is to start with aggressive process of elimination on the answer choices. Notice that the speed of the target vehicle is positive and since the target vehicle is approaching, T_1 must be greater than T_2. This eliminates choices B and D. The only difference between the remaining answer choices is the 250 or 500. A quick evaluation of the units of measure for $(T_1 - T_2)c$ yields units in meters and the question is asking for meters/second. So the coefficient must have units of 1/sec. The question states that there are 500 pulses per second and there have been two pulses emitted. Thus, the coefficient must be 250, eliminating choice C and leaving choice A as the correct answer.

MCAT PHYSICS TOPIC LIST[1]

Kinematics and Translational Motion

1. Dimensions
2. Vectors, components and addition
3. Speed, velocity, and acceleration
4. Bodies in free-fall

Force and Motion

A. Translational Systems and Gravitation
   1. Center of Mass
   2. Concept of force and its units
      a. Weight
      b. Static and kinetic friction
      c. Law of gravitation ($F = -GMm/r^2$)
      d. Gravitational field ($g = -GMm/r$)
   3. Newton's Laws
   4. Analysis of forces acting on an object
      a. Translational equilibrium
      b. Inclined planes and pulley systems
B. Rotational Systems
   1. Uniform circular motion
   2. Centripetal force
   3. Torque and rotational equilibrium

Work and Energy

1. Sign conventions and derived units (of work)
2. Kinetic energy and its units
3. Potential energy
      a. gravitational, local and general
4. Conservation of energy
5. Work-energy theorem
6. Path-independence of work done in gravitational field
      a. Conservative forces (gravity)
      b. Non-conservative forces (friction)
7. Power and its units
8. Mechanical advantage

Momentum

1. Momentum and impulse
2. Conservation of linear momentum
3. Elastic and inelastic collisions

Fluids and Solids

A. Fluids – Hydrostatics
   1. Density, specific gravity
   2. Buoyancy (Archimedes' principle)
   3. Hydrostatic pressure and Pascal's law
   4. Surface tension
B. Fluids – Hydrodynamics
   1. Continuity equation
   2. Poiseuille flow (viscosity)
   3. Turbulence
   4. Bernoulli's equation and principle
C. Solids
   1. Density
   2. Elastic properties and elastic limit
   3. Shear and compression
   4. Coefficient of thermal expansion

---

[1] Adapted from *The Official Guide to the MCAT Exam*, 2009 ed., 2009 Association of American Medical Colleges

Electrostatics

1. Charges, charge conversion
2. Insulators and conductors
3. Coulomb's law and sign conventions
4. Electric fields
5. Potential differences and absolute potential
6. Equipotential lines
7. Electric dipoles
8. Induction
9. Gauss' law

Electricity and Magnetism

A. Circuit Elements
    1. Current, its units and sign conventions
    2. Batteries
    3. Resistance
    4. Capacitance and dielectrics
    5. Discharge of a capacitor through a resistor
    6. Resistors/capacitors in series and in parallel
    7. Theory of conductivity
    8. Power in circuits
B. Alternating Currents and Reactive Circuits
C. Magnetism
    1. Magnetic field
    2. Force on a charge moving in a magnetic field

Waves and Periodic Motion

A. Periodic Motion
    1. Amplitude, period, frequency, velocity, phase
    2. Hooke's law
    3. Simple harmonic motion in pendulums and springs
    4. Potential energy of a spring system
B. Wave Characteristics
    1. Transverse and longitudinal waves
    2. Wavelength, frequency, wave speed
    3. Amplitude and intensity
    4. Superposition of waves, interference, wave addition
    5. Beat frequencies
    6. Standing waves
    7. Resonance in pipes and strings
        a. Harmonics

Sound

1. Production of sound
2. Relative speed of sound in different media
3. Sound intensity (decibels) and attenuation
4. Pitch
5. Doppler effect (and it's application to light)
6. Ultrasound

Light and Geometrical Optics

A. Electromagnetic radiation (Light)
    1. Properties of electromagnetic radiation
    2. Classification of electromagnetic spectrum (radio, infrared, UV, X-rays, etc.)
    3. Visual spectrum, color, energy and lasers
    4. Diffraction
    5. Interference, Young's double-slit experiment
    6. Polarization of light
B. Geometrical Optics
    1. Reflection from plane surface
    2. Refraction and Snell's law
    3. Total internal reflection
    4. Dispersion (change of index of refraction with wavelength)
    5. Spherical mirrors
    6. Thin lenses and combination of lenses
    7. Ray tracing and optical instruments

Atomic and Nuclear Structure[2]

A. Atomic Structure and Spectra
    1. Emission spectrum of hydrogen (Bohr model)
    2. Atomic energy levels
B. Atomic Nucleus
    1. Atomic number and weight
    2. Neutrons, protons, isotopes
    3. Nuclear forces
    4. Radioactive decay
    5. Fission and fusion
    6. Mass deficit, energy liberated, binding energy

---

[2] This information, while technically listed with the AAMC as Physics topics, is also relevant to General Chemistry.

Chapter 12
Physics
Practice Section

FREESTANDING QUESTIONS

1. A train is starting its trip from Paris to Frankfurt with an acceleration of x m/s^2. What is the ratio of its displacement traveled during the 5th second from ($t = 4$ s to $t = 5$ s) compared to the 10th second from ($t = 9$ s to $t = 10$ s)?

   A) 7 : 17
   B) 8 : 18
   C) 9 : 19
   D) 10 : 20

2. A 1 m horizontal wooden plank with mass m is perfectly balanced by two masses x and y at the ends of the plank. Which of the following is the correct relationship between x and y if the pivot is located 25 cm from mass x?

   A) $x = m + 3y$
   B) $x = 3y$
   C) $y = m + 3x$
   D) $x = (m + y) / 3$

3. A yo-yo is being swung in a vertical circular motion by a constant tension force applied through the string. Which of the following correctly describes the yo-yo's motion?

   A) The yo-yo moves at a constant speed and the net acceleration points towards the center of the circular path.
   B) The yo-yo moves at a variable speed and the net acceleration points towards the center of the circular path.
   C) The yo-yo moves at a constant speed and the centripetal acceleration points towards the center of the circular path.
   D) The yo-yo moves at a variable speed and the centripetal acceleration points towards the center of the circular path.

4. A microscopic particle, initially at a speed v_1, collides elastically with another particle, initially at rest. The first particle then comes to a stop, and the second particle moves with a speed v_2. If the first particle has a mass m_1 and the second a mass m_2, what is m_1/m_2?

   A) $v_1/2v_2$
   B) 1
   C) 2
   D) $2v_1/v_2$

5. A wooden cube of 8 cm length is partially submerged in a tank of canola oil with 2 cm of its length beneath the surface. If a hand suddenly pushes the cube so that the cube now has only 2 cm of its length above the surface, what is the magnitude of the new buoyant force compared to the previous one?

   A) ½ the previous magnitude
   B) Same as the previous magnitude
   C) 2 times the previous magnitude
   D) 3 times the previous magnitude

6. Two pipes of equal volume output per minute deliver water away from a water station to different areas of the city. Pipe A delivers the water to a mountain observatory while Pipe B delivers the water to a university at ground level. Given equal pressures in the pipes, which of the following is true?

   A) The cross section area of Pipe A is larger than that of Pipe B.
   B) The cross section area of Pipe A is smaller than that of Pipe B.
   C) The flow rate of water in Pipe A is larger than that of Pipe B.
   D) The flow rate of water in Pipe A is smaller than that of Pipe B.

7. You have three resistors of 3 Ω, 6 Ω and 8 Ω and a 50 V battery. You want to create a circuit where the current through the 8 Ω resistor is 5 A. How could you arrange the circuit?

A) All three resistors in parallel.
B) All three resistors in series.
C) The 3 Ω and 6 Ω resistors in parallel and the 8 Ω in series with it.
D) The 6 Ω and 8 Ω resistors in parallel and the 3 Ω in series with it.

8. If the time it takes for a proton to complete one circular revolution is T, what is the time needed for an alpha particle (helium nucleus) to complete one revolution in the same uniform magnetic field?

A) T
B) $2T$
C) $4T$
D) $8T$

9. A spring is compressed by a displacement x so that it stores a potential energy of 100 J. The force exerted by the spring is measured to be 500 N. Find the magnitude of x.

A) 10 cm
B) 20 cm
C) 30 cm
D) 40 cm

10. The harmonic frequencies of a glass tube, which has one end closed off, are empirically measured using a note-emitting device. The beat frequency (f_{beat}) between the third and fourth harmonic is 680 Hz. What is second harmonic frequency and what is the length of the glass tube?

A) 1020 Hz, 20 cm
B) 1360 Hz, 20 cm
C) 1020 Hz, 25 cm
D) 1360 Hz, 25 cm

11. A single speaker produces music at an intensity level of 160 dB at 1 meter away from itself. A student stands 10 meters away from the speaker, and puts on a pair of noise canceling headphones, capable of reducing the intensity by 99.9%. What is the intensity level that is student hears?

A) 100 dB
B) 110 dB
C) 120 dB
D) 130 dB

12. A wind-chime made up of colored flat glass pieces is swaying in the sunlight. A physics student wants to measure the angles of light as they are refracted through the glass and back into the air. If the angle of incidence of the sunlight is 30° on the glass which has an index of refraction of 1.50, at what angle does the ray emerge from the glass into the air at?

A) $\sin^{-1}(1/2)$
B) $\sin^{-1}(1/3)$
C) $\sin^{-1}(1/4)$
D) $\sin^{-1}(1/6)$

PRACTICE PASSAGE 1

A lab class performs an investigation of kinematic quantities through a series of tests. In addition to the quantities associated with uniform velocity and uniformly accelerated motion, the class considers the effect of changing acceleration. Just as acceleration is the rate of change of velocity, jerk is the rate of change of acceleration, given by:

$$j = \frac{\Delta a}{\Delta t}$$

Equation 1

Jerk bears exactly the same relationship to acceleration as acceleration bears to velocity, and just like acceleration, it is a vector. Jerk is known by several other names, including *jolt* and *surge*. It is important for certain applications in which not only acceleration but also jerk must be maintained below a maximum value to prevent breaking or damaging tools or machine parts. Also, excessive jerk can be a contributing factor in whiplash, a category of neck injuries.

In this lab, several numbered but otherwise identical toy race cars are given initial velocities and initial accelerations, and some are given constant, non-zero jerk as well. Selected race car data is given in the following table.

Table 1 Race Cars Used in Lab

Race car	Initial velocity (m/s)	Initial acceleration (m/s²)	Jerk (m/s³)
1	0	7	0
2	6	5	0
3	0	0	2
4	4	−2	2

1. If Cars 1 and 2 start at the same time from the same position, how long after their start will they have advanced the same forward distance?

   A) 3 seconds
   B) 6 seconds
   C) 9 seconds
   D) 12 seconds

2. Which of the following is the most likely reason that Car 4's initial acceleration is negative?

   A) It is initially facing the opposite direction as the other race cars.
   B) It is initially motionless, since the sum of its jerk and its initial acceleration is zero.
   C) It is initially slowing down.
   D) It is initially not accelerating, and it only begins to accelerate when its jerk brings its acceleration up to a positive value.

3. At a certain time, a fifth race car has only a Northward acceleration with a magnitude of a_1. A time Δt later, the same race car has only an acceleration Eastward with a magnitude of a_2. What was the magnitude of its average jerk during this time?

   A) $\dfrac{a_2 - a_1}{\Delta t}$

   B) $\dfrac{a_1 - a_2}{\Delta t}$

   C) $\dfrac{a_2 + a_1}{\Delta t}$

   D) $\dfrac{\sqrt{a_2^{\,2} + a_1^{\,2}}}{\Delta t}$

4. What would a jerk of 3 m/s^3 be in nanometers per millisecond?

A) 3
B) 3×10^3
C) 3×10^6
D) 3×10^9

5. For how many seconds does Car 3 have an acceleration between that of Car 1 and that of Car 2?

A) 0.25
B) 0.5
C) 1
D) 2

6. If Car 4's jerk were zero, how would its distance traveled compare to its displacement from its starting position, if both were measured after a long time?

A) The distance would be greater.
B) They would be equal.
C) The displacement would be greater.
D) It cannot be determined.

7. If Cars 1 and 2 start at the same time from the same position, how far has Car 1 traveled when it reaches the speed that Car 2 has after it has traveled two meters?

A) 3 m
B) 4 m
C) 5 m
D) 6 m

PRACTICE PASSAGE 2

When an object is in contact with a surface, it may experience a frictional force, which resists lateral movement. There are two major kinds of friction: *static* and *kinetic*. The latter applies to an object sliding or skidding along a surface, whereas the former acts when the two surfaces are at rest with respect to each other at their point of contact and prevents motion. Static friction applies not only to two objects that are both totally motionless but also to an object that is rolling without slipping on a surface.

The amount of frictional force experienced by an object depends both on the normal force that the object experiences and the coefficient of friction, μ, a measure of the molecular-level interactions between the object and the surface and usually corresponding to roughness. The coefficient of friction depends mostly on the materials interacting, though it can also vary with temperature, relative speed, and a variety of other factors. For example, at very high speeds, coefficients of friction are usually reduced.

Coefficients of friction cannot be calculated from fundamental physical equations and must be measured empirically for different surfaces. The following table contains coefficients of friction for certain materials under typical conditions.

Table 1 Coefficients of Friction for Certain Materials

Material	Coefficient of Static Friction	Coefficient of Kinetic Friction
PTFE on PTFE	0.04	0.04
Zinc on Cast Iron	0.85	0.21
Cast Iron on Cast Iron	1.1	0.15

Rubber can have an exceedingly high coefficient of friction, as high as 4. One of the properties of rubber is that its coefficient of friction actually decreases with greater applied force. This can be expressed in *Thirion's law*:

$$\frac{1}{\mu} = \frac{cF}{A} + b$$

Equation 1

in which F is the applied force, A is the area of contact between the object and the surface, and c and b are empirically measured constants that depend on the exact types of rubber used.

1. An object initially at a speed of 4 m/s skids to a halt on a surface after 2 meters. What is the coefficient of kinetic friction between the object and the surface?

    A) 0.3
    B) 0.4
    C) 0.5
    D) 0.6

2. When a copper pin slides against a copper surface, the force required to keep the pin sliding at constant speed is most likely:

    A) zero.
    B) greater at high speeds than at low speeds.
    C) greater at low speeds than at high speeds.
    D) equal at all speeds.

3. An object weighs 20 N and is sliding along a rough surface, experiencing a frictional force of 6 N. If an additional force of 40 N suddenly presses down on the top of the object, what is the magnitude of the frictional force that it experiences?

    A) 3 N
    B) 6 N
    C) 12 N
    D) 18 N

4. Which of the following best approximates the steepest angle at which a flat zinc surface can be tilted before a cast iron pot on it starts to slide?

    A) 40°
    B) 50°
    C) 60°
    D) 70°

5. When a car driving along a road encounters an icy patch, it becomes more likely to lose traction. Which of the following best accounts for this phenomenon?

A) The coefficient of kinetic friction is lower for the icy road than for normal road.
B) The coefficient of static friction is lower for the icy road than for normal road.
C) The coefficient of kinetic friction is higher for the icy than for normal road.
D) The coefficient of static friction is higher for the icy road than for normal road.

6. If a rubber object is on a rubber surface, and if the object's mass is increased by adding several weights inside it, which of the following is true of the magnitude of the force required to initiate horizontal movement (F_x) and the weight of the object (w)?

A) The ratio of F_x to w increases.
B) The ratio of F_x to w remains constant.
C) The ratio of F_x to w decreases.
D) The difference between F_x and w remains constant.

7. Which of the following best explains the reason why polytetrafluoroethylene (PTFE), better known by the brand name *Teflon*™, is often used to coat "non-stick" cookware?

A) The toxicity of fumes given off by PTFE-coated pots is less than the toxicity of standard cooking oils.
B) Its extremely low coefficient of friction reduces the occurrence of food sticking to the pans.
C) Its extremely low coefficient of friction reduces the heat lost to friction when food slides on PTFE-coated surfaces.
D) PTFE was also used in the Manhattan Project to coat parts of pipes holding radioactive uranium compounds.

PRACTICE PASSAGE 3

The problem of two massive bodies interacting solely with each other and solely via the gravitational force (a good approximation of, for example, a planet orbiting the Sun) can be simplified by examining not the two actual bodies in space but instead two hypothetical bodies. If the two actual bodies have masses of m_1 and m_2, the two relevant hypothetical bodies are the total mass, M, which, as the name implies, has a mass given by the sum of the two actual masses, and the reduced mass, which has a mass of m, given by:

$$\mu = \frac{m_1 m_2}{m_1 + m_2}$$

Equation 1

The hypothetical bodies are analyzed in *center-of-mass coordinates*, in which the position of the center of mass of the two actual masses is defined to be the origin. This origin remains fixed, for the center of mass of any set of objects that feel forces only from each other does not accelerate, and the two hypothetical objects are positioned such that the total mass is at the origin and the reduced mass orbits it. Thus, instead of a problem involving two objects both of which are free to move, using a reduced mass and center-of-mass coordinates simplifies to a problem involving two objects only one of which is free to move (the reduced mass).

From basic Newtonian gravitation, simplified by the reduced mass and center-of-mass coordinates, one can derive the length of time P that it takes either actual mass to orbit the fixed center of mass in terms of an orbital parameter, a, which in circular orbits is the radius of the circle:

$$P^2 = \frac{4\pi^2}{G(m_1 + m_2)} a^3$$

Equation 2

This, together with the value of the gravitational constant $G = 6.67 \times 10^{-11}$ N·m²/kg² and other basic physical principles, has allowed the masses of many celestial objects to be measured. Examples include: the Earth's mass of 5.97×10^{24} kg, the Sun's mass of 1.99×10^{30} kg, the gas giant Jupiter's mass of 1.90×10^{27} kg, and the Moon's mass of 7.36×10^{22} kg.

1. In center-of-mass coordinates defined by two objects m_1 and m_2 separated by a distance a, how far is object m_1 from the origin?

A) $\dfrac{1}{1 + m_1 / m_2} a$

B) $\dfrac{m_2}{m_1} a$

C) $\dfrac{m_1 + m_2}{m_2} a$

D) $\dfrac{m_2 m_1}{m_1 + m_2} a$

2. If Planet X and Planet Y are of equal mass and orbit in circles of radii R and $4R$ from the Sun, respectively, then how many times greater is the period of Planet Y's orbit than is that of Planet X?

A) 4
B) 8
C) 16
D) 64

3. Which of the following best explains the reason that the position of the Sun is often considered fixed in place while the planets move around it?

A) The torque exerted by planets moving counterclockwise around the Sun is approximately balanced by the torque exerted by planets moving clockwise around the Sun.
B) The mass of the Sun is large relative to all of the other mass in the solar system, so it is always near the fixed center of mass.
C) The Sun feels much smaller gravitational forces from the planets than they feel from it, due to its considerably greater mass.
D) The reduced mass of the Sun orbits the center of mass instead of the actual mass of the Sun.

4. The gas giant Saturn has a satellite, Rhea, which orbits in approximately a circle at a distance of 5.27×10^8 m and at a speed of 8480 m/s, both measured with respect to the center of mass of Saturn. What is the approximate mass of Saturn?

A) 6×10^{21} kg
B) 6×10^{25} kg
C) 6×10^{26} kg
D) 6×10^{29} kg

5. If both actual masses in orbit around each other are doubled, what will happen to the reduced mass?

A) It will decrease by a factor of 2.
B) It will remain constant.
C) It will increase by a factor of 2.
D) It will increase by a factor of 4.

6. Would moving objects with no net force on them move in straight lines at constant speed in center-of-mass coordinates?

A) Yes, because the center of mass is fixed in space for closed systems with no external forces.
B) Yes, because the principle of inertia requires that unforced objects travel with constant velocity in all coordinate systems.
C) No, because the reduced mass is an object in center-of-mass coordinates, and it moves in a circle.
D) No, because only hypothetical objects can exist in center-of-mass coordinates, and such objects need not obey physical laws.

7. How many full Earth years does it take for Jupiter to orbit the Sun, given that the Jupiter-Sun distance is 7.78×10^{11} m? (Note: 1 year is approximately 3.15×10^7 s.)

A) 1
B) 2
C) 12
D) 119

PRACTICE PASSAGE 4

Jack and Jill are running up a hill, at an incline of approximately 30° to the horizontal, along a path that is 450 m long to the top of the hill, as shown in Figure 1. Jack weighs 900 N and Jill is half his size. They are racing to the top of the hill, and Jill runs up in half the time it takes for Jack to scramble up the hill. Their good friend Ty-Mur measures how long it takes for them to get to the top of the hill and clocks in Jack at 3 minutes.

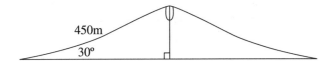

Figure 1   Jack and Jill's Hill

At the top of the hill is a well where they try to fetch a pail of water. The well is 15 m deep, but Jill cannot see the bottom. They decide to drop a penny down to check if there is water in the well. Then they lower the 2 L pail using a pulley system into the well and draw up a full bucket. Then they start walking back down the hill.

Unfortunately, Jack falls when they are almost at the bottom of the hill when they have travelled 440 m from the summit, and he slides down the hill for 6 m before coming to a stop. Jill drops the pail and races down after him. She trips just as she gets close to him, and they wind up sliding down the hill together with a coefficient of friction of 0.1 coming to a stop just as they reach the bottom of the hill.

1. When Jack has reached the top of the hill, how much work has he done?

   A) 202.5 kJ
   B) 405 kJ
   C) 2025 kJ
   D) 4050 kJ

2. What was Jill's power output going up the hill?

   A) 1.125 kW
   B) 2.250 kW
   C) 33.75 kW
   D) 67.50 kW

3. What did Ty-Mur's stopwatch read if he started it when Jill dropped the penny and stopped it when they heard the splash from the penny she dropped?

   A) 0.04 s
   B) 0.08 s
   C) 1.77 s
   D) 3.46 s

4. How fast was Jill running down the hill just before falling onto Jack?

   A) 2 m/s
   B) 3 m/s
   C) 6 m/s
   D) 8 m/s

5. What is Jill's change in potential energy from the start of the trip to the end of the trip?

A) 0 J

B) −101.25 kJ

C) 101.25 kJ

D) Cannot be determined

7. How fast was the penny going when it hit the water?

A) 15 m/s

B) 17 m/s

C) 20 m/s

D) 25 m/s

6. Ignoring the stop at the top of the hill, which one of the following diagrams best approximates the potential energy changes of Jack (solid line) and Jill (dotted line)?

A)

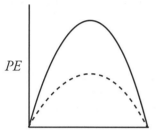

B)

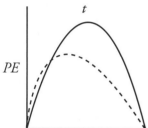

C)

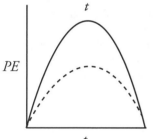

D)

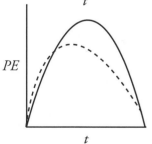

PRACTICE PASSAGE 5

Arterial blood pressure, measured in mm of mercury, is measured at two moments within the circulatory cycle: one during the maximum thrust of the heart (*systolic* pressure, normally around 120 mm Hg), and one when the heart is relaxed (*diastolic* pressure, normally around 80 mm Hg). Systolic and diastolic blood pressures vary throughout the day. They can change in response to stress, exercise, change in diet and other factors. Blood pressure decreases as blood moves through arteries, arterioles, capillaries and veins, as described by *Poiseuille's law*:

$$\frac{\Delta P}{L} = \frac{8\eta f}{R^4}$$

Equation 1

where $\Delta P/L$ is the pressure drop per length, η is the viscosity coefficient, f is the volume flow rate and R is the radius of the artery.

One factor that affects blood pressure is the buildup of fatty deposits or plaque on the arterials walls. The effective diameter is decreased which increases the speed of blood flow. The increase in speed, in turn, decreases the pressure inside that section of the artery.

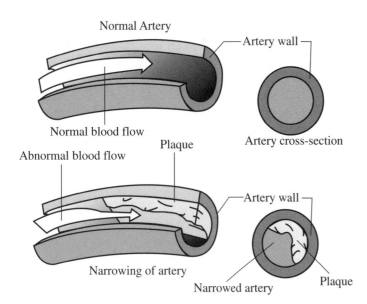

Figure 1

If the fluid pressure decreases too much, the artery will collapse on itself. Then, when the flow of blood has ceased, the artery opens up again. This process repeats in what is known as *vascular flutter*. This repetitive opening and closing of the artery can act as a pump, which may dislodge the plaque and send it through the artery where it may potentially entirely block a down-stream vessel in the body.

While plaque decreases the fluid pressure along a section of artery, the average blood pressure in the body as a whole increases.

1. A bag contains a glucose solution with specific gravity 1.02. If the average gauge pressure of an artery is 1.33×10^4 Pa, what is the minimum height the bag needs to be placed to infuse the glucose solution into the artery?

   A) 1.30 m
   B) 1.36 m
   C) 13.0 m
   D) 13.6 m

2. Which of the following would increase the pressure drop per length as blood moves through an artery?

   I. Using a blood thinner to decrease the viscosity
   II. Inserting a stent to widen the artery
   III. Increasing the blood flow rate

   A) I only
   B) II and III
   C) III only
   D) I, II and III

3. During the systole, the heart produces a *vascular pressure wave*, which travels through the vessel walls to the peripheral arteries. These waves are reflected at the peripheral veins and interfere with the incoming waves, causing pressure readings that differ from the true aortic pressure. A high pressure reading would occur at:

A) a displacement node.
B) a displacement antinode.
C) halfway between a displacement node and antinode.
D) a pressure node.

4. A hypodermic syringe, positioned horizontally, contains medicine with specific gravity 1.0, initially at 1 atm. The barrel of the syringe has a cross-sectional area of 25 mm². A force of 5 N is exerted on the plunger. If the medicine leaves the needle at 1 atm, with what speed is it ejected? (Assume the needle cross-sectional area is much smaller than the barrel cross-sectional area.)

A) 2.0 cm/s
B) 63 cm/s
C) 20 m/s
D) 25 m/s

5. If blood traveling through a vessel encounters a region where plaque has decreased the effective diameter by one third its normal value, then the average speed of blood flow will increase by:

A) one third.
B) a factor of 3.
C) a factor of 9/4.
D) a factor of 9.

6. Certain foods, such as salt, can increase the amount of blood pumped out from the heart during each contraction. This would most likely:

A) decrease the frequency of flutter due to the increase in flow rate.
B) increase the frequency of flutter due to the increase in flow rate.
C) decrease the frequency of flutter due to the change in blood density.
D) increase the frequency of flutter due to the change in blood density.

7. Early heart defibrillators used a bank of capacitors connected to a 1000 volt DC power source, storing 100–200 J of potential energy. What is the minimum total capacitance needed to restart a heart that has stopped beating?

A) 200 μF
B) 400 μF
C) 200 mF
D) 400 mF

PRACTICE PASSAGE 6

Coulomb's law describes the force between two point charges. Using the *principle of superposition*, the forces involved in configurations of more than two point charges can be fully described by summing the individual contributions of each discrete point charge. Additionally, the electric field generated by any such configuration of charges at some point in space can be found by summing the field contributions of each charge according to the equation $\mathbf{F} = q\mathbf{E}$. For example, it can be shown that, at distances much greater than the separation between the two charges in an electric dipole, the field is inversely proportional to the cube of the distance.

Other charge distributions are possible than discrete point charges. One example is the long straight line of continuous charge, described in terms of its charge per unit length, λ. For such a charge distribution, the electric field is given by

$$E = \frac{2k\lambda}{r}$$

Equation 1

where k is Coulomb's constant (9×10^9 N·m^2/C^2) and r is the radial distance from the line of charge. This equation is subject to the constraint that $r \ll L$, where L is the length of the line of charge. The electric potential field due to a line of charge is given by

$$\phi = -2k\lambda \ln(r)$$

Equation 2

Another common example of a charge distribution is the uniformly charged plane (with charge distribution σ in C/m^2), such as one encounters in the charged plates of a parallel-plate capacitor. The electric field generated by such a plane is constant over distances d from the plane such that d is much less than the linear extension of the plane (the plane can be described as infinite to avoid complications). That field is given by

$$E = 2\pi k \sigma$$

Equation 3

with the field lines normal to the plane. The electric potential field due to an infinite uniform plane of charge is given by

$$\phi = -2\pi k \sigma d$$

Equation 4

1. A test charge q_0 is used to determine the electric field strength at a distance of 10 cm from a long line of charge. The electric field strength is discovered to be 900 N/C directed radially inward toward the wire. What is the linear charge density of this line of charge?

A) 5×10^{-8} C/m
B) 5×10^{-9} C/m
C) -5×10^{-8} C/m
D) -5×10^{-8} C/m

2. Suppose that a metal sphere of mass m_0 is given a charge $+Q_0$. If this charge is set a distance d above the surface of a large horizontal uniformly charged plate with surface charge $+\sigma$, for what ratio of charge to mass will the sphere float at that height?

A) $\dfrac{g}{2\pi k \sigma}$

B) $\dfrac{gd}{2\pi k \sigma}$

C) $\dfrac{2\pi k \sigma}{gd}$

D) $\dfrac{2\pi k \sigma}{g}$

3. Which of the following graphs best represents the electric potential and electric potential energy of an electron proximate to a long line of uniformly distributed positive charge as a function of radial distance from that line?

A)

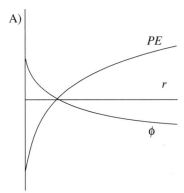

B)

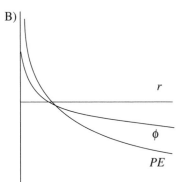

C)

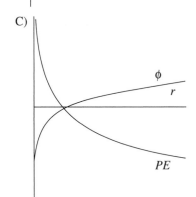

D)

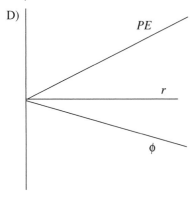

4. Suppose a positive ion is ejected with minimal initial kinetic energy from a large uniformly positively charged plate. How will its kinetic energy change as a function of distance from the plate?

A) It will be constant.
B) It will increase linearly as a function of distance.
C) It will increase as the square of the distance from the plate.
D) It will decrease as the square of the distance from the plate.

5. Liquid water is composed of randomly aligned H_2O dipoles. If a long uniformly charged rod were lowered rapidly into a water bath, which of the following best describes the effect on the average water molecule due to its presence?

A) It would experience neither force nor torque.
B) It would experience a force but no torque.
C) It would experience no force but would experience a torque.
D) It would experience both a force and a torque.

6. A charge $-q_0$ of mass m_0 orbits a long line of uniform positive charge with linear charge density $+\lambda$ in a circular path. What is its orbital period?

A) $\pi r^2 \sqrt{\dfrac{2k\lambda q_0}{m_0}}$ seconds

B) $2\pi r \sqrt{\dfrac{2k\lambda}{m_0}}$ seconds

C) $2\pi r \sqrt{\dfrac{m_0}{2k\lambda q_0}}$ seconds

D) $2\pi r \sqrt{\dfrac{m_0}{4k\lambda q_0 \ln(r)}}$ seconds

7. A charged parallel plate capacitor is composed of two oppositely charged uniform planes of charge densities $+\sigma$ and $-\sigma$ ($\sigma = 10^{-4}$ C/m) separated by air. If the area of each plate is 2 cm^2 and their separation is 1 mm, how much work is done by the electric field in moving a charge of 1 nC from the positive plate to the negative plate ($\varepsilon_0 = 8.85 \times 10^{-12}$ C^2/N·m^2)?

A) 1.1×10^{-4} J
B) 2.2×10^{-5} J
C) 1.1×10^{-5} J
D) 5.4×10^{-6} J

PRACTICE PASSAGE 7

A cloud chamber is a device for studying subatomic particles. It is called a cloud chamber because it is filled with a pressurized vapor. When a charged particle enters the vapor it ionizes the atoms by which it passes. These ions cause the vapor to condense into droplets, leaving a track behind the charged particle. Photographs of these tracks are taken and used to study the particles. Heavier particles, like alpha particles and protons, interact more strongly with the vapor causing more droplets to form. This results in alpha particles and protons leaving thicker tracks than electrons. However, the stronger interaction causes the heavier particles to lose energy and come to a stop more quickly. Also, the greater the charge of a particle the more strongly it will interact with the vapor causing more atoms to ionize.

Placing the cloud chamber in a constant magnetic field causes the charged particles to curve in a circular path of radius

$$r = \frac{mv}{qB}$$

where m is the mass of the particle, v is its speed, q is its charge, and B is the strength of the magnetic field. Positive and negative charges will curve in opposite directions. To determine from the photograph the direction in which the particles are traveling, a thin lead plate is placed in the chamber. When the particles pass through the plate they slow down, causing their radius of curvature to decrease on the opposite side of the lead plate.

A cloud chamber with a magnetic field and lead plate was used to discover the positron, the electron's antiparticle. Antiparticles have the same mass as their counterparts but opposite charge. Figure 1 is a diagram of what a photograph from such an experiment might look like. In this picture the magnetic field points into the page.

1. Which of the tracks in Figure 1 was most likely left by a positron?

A) 1
B) 2
C) 3
D) 4

2. If an electron and a proton have the same kinetic energy, the proton will:

A) curve in a smaller circle and have a longer track length.
B) curve in a larger circle and have a shorter track length.
C) curve in a smaller circle and have a shorter track length.
D) curve in a larger circle and have a longer track length.

3. Which track was left by a neutron?

A) 1
B) 3
C) 4
D) None of the above

4. Suppose the magnetic field was turned off and was replaced with an electric field pointing from left to right. Which track would curve in the opposite direction than it did with the magnetic field?

A) None of them
B) 1 only
C) 2, 3, and 4 only
D) All of them

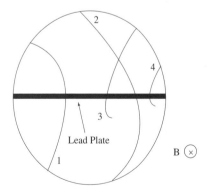

Figure 1   Photograph from a cloud chamber experiment

5. Suppose an electric field, of strength E, pointing from left to right was added to the experiment in addition to the magnetic field pointing into the page. If a negatively charged particle were observed to move in a straight line it would

A) be moving upward with speed E/B.
B) be moving upward with speed B/E.
C) be moving downward with speed E/B.
D) be moving downward with speed B/E.

6. If q is the charge of the particle, d is the distance traveled, and m is the mass of the particle, which formula would most accurately describe the kinetic energy loss of a charged particle as it passes through the vapor?

A) $\Delta KE \propto q^2 d$

B) $\Delta KE \propto q^2 d$

C) $\Delta KE \propto \dfrac{q^2 d}{m}$

D) $\Delta KE \propto \dfrac{md}{q^2}$

7. Compared to a proton with the same momentum, an alpha particle will leave:

   I.   A track with a larger radius of curvature.
   II. A wider track.
   III. A shorter track.

A) I only
B) III only
C) II and III
D) I, II, and III

PRACTICE PASSAGE 8

Simple harmonic motion occurs when the restoring force on an oscillating mass is directly proportional to displacement. An example of a simple harmonic oscillator can be made using a mass m attached to an ideal spring of spring constant k suspended from a ceiling. Once the new equilibrium length of the spring is achieved by gently lowering and releasing the mass, the system can be set into motion by pulling the spring down an additional displacement A and releasing it. The period of oscillation of this system is given by

$$T = 2\pi\sqrt{\frac{m}{k}}$$

Equation 1

Due to the assumption of direct proportionality between force and displacement, simple harmonic motion necessarily ignores the contribution of frictional forces. In many cases this assumption of negligible friction yields poor approximations of the behavior of the oscillating system. One such case is shown below, where the oscillating mass is attached by a rigid, low-mass rod to a rigid plate submerged in a tank filled with a low-viscosity liquid.

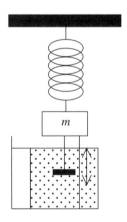

Figure 1

To a close approximation, the effect of the drag force on the oscillating submerged plate is directly proportional to its velocity, $\mathbf{v}$. Thus in place of Hooke's law for the restoring force of ideal springs we have the following force equation for *damped harmonic motion*:

$$\mathbf{F} = -k\mathbf{y} - b\mathbf{v}$$

Equation 2

where $\mathbf{y}$ is the displacement from equilibrium of the spring-mass system and b is a *damping coefficient*, a measure of the frictional effects on the system due to the movement of the submerged plate through the fluid. Using Newton's second law and assuming a small value for b, one finds the following solution for the position of the mass as a function of time:

$$y = Ae^{-bt/2m}\cos\left(t \cdot \sqrt{\frac{k}{m} - \left(\frac{b}{2m}\right)^2}\right)$$

Equation 3

The graph of this equation is a sinusoidal curve whose amplitude is a decaying exponential, as shown below.

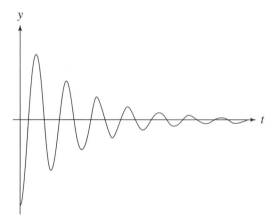

Figure 2

1. How does the frequency of oscillation of the damped harmonic oscillator change over time?

A) It is constant.
B) It decreases.
C) It increases.
D) It initially decreases, then becomes constant.

2. If the equilibrium length of the hanging spring before the mass is attached is L, what is the length of the spring that corresponds to $y = 0$ in Equation 3 and Figure 2?

A) $L + A$

B) $L + \dfrac{mg}{k}$

C) $L + \dfrac{k}{mg}$

D) $L - \dfrac{mg}{k} + A$

3. What does the slope of the sinusoidal curve in Figure 2 represent?

A) The distance traveled by the oscillating mass
B) The velocity of the oscillating mass
C) The work done by gravity on the system
D) The decay rate of the amplitude of the oscillations

4. Which of the following would likely result from increasing the viscosity of the fluid in which the plate is submerged?

A) The amplitude of oscillations would decay more rapidly and their frequency would decrease.
B) The amplitude of oscillations would decay less rapidly and their frequency would decrease.
C) The amplitude of oscillations would decay more rapidly and their frequency would increase.
D) The amplitude of oscillations would decay more rapidly and their frequency would remain the same.

5. As the maximum amplitude of the oscillations decreases with time, so does the total mechanical energy of the system. At what time will this energy be one quarter its initial value?

A) $t = \dfrac{\pi}{2\sqrt{\dfrac{k}{m} - \left(\dfrac{b}{2m}\right)^2}}$

B) $t = \dfrac{2m\ln(4)}{b}$

C) $t = \dfrac{2m\ln(2)}{b}$

D) $t = \dfrac{2m}{b}$

6. Each of the following changes would affect the rate of decay of the amplitude of oscillations EXCEPT:

A) increasing the suspended mass.
B) changing the surface area of the submerged plate.
C) draining the liquid from the tank.
D) increasing the stiffness of the spring.

7. The rod and plate are removed from the mass, and the mass is then pulled down by a displacement A from its hanging equilibrium length (such that no part of it touches the liquid in the container) and released. If $A = 10$ cm, $k = 100$ N/m, and $m = 4$ kg, what best approximates the period of the resulting oscillations?

A) 0.83 seconds
B) 1.0 second
C) 1.2 seconds
D) 12 seconds

PRACTICE PASSAGE 9

Early in the 20th century, several crucial experiments established the dual wave-particle nature of light and the ways that electromagnetic radiation interacts with matter. In 1923, Arthur H. Compton conducted an important experiment showing how photons in the X-ray and gamma-ray portion of the spectrum interact with free electrons. Compton's experiment provided further verification of the photonic nature of electromagnetic phenomena.

Compton scattering occurs when incident photons strike electrons in elastic collisions, imparting momentum and kinetic energy to the electrons and thereby reducing the momentum and energy of the scattered photons. The reduced energy of the photon implies a reduced frequency according to the photon energy equation $E = hf$, where h is *Planck's constant* ($h = 4.14 \times 10^{-15}$ eV·s). This change in frequency implies a corresponding change in wavelength; this shift in wavelength of Compton scattered photons is given by the Compton Shift equation:

$$\Delta\lambda = \frac{h}{m_e c}(1 - \cos\phi)$$

Equation 1

Here ϕ represents the *scattering angle*, or the angle between the photon's original path and its path after the collision, and m_e is the rest mass of the electron.

To study Compton scattering in the lab, a student conducts the following experiment. Using a radioactive source (Americium-241, a commonly manufactured radioactive isotope used in household smoke detectors with a peak gamma emission of 59.5 keV), a metallic target shaped into a circular arc, and an X-ray detector that converts incident X-ray photons into electric current by means of the *photoelectric effect*, the student counts the number of scattering events at various angles over set durations. So long as the source, detector, and target all lie on a circle on a flat surface, the student can be relatively assured of receiving only photons scattered at particular angles due to the geometric rule that inscribed angles in a circle are equal to half the intercepted arc. The experimental set-up is shown below.

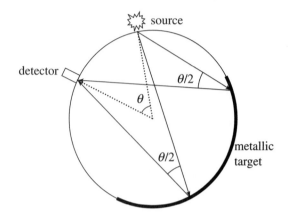

Figure 1

The student conducts experimental runs at four different scattering angles over four different durations. The following data record the scattered energy peaks in terms of scattering angle and photon counts (only the peak counts are included, not the entire energy spectrum for each scattering angle).

Table 1

Scattering angle ϕ	Energy of peak	# of detections at peak energy	Duration of exprimental run
60°	57.0 ± 0.4 keV	1242	4 hours
75°	55.2 ± 0.6 keV	989	4 hours
90°	53.5 ± 0.6 keV	1411	8 hours
120°	50.5 ± 0.5 keV	1206	8 hours

1. What is the scattering angle ϕ in terms of the circular arc θ (see Figure 1)?

A) $\theta/2$
B) $90 - \theta/2$
C) $180 - \theta/2$
D) $180 - \theta$

2. If incident photons from a green light source undergo Compton scattering off of electrons at rest, which of the following could NOT be true of the scattered photons?

A) They appear blue.
B) They appear yellow.
C) They have a longer wavelength than the incident photons.
D) They have a lower energy than the incident photons.

3. What is the maximum change in wavelength of a Compton-scattered photon?

A) $\Delta\lambda_{max} = \dfrac{h}{m_e c}$

B) $\Delta\lambda_{max} = \dfrac{2h}{m_e c}$

C) $\Delta\lambda_{max} = \dfrac{h}{2m_e c}$

D) $\Delta\lambda_{max} = 0$

4. During experimental runs, the student places a thin sheet of lead directly between the Amercium-241 source and the scintillation detector. Which of the following best explains the purpose of this measure?

A) It prevents electrons scattered in the air between the source and the detector from entering the detector and corrupting the data.
B) It ensures that photons scattered off the metallic target at angles different from the desired angle do not enter the detector.
C) It prevents high energy photons from cosmic radiation from entering the detector and corrupting the data.
D) It prevents photons emitted from the source from entering the detector directly without scattering off the target.

5. According to Table 1, for which scattering angle was the rate of detection events at the peak energy highest?

A) 60°
B) 75°
C) 90°
D) 120°

6. Suppose another trial of the experiment were conducted set up to record scatterings at an angle of 105°. If the experiment were allowed to run overnight (for a duration of 12 hours), which of the following would most likely correspond to the peak energy detected and the number of detections?

A) 51.8 ± 0.3 keV and 1320 detections
B) 51.8 ± 0.3 keV and 1935 detections
C) 54.3 ± 0.6 keV and 1320 detections
D) 54.3 ± 0.6 keV and 1935 detections

7. *Inverse Compton Scattering* occurs when photons scatter off of relativistic electrons in extremely fast-moving gases around astrophysical phenomena like black holes and gamma ray bursts. Which of the following might you expect to observe as a result of such scattering?

A) An increase in the number of electrons detected from that direction in the sky
B) An increase in the velocity of the scattered photons
C) An increase in the energy of the scattered photons
D) An increase in the relative population of radio photons to gamma ray photons

Chapter 13
Physics Practice
Section Solutions

Solutions to Freestanding Questions

1. **C**   The formula $d = v_0 t + \frac{1}{2} at^2$ is used to calculate the displacement traveled at the 5th second and at the 10th second. Express the displacement traveled at the 5th second, Δd_5, by finding the difference between the total displacement traveled in 5 seconds, d_5, by the total displacement traveled in 4 seconds, d_4. Thus, $\Delta d_5 = d_5 - d_4$. Applying the formula $d = v_0 t + \frac{1}{2} at^2$ with respect to d_5 and d_4, the equation becomes $\Delta d_5 = (v_0 t_5 + \frac{1}{2} at_5{}^2) - (v_0 t_4 + \frac{1}{2} at_4{}^2)$. Since the train was initially at rest, $v_0 = 0$. The acceleration, a, is a constant, and is equal to x,

$$\Delta d_5 = (\tfrac{1}{2} x(5)^2) - (\tfrac{1}{2} x(4)^2)$$
$$= (\tfrac{25}{2})x - (\tfrac{16}{2})x$$
$$= \frac{9x}{2}$$

Likewise, the equation for the displacement traveled at the 10th second, Δd_{10}, is as follows,

$$\Delta d_{10} = d_{10} - d_9$$
$$= (v_0 t_{10} + \tfrac{1}{2} at_{10}{}^2) - (v_0 t_9 + \tfrac{1}{2} at_9{}^2)$$

Since $v_0 = 0$, $a = x$,

$$\Delta d_5 = (\tfrac{1}{2} x(10)^2) - (\tfrac{1}{2} x(9)^2)$$
$$= (\tfrac{100}{2})x - (\tfrac{81}{2})x$$
$$= \frac{19x}{2}$$

The ratio $d_5 : d_{10}$ could be expressed as a fraction d_5/d_{10},

$$\frac{d_5}{d_{10}} = \frac{\frac{9x}{2}}{\frac{19x}{2}}$$
$$= \frac{9x}{19x}$$
$$= \frac{9}{19}$$

and therefore, the ratio $d_5 : d_{10}$ is equal to 9 : 19.

2. **A**   When calculating questions related to the center of mass, the center of mass of the plank is always taken into account unless assumed negligible. According to the scenario, mass y is 25 cm + 50 cm = 75 cm from the pivot point, whereas mass x is 25 cm on the opposite side. Therefore, if the pivot point is chosen as the origin, applying the formula for center of mass for point masses:

$$x_{cm} = \frac{(m_1 x_1 + m_2 x_2 + m_3 x_3)}{(m_1 + m_2 + m_3)}$$

$$0 = \frac{(-25x + 25m + 75y)}{(x + m + y)}$$

$$0 = \frac{25(-x + m + 3y)}{(x + m + y)}$$

Since the fraction must be equal to zero, this implies that the numerator must be equal to zero. That is, $-x + m + 3y = 0$. Solving for x, we get the equation $x = m + 3y$, which is choice A.

3. **D**   This is another two-by-two question. In a vertical circular motion, the yo-yo is under the influence of both the tension force of the string, and the gravity of the yo-yo. Therefore, its speed is not constant and increases as the yo-yo swings down and decreases as it swings up. This eliminates choices A and C. In this scenario, the weight of the yo-yo could be split into a component force that is parallel to the tension of the string, and a force perpendicular to the tension force. The net force of the tension and the parallel component of the yo-yo's weight would be the centripetal acceleration. However, the perpendicular component of gravity introduces a tangential acceleration to the yo-yo. This results in a net acceleration that does not point toward the center of the circular path.

4. **B**   This question is a bit of an oddball, but begin with the usual equations for elastic collisions. Elastic collisions are ones in which both momentum and kinetic energy are conserved, so $m_1 v_1 = m_2 v_2$ and $\frac{1}{2} m_1 v_1^2 = \frac{1}{2} m_2 v_2^2$ (already noting that the velocity of the second mass before the collision and the velocity of the first mass after the collision are both zero). These are two equations with two unknowns (m_2 and v_2), so the next step, working forwards, would be to solve them simultaneously. However, it would be easiest here to work backwards from the answers: equal masses, as in choice B, would work, since that would give that $v_1 = v_2$, and there is no reason that this shouldn't be so. If that is not apparent, proceed forwards: from the first equation, $v_1 = \frac{m_2 v_2}{m_1}$, which plugged into the second equation yields $\frac{1}{2} m_1 (\frac{m_2 v_2}{m_1})^2 = \frac{1}{2} m_2 v_2^2$. When appropriate cancellations are made, this becomes $m_1 = m_2$.

5. **D**   This is an application of Archimedes' principle, in which the magnitude of the buoyant force is equal to the weight of the fluid displaced by the object. Choices A and B can be eliminated first because the more the object is submerged in the fluid, the larger the buoyant force. In the original scenario, the wooden cube, having a volume V, has a proportion of 2 cm / 8 cm = ¼ under the surface. The original buoyant force $F_1 = \rho\,\frac{1}{4}Vg$. When pushed by the hand, the cube is now 8 cm − 2 cm = 6 cm submerged from the surface in length. This tells us that the new buoyant force is $F_2 = \rho\,\frac{3}{4}Vg$, which is three times the original magnitude of the buoyant force.

6. **A**   Since the pipes are delivering water at equal volume output per minute, the flow rate is the same in both pipes, eliminating choices C and D. According to Bernoulli's equation: $P_A + \frac{1}{2}\rho v_A^2 + \rho g y_A = P_B + \frac{1}{2}\rho v_B^2 + \rho g y_B$, and $P_A = P_B$, the equation becomes $\frac{1}{2}\rho v_A^2 + \rho g y_A = \frac{1}{2}\rho v_B^2 + \rho g y_B$. We know that $y_A > y_B$, so $v_A < v_B$. For a constant flow rate f, if $v_A < v_B$, that means that $A_A > A_B$, according to $f = Av$, which makes choice A the correct answer.

7. **C**   If the current through the 8 Ω resistor is 5 A, then the voltage across it is 40 V. This eliminates choice A as the voltage across each of the resistors in parallel is the same. If all the resistors were in series, the total resistance would be 17 Ω, leading to a voltage across each resistor approximately 3 A, which eliminates choice B. If the 6 Ω and 3 Ω resistors were in parallel this gives a resistance of 2 Ω and a total of 10 Ω. The current across the resistances would then by 5 A. Thus, the correct answer is choice C. If the 6 Ω and 3 Ω resistors are in parallel, this gives an equivalent resistance of 2 Ω for the parallel set, and a total of 10 Ω for the circuit. The current across the 8 Ω resistor and the parallel resistor set would then be 5 A. Thus, the correct answer is choice C. A similar approach can be used to figure out choice D. If the 6 Ω and 8 Ω resistors are in parallel, this gives an equivalent resistance of 24/7 ≈ 3.5 Ω, and a total of 6.5 Ω for the circuit. In this case, the current across the 3 Ω resistor and the parallel resistor set would then be approximately 7.7 A, and splitting this current between the branches of the parallel circuit would give approximately 3.3 A across the 8 Ω resistor and 4.4 A across the 6 Ω resistor. This makes choice D incorrect.

8. **B**   A charged particle that moves in a circle due to magnetic force will travel at a speed of $v = qBr/m$ (a formula which can be derived from $qvB = mv^2/r$). Since the particle must travel a distance $2\pi r$ in time T, we have $T = 2\pi m/qB$, where m is the mass of the particle, q is the charge of the particle and B is the magnetic field strength. According to this formula, if m is the mass of the proton, and q is the charge of the proton, then the mass of the alpha particle will be $4m$, and its charge will be $2q$. If we substitute these variables into the formula, the cyclotron period of the alpha particle becomes $T_\alpha = 2\pi\,(4m)/2qB = 2(2\pi m/qB) = 2T$.

9. **D**   To solve this problem, it is necessary to apply two equations simultaneously. We know that $PE = \frac{1}{2}kx^2 = 100$ J, and $F = -kx = 500$ N. Using these two equations, we know that if we multiply 500 by $\frac{1}{2}x$, it would yield a value of 100, meaning that $\frac{1}{2}x = 0.2$. Therefore, $x = 0.4$ m, or 40 cm.

10. **C** The equation for beat frequency is given by $f_{beat} = |f_1 - f_2|$. In this example, f_1 is the fourth harmonic frequency and f_2 is the third harmonic frequency, due to how the fourth harmonic is greater than the third. For a pipe with one end closed off, the resonance frequencies are calculated using the equation $f_n = nv/4L$ ($n = 1, 3, 5...$). The fourth harmonic frequency has $n = 7$, while the third harmonic frequency has $n = 5$. With these equations in mind, we begin to plug in:

$$f_{beat} = |f_{n2} - f_{n1}| = |f_7 - f_5|$$

$$f_{beat} = |[7v/4L] - [5v/4L]| = 2v/4L = v/2L$$

$$L = v/2f_{beat}$$

$$L = 340/(2 \times 680) = 0.25 \text{ m} = 25 \text{ cm}$$

Now that we have the length of the tube, we can use $f_n = nv/4L$ ($n = 1, 3, 5...$) to find the second harmonic frequency. For a tube with one end closed, the second harmonic frequency has $n = 3$.

$$f_n = nv/4L, \text{ with } n = 3$$

$$f_3 = (3 \times 340) / (4 \times 0.25) = 1020 \text{ Hz}$$

11. **B** This question has two parts to it. In the first part, the intensity (I) is inversely proportional to the area over which the sound is produced ($I = W/m^2$). Sound travels from the speaker to the student in a spherical shape. When it reaches the student, its radius has increased ten times (from 1 meter to 10 meters). Since area is proportional to r^2, the area of the sphere increases $10^2 = 100$ times. A 100-fold increase in area translates to a 100-fold decrease in intensity ($I \propto 1/\text{area}$). Since intensity is decreased by a factor of 100, which is 10×10, then the intensity level must decrease by $10 + 10 = 20$ dB. Therefore, the intensity level before the sound enters the headphones is $160 - 20 = 140$ dB. In the second part, the headphones remove 99.9% of the intensity, or the intensity is 1/1000 of the original intensity. Therefore, the intensity is decreased by a factor of 10^3, meaning the intensity level is decreased by 30 dB. The intensity level before entry into the headphones is 140 dB, so the intensity level which is heard is 140 dB − 30 dB = 110 dB.

12. **A** This question relies on an understanding of Snell's law. The light ray is first incident from the air onto the glass and then incident from the glass into the air. Since the index of refraction of the air does not change from one side of the glass to the other, the index of refraction of the glass does not change, and the angle that the light ray travels throughout the glass does not change, the angle at which the ray emerges into the air is unchanged from the angle at which it originally entered from the air. To see this proven mathematically, first take stock of the known information: the index of refraction of the air (n_1) is 1.00, the index of refraction of the glass (n_2) is 1.50, and the angle of incidence (θ_1) is 30°. Applying Snell's law for the light incident on the piece of glass from the air,

$$n_1 \sin \theta_1 = n_2 \sin \theta_2$$
$$\sin \theta_2 = n_1 \sin \theta_1 / n_2$$
$$= 1.00(\sin 30°) / 1.50$$
$$= 1/6$$

Applying Snell's law for the light incident on the air from the piece of glass,

$$n_1 \sin \theta_1 = n_2 \sin \theta_2$$
$$\sin \theta_2 = n_1 \sin \theta_1 / n_2$$
$$= 1.00 \cdot (1/6)/1.50$$
$$\theta_2 = \sin^{-1} 0.5 = 30°$$

The angle of incidence for the ray emerging is now the reversed equation. Thus, the angle of the ray emerging from the glass into the air is the same as the angle of the ray entering the glass from the air.

Solutions to Practice Passage 1

1. **B**   Since initial velocities and accelerations are given and distance and time are said to be the same, the kinematic variable neither given nor asked for is final velocity. This suggests using $d = v_0 t + \frac{1}{2} a t^2$. Since they are going to travel the same distance in the same time, d for Car 1 and d for Car 2 should be equal, so $v_{01} t + \frac{1}{2} a_1 t^2 = v_{02} t + \frac{1}{2} a_2 t^2$. One solution to this equation is $t = 0$, but that just says that the cars are in the same place when they begin moving. The question stem asks about a time for which t does not equal 0, so divide by t: $v_{01} + \frac{1}{2} a_1 t = v_{02} + \frac{1}{2} a_2 t$. Then solve for t: $t = \dfrac{2(v_{02} - v_{01})}{a_1 - a_2}$. Plug in, and $t = \dfrac{2(6-0)}{7-5} = 6$ seconds.

2. **C**   The velocity is positive and the acceleration is negative. This suggests that they are in opposite directions from each other, and an acceleration against the direction of the velocity makes an object slow down (as, for example, when an object is initially tossed straight up in the air: the velocity is up but gravity is causing a downward acceleration, so the object slows). Choice A is wrong because the table gives no information about the direction the cars are facing: they could be in reverse (or otherwise rolling backwards) as easily as rolling forwards. Choice B is wrong because it is not initially motionless, since it has an initial velocity, and the acceleration and jerk have different units and cannot be added anyway. Choice D is wrong because any non-zero acceleration is an acceleration, whether it is negative or not.

3. **D**   It is important to note that jerk is a vector, but the quantities given are magnitudes. Thus, even though choice A would be perfectly true if the accelerations given were the vector accelerations, it is not true for the magnitudes of the accelerations. The actual appearance of $\mathbf{a}_2 - \mathbf{a}_1$ as vectors would be:

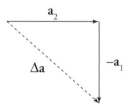

Thus, one must use the Pythagorean theorem to find the magnitude of Δa:

$(\Delta a)^2 = (a_2)^2 + (-a_1)^2$. As a result, $\Delta a = \sqrt{(a_2)^2 + (a_1)^2}$, and $j = \dfrac{\Delta a}{\Delta t} = \dfrac{\sqrt{(a_2)^2 + (a_1)^2}}{\Delta t}$.

4. **A** To convert from 3 m/s³, multiply: $\left(3\frac{m}{s^3}\right)\left(10^9 \frac{nm}{m}\right)\left(10^{-3}\frac{s}{ms}\right)^3 = 3\frac{nm}{ms^3}$. Be careful to cube the seconds-to-milliseconds conversion factor! One second is a thousand milliseconds, but one second cubed is one billion milliseconds cubed. Note: This question does not require any information from the passage.

5. **C** An intuitive way to think about this is that Car 3 gains 2 m/s² every second (that's what m/s³ means). Since there are 2 m/s² between Car 1's acceleration and Car 2's acceleration, it will take one second to close that gap. A more computational way is the following: Equation 1 can be rearranged to $\Delta a = j\Delta t$. Since $\Delta a = a_{final} - a_{initial}$ by definition, and since Car 3 is starting from an initial acceleration of zero, Car 3's acceleration, a_3, can be expressed as $a_3 = j\Delta t$. Since $j = 2$ m/s³, a_3 will equal 5 m/s² (Car 2's acceleration) after 2.5 seconds and 7 m/s² (Car 1's acceleration) after 3.5 seconds. There is a difference of 1 second between 2.5 seconds and 3.5 seconds, so it will take one second to go from Car 2's acceleration to Car 1's acceleration.

6. **A** Car 4 has a positive velocity and a negative acceleration. Without a jerk (a changing acceleration), the acceleration will continue to be negative, so the car will slow down, stop, and turn around. When it does this, its displacement will decrease for a time while its distance traveled will continue to increase. If the car travels for long enough to return back to its starting position, the displacement will be zero and the total distance traveled will be positive. After that, if the car continues to travel, the displacement will grow at the same rate as the distance traveled and never catch back up to it. The question stem specifies "a long time," which must mean long enough for the car to turn around, at which point the displacement is less than the distance. Note: choice C is impossible under any circumstances. One cannot be displaced farther from one's start than the distance that one travels.

7. **B** One way to do this question is to take it in bite-sized pieces. First, how fast is Car 2 going after it has traveled 2 m? To find this, use $v^2 = v_0^2 + 2ad$, since time is neither needed nor given and this equation does not involve time. Then $v = \sqrt{6^2 + (2)(5)(2)} = \sqrt{56}$. (Note that there is no need to find what the square root of 56 is; this number will be squared in the next equation anyway.) Next, how far has Car 1 traveled when it reaches this speed? Again, time is neither given nor asked for, so use the same equation, and solve for d:

$$d = \frac{v^2 - v_0^2}{2a} = \frac{\left(\sqrt{56}\right)^2 - 0^2}{(2)(7)} = 4 \text{ m}.$$

Solutions to Practice Passage 2

1. **B** Begin by finding the acceleration caused by the frictional force. The equation $v^2 = v_0^2 + 2ad$, when the final velocity is set to zero and when the equation is solved for a, yields that the magnitude of the acceleration is $a = \dfrac{v_0^2}{2d}$. Now apply $F_{net} = ma$: the net force is supplied by kinetic friction, so $\mu mg = ma$, and thus $a = \mu g$. Combining the two equations gives $\mu g = \dfrac{v_0^2}{2d}$ and then $\mu = \dfrac{v_0^2}{2dg}$. Plugging in $v_0 = 4$, $d = 2$, and $g = 10$ gives a result of $\mu = 0.4$. Additional note: this problem does not require any information from the passage; it is a disguised free-standing question.

2. **C** The passage states that coefficients of friction are usually lower at very high speeds. Consequently, the force of kinetic friction is lower at very high speeds. Therefore, the force required to counter kinetic friction is lower at very high speeds. Choice A is a trap, because the net force on an object at constant speed is zero, but there will be a frictional force slowing the object down, so it needs an additional push to keep going. Choice B is backwards. choice D would be true if the coefficient of friction were constant at all speeds, which is the usual approximation on the MCAT, but the passage indicates that the coefficient of friction should not be considered constant here.

3. **D** Since the object is sliding, it is experiencing a kinetic friction force, which is equal to μF_N. Since it is not accelerating vertically, the sum of the forces in the vertical direction is zero, which means that the normal force upwards initially balances only the weight of the object downwards (that is, $F_N = w$). Thus, the force of kinetic friction is μw, which equals 20μ. After the additional pressing down, the normal force balances the weight and the extra downward force, so the force of kinetic friction is $(\mu)(20 + 40)$, which equals 60μ. That's three times as large, so the new force must be 18 N, three times as large as it was before. (One could solve for what the coefficient of friction actually is to cause this force, which is 0.3, but it is not necessary to do so in this case; proportions are sufficient here.) Additional note: this problem does not require any information from the passage; it is a disguised free-standing question.

4. **A** This is an inclined plane problem involving a flat tilted surface. From typical inclined plane analysis, the forces on the pot parallel to the plane are $mg \sin\theta$ down the plane and static friction up the plane. Right before the pot starts to slide, static friction is at its maximum and the two forces are equal, so $mg \sin\theta = \mu mg \cos\theta$, which yields that $\mu = \tan\theta$. From Table 1, the coefficient of static friction between zinc and cast iron is 0.85. Compare this to $\tan(45°)$, which is equal to 1; 0.85 is smaller, so the angle must be less than 45°. Thus, it must be $\tan(40°)$, since 40° is the only choice less than 45° available.

5. **B** This is a two-by-two question: two answer choices say that the coefficient of friction is lower and two say that it is higher, and two answer choices say that the operative friction is static and the other two say that it is kinetic. First, the coefficient of friction is lower on an icy road. As the passage indicates, the coefficient of friction is usually a measure of roughness, and icy roads are smoother than non-icy roads. Also, the question stem says that cars are more likely to slip on the ice, and rolling objects slip because the frictional force does not

provide enough torque to keep the objects rolling; here, the force is reduced because the coefficient of friction drops. This eliminates choices C and D. Second, the first paragraph of the passage indicates that objects that are rolling without slipping are being moved by static friction, so static friction is the relevant type here, eliminating choice A.

6. **C** First, decipher the wording of the question. The variable F_x refers to the amount of force required to initiate horizontal movement, which means the force required to overcome static friction. The force to overcome static friction is equal to the maximum force of static friction, μF_N, which in turn is equal to μw. The ratio that several of the answer choices talk about is $F_x{:}w$, which is $\mu w{:}w$, which is the same thing as $\mu{:}1$. In other words, all that this question is asking is what happens to the coefficient of friction as more weight is added to the rubber object. Now, refer to the passage: Equation 1 describes how the coefficient of friction changes for rubber when more force is applied to the surface. In particular, the reciprocal of the coefficient of friction increases linearly with the applied force, so the coefficient of friction must decrease with applied force; more weight means less coefficient of friction. Therefore the ratio goes down.

7. **B** Begin by referring to the passage. PTFE is mentioned in the table, and it has a coefficient of friction of 0.04, which is much lower than anything else in the table. The answer is likely to have to do with this low coefficient of friction. A might be tempting because it suggests that PTFE is not very toxic, but lack of toxicity itself is not a major reason why PTFE is applied to cookware; any other non-toxic substance might equally be applied if that were its only useful property. Choice B addresses the low coefficient of friction and at least is physically possible, because low coefficients of friction enable sliding more easily than high coefficients of friction, and easy sliding means less sticking. Choice C is non-physical: low friction means less heat generated by friction, not less heat lost to friction. Choice D is off-topic; this may or may not have anything to do with cooking.

Solutions to Practice Passage 3

1. **A** If we use the center of mass coordinate system mentioned in the passage, X_{COM} would be 0 and either x_1 or x_2 would be negative and the other would be positive (note that x_1 and x_2 represent coordinates rather than distances). An easier way of finding the distance from the center of mass to x_1 would be to move the origin to the location of m_1 and then find the distance from the new origin to the center of mass. Therefore, $X_{COM} = [(0)(m_1) + (a)(m_2)]/(m_1 + m_2)$, which equals $am_2/(m_1 + m_2)$ or $a/(1 + m_1/m_2)$.

Alternatively, consider extreme cases: if m_1 is small compared to m_2, then the center of mass should be near the other (much larger) mass, and the answer should be near a: the distance between object m_1 and the center of mass (the origin) should be close to the distance between the objects. This is possible in choice A, since a small m_1 gives approximately $1a / (1 + 0)$. A small m_1 in choice B gives an infinite distance, which is not right, so it can be eliminated. A small m_1 in choice C gives approximately a. A small m_1 in choice D gives zero distance, which is also not right; eliminate this, too. At this point, only choices A and C remain. Next, consider a large m_1: the answer should be near 0, because the origin should be approximately at the large mass. Choice A still yields the correct answer, but choice C gives infinity for a large m_1, so it cannot be right.

2. **B** This is a proportions question, albeit a strange one. Equation 2 relates orbital radius (*a*, according to the text of the passage preceding the equation) and period (*P*). The relationship is: $P^2 = ka^3$, if all the constants in the equation are set equal to *k*. For Planet X, which has a radius of *R*, the period is: $P_X = \sqrt{kR^3}$. For Planet Y, which has a radius of 4*R*, this gives: $P_Y^2 = k(4R)^3 = 64kR^3$. Thus, the period of Planet Y is: $P_Y = \sqrt{64kR^3} = \sqrt{64} \times \sqrt{kR^3} = 8 \times \sqrt{kR^3}$. This is 8 times as large as the period of Planet X.

3. **B** Use Process of Elimination. Choice A is wrong because there is no torque from planets on the Sun. They interact gravitationally, and in the equation for torque, $\tau = rF \sin\theta$, *r* is from the planet to the Sun and *F* acts from the Sun to the planet; these are anti-parallel, so $\theta = 180°$ and sin 180° = 0. (As an aside, all planets in the Solar System orbit in the same direction, so even if their motions could somehow exert torque, this still wouldn't be true.) Choice B is correct because the Sun is much larger than the other masses (the next largest mass listed in the passage is Jupiter, and it has only 1/1000th the mass of the Sun) and therefore the center of mass will be very near its center. Furthermore, if the center of mass is fixed, and the Sun is near the center of mass, the Sun must be nearly fixed as well. Choice C is almost right, but by Newton's third law (action-reaction pairs), the Sun feels the same force from each of the planets as each planet does from it; this answer would be true (and correct) if it said that the Sun does not accelerate nearly as much, because of its greater mass. Choice D is wrong because, first, the reduced mass is a mathematical construct and can't change the nature of reality; it can't orbit in place of something else. Second, there is no such thing as "the reduced mass of the Sun" anyway; the reduced mass is calculated based on two objects, so there could be a reduced mass of the Sun and the Earth, but not just the Sun.

4. **C** Since the satellite orbits in approximately a circle, there is a centripetal force present. The only force of note here is gravitation, so gravity must supply the centripetal force. Therefore, $G\dfrac{Mm}{r^2} = \dfrac{mv^2}{r}$. Canceling and rearranging, the mass of Saturn is given by $M = \dfrac{v^2 r}{G}$. Since the answer choices are so dramatically apart in size, it is easiest to round all coefficients to the nearest integer: $M = \dfrac{(8\times10^3)^2(5\times10^8)}{7\times10^{-11}}$. Working out the arithmetic yields 5×10^{26} kg, which is close enough to choice C. (More exact calculations with the given numbers result in a number closer to 6.) Note: This question can be solved almost independently of the passage, except for fetching the value of *G* from the final paragraph. However, as a quick check, one could also compare to the given value of Jupiter's mass, since Jupiter is also described as a gas giant, and choice C is about half the mass given for Jupiter, which is reasonable. Choice A is doubtful, since it is less than the given mass of the Earth, and so is choice D, which is close to the given mass of the Sun.

5.   **C**   Plug 2's into the equation for reduced mass, Equation 1: $\mu = \dfrac{(2m_1)(2m_2)}{(2m_1)+(2m_2)}$. Next, factor and reduce: $\mu = \dfrac{(4)m_1 m_2}{(2)(m_1+m_2)} = 2\dfrac{m_1 m_2}{m_1+m_2}$. This shows that the reduced mass doubles. Be careful not to select choice B! Even though both numerator and denominator contain m_1 and m_2, the 2's do not cancel, because the terms are multiplied in the numerator but added in the denominator.

6.   **A**   Consider what would have to hold for objects to move in straight lines with constant speed in center-of-mass coordinates. This is certainly normal behavior, under Newton's first law, but the limitation on Newton's first law is that it only applies to a coordinate system that is not accelerating. As viewed from inside a car going around a turn, for example, objects will not move with constant velocity even if they have no net force on them. This suggests that the answer is "yes," and the reason is that the center of mass that defines the origin is not accelerating. This best matches choice A. Alternatively, consider Process of Elimination: eliminate choice B because the "all" is extreme, which should make you suspicious (and, indeed, the principle of inertia only applies in non-accelerating coordinate systems). Eliminate choice C because the justification given, while true, is not relevant: the reduced mass moves under the influence of gravity, even in center-of-mass coordinates, so it feels a net force. Eliminate choice D because both halves are wrong: any object can exist in center-of-mass coordinates, though the passage suggests that it is most useful to examine hypothetical objects in them, and the whole point of using these hypothetical objects is that they do obey physical laws.

7.   **C**   This question asks for the period of Jupiter's orbit, which is what Equation 2 describes. Plug in the given numbers, all rounded to the nearest integer coefficient (and since the mass of the Sun is so much larger than the mass of Jupiter, use the Sun's mass for the total mass):

$P^2 = \dfrac{(4)(3)^2}{(7\times10^{-11})(2\times10^{30})}(8\times10^{11})^3$. The task here is to approximate what this is. One way to do this is to compute the numerator, re-group the denominator, and consider 8×10^{11} fairly close to 10×10^{11}: $P^2 = \dfrac{(36)(10^{12})^3}{7\times2\times10^{-11}\times10^{30}}$. Next, $36/7$ is nearly 5, and $(10^{12})^3 = 10^{36}$ $= 10\times10^{35}$, so this simplifies to $P^2 = \dfrac{25\times10^{35}}{10^{-11}\times10^{30}} = 25\times10^{16}$. Thus, $P = 5\times10^8$ seconds, which (given the conversion between seconds and years in the question stem) is between 10 and 20 years. Thus, the correct answer is choice C.

Solutions to Practice Passage 4

1. **A**   This question can be tackled using the work-energy theorem. That is, the change in gravitational potential energy is the opposite of the work done by gravitational force. Be sure to read the question carefully and use Jack's information; further, his weight is given not his mass. In order to use the formula, we must calculate his altitude when he is at the top of the hill: $\sin 30° = h/450$, and $h = 450 \sin 30° = 225$ m. Then we can plug this information into the work-energy theorem.

    $$W_{Jack} = -W_{gravity} = \Delta PE = mgh = (900)(225) = 202.5 \text{ kJ}$$

2. **A**   This is another straight calculation question. Recall the formula for power and the formula for work: $P = W/t$. To calculate the work done by Jill, we need to determine how high up the hill she went. Since we know the time it took for her to do the entire trip, we can use the height of the hill, $h = 225$ m. Now, we can calculate the work done by Jill. $W_{Jill} = -W_{gravity} = \Delta PE = mgh = (450)(225) = 101,250$ J $= 101.25$ kJ. Next, we calculate how much time was used by Jill to climb the hill. The passage states that it took Jill half the time it took Jack to climb the hill. Therefore, she took 1.5 minutes or 90 seconds in total. Thus, Jill's power output is $P = W/t = 101,250/90 = 1125$ W $= 1.125$ kW. Choice B is incorrect because it uses the wrong height of the hill. (It uses the length given in the passage as the height of the hill.) Choice C is incorrect because it uses the time (in minutes, not seconds) given in the passage (3 minutes) as the time that Jill spent going up the hill; be careful when reading a passage not just to use the numbers that are given. Choice D is incorrect because it uses the time for Jill to go up the hill, but in minutes not seconds (1.5 minutes).

3. **C**   We need to calculate the total time for the "round trip" for the penny being dropped and then the sound being heard by Jill. Let t_1 be the time it takes for the penny to hit the water below. Note that this is only part of the trip. The penny is dropped under gravity, so its speed can be calculated using the kinematics equation:

    $$d = v_0 t_1 + \tfrac{1}{2} a t_1^2$$
    $$15 = 0 + \tfrac{1}{2} g t_1^2$$
    $$15 = 5 t_1^2$$
    $$t_1^2 = 3$$
    $$t_1 = 1.73$$

    Given that the sound would have to travel back to Jill's ear the total time would be slightly more than 1.73 sec (choice C). However, to be more accurate, one can calculate the time it takes for the sound to travel from the bottom of the well up to Jill's ear.

    Recall the formula for speed $= d/t$. Let t_2 be the time it takes for the sound to reach Jill's ear after the penny hits the water: $t_2 = d / v_{sound} = 15/340 = 0.04 \text{ s}$. Thus, the total time for the trip is about 1.77 sec. Choice A is incorrect because it only accounts for one direction of the sound to travel back to Jill's ear. Choice B is incorrect because it only uses the speed of sound for the calculation of the total trip time and does not account for the fact that the time for the penny to drop is different than the time it takes for the splash sound to travel back to Jill's ear. Choice D is incorrect because it only takes into account the time it takes for the penny to drop and hit the water and then incorrectly assumes it takes the same amount of time for the sound to travel back to Jill's ear.

4. **D** This question relies on us remembering that perfectly inelastic collisions involve the two objects that collide sticking together afterwards. When Jack and Jill collide, it is a perfectly inelastic collision since they slide down the hill together. Thus, total momentum is conserved but total kinetic energy is not conserved. Let Object 1 be Jill and Object 2 be Jack. The total momentum before the collision must be equal to the total momentum after the collision.

$\mathbf{P}_{\text{total before}} = \mathbf{P}_{\text{total after}}$, or $m_1 v_1 + m_2 v_2 = (m_1 + m_2) v_3$

Since Jack was at rest when Jill collided into him, the second term on the left hand side of the equation is 0. Also, we are given the weights of Jack and Jill and must convert these to masses (divide by 10 m/s² for gravity). The equation reduces down to

$$45v_1 = (45 + 90)v_3$$

$$v_1 = 135v_3/45 = 3v_3$$

To determine v_3, we can use the length of time they slide down the hill, 10 s, and the coefficient of friction, 0.8. The total distance that they slide down the hill can be calculated based on the length of the hill (that is, 450 m), where Jack started his tumble (440 m of the way down), and how far Jack tumbled (6 m). Therefore, Jack and Jill slide down the hill for 450 − 440 − 6 = 4 m. We can calculate the amount of work done by friction to stop the pair.

$$W_{\text{by friction}} = Fd$$
$$= (\mu mg \cos \theta)d$$

Then we use the Work-Energy Theorem to calculate the speed of the pair.

$$W_{\text{by friction}} = \Delta KE = \tfrac{1}{2}mv_3^2 = (\mu mg \cos \theta)d$$
$$v_3 = \sqrt{2(\mu mg \cos \theta)d}$$
$$= \sqrt{2(0.1)(10)(4)\cos 30°}$$
$$= \sqrt{8 \cos 30°}$$
$$= \sqrt{6.9}$$
$$= 2.6 \ m/s$$

Now this information can be put back into the original equation and the speed of Jill estimated.

$$v_1 = 3v_3 = 3\,(2.6) = 8 \text{ m/s}$$

5. **A** Gravitational potential energy is only meaningful in terms of a reference point and then we gain potential energy the higher we go from that point and we lose potential energy the lower we go from that point. Jill starts her trip at the bottom of the hill ($PE_{\text{initial}} = 0$), then climbs up the hill ($PE_{\text{hill}} = mgh$), her potential energy at the top of the hill is 101,250 kJ as calculated in Question 2. However, then she comes back down the hill, and she returns to her initial height (0 m). Therefore, her change in potential energy of her initial position compared to her final position is choice A (0 J) since the positions are the same. Remember that gravity is a conservative force, which means it depends only on position and not the path Jill has taken to climb up and down the hill.

6. **B** This is a two-by-two graph question. Looking at the graphs, the first half of graph A and graph C are the same, whereas the first half of graph B and D are the same. The latter half of graph A and B are the same and the latter half of graph C and D are the same. Looking back at the question, we see that Jill arrives up to the summit first (in half the time it takes for Jack to make it up the hill). Thus we can eliminate graphs A and C. Looking at graphs B and D, the difference lies in whether Jack and Jill have the same potential energy at the end of their trip when they reach the bottom of the hill. At the very end, they do indeed have the same potential energy (their heights above the ground are both 0 m); however up until the very end of their trip, they both have their individual potential energies with Jill's being less given her smaller mass. Thus, graph B is the best choice. Note that it does not matter that both Jack and Jill are moving down the hill at the same rate at the end (they collided) since we can still graph each of their individual potential energies.

7. **B** This question can be solved using either the kinematics Big 5 equations or using the Conservation of Energy with the same result.

Using kinematics:

$v^2 = v_0^2 + 2ad$, where v_0 is 0 m/s, $a = g = 10$ m/s^2, and $d =$ the depth of the well (15 m):

$$v = \sqrt{0 + 2gd} = \sqrt{2(10)(15)} = \sqrt{300} = 17 \tfrac{m}{s}.$$

Using the Conservation of Energy:

Since the penny is dropped, its initial *KE* is 0 J. We can call the point where it hits the water the point where the height is baseline (0 m) so we can say its *PE* at that point is 0 J. Thus,

$$KE_i + PE_i = KE_f + PE_f$$

$$PE_i = KE_f$$

$$mgh = \tfrac{1}{2}mv^2$$

$$gh = \tfrac{1}{2}v^2$$

$$v = \sqrt{2gh} = \sqrt{2(10)(15)} = \sqrt{300} = 17 \text{ m/s}$$

Solutions to Practice Passage 5

1. **A** For the glucose solution to enter the bloodstream, its gauge pressure must be at least as large as the gauge pressure within the artery. Hydrostatic gauge pressure is ρgd, where ρ is the density of the fluid (which equals the specific gravity of the fluid times the density of water), g is acceleration due to gravity, and d is the depth of the fluid. Therefore, 1.33×10^4 Pa = $(1.02)(1000$ kg/m$^3)(10$ m/s$^2)(h)$. Solving for h we get approximately 1.30 m, which is choice A. Note that choices B and D can be eliminated since we expect the answer to be less than 1.33 times ten to the something. Also, as a practical matter, choices C and D could be eliminated since 13 m is very large.

2. **C** Item I is false: Equation 1 describes the pressure drop per length in an artery. It varies directly with viscosity, therefore a decrease in viscosity would *decrease* the pressure drop per length (choices A and D can be eliminated). Item II is false: In a similar fashion, since R is in the denominator, widening the artery would also decrease $\Delta P/L$ (choice B can be eliminated). Item III is true: Increasing the flow rate also increases $\Delta P/L$ (choice C is correct).

3. **A** Choice C can be eliminated because we expect the answer to be at an extreme location, a node or antinode. Choice D can be eliminated given that an increase in pressure indicates the individual pressure amplitudes must have added together, which corresponds to a pressure antinode. A pressure antinode occurs at a displacement node, which is choice A.

4. **C** The equation relating pressure and fluid speed is Bernoulli's Equation. Since the syringe is horizontal, the potential energy term can be neglected: $P_{barrel} + (1/2)\rho v_{barrel}^2 = P_{needle} + (1/2)\rho v_{needle}^2$. Also, since the area of the barrel is so much larger than the area of the needle, then v_{barrel} is negligible (due to the continuity equation, $A_1 v_1 = A_2 v_2$). Therefore, $(1/2)\rho v_{needle}^2 = P_{barrel} - P_{needle}$ which is equal to the force on the plunger divided by the area. So $(1/2)(1000$ kg/m$^3)(v_{needle})^2 = (5$ N$)/(25 \times 10^{-6}$ m$^2)$. Thus, $v_{needle} = 20$ m/s, which is choice C.

5. **C** The continuity equation states that $A_1 v_1 = A_2 v_2$. If the diameter decreases by one third its previous value, it is now 2/3 of its previous value. The area is therefore $(2/3)^2 = 4/9$ its previous value. Because A and v are inversely proportional, v is now 9/4 its previous value.

6. **B** The passage states that a blood vessel collapses when the pressure drops too low. It follows that the more rapidly pressure drops, the higher the frequency of collapse. Equation 1 shows which factors cause a drop in pressure. More blood being pumped from the heart increases the flow rate, which in turn increases the pressure drop per length, making choice B the correct answer. Choices C and D concern density, which does not appear in Equation 1.

7. **A** The equation that relates potential energy and capacitance is $PE = (1/2)CV^2$. Since we're looking for the minimum capacitance, we need to use the minimum value of PE, 100 Joules. 100 J $= (1/2)(C)(1000)^2$, so $C = 2 \times 10^{-4}$ F or 200 μF.

Solutions to Practice Passage 6

1. **D**   Because the field is directed inward toward the wire, the charge must be negative, eliminating choices A and B. Find the magnitude of the charge density using Equation 1:

$$E = \frac{2k\lambda}{r} \rightarrow \lambda = \frac{rE}{2k} = \frac{10^{-1}(900)}{2(9 \times 10^9)} = 0.5 \times 10^{-8} = 5 \times 10^{-9} \frac{C}{m}$$

2. **A**   In order for the sphere to float, it must be in translational equilibrium, so the force of gravity is equal and opposite the electrostatic repulsion from the plate. Note also that the problem asks for the charge to mass ratio: you should get in the habit of writing out such ratios algebraically when you read them so that you don't lose track of what you're being asked to find. Using equation 1 and $F = qE$, we have $F_{grav} = F_E \rightarrow m_0 g = Q_0(2\pi k\sigma) \rightarrow \frac{Q_0}{m_0} = \frac{g}{2\pi k\sigma}$.

3. **A**   This problem essentially asks for the graph of Equation 2 and for the graph of $PE = q\phi$. If you know what the graph of the natural log looks like, you can immediately get the answer (note the negative sign). If not, process of elimination removes choice B on the basis of the negative charge of the electron (meaning that the graphs of PE and ϕ must trend in opposite directions), choice C because the electron will be *attracted* to the positive line of charge (and therefore PE should *decrease* as r decreases), and choice D because straight lines don't fit the logarithmic form of Equation 2.

4. **B**   Conservation of energy yields the solution to this problem: don't let the fact that kinetic energy goes as the square of speed confuse you, because the functional dependence mentioned in this problem is distance from the plate, not speed. $\Delta PE + \Delta KE = 0 \rightarrow q\Delta\phi + KE_f = 0 \rightarrow KE_f = -q(-2\pi k\sigma d) = 2\pi qk\sigma d$, so kinetic energy is linearly proportional to distance d.

5. **D**   A randomly chosen dipole will not be aligned parallel or perpendicular to the radial electric field emitted by the charged rod. The oppositely charged end of the dipole will be attracted to the rod, and the like-charged end will be repelled. Because one end in this randomly aligned dipole will be closer to the rod than the other, the fact that the field strength drops off as radial distance from the rod means that there will be a net force on the dipole. Because the randomly aligned dipole is not already parallel to the field, there will also be a net torque.

6.   This is a uniform circular motion problem, with the centripetal force being provided by the interaction of the orbiting charge with the electric field of the line of charge (note that you cannot legitimately set $KE = PE$ to find the value of mv^2, which would lead to choice D, because there is no reason those values should be equal even though energy is conserved). $F_E = qE = \frac{2k\lambda q_0}{r} = \frac{m_0 v^2}{r} \rightarrow v = \sqrt{\frac{2k\lambda q_0}{m_0}}$. With speed, one can

determine the orbital period T by recalling the basic relation: distance = rate × time.

$T = \dfrac{2\pi r}{v} = \dfrac{2\pi r}{\sqrt{2k\lambda q_0 / m_0}} = 2\pi r \sqrt{\dfrac{m_0}{2k\lambda q_0}}$. Note that choices A and B could be eliminated on

the basis of the units not working out to seconds (choice A uses the area of a circle instead of

circumference, and choice B neglects to include the charge of the orbiting particle).

7. C There are two equally appropriate approaches to this problem, both of which make use of

the fact that the work done by the field equals $-\Delta PE = -q\Delta\phi = qV$ ($\Delta\phi$ is negative going

from the positive to the negative plate). Note that this value must turn out positive in this

case because the positive charge is moving in the direction of the force acting on it: we can

thus ignore the signs in subsequent equations to avoid complication (more pragmatically,

all the answer choices are positive). One approach is to consider the capacitor equations:

$W = qV = 10^{-9}\left(\dfrac{Q}{C}\right) = 10^{-9}\left(\dfrac{\sigma A}{\kappa\varepsilon_0 \, A/d}\right) = 10^{-9}\dfrac{\sigma d}{\varepsilon_0} = \dfrac{10^{-9}\times 10^{-4}\times 10^{-3}}{8.85\times 10^{-12}} \approx 1.1\times 10^{-5}\,\text{J}.$

Note the use of $\kappa = 1$ for air. Another approach is simply to use $-q\Delta\phi$ directly with Equa-

tion 4, recognizing the sign difference in σ between the two plates:

$$-q\Delta\phi = -10^{-9}\left[-2\pi k\sigma d - (2\pi k\sigma d)\right] = 10^{-9}(4\pi k\sigma d)$$
$$\approx 12 \cdot 9(10^{-9}\cdot 10^{9}\cdot 10^{-4}\cdot 10^{-3}) = 108\times 10^{-7}$$
$$\approx 1.1\times 10^{-5}\,\text{J}$$

Solutions to Practice Passage 7

1. A The positrons are lightweight particles like electrons, so they will leave long thin tracks.
This eliminates choices C and D. Due to the decrease in the radius of curvature after crossing the plate we can tell that the direction of the Track 1 is up and Track 2 is down. Using
the right hand rule, and that the magnetic field points into the page, we see that a positive
charge moving down would curve to the right. This eliminates choice B, leaving A as the
correct answer.

2. B This is a two-by-two question meaning that there are two different quantities in the answer

and two choices for each quantity. The best way to solve these questions is to solve the easy

quantity first eliminating two of the choices. In this case the easy quantity is the track

length. The passage states that heavier particles will interact more strongly and thus come to a stop more quickly. Thus the proton will leave a shorter track, eliminating choices A and D. Setting the kinetic energies equal we have $\frac{1}{2} m_p v_p^2 = \frac{1}{2} m_e v_e^2$, giving $v_p = \sqrt{\frac{m_e}{m_p}} v_e$. Thus $m_p v_p = \sqrt{m_p \cdot m_e} \cdot v_e > m_e v_e$ and the proton moves in a larger radius because its momentum is larger.

3. **D** The passage states that charged particles ionize the vapor and leaves tracks. The neutron is neutral so it won't ionize the vapor and will leave no track; also, it would not curve in the magnetic field. Therefore the correct answer is D.

4. **B** If the electric field is pointing left to right, then positive charges will move to the right while negative charges will move to the left. Track 1 is moving upwards (the radius of curvature is smaller above the plate); using the right hand rule we see that it is positive. Since it is positive it would move to the right under the electric field, thus switching directions (this eliminates choices A and C; they don't include Track 1 switching directions). Using the same analysis we see that Track 2 is negative, and that both Tracks 3 and 4 are positive. Thus Track 2 will still curve to the left and Tracks 3 and 4 will still curve to the right. Thus, the correct answer is choice B.

5. **A** This is another two-by-two question. The electric field points from left to right so a negatively charged particle will be pulled to the left by the electric field. For the particle to move in a straight line the net force on it must be zero so the magnetic force must point to the right. Using the right hand rule and flipping directions (or using the left hand rule) the negatively charged particle must be moving upwards. This eliminates choices C and D. Setting the electric force equal to the magnetic force we have $qE = qvB$. This gives $v = E/B$.

6. **A** There is no way to derive this formula from the information we have so we have to eliminate answers that contradict the information in the passage. Choice B can be eliminated because it has the distance in the denominator. The farther the particle travels through the vapor the more energy it will lose. The passage states that heavier particles and particles with more charge interact more strongly and lose their energy sooner, so choice C can be eliminated because it has the mass in the denominator and choice D can be eliminated because it has the charge in the denominator. Therefore, the correct answer must be choice A.

7. **C** The alpha particle consists of two protons and two neutrons. Since the alpha particle is heavier and has more charge than the proton, it will leave a thicker and shorter track. Both Items II and III are true, eliminating choices A and B. Since they have the same momentum, the only thing influencing the radius of curvature is the charge. Since the alpha particle has more charge its radius of curvature is smaller, meaning Item I is false, eliminating choice D. The correct answer is choice C.

Solutions to Practice Passage 8

1. **A** One should not typically rely on figures for precise answers, but Figure 2 does reveal that the period of oscillation is at least approximately constant. The key to this question is to notice that the term inside the argument of the cosine is of the form (ωt), or a constant (for any given set of values k, b, and m) times t, and thus the frequency of the cosine is itself constant ($\omega/2\pi$).

2. **B** Equilibrium occurs when the net force acting on the system is zero. Thus to find the equilibrium length of a spring with a hanging mass, we find the displacement Δs for which the restoring force of the spring equals the weight of the mass. This give us $k\Delta s = mg \rightarrow \Delta s = \frac{mg}{k}$. Adding this to the equilibrium length of the unencumbered hanging spring L gives the correct answer.

3. **B** As always, slope is rise over run, which in this case yields y/t. Taking the units of this quantity we find $[y]/[t] = $ m/s, which are of course the units of velocity.

4. **A** This is a slight variation on the classic two-by-two Process of Elimination question, because in this case the amplitude decays either more or less rapidly than in the experimental set up with a less viscous liquid, whereas the frequency can, among the choices, decrease, increase, or remain the same. The passage defines b, the *damping coefficient*, as "a measure of the frictional effects on the system due to the movement of the submerged plate through the fluid." Because a more viscous liquid provides greater fluid friction, b should increase with increased viscosity. A larger b means a larger negative exponent in Equation 3, meaning a more rapid decrease in amplitude. It also means a smaller coefficient of t in the argument of the cosine function (because the term containing b is subtracted from k/m), which means a lower frequency of oscillation.

5. **C** The total mechanical energy of a harmonic oscillator, the sum of its kinetic and potential energies at any time t, is equal to its maximum potential energy at that time t, or $\frac{1}{2}kA_t^2$ (this is just another way of saying that the energy in an oscillating system like a wave goes as the square of the amplitude). For the case of a simple harmonic oscillator, that energy is constant because amplitude is constant, but for this damped harmonic oscillator the amplitude varies as the exponential term in Equation 3. The question asks at what time the energy will be one quarter its original value, which means we are looking for the time at which the amplitude will be half its original value (the square root of a quarter). Thus we have

    $$Ae^{-bt/2m} = \frac{1}{2}A \rightarrow \ln(e^{-bt/2m}) = \ln(\frac{1}{2}) = -\ln(2) \rightarrow \frac{bt}{2m} = \ln(2) \rightarrow t = \frac{2m\ln(2)}{b}.$$

    Note that choice A corresponds to the time at which the oscillator first crosses its equilibrium length (that is, when cosine is zero).

6. **D** The rate of decay of the amplitude of oscillations is determined by the exponential term, which contains b and m but not k. Thus the stiffness of the spring has no effect on the amplitude. Choices B and C, changing the area of the plate or draining the liquid from the tank, would each alter the value of b.

7.   C   If the hanging mass is not interacting with the liquid in the container, we can approximate its motion as simple harmonic. Thus we use Equation 1 in the passage and simply plug in given values for k and m (the given value for A does not influence our answer because for simple harmonic motion, period is independent of amplitude). We have the following:

$$T = 2\pi\sqrt{\frac{4}{100}} \approx 6\sqrt{\frac{1}{25}} = \frac{6}{5} = 1.2 \text{ seconds.}$$

Solutions to Practice Passage 9

1.   C   The passage defines the scattering angle as "the angle between the photon's original path and its path after the collision." Drawing a continuation of any original path in the diagram shows that $\theta/2$ is the supplement of this angle.

2.   A   After any collision with an object at rest, a moving object will lose energy (that Compton scattering is elastic simply guarantees that this lost energy will be imparted to the second object). Thus when the green photons collide with the at-rest electrons, they must lose energy and thus decrease in frequency according to $E = hf$. Blue photons have a higher frequency than green photons (ROYGBV), and thus could not result from such a scattering. All other choices correctly correspond to an energy loss after scattering.

3.   B   The maximum value of $\Delta\lambda$ will occur at the maximum value for $(1 - \cos\phi)$, as that is the term in Equation 1 subject to change for a given incident wavelength. Because cosine varies between 1 and −1 inclusive, the maximum value of this term is 2, hence the answer is twice the fractional coefficient.

4.   D   This problem can be solved using process of elimination. Choice A is wrong because there is nothing in the passage to indicate that Compton scattering occurs with any regularity in the air (indeed there are far fewer free electrons in air than on the surface of a metal, making Compton scattering that much less likely). Moreover, the scintillation detector is designed to detect photons, not electrons. Choice B is wrong because the desired scattering angle is achieved by the experimental set up using the circular arced target. Choice C is wrong because cosmic rays would arrive at the detector from all directions above the experimental surface with equal probability, so placing the shield between the Am-241 source and the detector would not especially screen them out (if the problem had said that the lead shield formed a dome over the detector, choice C could be a viable choice). Choice D is correct because the experimenter desires not to allow photons leaving the Am-241 source to enter the detector directly without first scattering off the target.

5.   A   The rate of scattering events can be determined by taking the ratio of number of detections to the duration over which those detections occurred. The ratio of 1242 : 4 hours is greater than any of the remaining three ratios.

6. **B**   This is a classic two-by-two MCAT question, in which the two differing options are the peak energy and the number of detections (the error factor is a trap—there is no information explicitly in the passage or table to indicate how it arises). Because the trend in peak energies is steadily decreasing as scattering angle increases, one should interpolate that the peak energy at 105° will fall between the peak energies at 90° and 120°, thus eliminating choices C and D. Determining the likely number of detections requires looking at the ratio between detection number and experimental duration. For a 12-hour run, one would expect about 1.5 times as many detections as in an 8 hour run at a scattering similar angle. Picking a number of detections between 1411 and 1206 (say around 1300) and multiplying that by 1.5 yields 1950, which is closest to 1935.

7. **C**   This can be solved by process of elimination. Choice A is wrong because there is nothing to suggest that electrons are more or less likely to come from one part of the sky than another due to these phenomena, both because scattering events would not push electrons in any privileged direction and because the question mentions electrons in gases moving *around* astrophysical phenomena (as opposed to radially outward from them). Choice B is wrong because the velocity of photons is simply the speed of light, irrespective of scattering (which changes frequency, not velocity). Differentiating between choices C and D requires more careful consideration of what makes *inverse* Compton scattering different from what the passage has previously discussed. The key is to recognize in the words "relativistic" and "extremely fast moving" that, rather than approximating these scatterings (as we do with normal Compton scattering) as elastic collisions between moving photons and stationary electrons, for inverse Compton scattering we treat the electrons as moving extremely fast and therefore having much more energy than the photons with which they are colliding (because electrons have mass and therefore kinetic energy, as opposed to photons which have energy only due to their frequency). The point is that these collisions will *impart* energy to the photons rather than remove it, and thus choice C is correct and choice D, which would imply the opposite effect, is wrong.

Chapter 14
General Chemistry on the MCAT

General Chemistry makes up approximately 50 percent of the Physical Sciences section. Unlike Physics however, MCAT G-Chem does not require you to memorize a large number of equations. In general, if an equation is required to answer a G-Chem question, it is provided in the passage.

In fact, the majority of questions in the G-Chem part of the test are not based on rote memory. About 75 percent of the General Chemistry questions require you to retrieve information from the passage and use some deductive reasoning skills. Thus, in order to succeed in this section, you not only need solid knowledge of fundamental principles of chemistry, but also strong critical reasoning and reading comprehension skills. These three components may be stressed differently depending on the passage type.

PASSAGE TYPES AS THEY APPLY TO G-CHEM

Information/Situation Presentation

These passages assume knowledge of basic scientific concepts, and also present new information that builds on these basic concepts. The new information may be presented in a way that is very similar to how it would appear in a textbook or other scientific reference. The questions may be about basic scientific facts that you already know, but often the passage will present topics or subtopics with which you are unfamiliar. Information/Situation Presentation passages can be intimidating, as they often explore topics in a greater level of detail than the scope of your MCAT preparation. However, keep in mind that the whole point of these types of passages is to force you to use critical reasoning and apply your basic scientific knowledge to new topics. It is not to see how much advanced scientific coursework you have memorized. Therefore, it is important when you see a passage on, say, molecular orbital theory, that you don't think to yourself, "Oh no!! I forgot to study molecular orbital theory!!!" Rather, look at the information in the passage, and consider how your knowledge about more basic chemical concepts, such as electron configurations, can be applied in order to answer the questions. The new information in the passage can supplement your basic knowledge.

This type of passage may also present information in the context of a specific situation, such as the results of a research study or an experiment. In this case, the questions may ask you to distinguish between data that supports or refutes the result being presented. In some passages, an apparently contradictory or erroneous result is presented and questions may ask what mistakes could have been made over the course of the experiment to cause such a result. Thus, these passages require to you think critically about the importance of each chemical and physical element of an experiment. Note however, that they do not present the steps of an experiment in great detail; that style is reserved for Experiment/Research Presentation passages.

Experiment/Research Presentation

These passages present an experimental set up in great detail; they describe the rationale behind an experiment, how it is set up and executed, and its results. In these passages you are often asked to analyze data given in the form of charts and graphs. In addition, questions may ask you how the results of the experiment would differ if a certain variable were changed; this requires you to think critically about the role of each element of the experiment. In this passage type, be careful not to gloss over important experimental details as you retrieve information from the passage. For example, comparing the colligative properties of a set of reagents whose concentrations are all 10 g/mL is very different than comparing the same set of reagents with concentrations of 10 m. Be aware that details such as units can make the difference between answering a question correctly or incorrectly, and be vigilant about these experimental details as you work through the questions and look back to the passage.

Persuasive Argument

In a Persuasive Argument passage, two perspectives on a problem are presented. It may be different researchers putting forth two different methodologies for conducting an experiment, or two different explanations for an experimental result or phenomenon.

The questions may ask how the authors came to develop different perspectives, or ask you to evaluate the credibility of each of their arguments. Persuasive Argument passages are the least common passage type in G-Chem.

READING A G-CHEM PASSAGE

Reading a G-Chem passage is not like reading a scientific paper or a textbook. That is, you are not reading thoroughly and trying to understand the relevance of each sentence. Instead, your goal is to take 30 to 60 seconds and skim the passage in order to determine the general topic area being tested and create a brief passage map. To do this as efficiently as possible, focus on the first sentence of each paragraph and any bolded or italicized words. In addition, chemical equations and figures may provide insight as to the general topic of the passage. For example, if you see a titration curve, it is likely that the passage will test acid-base chemistry.

G-Chem passages often include complex graphs and data tables. Avoid the temptation to analyze this data on your first pass through the passage. Rather, wait until you find a question that requires the use of the data in the graph or table, then analyze the data in the context of that question. This approach is more efficient and productive than trying to preemptively interpret data.

The bottom line: You can always go back and reread more details from the passage. Furthermore, not all of the details from the passage are necessary to answer the questions. Therefore, it is a waste of your time to read and attempt to thoroughly understand the passage the first time you read it.

MAPPING A G-CHEM PASSAGE

As you skim through a G-Chem passage, the highlighter is a useful way to visually note a few key words that relate to the general topic of the passage or some unusual or new term that is introduced. Use the highlighter sparingly, and keep in mind that any highlighting you do will not persist as you move from passage to passage. An example of a highlighted passage is shown below. This is an Information Presentation passage:

The batteries that start an automobile or power flashlights are devices that convert chemical energy into electrical energy. These devices use spontaneous oxidation-reduction reactions (called half-reactions) that take place at the electrodes to create an electric current. The strength of the battery, or electromotive force, is determined by the difference in electric potential between the half cells, expressed in volts. This voltage depends on which reactions occur at the anode and the cathode, the concentrations of the solutions in the cells, and the temperature. The cell voltage, E, at a temperature of 25°C and nonstandard conditions, can be calculated from the Nernst equation, where $E°$ is the standard potential, n denotes the number of electrons transferred in the balanced half reaction, and Q is the reaction quotient.

$$E = E° - \frac{0.0592}{n} \log_{10} Q$$

Equation 1

The lead storage battery used in automobiles is composed of six identical cells joined in series. The anode is solid lead, the cathode is lead dioxide, and the electrodes are immersed in a solution of sulfuric acid. As each cell discharges during normal operation, the sulfate ion is consumed as it is deposited in the form of lead sulfate on both electrodes, as shown in Reaction 1:

Reaction 1:

$$Pb(s) + PbO_2(s) + 4\ H^+(aq) + 2\ SO_4^{2-}(aq)$$
$$\downarrow$$
$$2\ PbSO_4(s) + 2\ H_2O(l)$$

Each cell produces 2 V, for a total of 12 V for the typical car battery. Unlike many batteries, however, the lead storage battery can be recharged by applying an external voltage. Because the redox reaction in the battery consumes sulfate ions, the degree of discharge of the battery can be checked by measuring the density of the battery fluid with a hydrometer. The fluid density in a fully charged battery is 1.2 g/cm^3.

Table 1 Standard Reduction Potentials at T = 25°C

Half-reaction	$E°$ (V)
$F_2(g) + 2e^- \rightarrow 2F^-(aq)$	+2.87
$Cl_2(g) + 2e^- \rightarrow 2Cl^-(aq)$	+1.36
$Cu^+(aq) + e^- \rightarrow Cu(s)$	+0.52
$Cu^{2+}(aq) + 2e^- \rightarrow Cu(s)$	+0.34
$Zn^{2+}(aq) + 2e^- \rightarrow Zn(s)$	–0.76
$Al^{3+}(aq) + 3e^- \rightarrow Al(s)$	–1.66
$Li^+(aq) + e^- \rightarrow Li(s)$	–3.05

Note that only a few words are highlighted. In the first paragraph, "batteries," and "spontaneous oxida-tion-reduction," relate to the general topic of the passage, and serve as a reminder that batteries contain a spontaneous redox reaction. In the last paragraph, the voltage of a car battery is highlighted. Since this is a specific and unusual piece of information, it is likely to come up in a question.

Rather than highlighting large portions of the passage as you skim it, use your scratch paper to create a simple passage map to help organize where different types of information are in the passage. As you skim the passage, note the subject of each paragraph and any key words or values. A well-constructed passage map makes it easier and more efficient to go back and retrieve specific information as you work through the questions. Here is an example of a passage map for the passage shown above:

> *P1 – Batteries, general information, background, Nernst equation in Equation 1*
> *P2 – Automobile batteries, more specific information about them*
> *P3 – Recharging car battery, Reduction Potentials in Table 1*

As you can see, your passage map does not need to be particularly detailed, nor should it be, as reading and mapping the passage should only take a minute of your time. However, this does provide a valuable framework for efficiently locating information within the passage.

Let's look at another passage and how to map it. This is an Experiment/Research Presentation passage from The Princeton Review's free online demo MCAT:

Two cube-shaped compartments, X and Y, each with a volume of one cubic meter, were used in several experiments to study the properties of gases. Compartment X was fitted with a piston of negligible mass which fit snugly against the walls of the container. The compartments were connected by a pinhole which could be opened or closed at will (see Figure 1). The pressure and temperature could be measured in either compartment. At the start of each experiment, Compartment X contained equal molar quantities of four gases (helium, oxygen, nitrogen, and carbon dioxide), the temperature in Compartment X was 25°C and the pressure was 1 atm. Initially, Compartment Y was evacuated. The behavior of all the gases can be assumed to be ideal. (Note: 1 atm ≈ 105 Pa.)

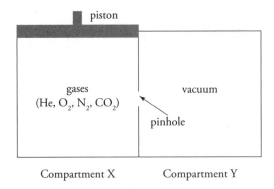

Figure 1 Experimental apparatus

Experiment 1:

With the pinhole closed, the temperature of the gases in Compartment X was gradually increased to 50°C, and the pressure of the gas inside the compartment was measured.

Experiment 2:

With the pinhole closed, the piston was gradually lowered into Compartment X until it had dropped a distance of 0.5 m. The pressure of the gas in the container was then measured.

Experiment 3:

The pinhole was opened, and the pressure change in each compartment was measured until equilibrium was reached.

Here, the highlighter tool can be used to emphasize that this passage is about the behavior of gases. Any time a passage is about gases, it's useful to know if the gas behaves in a real or ideal manner; therefore the phrase "assumed to be ideal" is also highlighted. In experimental passages, if important details jump out at you on your initial skim of the passage, it's useful to highlight them. For example, Figure 1 makes it fairly obvious that compartment X contains four gases, while compartment Y is a vacuum with no gas, however the "equal molar quantities" of the four gases in compartment X is a useful detail to highlight. Here's how you might map this passage on your scratch paper:

P1 – Experimental setup
E1 – Temp change
E2 – Pressure change
E3 – Pressure change, equilibrium

As was true of our last passage map, the main purpose is to create an outline so that it will be easier to retrieve necessary information as you work through the questions. Since this is an Experiment Presentation passage, the map points out the location of the main experimental details. Note that on the first pass, it is not important to note the specific details of each individual experiment. If possible, however, it may be helpful to note the general variable being changed.

Let's look at one more example of passage mapping. This passage is a Persuasive Argument Passage:

Two theoretical chemists attempted to explain the observed trends of acidity by applying two interpretations of molecular orbital theory. Consider the pKa's of some common acids listed along with each acids conjugate base:

acid	pK_a	conjugate base
H_2SO_4	< 0	HSO_4^-
H_2CrO_4	5.0	$HCrO_4^-$
H_3PO_4	2.1	$H_2PO_4^-$
HF	3.9	F^-
HOCl	7.8	ClO^-
HCN	9.5	CN^-
HIO_3	1.2	IO_3^-

Recall that acids with a pKa < 0 are called strong acids, and those with a pKa > 0 are called weak acids. The arguments of the chemists are given below.

Chemist #1:

"The acidity of a compound is proportional to the polarization of the H—X bond, where X is some nonmetal element. Complex acids, such as H2SO4, HClO4, and HNO3 are strong acids because the H—O bonding electrons are strongly drawn towards the oxygen. It is generally true that a covalent bond weakens as its polarization increases. Therefore, one can conclude that the strength of an acid is proportional to the number of electronegative atoms in that acid."

Chemist #2:

"The acidity of a compound is proportional to the number of stable resonance structures of that acid's conjugate base. H2SO4, HClO4, and HNO3 are all strong acids because their respective conjugate bases exhibit a high degree of resonance stabilization."

For a Persuasive Argument passage, the goal of passage mapping and highlighting is to identify the issue being addressed, and the main points of each of the opposing lines of reasoning. This can be accomplished using the highlighter tool to emphasize that the passage is about "trends of acidity", and that Chemist #1 atributes the behavior of acids to "polarization of the H—X bond," while Chemist #2 focuses on "stable resonance structures."

In this case, a passage map would be very similar to the results achieved by highlighting. However, keep in mind that while highlighting does not persist as you move from passage to passage, a passage map can permanently be referred to on well-organized scratch paper. Also, the very act of writing things down helps clarify it in your head:

P1/Main issue: Trends of acidity, interpretation of molecular orbital theory
Chemist #1: acidity ∝ polarization of H—X bond
Chemist #2: acidity ∝ # of stable resonance structures for conjugate base.

As you can see from the examples above, effective passage-mapping requires a combination of highlighting and jotting down notes in an organized fashion on your scratch paper. The best way to improve your passage mapping, and to determine which combination of these skills works best for you, is to practice, practice, practice.

TACKLING THE QUESTIONS

In general, G-Chem questions require a combination of basic knowledge, passage retrieval, and critical reasoning. The more difficult G-Chem questions tend to weigh the last two skills more heavily. Therefore, if you have a sound basis in the fundamental principles of General Chemistry, it is safe to assume that a tough question will be best addressed by looking back to the passage for information that is either explicitly stated or implied.

In the section on passage mapping, we reviewed an Information/Situation Presentation passage on batteries and redox reactions. We will draw on questions from this passage in order to illustrate the different question types.

Memory Questions

These questions test background knowledge and require you to recall a specific definition or relationship. Memory questions are often freestanding questions, either on their own or within a set of questions that accompany a passage. In the latter instance, the information they require is not given in the passage. For example, a question from the car battery passage shown above asked:

> If the reaction in a concentration cell is spontaneous in the reverse direction, then:
>
> A) $Q < K$, ΔG for the forward reaction is negative, and the cell voltage is positive.
> B) $Q < K$, ΔG for the forward reaction is positive, and the cell voltage is negative.
> C) $Q > K$, ΔG for the forward reaction is negative, and the cell voltage is positive.
> D) $Q > K$, ΔG for the forward reaction is positive, and the cell voltage is negative.

In order to answer this question correctly, you need to know the connection between ΔG and spontaneity. A spontaneous reaction has a negative ΔG, and a nonspontaneous reaction has a positive ΔG. Since the reaction is spontaneous in the reverse direction, it must be nonspontaneous in the forward direction. Therefore, the ΔG of the forward reaction is positive, eliminating choices A and C. Alternatively, you could know that cell voltage applies to the forward direction, and that a nonspontaneous cell has a negative voltage, also eliminating choices A and C.

To distinguish between choices B and D, you must have a fundamental understanding of equilibrium and Le Chatelier's Principle. The reaction quotient, Q, always approaches the equilibrium constant, K, and if $Q > K$ the reaction will be pushed in the reverse direction, toward the reactants side of the equilibrium, in order to decrease the value of Q. Thus, since the question says the reaction is spontaneous in the reverse direction, Q must be greater than K. This makes choice D the best answer.

Also, note that this question asks about concentration cells, which are not mentioned in the passage, and therefore this problem is essentially a free-standing question.

Explicit Questions

Explicit questions require direct retrieval of information from the passage. Sometimes, the answers to Explicit questions are definitions or relationships that are clearly stated in the passage. However, these types of questions may also require some background knowledge or a simple step of logical reasoning. Here is another example from the car battery redox passage shown above:

Of the following, which is the best reducing agent?

A) Li^+
B) Li
C) Cl^-
D) F^-

To answer this question, you must have fundamental knowledge of redox definitions and relationships, but you also need to retrieve information from the passage. The best reducing agent is the species that has the highest oxidizing potential, and Table 1 gives the reduction potentials for these reagents. However, you also need the knowledge that the oxidation potential is the same as the reduction potential, but with the opposite sign. Since the oxidation of Li has the highest positive potential (3.05 V), Li is the strongest reducing agent.

The best way to approach Explicit questions is to refer to your passage map to find the location of the information you need. Then, go back to the passage and read that section in greater detail. There are two instances when retrieval of information for Explicit questions can be especially tricky. First, in research study passages, be cautious when retrieving information tables and graphs. Rather than simply pulling data directly from the figures, be sure to read the text just before and after the figures as well, as it may contain important information that changes the way the data should be interpreted. Second, when a passage goes into greater detail about a subject that you already have fundamental knowledge of, avoid the temptation to answer questions directly from memory. Often, these types of passages will provide some obscure detail or anomalous situation that will be tested in the questions, and require you to retrieve information from the passage in order to select the correct answer.

Implicit Questions

Implicit questions require you to work through two or more steps of critical reasoning based on your background knowledge and information given in the passage. In other words, the answer is not directly stated in the passage, but is implied by the information provided. The distinction between an Implicit and an Explicit question can be subtle, as both require you to retrieve information from the passage, and Explicit questions may also require you to make a simple critical reasoning decision. The difference is that in Implicit questions, the reasoning step required is not as direct or obvious, and more than one step is usually required. For example:

> When a lead storage battery recharges, what happens to the density of the battery fluid?
>
> A) It decreases to 1.0 g/cm^3.
> B) It increases to 1.0 g/cm^3.
> C) It decreases to 1.2 g/cm^3.
> D) It increases to 1.2 g/cm^3.

First, information on the density of the battery fluid must be retrieved from the passage. Our passage map tells us that specific information on car batteries can be found in paragraphs two and three. Re-skimming these sections reveals that in the third paragraph of the passage, it states that the density of fluid in a fully charged battery is 1.2 g/cm^3. Therefore, as the battery is recharging, its density is approaching this value, eliminating choices A and B.

The difference between choices C and D is whether the density of the solution is increasing or decreasing to 1.2 g/cm^3 during recharge. To determine this, we can look for additional information in the passage that may relate to changing density of the battery fluid. The second paragraph of the passage states that as the battery discharges, sulfate ions are consumed and deposited in the form of lead sulfate. The removal of ions from solution implies that the amount of mass in the solution is going down, and therefore its density is also decreasing. Therefore, density is decreasing during discharge, and increasing during recharge. This makes choice D the best answer.

The key step here is focusing on the differences among answer choices. What can be difficult about approaching implicit questions is that it often hard to determine which information is supposed to "imply" something about the answer. Zeroing in on differences among the answer choices can help you determine which information from the passage is most relevant, and may help you rephrase what the question is really asking. Also, note that the first step of our analysis, eliminating the choices with 1.0 g/cm^3 density, was basically just answering an explicit question via direct passage retrieval. Many implicit questions begin this way, and it is much easier to eliminate answer choices first based on explicit information than it is to try to make a decision based on implicit information.

MCAT GENERAL CHEMISTRY TOPIC LIST[1]

Stoichiometry

1. Metric units
2. Density
3. Molecular weight
4. Mole concept, Avogadro's number
5. Empirical formulas
6. Percent composition by mass
7. Reactions and chemical equations
    a. writing and balancing chemical equations
    b. limiting reactants and theoretical yields
8. Oxidation states

Atomic Structure and Periodic Table

A. Atomic Structure
    1. orbital structure of H
    2. number of electrons per orbital
    3. ground and excited states
    4. electron quantum numbers
    5. common names and geometric shapes for orbitals *s, p, d*
    6. conventional notation for electronic structure
    7. emission and absorption spectra
    8. the Bohr model of an atom

B. The Periodic Table
    1. alkali metals
    2. alkaline earth metals
    3. halogens
    4. noble gases
    5. transition metals
    6. representative elements
    7. metals and nonmetals
    8. oxygen group

C. Periodic Trends
    1. valence electrons
    2. ionization energies
    3. electron affinity
    4. electronegativity
    5. electron shells and atomic size

Bonding

A. Covalent
    1. sigma and pi bonds
    2. hybrid orbitals
    3. VSEPR
    4. Lewis dot symbols
    5. resonance and formal charge
    6. polar covalent bonds
B. Ionic
    1. Electrostatic energy ($q_1 q_2/r$) and force ($q_1 q_2/r^2$)
C. Intermolecular forces
    1. Hydrogen bonding
    2. Dipole interactions
    3. London dispersion forces

Phases

1. Phase transition
2. Phase diagrams
3. Heats of phase change
4. Calorimetry, heat capacity, specific heat

Gases

1. Units of volume, temperature, and pressure
2. Standard temperature and pressure
3. Ideal gases and the Ideal gas law
4. Other gas laws (Henry's, Boyle's, Charles', Avogadro's)
5. Deviation of real-gas behavior from ideal gas law
6. Partial pressure, mole fraction
7. Dalton's law of partial pressures

---

[1] Adapted from *The Official Guide to the MCAT Exam*, 2009 ed., © 2009 Association of American Medical Colleges

Solutions and Solution Chemistry

A. Solubility
    1. molarity vs molality
    2. Complex ion formation and solubility
    3. effects of pH
    4. electrolytes

B. Colligative properties
    1. vapor pressure lowering
    2. boiling point elevation
    3. freezing point depression
    4. osmotic pressure

C. Colloids

Kinetics and Equilibrium

A. Kinetics
    1. reaction rates
    2. rate-determining step
    3. activation energy and transition state
    4. catalysts
    5. rate laws
    6. reaction coordinate graphs
    7. kinetics vs thermodynamics in a reaction

B. Equilibrium
    1. equilibrium constant and reaction quotient
    2. law of mass action
    3. Le Châtelier's principle
    4. solubility product constant
    5. the ion product
    6. common ion effect

Acids and Bases

1. Definitions (Lewis, Brønsted-Lowry, Arrhenius)
2. Conjugates
3. Strong acids and bases, common examples
4. Weak acids and bases, common examples
5. Equilibrium constants K_a and K_b (pK_a and pK_b)
6. Ionization of water and K_w
7. pH definition and calculations
8. Hydrolysis of salts of weak acids or bases
9. Buffers
10. Titrations
    a. indicators
    b. titration curves

Thermodynamics

1. Thermodynamic system, state function
2. "Zeroth" law (concept of temperature), temperature scales
3. First law
    a. heat transfer, heats of fusion and vaporization
    b. PV diagram
4. Second law
5. Enthalpy
    a. Hess's law
    b. endothermic and exothermic reactions
    c. bond dissociation energy
6. Reaction energy diagrams
    a. kinetics vs thermodynamics
    b. free energy and spontaneous reactions

Electrochemistry

1. Oxidation reduction reactions
2. Standard reduction potentials
3. Galvanic cells
4. Electrolytic cells
5. Faraday's law

Chapter 15
General Chemistry
Practice Section

FREESTANDING QUESTIONS

1. Given the masses in amu of $^{238}U = 238.051$, $^{234}Th = 234.044$, and $\alpha = 4.003$; what is the maximum velocity of the α particle emitted in the following reaction: $^{238}U \rightarrow {}^{234}Th + \alpha$

   (Note: 1 amu = 1.7×10^{-27} kg and 1.5×10^{-10} J of energy)

   A) 6100 m/s
   B) 3.2×10^5 m/s
   C) 1.3×10^7 m/s
   D) 4.4×10^{14} m/s

2. What is the correct ranking of the following compounds in terms of decreasing basicity?

   I. NH_3
   II. CH_3^-
   III. AsH_3
   IV. PH_3

   A) II > I > IV > III
   B) I > IV > III > II
   C) II > IV > I > III
   D) I > III > IV > II

3. What is the difference between electronegativity and electron affinity?

   A) Electronegativity is the energy change when a mole of neutral atoms become –1 anions whereas electron affinity quantifies how much an atom pulls electron density toward itself in a covalent bond.
   B) Electronegativity measures the tendency of an atom to gain an electron whereas electron affinity quantifies how strongly electrons are attracted to an atom.
   C) Electronegativity quantifies how much an atom pulls electron density toward itself in a covalent bond whereas electron affinity is the energy change when a mole of neutral atoms become –1 anions.
   D) There is no difference between electronegativity and electron affinity.

4. A 36 gram sample of water requires 93.4 kJ to sublime. What are the heats of fusion (ΔH_{fus}) and vaporization (ΔH_{vap}) for water?

   A) $\Delta H_{fus} = -20$ kJ/mol, $\Delta H_{vap} = 66.7$ kJ/mol
   B) $\Delta H_{fus} = 40.7$ kJ/mol, $\Delta H_{vap} = 6.0$ kJ/mol
   C) $\Delta H_{fus} = 6.0$ kJ/mol, $\Delta H_{vap} = 40.7$ kJ/mol
   D) $\Delta H_{fus} = 12.0$ kJ/mol, $\Delta H_{vap} = 81.4$ kJ/mol

5. At 1 atm, deionized water can remain a liquid at temperatures down to –42°C. If a foreign body is added to the supercooled liquid, it will immediately turn into ice. Which of the following is true about this process?

   A) The reaction is exothermic.
   B) Tap water could also be supercooled to –42°C.
   C) The transformation of a supercooled fluid to a solid is nonspontaneous.
   D) Water's unique phase diagram allows it to be supercooled.

6. In the commercial production of caramel, sucrose (a glucose/fructose disaccharide) and water are boiled together to form a supersaturated solution in which sucrose decomposition occurs. In addition, manufacturers add a small quantity of pure glucose to ensure a homogenous mixture. What is a possible explanation for this addition?

   A) Free hydroxyl groups on glucose dissociate, lowering pH and preventing sucrose degradation.
   B) Glucose addition destabilizes nucleating sucrose clusters.
   C) Adding glucose causes an equilibrium shift to the right favoring the hydrolysis of sucrose.
   D) Glucose sequesters free water to prevent microbial growth during storage.

7. For any chemical reaction, which of the following will NOT affect both the reaction rate and the rate constant?

   A) Activation energy
   B) Orientation of reactant molecules
   C) Temperature
   D) Concentration of reactants

8. Consider the following reaction at 1650°C:

$$C(s) + H_2O(g) \rightleftharpoons H_2(g) + CO(g)$$

When equilibrium is reached at a total pressure of 260 atm, there are 4 moles each of carbon and water and 40 moles each of hydrogen gas and carbon monoxide. What is the value of the equilibrium constant at this temperature?

A) 400
B) 1238
C) 2396
D) 104,000

9. The K_a of HSCN is equal to 1×10^{-4}. The pH of a HSCN solution:

A) will be approximately 4.
B) will be approximately 10.
C) will increase as [HSCN] increases.
D) cannot be determined from the information given.

10. A 25.0 mL solution of 0.2 M acetic acid ($pK_a = 4.76$) is mixed with 50 mL of 1.0 M sodium acetate ($pK_b = 9.24$). What is the final pH?

A) 4.8
B) 5.8
C) 9.2
D) 10.2

11. All of the following could apply to the closed, gaseous, thermodynamic process in the graph shown above EXCEPT:

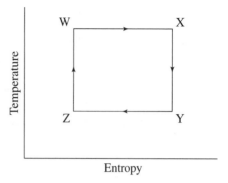

A) Heat is exchanged between points W and X.
B) No heat is exchanged between points Y and Z.
C) Work is done between points X and Y.
D) Gas is expanding from point W to X.

12. An electrochemical cell is constructed using two inert electrodes in one chamber with an inert electrolyte. The binary compound ICl is dissolved in the electrolyte, current is applied, and I_2 and Cl_2 are produced. Which of the following statements is true?

A) Cl_2 was produced by reduction at the cathode.
B) I_2 was produced by oxidation at the cathode.
C) Cl_2 was produced by oxidation at the cathode.
D) I_2 was produced by reduction at the cathode.

PRACTICE PASSAGE 1

Electrons within atoms occupy quantized energy levels. Atoms can absorb photons with the right amount of energy, bringing about an excited state in which electrons are promoted to higher energy levels. The excited atoms can slowly relax and reemit these photons, typically at the same frequency. When passed through a prism or other appropriate refractive material, this quantized emission produces a spectral line pattern unique for each atom. The emissions for the hydrogen atom have been well characterized and are depicted in Figure 1 below.

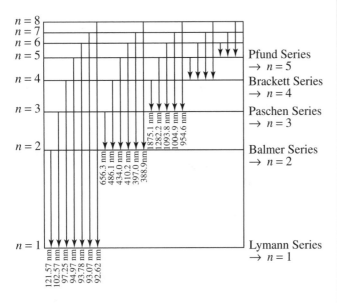

Figure 1

The wavelength in nanometers associated with each emission is labeled, and the emissions are grouped into series corresponding to the final level to which an excited electron relaxes. Planck's constant (h) has a value of $6.6 \times 10^{-34}\,\mathrm{m^2 \times kg/s}$.

Spectral lines exist over a range of frequencies rather than a single frequency due to a number of broadening effects. Thermal Doppler broadening arises from the distribution of velocities of individual atoms within a sample of a gas at a particular temperature. The Doppler effect predicts either an up shifting or down shifting of emitted frequency for each atom depending upon its motion relative to the observer. Interaction with nearby particles provides additional sources of line broadening. Stark broadening arises from the interaction of an emitting atom with an electric field. This effect can be both linearly and quadratically dependent upon the strength of the field. Resonance broadening occurs by energy transfer between similar particles and exhibits an inverse cubic dependence on

the distance of separation between the particles. Van der Waal forces can also perturb the emission of atoms. This effect exhibits an inverse sixth power dependence on the distance of separation between the interacting atoms.

1. The Balmer series contains wavelengths within the visible spectrum. Which of the following series contain wavelengths within the ultraviolet spectrum?

    I.   Lymann series
    II. Paschen series
    III. Brackett series

A) I only
B) II only
C) II and III only
D) I, II and III

2. White light is used to irradiate a hydrogen gas sample in the presence of two optical detectors. Detector A is positioned to receive frequencies of the white light beam not absorbed by the gas. Detector B is positioned to receive light emitted from the gas, but not the original white light beam. Which of the following describes the appearance of the spectra formed at these two detectors?

A) Detector A will have narrow, bright bands of colored light superimposed on an otherwise dark background while detector B will have narrow, dark bands superimposed on an otherwise continuous background of colored light.
B) Detector A will have narrow, dark bands superimposed on an otherwise continuous background of colored light while detector B will have narrow, bright bands of colored light superimposed on an otherwise dark background.
C) Both detectors will display narrow, bright bands of colored light superimposed on an otherwise dark background
D) Both detectors will display narrow, dark bands superimposed upon an otherwise continuous background of colored light.

3. Approximately how much energy is released when an electron falls from the $n = 7$ to the $n = 2$ level in the hydrogen atom?

A) 5×10^{-17} J
B) 5×10^{-19} J
C) 1.6×10^{-27} J
D) 2.6×10^{-40} J

4. Rank the relative contribution of the following broadening effects as the distance from an emitting atom increases.

    I.   Linear Stark broadening
    II.   Quadratic Stark broadening
    III. Resonance broadening
    IV. Van der Waal's broadening

A) I > III > II > IV
B) I > II > IV > III
C) II > IV > III > I
D) IV > II > III > I

5. All of the following are accurate statements about photon emissions EXCEPT:

A) thermal Doppler broadening effects increase with increasing temperature.
B) all of the noble gases can be distinguished from each other by their emission spectra.
C) a star approaching the Earth emitting yellow light could appear orange to an observer on Earth.
D) hydrogen bonding does not contribute to emission broadening in a sample of hydrogen gas.

6. For an electron transitioning between two energy levels ($n_{initial} \rightarrow n_{final}$) with an accompanying absorption or emission of radiation of wavelength λ, which of the following relationships is accurate?

A) $\lambda \propto |n_{final} - n_{initial}|$
B) $\lambda \propto |1/n_{final} - 1/n_{initial}|$
C) $\lambda \propto |1/n_{final}^2 - 1/n_{initial}^2|$
D) $1/\lambda \propto |1/n_{final}^2 - 1/n_{initial}^2|$

7. The energy level n is also the principal quantum number for an electron. What physical information is provided by this quantum number?

A) Shape of the orbital in which the electron resides
B) Orientation of the orbital in which the electron resides
C) Radial distance of the electron from the nucleus of the atom
D) Direction of the electron spin

PRACTICE PASSAGE 2

Molecules are not rigid, unchanging structures. Their atoms are in constant motion even relative to each other, ceaselessly oscillating around their average bond lengths and bond angles. For instance, in non-linear triatomic molecules there are three possible modes of vibration. There is the symmetric stretch in which both bonds in the molecule lengthen and contract in unison. In the asymmetric stretch, one bond lengthens while the other contracts. Finally, there is the bend in which the bond angle alternately widens and narrows.

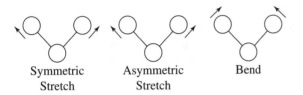

Symmetric   Asymmetric   Bend
Stretch   Stretch

Figure 1   Vibrations of a Triatomic Molecule

More generally, each atom in a molecule is capable of moving in three distinct directions, often represented by x, y and z. In a molecule with N atoms, there will be $3N$ possible atomic movements. However, if all the atoms in a molecule move in the same direction, translational movement and not vibration will result. Likewise, there are some combinations of atomic motions that result in rotation of the molecule and not vibration. Taking this into account, in a molecule containing N atoms there will be $3N - 6$ normal modes of vibration in non-linear molecules and $3N - 5$ normal modes of vibration in linear molecules.

If we make the rough approximation that atoms in a molecule are harmonic oscillators, then the energy of their vibration is given by:

$$E = \left(v + \frac{1}{2}\right)\left(\frac{h}{2\pi}\right)\sqrt{\frac{k}{u}} \text{ for } v = 0,1,2,...$$

where v is the quantum vibrational number, h is Planck's constant, k is the force constant of the bond which increases with bond strength, and u is the reduced mass of the molecule. Changes in the vibrational quantum state are associated with energies similar to infrared photons. Thus, IR spectroscopy is the study of the energetics of a molecule's vibrational quantum states. However, only those normal modes of vibration that induce a change in the dipole moment of a molecule can be excited with IR light.

Table 1   Bond Energies of Select Diatomic Elements

Molecule	Bond Energy (kJ/mol)
H_2	436
N_2	946
O_2	497
F_2	155

1. Which of the following molecules has nine normal modes of vibration?

A) NI_3
B) CH_4
C) PF_5
D) SCl_6

2. A change in which of the following combinations of molecular movement can never produce a peak in an IR spectrum?

A) Translation and rotation
B) Stretching and bending
C) Vibration and translation
D) Rotation and bending

3. Assuming their reduced masses are the same, which molecule will have the highest energy of vibration in the $v = 0$ state?

A) N_2
B) O_2
C) F_2
D) Cannot be determined from the information given.

4. All of the following molecules will display absorption peaks in an IR spectrum EXCEPT

A) $HClO_4$
B) SO_3
C) CO
D) O_2

5. In VSEPR theory, T-shaped is a sub-class of the trigonal bipyramidal geometric family in which the central atom has exactly three atoms bound to it. Which of the following molecules is T-shaped?

A) SF_4
B) NH_3
C) FCl_3
D) FO_3^-

6. For a diatomic molecule, the reduced mass is given by $u = (m_1 \times m_2) / (m_1 + m_2)$ where m_1 and m_2 are the atomic weights of the two bonded atoms. What will be the ratio of the ground state vibration energies of D_2 to H_2 assuming the force constant k is the same for both?

A) 0.5
B) 0.7
C) 1.4
D) 2.0

7. Nitrate is best described by a resonance average of three structures:

What best describes the peaks in an IR spectrum that result from the three N¾O bond stretches?

A) One peak at the double bond N=O stretch frequency and two peaks at the single bond N3—4O stretch frequency
B) One peak at the double bond N=O stretch frequency and one peak at the single bond N3—4O stretch frequency
C) One peak at the double bond N=O stretch frequency and one peak between the single N3—4O and double bond N=O stretch frequencies
D) One peak between the single N3—4O and double bond N=O stretch frequencies

PRACTICE PASSAGE 3

Phase change materials (PCM) are substances that possess high heats of fusion (H_f) and are capable of storing and releasing large amounts of heat at a constant temperature when they freeze or melt. When the surrounding temperature rises above the melting temperature of the material, heat will be absorbed by the material as it undergoes the solid to liquid transition When the surrounding temperature falls below the freezing point of the material, heat will be released by the material as it undergoes the liquid to solid transition. These materials are often used as thermal storage devices, temperature regulators, and coolants. When a PCM is contained within a suitable material through a process called *microencapsulation*, it can be incorporated into building materials and even clothing to add thermoregulatory capability.

The primary consideration in choosing a PCM is ensuring that its melting point is close to the desired temperature of the system or process to which it is being applied, since the isothermal heat transfer during phase change will occur at this temperature. Other considerations include the magnitude of H_f, density, thermal conductivity, toxicity, flammability, and cost. Advances in packaging have overcome non-optimal toxicity or flammability profiles and the addition of highly conducting additives has enhanced the thermal conductivity of many PCMs.

Figure 1 below is a representative phase change diagram for a PCM, depicting how temperature (T) varies with the addition of heat (q). A related concept is how the specific heat of a substance varies with its phase. For example the specific heat of $H_2O(s)$ is 2.108 kJ/kg $\times$ K while that for $H_2O(l)$ is 4.187 kJ/kg $\times$ K.

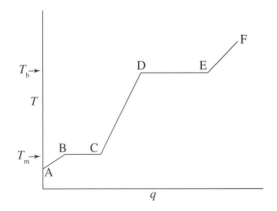

Figure 1   Representative Phase Change Diagram

1. Most practical applications of phase transfer materials exploit the energy transfer during the solid-liquid transition rather than the liquid-vapor transition. Which of the following is the most reasonable explanation for this?

A) Substances exhibit a smaller change in temperature during their solid-liquid phase transition than during their liquid-vapor phase transition.
B) Substances typically absorb or release more heat during their solid-liquid phase transition than during their liquid vapor phase transition.
C) The volume change associated with the solid-liquid phase transition is much less than the volume change associated with the liquid-vapor phase transition.
D) The critical point for many materials occurs at relatively extreme temperatures and pressures.

2. Which of the following correctly describes the primary mechanism of heat transfer through solids and liquids?

A) Convection within solids and conduction within liquids
B) Convection within both solids and liquids
C) Conduction within solids and convection within liquids
D) Conduction within both solids and liquids.

3. Which of the following is true concerning the graph in Figure 1?

   I.   The heat capacity of the solid phase can be obtained by measuring the area under the segment between points A and B.
   II. The heat capacity of the substance is smallest while it is a liquid.
   III. The average kinetic energy of the material increases while heat is transferred to it between points D and E.

A) I only
B) II only
C) II and III only
D) I, II, and III

4. As a substance transitions from solid to liquid to vapor, which of the following is true?

A) Heat is absorbed, entropy decreases, and intermolecular forces are increased.
B) Heat is absorbed, entropy increases, and intermolecular forces are decreased.
C) Heat is released, entropy decreases, and intermolecular forces are decreased.
D) Heat is released, entropy increases, and intermolecular forces are increased.

5. A clothing designer manufactures a new line of thermoregulatory apparel using a PCM microencapsulated in flame retardant pellets woven into the fabric. Which of the following was the most critical property considered in choosing the PCM?

A) A melting point in the range of 30 to 45°C
B) Low thermal conductivity
C) High density
D) Low solubility in aqueous solution

6. An ice cube weighing 18 grams is removed from a −10°C freezer. How much heat energy would be required to transform this ice cube into an equal mass of liquid water with a temperature of 10°C (molar heat of fusion of water = 6.009 kJ/mol)?

A) 1.1 kJ
B) 5.0 kJ
C) 7.1 kJ
D) 1086 kJ

7. In contrast to microencapsulation, initial attempts at macroencapsulation (containment of PCMs in large volume units) were largely unsuccessful. This led to the realization that PCMs function best in small volume cells. Which of the following is the most likely explanation?

A) The corrosive nature of many PCMs makes it difficult to identify suitable materials to contain them.
B) The increase in weight experienced when PCMs solidify makes large volume containment unfeasible.
C) The high cost of many PCMs makes high volume containment unfeasible.
D) The poor thermal conductivity of most PCMs causes them to solidify at the edges of large volume containers, preventing efficient heat transfer to the interior of larger cells.

PRACTICE PASSAGE 4

In the study of gases, the assumption of ideal behavior significantly simplifies calculations. This does not yield sufficiently accurate results in many cases as gases violate the assumed aspects of ideal behavior to varying degrees. To correct for real gas behavior, scientists use several methods including evaluating the compressibility factor (Z) for a gas, and using a modified ideal gas equation. The compressibility factor, a measure of deviation from ideal gas behavior, can be calculated using Equation 1. At low temperatures, gas molecules move more slowly. At high pressures, gas molecules are closer together. The interactions of gas molecules are therefore most pronounced in these circumstances. A researcher wishes to characterize the differences for several real gases and performs a series of experiments. The compressibility factor for an unknown gas at varying temperatures is shown in Figure 1.

$$Z = \frac{PV}{nRT}$$

Equation 1

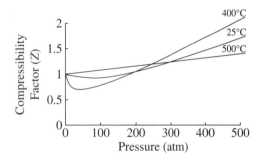

Figure 1

The van der Waals equation (Equation 2), a modification of the ideal gas equation to account for deviations in real gas behavior, allows for corrections to be made for real gases based on measured pressures and volumes. The researcher next takes several measurements of known gases under varied conditions to determine the constants (a and b) found in the van der Waals equation where P is the measured pressure, V is the measured volume, n is the number of moles, and T is temperature. Results are recorded in Table 1.

$$\left(P + \frac{an^2}{V^2}\right)(V - nb) = nRT$$

Equation 2

Table 1

Gas ($T = 273$ K)	a (atm·L²·mol⁻²)	b (L·mol⁻¹)
He	0.03	0.03
Ar	1.3	0.04
O_2	1.3	0.04
CO	1.5	0.05
CH_4	2.4	0.05
H_2O	5.8	0.05

1. From the ideal gas equation, the following relationship can be established:

$$\overline{E}_{trans} = \frac{3}{2}k_B T$$

where $\overline{E}_{trans}$ is the average kinetic energy of the gas and k_B is the Boltzmann constant. All of the following are true regarding this relationship EXCEPT:

A) temperature is related to molecular momentum.
B) gases with equal temperature posses equal molecular velocities.
C) k_B does not vary with temperature change.
D) decreased $\overline{E}_{trans}$ at high pressures results in an increased compressibility factor (Z).

2. What is a possible explanation for the initial decrease then increase in Z observed as pressure is increased at lower temperatures?

A) Attractive forces giving way to repulsive forces with increased pressure
B) Repulsive forces giving way to attractive forces with increased pressure
C) Attractive forces giving way to repulsive forces with increased temperature
D) Repulsive forces giving way to attractive forces with increased pressure

3. Which of the following compressibility factor vs. pressure curves best characterizes an ideal gas?

A)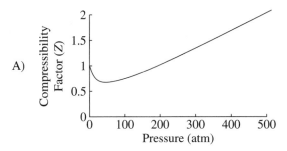

B)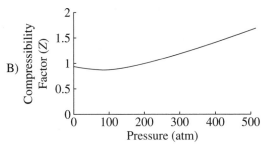

C.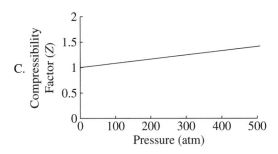

D.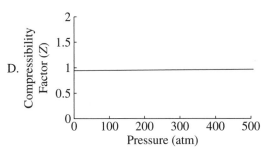

4. In van der Waals equation, which properties are most likely accounted for by a and b?

A) Attractive forces and molecular volume respectively
B) Attractive forces and molecular speed respectively
C) Molecular volume and collision elasticity respectively
D) Molecular volume and boiling point respectively

5. Which of the following best explains the changes that were made to the ideal gas equation to obtain the van der Waals equation?

A) Real gases have increased pressure due to inelastic collisions and decreased volume due to diminished repulsive forces.
B) Real gases have increased pressure due to decreased momentum and increased volume due to increased molecular mass.
C) Real gases have decreased pressure due to decreased momentum and increased volume due to molecular volume.
D) Real gases have decreased pressure due to decreased molecular mass and increased volume due to inelastic collisions.

6. The researcher performs an additional set of experiments where he quantifies the compressibility factor for several known gases at room temperature and 100 atm.

Gas	Z
H_2	1.1
N_2	0.9
CO_2	0.4

Given these values, what is the most likely identity of an unknown gas with a compressibility factor of 0.8?

A) Br_2
B) NH_3
C) CH_4
D) H_2O

7. The temperature at which a gas can no longer condense with increasing pressure is known as the critical temperature and is a direct result of the non-ideal behavior of gases. Which of the following is/are true of a critical temperature?

I. The attractive forces of the gas cannot overcome its kinetic energy
II. A decrease in volume results in a decrease in critical temperature
III. The critical temperatures for ideal gases are higher than those for real gases

A) I
B) I and II only
C) I and III only
D) II and III only

PRACTICE PASSAGE 5

A student conducted an experiment to study the effects of mercury poisoning on marine life. After preparing four beakers with 1 L of deionized water and labeling them "1" through "4", the student added 2 moles of a mercury salt into the first beaker. This process was repeated three times using different mercury based salts, derived from both its +1 and +2 oxidation states. The student allowed each system to reach equilibrium before filtering out any undissolved salt. The findings are recorded below in Table 1.

Table 1   Observations on Various Mercury Salts

Beaker	Observations
1	Completely dissolved
2	Completely dissolved
3	Partially dissolved
4	Did not dissolve

To determine if these solutions might share any similar physical properties to seawater, the student conducted an osmotic pressure (Π) test. After obtaining a U-tube divided by a semipermeable membrane, the student filled the left half with Solution 1, and the right half with an equal amount of deionized water. Using a hydrostatic piston, the student found that it required 147 atm to stop osmosis at 25°C. Since this pressure is approximately half of the pressure needed to prevent osmosis to occur using seawater, the student used the formula $\Pi = MiRT$ (where M is molarity, i is the van't Hoff factor, and T is temperature) to determine the composition of a solution which would be more similar to seawater. Given that $R = 0.0821$ L·atm/K·mol, the student discovered that doubling the temperature or molarity would yield a solution with the desired properties.

1. A possible formula for the salt in Beaker 1 is:

A) $HgNO_3$.
B) $HgClO_4$.
C) $Hg(CH_3COO)_2$.
D) $Hg(CN)_2$.

2. Adding which of the following compounds would increase the dissociation of $Hg(NO_3)_2$ in a 5 M solution?

A) $HgCl_2$
B) $NaCl$
C) $AgNO_3$
D) $Hg(ClO_4)_2$

3. The K_{sp} of mercury (I) carbonate, Hg_2CO_3, is 3.6×10^{-17}. How many moles of Hg^+ will be produced if an excess of Hg_2CO_3 is dissolved in 1 L of water?

A) 9.0×10^{-4}
B) 4.2×10^{-6}
C) 1.2×10^{-8}
D) 6.0×10^{-9}

4. If 1 L of deuterated water (density = 1.1 g/cm³) was used instead of normal water, the resulting solutions would have a:

A) smaller change in freezing point.
B) smaller change in osmotic pressure.
C) greater vapor depression.
D) greater change in boiling point.

5. If HgF_4 and XeF_4 have similar structures, which of the following is true regarding these molecules?

A) The central atom is sp^3d hybridized and the molecule has a trigonal pyramidal shape.

B) The central atom has a +4 formal charge and the molecule has a square planar shape.

C) The central atom has filled subshells and the molecule has tetrahedral geometry.

D) The central atom has a +4 oxidation state and the molecule has octahedral geometry.

6. A fifth solution was prepared by bubbling mercury vapor though 1 L of water. Decreasing which of the following will increase the solubility of the gaseous mercury?

A) Temperature of the water

B) Pressure on the water

C) Volume of the water

D) Rate of mercury bubbling through the water

7. If $CaCl_2$ contaminated one of the beakers, what would happen to the aqueous solution containing $Hg(ClO_4)_2$?

A) The $Hg(ClO_4)_2$ equilibrium would shift resulting in less dissociation.

B) $Ca(ClO_4)_2$ would react to form a white crystalline precipitate.

C) $HgCl_2$ would react to form a white crystalline precipitate.

D) $Cl_2(g)$ would be produced.

PRACTICE PASSAGE 6

A bimolecular reaction occurs when two reactants collide, forming one activated complex. An example of a bimolecular reaction is given in Reaction 1.

$$Cl(g) + Br_2(g) \rightarrow BrCl(g) + Br(g)$$

Reaction 1

The rate of a bimolecular reaction depends in part on the frequency of collisions between two molecules that occur with sufficient energy to create a reactive intermediate. The change in concentration of the reactants and products can be monitored over time, as depicted in Figure 1, and can be used to approximate the rate of a reaction. A tangential line to the initial portion of the slope can approximate the initial rate of the reaction.

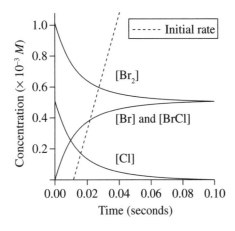

Figure 1 Reaction between Br_2 and Cl at 304 K

Although the rate constant is determined experimentally, for a bimolecular reaction in the gas phase, it can be estimated using Equation 1:

$$k_T = Z\rho e^{\left(\frac{-E_a}{RT}\right)}$$

Equation 1

where ρ is the steric factor, E_a is the activation energy, R is the gas constant, T is the temperature and Z is the collision frequency. The steric factor is the ratio between the experimental and predicted rate constant, and takes into consideration that the probability of a reaction occurring depends on the orientation of the reactant molecules. The collision frequency is the average collisions per unit time, and is determined using Equation 2:

$$Z = N_A^2 \sigma_{AB} \sqrt{\frac{8k_B T}{\pi\mu_{AB}}}$$

Equation 2

where N_A is Avogadro's number (6.02×10^{23} mol^{-1}), σ_{AB} is the reaction cross-section, k_B is Boltzmann's constant (1.38×10^{-23} J $\cdot$ K^{-1}), and μ_{AB} is the reduced mass.

Although Equation 1 is a good prediction of bimolecular reactions, it cannot be used for reactions that are non-elementary reactions. In these cases, the reaction mechanism can be used to determine the rate expression.

Step 1	$BrO_3^- + H^+ \rightleftharpoons HBrO_3$
Step 2	$HBrO_3 + H^+ \rightleftharpoons H_2BrO_3^+$
Step 3	$Br^- + HBrO_3^+ \rightleftharpoons HBrO_2 + HOBr$
Step 4	$HBrO_2 + H^+ \rightleftharpoons {}^+H_2BrO_2^+$
Step 5	$H_2BrO_2^+ + Br^- \rightleftharpoons 2HOBr$
Step 6	$3\,(HOBr + H^+ \rightleftharpoons H_2O \cdot Br^+)$
Step 7	$3\,(H_2O \cdot Br^+ + Br^- \rightleftharpoons Br_2 + H_2O)$

Mechanism 1

1. Which of the following is the general formula for a bimolecular reaction?

A) $A + B \rightarrow X^{\ddagger} \rightarrow C + D$
B) $A + B + C \rightarrow X^{\ddagger} \rightarrow D + E$
C) $A + 2B \rightarrow (A\text{-}B\text{-}A)^{\ddagger} \rightarrow AB2$
D) $A + B \rightarrow X^{\ddagger} + Y^{\ddagger} \rightarrow C + D$

2. What is the rate constant of Reaction 1 at 304 K?

A) $8 \times 10^{1} \ M^{-1}s^{-1}$
B) $8 \times 10^{10} \ M^{-1}s^{-1}$
C) $8 \times 10^{10} \ s^{-1}$
D) Cannot be determined with the given information.

3. With regards to the overall reaction described by Mechanism 1:

A) BrO_3^- is an intermediate.
B) $HBrO_2$ is a catalyst.
C) H_2O is a product.
D) HOBr is a reactant.

4. An increase in temperature by a factor of 4 would:

A) increase Z by a factor of 2 and decrease k_T overall.
B) increase Z by a factor of 2 and increase k_T overall.
C) increase Z by a factor of 4 and decrease k_T overall.
D) increase Z by a factor of 4 and increase k_T overall.

5. Which of the following statements regarding reaction kinetics is most accurate?

A) The activated complex can be measured in solution, although it is not a net product of the reaction.
B) The steric factor for more complex reactions is less than that for simpler reactions.
C) The rate constant depends on the initial concentration of the reactants.
D) The reaction order of a bimolecular reaction cannot be determined using stoichiometry, but rather can only be calculated experimentally.

6. What effect would doubling the concentration of BrO_3^- have on the rate of the reaction depicted by Mechanism 1?

A) The rate of the reaction will increase by a factor of $2^{1/2}$.
B) The rate of the reaction will increase by a factor of 2.
C) The rate of the reaction will increase by a factor of 4.
D) This cannot be determined with the given information.

7. Which of the following equations gives the rate law for the reaction between Cl and Br_2?

A) rate $= k[Cl_2][Br_2]$
B) rate $= k[ClBr][Br]$
C) rate $= k[Cl][Br_2]$
D) Cannot be determined

Practice Passage 7

Ocean acidification is a consequence of ocean waters absorbing atmospheric CO_2 at the air-water interface to form carbonic acid. This acid ultimately dissociates to form bicarbonate and carbonate ions:

$$CO_2(g) + H_2O(l) \rightarrow H_2CO_3(aq)$$

Reaction 1

$$H_2CO_3(aq) \rightleftharpoons H^+(aq) + HCO_3^-(aq) \quad K_a = 2.5 \times 10^{-4} \,(\text{at } 25°C)$$

Reaction 2

$$HCO_3^-(aq) \rightleftharpoons H^+(aq) + CO_3^{2-}(aq) \quad K_a = 5.6 \times 10^{-11} \,(\text{at } 25°C)$$

Reaction 3

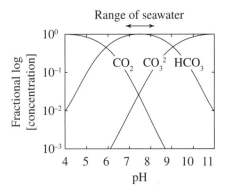

Figure 1 Measurements of CO_2, Bicarbonate, and carbonate ions over a range of seawater pH

This phenomenon is of great interest for marine biologists because of its effects on the calcium carbonate exoskeletons of mollusks and corals. The equilibrium governing the mineralization and dissolution of calcium carbonate exoskeletons is described by the following equation:

$$CaCO_3(s) \rightleftharpoons Ca^{2+}(aq) + CO_3^{2-}(aq) \quad K_{sp} = 8.7 \times 10^{-9} \,(\text{at } 25°C)$$

Reaction 4

The solubility of calcium carbonate decreases with increasing temperature. Organisms that need to generate calcium carbonate for their exoskeletons are usually found in shallow waters due to the relative saturation of carbonate ions at this depth. However, it is hypothesized that ocean acidification and its effects on carbonate availability may lead to mass migrations of these organisms.

1. Which of the following is a consequence of increased CO_2 absorption in ocean water?

   A) A decrease in seawater pOH
   B) A decrease in the K_a of Reaction #2
   C) A decrease in the hardness of mollusk shells
   D) A decrease in calcium ions in seawater

2. If the natural environment of mollusks continues to experience an increase in CO_2 absorption, which location would be their most probable destination if they migrate?

   A) Shallower waters
   B) Deeper waters
   C) Polar waters
   D) Tropical waters

3. Titration of carbonic acid with sodium hydroxide will result in two plateaus close to which pH values?

   A) 2.5 and 4
   B) 2.5 and 5.6
   C) 3.6 and 10.2
   D) 5.6 and 11

4. Groundwater, often found with dissolved calcium and carbonate ions, may contain high levels of carbon dioxide while underground. Which of the following will occur when this water surfaces and expels the excess carbon dioxide?

A) Water acidity increases and calcium carbonate remains in solution
B) Water acidity increases and calcium carbonate precipitates
C) Water acidity decreases and calcium carbonate remains in solution
D) Water acidity decreases and calcium carbonate precipitates

5. A scientist samples a liter of seawater and notices calcium carbonate precipitate at the bottom of the flask when placed in a 25°C water bath. The number of moles of calcium carbonate soluble in solution is closest to:

A) 3×10^{-3} moles.
B) 9×10^{-5} moles.
C) 9×10^{-9} moles.
D) 9×10^{-18} moles.

PRACTICE PASSAGE 8

Artificial snowmaking illustrates the Joule-Thomson effect as a mixture of air and water vapor is throttled from 20 atm of pressure through an insulated valve into the surrounding atmosphere. Snowmaking is costly, and its efficiency is dependent on appropriate weather conditions.

The *wet bulb temperature* is used to determine when snowmaking is possible. The bulb of a standard, dry bulb thermometer is wrapped in wet cloth. The wet bulb temperature reading results from the evaporation of the water on the cloth in a manner dependent on the relative humidity or moisture content of the surrounding air passing by. Humidity levels also influence the *dew point*, or maximum temperature where condensation can occur.

An engineer refers to the data in Table 1 and Figure 1 to plan snowmaking operations at a mountain ski resort. The snowmaking curves in Figure 1 mark the boundaries between good, possible, and impossible conditions to make snow.

Table 1 Physical Properties of Water

Enthalpy of formation	-285.85 kJ mol^{-1} (at 25°C)
Enthalpy of vaporization	45.05 kJ mol^{-1} (at 0°C)
	40.66 kJ mol^{-1} (at 100°C)
Enthalpy of fusion	6.01 kJ mol^{-1} (at 0°C)
	6.35 kJ mol^{-1} (at 82°C)

Snow Making Curves

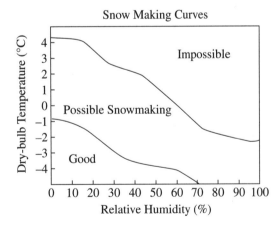

Figure 1

1. Throttling best approximates what kind of process?

A) Isothermal
B) Isochoric
C) Isobaric
D) Adiabatic

2. At any point in time, all of the following can be true regarding wet bulb temperature EXCEPT that it may:

A) exceed the dry bulb temperature.
B) be exceeded by the dry bulb temperature.
C) equal the dew point.
D) exceed the dew point.

3. Which of the following best approximates the molar enthalpy of deposition during snowmaking operations?

A) 51 kJ
B) −51 kJ
C) 47 kJ
D) −47 kJ

4. With increasing relative humidity, which of the following observations is expected?

A) The difference between wet and dry bulb temperature increases.
B) The difference between wet and dry bulb temperature decreases.
C) The temperature range for possible snowmaking increases.
D) The heat of vaporization of water decreases.

5. Given the change in internal energy (U), work (w) and heat (q) of water vapor turning to snow during throttling, which of the following is true?

A) $q > U$
B) $q = w$
C) $w > q$
D) $w > U$

6. In a wet bulb thermometer, which of the following is true during the initial vaporization of water from the cloth?

A) Average kinetic energy of the thermometer bulb increases
B) Internal energy of the cloth remains constant
C) Work is done by the expanding water vapor
D) Heat is released from the cloth

7. According to the passage, snowmaking is least likely to be possible for which of the following wet bulb temperature and relative humidity values?

A) 0°C, 50%
B) –4°C, 50%
C) –3°C, 100%
D) –5°C, 100%

PRACTICE PASSAGE 9

Electrolysis of water can be used to produce hydrogen or oxygen gas. Industrial applications primarily focus on hydrogen gas production. In addition, electrolysis of water is an important method for creating oxygen in enclosed atmospheres such as on a submarine.

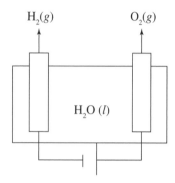

Figure 1

Figure 1 shows a schematic for electrolysis. An electric current is passed to electrodes submerged in water. The overall reaction is:

$$H_2O(l) \rightarrow H_2(g) + \frac{1}{2}O_2(g)$$

($\Delta H = 286$ kJ and $\Delta S = 0.16$ kJ/K at STP)

At room temperature the energy required for this process provides for both the generation of the gas molecules and their subsequent expansion. Efficiency can be affected by changing the ambient temperature. This is particularly important in the case of hydrogen gas production because of its potential as a source of fuel. Under non-standard conditions, the cell potential can be calculated using the Nernst equation:

$$E_{cell} = E_{cell}^{\circ} - \frac{RT}{zF}\ln Q$$

where E°_{cell} is the standard cell potential, $R = 8.31$ J K^{-1} mol^{-1}, z is the number of electrons transferred per mole, $F = 96,500$ C mol^{-1}, and Q is the reaction quotient.

Table 1 Standard Electrode Potentials

Half-reaction	E° (V)
$Na^+(aq) + e^- \rightleftharpoons Na(s)$	-2.71
$2 H_2O(l) + 2 e^- \rightleftharpoons H_2(g) + 2 OH^-(aq)$	-0.83
$2 H^+(aq) + 2 e^- \rightleftharpoons H_2(g)$	0.00
$O_2(g) + 2 H_2O(l) + 4 e^- \rightleftharpoons 4 OH^-(aq)$	0.40
$O_2(g) + 4 H^+(aq) + 4 e^- \rightleftharpoons 2 H_2O(l)$	1.23
$Cl_2(g) + 2 e^- \rightleftharpoons 2 Cl^-(aq)$	1.36

1. What is the Gibb's Energy (G) requirement on the circuit to carry out the electrolysis of 1 mole of liquid water at 25°C and 1 atm?

A) 238 kJ
B) 282 kJ
C) 286 kJ
D) 334 kJ

2. As electrolysis of pure water proceeds, what observation is expected?

A) Increasing positive charge around the cathode
B) Increasing negative charge around the anode
C) Increasing pH around the cathode
D) Increasing pH around the anode

3. The standard cell potential for electrolysis of water is:

A) -1.23 V.
B) -0.83 V.
C) 0.40 V.
D) 1.23 V.

4. During an experiment on the electrolysis of pure water, $E_{cell} = 0$ when $T = 400$ K. This is consistent with which of the following?

A) The reaction is no longer at equilibrium.
B) The K_{eq} at 400 K is greater than the K_{eq} at 298 K.
C) More free energy is required from the circuit at 400 K compared to 298 K.
D) $E°_{cell}$ is greater at 400 K compared to 298 K.

5. NaCl(s) is added to pure water in an electrolysis unit with the goal of increasing the rate of oxygen production. Will this be effective?

A) No, because the standard reduction potential of $Na^+(aq)$ is less than that of $H^+(aq)$.
B) No, because $Cl^-(aq)$ will be preferentially oxidized at the anode to produce chlorine gas.
C) Yes, because $Na^+(aq)$ will migrate to the cathode and alleviate the buildup of negative charge.
D) Yes, because the overall conductivity of water will be decreased with the addition of solute.

6. Which of the following is true about the electrolysis of water?

    I.   Oxygen gas is formed at the cathode
    II. Electrons flow from anode to cathode
    III. The anode is positively charged

A) I only
B) II only
C) I and II only
D) II and III only

7. When adding an electrolyte to water during the production of hydrogen gas, it is important to choose one that contains:

A) a cation with a higher reduction potential than hydroxide.
B) a cation with a higher reduction potential than hydronium.
C) an anion with a higher reduction potential than hydronium.
D) an anion with a higher reduction potential than hydroxide.

Chapter 16
General Chemistry
Practice Section
Solutions

SOLUTIONS TO FREESTANDING QUESTIONS

1. **C**   First, solve for the change in mass from reactants to products to find that 0.004 amu of mass is lost: $[234.044 + 4.003] - [238.051] = -0.004$ amu.

    Next, convert this mass into energy: $(0.004 \text{ amu})(1.5 \times 10^{-10} \text{ J/amu}) = 6.0 \times 10^{-13}$ J

    Finally, assume all of the energy released goes into the kinetic energy (*KE*) of the alpha particle and solve for its velocity:

    $$KE = \frac{1}{2}mv^2$$

    $$v = \sqrt{\frac{(2)(KE)}{m}}$$

    $$v = \sqrt{\frac{(2)(6.0 \times 10^{-13} \text{ J})}{(4.003 \text{ amu})(1.7 \times 10^{-27} \text{ kg/amu})}}$$

    $$v \approx \sqrt{\frac{(3 \times 10^{-13})}{(1.5 \times 10^{-27})}} \text{ m/s}$$

    $$v \approx \sqrt{2 \times 10^{14}} \text{ m/s}$$

    $$v \approx 1.44 \times 10^{7} \text{ m/s}$$

    The only answer choice close to this is C.

2. **A**   Ranking questions are best answered by evaluating extremes. CH_3^- is the strongest base because of its negative charge (it has a high probability to attract a positive H^+ ion). Thus, choices B and D can be eliminated. Since Choices A and C have molecule III at the other extreme, we must deduce the relationship of the middle choices (i.e., molecules I and IV) to answer this question. Both are bound to H_3 so we need to find a relationship between nitrogen and phosphorus. Since acidity increases to the right and down in the periodic table, basicity increases to the left and up. Since nitrogen is in a higher period than phosphorus, it must be more basic, making Choice A the correct answer.

3. **C**   Choice D can be eliminated first because the two terms have different meanings. Since choices A and C are opposites, there is a reasonably good chance that one of them is correct. Choice B implies that electronegativity relates to ionization whereas electron affinity relates to density in a covalent bond which is not the case. Electronegativity only has meaning for atoms that are covalently bound. Electron affinity is the energy change when atoms gain an electron. Therefore, choice A is eliminated and choice C is the best answer.

4. **C** Both fusion (melting) and vaporization (boiling) require energy and are endothermic, eliminating choice A. Comparing both processes, vaporization takes substantially more energy. During vaporization, intermolecular forces are essentially completely overcome, and gaseous molecules separate widely due to their increased kinetic energy. Choice B is therefore eliminated. A 36 gram sample of water is 2 moles, so the heat of sublimation of 1 mole is half of 93.4 kJ, or 46.7 kJ/mol. This eliminates choice D. Examining the fusion and vaporization of water and adding their enthalpies by Hess's law gives choice C as the correct answer:

$$H_2O(s) \rightarrow H_2O(l) \qquad \Delta H_{fus} = X \ (6.0 \ kJ/mol)$$

$$H_2O(l) \rightarrow H_2O(g) \qquad \Delta H_{vap} = Y \ (40.7 \ kJ/mol)$$

$$H_2O(s) \rightarrow H_2O(g) \qquad \Delta H_{vap} = X + Y = 46.7 \ kJ/mol$$

5. **A** Upon nucleation with a foreign body, supercooled water will transition from liquid to solid phase. This phase transition (crystallization) requires heat to be released since intermolecular bonding interactions are formed. Choice B is eliminated because tap water contains many dissolved particles that can serve as sites of nucleation. Choice C is incorrect because the supercooled fluids are only kinetically stabilized against freezing, and their transformation to a solid form is thermodynamically spontaneous. Since pressure remains constant, the negative sloped solid-liquid equilibrium line in water's phase diagram does not play a role in supercooling, eliminating Choice D.

6. **B** Glucose interferes with the crystallization of sucrose, thereby helping maintain a homogenous mixture. Glucose is not a significant proton donor or acceptor and would have a negligible effect on pH, eliminating choice A. Addition of glucose (a product in the hydrolysis of sucrose) causes a left shift in the equilibrium of sucrose decomposition since it is a product, eliminating choice C. Glucose does sequester free water and prevent microbial growth, but this does not explain how it ensures a homogenous mixture, eliminating choice D.

7. **D** According to the Arrhenius equation, the rate constant $k = Ae^{-(Ea/RT)}$ where E_a is the activation energy, T is the temperature, and A is the Arrhenius factor (which takes into account the orientation of the colliding molecules). All of these factors affect k and consequently the reaction rate, eliminating choices A, B, and C. The concentration of the reactants affects the reaction rate; the greater the concentration, the higher the frequency of molecular collisions. However, reactant concentrations do not change the rate constant.

8. **B** Only gases are included in the equilibrium expression because C(s) does not change in concentration or pressure. The partial pressure of each gas at equilibrium can be determined from the moles present and the total pressure. Then, K_{eq} can be calculated:

$$K_{eq} = \frac{P_{H_2} \cdot P_{CO}}{P_{H_2O}} = \frac{X_{H_2}P_{total} \cdot X_{CO}P_{total}}{X_{H_2O}P_{total}} = \frac{\dfrac{moles_{H_2}}{moles_{total}}P_{total} \cdot \dfrac{moles_{CO}}{moles_{total}}P_{total}}{\dfrac{moles_{H_2O}}{moles_{total}}P_{total}} = \frac{\dfrac{moles_{H_2}}{moles_{total}}P_{total} \cdot moles_{CO}}{moles_{H_2O}}$$

$$K_{eq} = \frac{\left(\dfrac{40 \text{ moles } H_2}{84 \text{ total moles}}\right)(260 \text{ atm})(40 \text{ moles CO})}{(4 \text{ moles } H_2O)} \approx \left(\frac{40}{80}\right)(250)(10) = 1250$$

Choice B is the closest answer.

9. **D** The K_a of an acid is a measure of its ability to dissociate in water, not the pH of a solution (the smaller the K_a the weaker the acid). If we know the [H⁺] of a solution we can find the pH by finding –log [H⁺], but we cannot find the pH of a weak acid solution from only the K_a. We must also know the concentration of the acid. Choice A is a trap answer if you confuse pK_a with pH. The greater the concentration of an acid, the more H⁺ ions will be in solution. However, this will *decrease* the pH of the solution, not increase it (choices B and C can be eliminated). By process of elimination, choice D is the best answer.

10. **B** The sodium acetate solution will be completely ionized:

$$NaC_2H_3O_2 \rightarrow Na^+ + C_2H_3O_2^-$$

However, acetic acid will have negligible dissociation in solution:

$$HC_2H_3O_2 \rightleftharpoons H^+ + C_2H_3O_2^- \quad (K_a \approx 1 \times 10^{-5})$$

Therefore, for the combined solution, it is reasonable to assume that all of the $HC_2H_3O_2$ is contributed from the acid solution, and all of the $C_2H_3O_2^-$ is contributed from the salt solution:

$$(0.2 \; M \; HC_2H_3O_2)(0.025 \text{ L}) = 5 \times 10^{-3} \text{ mol } HC_2H_3O_2$$

$$(1 \; M \; NaC_2H_3O_2)(0.05 \text{ L}) = 5 \times 10^{-2} \text{ mol } C_2H_3O_2^-$$

The new volume of 0.075 L cancels out when solving for the pH using the Henderson-Hasselbalch equation:

$$pH = pK_a + \log\frac{[C_2H_3O_2^-]}{[HC_2H_3O_2]}$$

$$pH = 4.76 + \log\frac{\left(\dfrac{5 \times 10^{-2} \text{ mol}}{0.075 \text{ L}}\right)}{\left(\dfrac{5 \times 10^{-3} \text{ mol}}{0.075 \text{ L}}\right)}$$

$$pH = 4.76 + \log(10) = 5.76$$

11. **B** The process in the diagram is a Carnot cycle. Applying the first law ($E = q + w$):

1) W → X: Entropy increasing at constant temperature represents an isothermal volume expansion. E is constant, but heat is exchanged; $q = -w$ (eliminate A and D).

2) X → Y: Temperature decreasing at constant entropy is an adiabatic volume expansion. No heat is exchanged; $E = w$ (eliminate C).

3) Y → Z: Entropy decreasing at constant temperature is an isothermal volume contraction. E is constant, but heat is exchanged; $q = -w$. B is correct because heat must be exchanged to change volume at constant temperature.

4) Z → W: Temperature increasing at constant entropy is an adiabatic volume contraction. No heat is exchanged; $E = w$.

12. **D** In the compound ICl, I has an +1 oxidation state, and Cl has a −1 oxidation state owing to the greater electronegativity of Cl. Therefore, production of Cl_2 must be an oxidation, and production of I_2 must be a reduction eliminating choices A and B. Moreover, reduction always takes place at the cathode, eliminating choice C.

SOLUTIONS TO PRACTICE PASSAGE 1

1. **A** Ultraviolet radiation has higher energy, and therefore higher frequency and lower wavelength than visible light. Of the choices, the Lymann series is the only group of emissions that represents higher energy and lower wavelength than the Balmer series.

2. **B** Because of its position, Detector A will receive any incident irradiating light that is not absorbed by the gas sample. Since the gas will absorb only those frequencies allowed by its quantized energy levels, this detector will display all of the white light colors except those that were absorbed. This eliminates choices A and C. Detector B is positioned only to receive emitted light from the gas sample, so it should display spectral emission bright bands superimposed on an otherwise dark background. This eliminates choice D and makes choice B the best answer.

3. **B** The wavelength of light emitted by the $n = 7$ to $n = 2$ transition can be obtained from Figure 1 as 397 nm or 3.97×10^{-7} m. The energy of light can be solved by:

$$E = hf$$
$$E = h\left(\frac{c}{\lambda}\right)$$
$$E = (6.6 \times 10^{-34}\, m^2 \cdot kg/s)\left(\frac{3 \times 10^8\, m/s}{3.97 \times 10^{-7}\, m}\right)$$
$$E \approx (7 \times 10^{-34})(7.5 \times 10^{14}) \approx 5 \times 10^{-19}\, J$$

4. **A** The dependence of each of the broadening effects on distance (r) is provided or can be deduced from information in the passage. As in all ranking questions, starting with the extremes is the best approach. The passage states that the van der Waal effect is proportional to $1/r^6$. Therefore it extinguishes the most rapidly, eliminating choices B, C, and D. Electric field strength is proportional to $1/r^2$. Therefore, the linear Stark effect is also proportional to $1/r^2$ and the quadratic Stark effect is proportional to $(1/r^2)^2$ or $1/r^4$. The resonance effect is stated in the passage as proportional to $1/r^3$. These facts explain the rest of the ranking in choice A.

5. **C** As the emitter and observer approach each other, the Doppler effect predicts an upward shift in frequency. Orange light is lower frequency than yellow light, and is thus not a possible color that the earthbound observer could perceive. With increasing temperature, atoms exhibit a wider range of velocities, and thus emissions would exhibit greater broadening, eliminating choice A. The passage indicates that all atoms have unique emission spectra, eliminating choice B. Hydrogen bonding only occurs if the donor hydrogen is bonded to F, O, or N, eliminating choice D.

6. **D** Consider a situation where n_{final} is always 1. For increasing values of $n_{initial}$, λ should decrease because the energy transition is larger and wavelength is inversely related to energy. Therefore, choices A, B, and C are not possible because they would result in increasing λ for increasing energy level transitions. As evident from Figure 1, the energy gap between adjacent energy levels decreases with increasing values of n. Mathematically, $E \propto |1/n_{final}^2 - 1/n_{initial}^2|$. Since $E \propto 1/\lambda$, choice D is the best answer.

7. **C** The principal quantum number, n, defines the energy level as a function of increasing radial distances from the nucleus. The shape of orbitals is given by the l quantum number, eliminating choice A. The orientation of orbitals is given by the m_l quantum number, eliminating choice B. Electron spin, m_s, is its own quantum number, eliminating choice D.

SOLUTIONS TO PRACTICE PASSAGE 2

1. **B** None of these molecules are linear. The passage states that the number of normal modes of vibration is $3N - 6$ for non-linear molecules. If there are nine normal modes of vibration, $3N - 6 = 9$, and $N = 5$. Only methane, choice B, has 5 atoms.

2. **A** From the passage, stretching and bending are types of vibration, while translation and rotation are not. All vibrations can potentially produce peaks in IR spectra, so choices B, C, and D are eliminated. Changes in translational and rotational movements alone do not show up in IR.

3. **A** If $v = 0$ and h and u are constant, the equation for vibration energy reduces as follows:

$$E = \left(v + \frac{1}{2}\right)\left(\frac{h}{2\pi}\right)\sqrt{\frac{k}{u}}$$

$$E \propto \sqrt{k}$$

The energy of the ground state is proportional to the square root of the force constant k. The passage states that k is larger for stronger bonds, and the bond in N_2 is strongest since it has the highest bond energy (see Table 1). N_2 must have the highest vibrational energy in the ground state.

4. **D** The passage states that only those normal modes of vibration that produce a change in the dipole moment of a molecule will absorb IR light. Since O_2 has no dipole, it will not have any peaks in an IR spectrum. Note that while the molecule SO_3 as a whole has no dipole, its individual bonds do have detectable dipoles.

5. **C** T-shaped requires trigonal bipyramidal geometry along with three atoms and two lone pairs of electrons around the central atom. SF_4 has trigonal bypyramidal geometry but has four atoms bound so it is see-saw and not T-shaped, eliminating choice A. Both FO_3^- and NH_3 have three atoms bound and one lone pair so they belong to the tetrahedral geometric family, eliminating choices B and D. FCl_3 has three atoms bound to it and two lone pairs, making choice C the correct answer.

6. **B** Deuterium (D) has one proton, one neutron, and an atomic mass of 2. For D_2, $u = 2 \times 2 /(2 + 2) = 1$. For H_2, $u = 1 \times 1 / (1 + 1) = 1/2$. Since v, h, and k are all constant in this comparison, the vibration energy equation in the passage reduces as follows:

$$E = \left(v + \frac{1}{2}\right)\left(\frac{h}{2\pi}\right)\sqrt{\frac{k}{u}}$$

$$E \propto \frac{1}{\sqrt{u}}$$

The ratio of this energy for D_2 to H_2 is:

$$\frac{E_{D_2}}{E_{H_2}} = \frac{\dfrac{1}{\sqrt{1}}}{\dfrac{1}{\sqrt{1/2}}} = \frac{1}{\sqrt{2}}$$

The quantity must be greater than 0.5 but less than 1, so only choice B is possible.

7. **D** A molecule essentially exists as an average of its resonance structures. No individual resonance structure exists in isolation. In nitrate there are three bonds of equal strength, containing about 33% N=O double bond character and about 67% N—O single bond character. Therefore, there will be only one stretch peak in the IR spectrum intermediate to the N—O and N=O stretches that accounts for all three of these bonds in nitrate.

SOLUTIONS TO PRACTICE PASSAGE 3

1. **C** Because the gas phase of a substance occupies a much larger volume than its liquid phase, high volume or high pressure containment would be required if the liquid-vapor phase transition were to be exploited. The volume change accompanying a liquid-solid transition is much more modest by contrast. While B seems an attractive explanation, it is a false statement. Substances have higher heats of vaporization than heats of fusion because more intermolecular interactions need to be formed or broken in the liquid-vapor transition than in the solid-liquid transition. Phase change is an isothermal process, so A is incorrect. The critical point is the temperature and pressure above which a substance takes on the characteristic of a supercritical fluid, which is neither gas nor liquid, and thus not relevant to the question.

2. **C** Conduction describes heat transfer by direct contact between atoms or molecules, while convection describes heat transfer by bulk movement of the material medium. Since atoms or molecules in a solid are relatively constrained in their positions by an extensive network of intermolecular forces, they are unable to transfer heat by bulk movement required for convection, but well situated to participate in conductive transfer. By contrast, molecules in a fluid have much greater freedom to move, and thus transfer heat primarily by convection.

3. **B** This is best approached by establishing the correctness of each numbered statement and using it to eliminate answer choices. Item I is not correct, because in the equation relating temperature to heat, $q = mc\Delta T$, the specific heat c equals $q/m\Delta T$ which does not equal the area underneath the curve on a T vs. q graph. Thus, answer choices A and D can be eliminated. As both remaining answer choices contain Item II, it must be correct. The segment corresponding to heating of the liquid phase has the steepest slope, meaning that a small amount of heat is required to cause a large change in temperature. Item III is false because the segment described represents a phase change, which is isothermal. This is confirmed by the horizontal nature of this graph segment. Since temperature is a measure of average kinetic energy, an isothermal process implies no change in average kinetic energy. During phase change, energy is used to overcome intermolecular forces, not contribute to increased molecular motion.

4. **B** A gas is characterized by its absence of intermolecular forces while a solid is characterized by its abundance of intermolecular forces. Thus, the transition described requires the absorption of energy to overcome these forces (eliminate choices C and D). Because gas molecules are unconstrained by intermolecular forces, they have the greatest freedom of movement in this phase, and thus a gas is maximally disordered indicating an increase in entropy (Choice B).

5. **A** The passage points out that the primary consideration in choosing a PCM is ensuring that its melting point is close to the desired temperature of the system or process to which it is being applied. Thus, since 30 to 45°C is a range around normal body temperature (37°C), this was the defining criteria for choosing the material. Low thermal conductivity would reduce the ability of the PCM to absorb or release heat, so B is eliminated. High density would not be practical for a garment, so C is eliminated. No mention is made of phase change materials needing to be in aqueous solution or water soluble. Thus D can be eliminated.

6.   C   The solution to this question involves calculating and summing the heat transfer in 3 parts. The first (q_1) accounts for the heat needed to warm the ice from $-10°C$ to $0°C$:

$$q_1 = mc_{ice}\Delta T = (0.018\text{kg})(\sim 2 \text{ kJ/kg} \times \text{K})(10 \text{ K}) \approx 0.36 \text{ kJ}$$

The second (q_2) accounts for the heat absorbed during the melting transition:

$$q_2 = n(\Delta H_f) = [(18 \text{ g})/(18 \text{ g/mol})](\sim 6 \text{ kJ/mol}) \approx 6 \text{ kJ}$$

The third (q_3) accounts for the heat needed to warm the resulting water from $0°C$ to $10°C$:

$$q_3 = mc_{water}\Delta T = (0.018\text{kg})(\sim 4 \text{ kJ/kg} \times \text{K})(10 \text{ K}) \approx 0.72 \text{ kJ}$$

Summing the heats for each step yields $q_1 + q_2 + q_3 = 0.36 \text{ kJ} + 0.72 \text{ kJ} + 6 \text{ kJ} \approx 7 \text{ kJ}$, which is closest to answer C.

7.   D   The correct answer to this question should explain specifically why phase change materials function more effectively in small volume cells than large volume units. A is incorrect because if a material were corrosive, it would be equally difficult to find suitable materials to make either small or large cells. B is incorrect because this statement violates the principle of conservation of mass. While many phase change materials are costly, this does not explain why small cells *function* more effectively than large cells. Thus C is not the best answer. This leaves D as the only reasonable explanation. Thermal conductivity directly affects the PCM's ability to transfer heat with the surroundings.

SOLUTIONS TO PRACTICE PASSAGE 4

1.   B   Choice B is correct because gases at equal temperatures have equal average kinetic energies $\frac{1}{2}mv^2$, but not necessarily equal velocities (v) because their masses (m) may differ. From the equation in the question, temperature is related to molecular momentum (mv) since it is related to average kinetic energy, so choice A is a true statement and eliminated. The Boltzmann constant, with units of J/K, relates energy per unit temperature. It is therefore independent of the absolute quantity of temperature, eliminating choice C as a true statement. Finally, Figure 1 shows that Z and T (average kinetic energy) are inversely related at high pressures, eliminating choice D as a true statement.

2.   A   The question is asking about the changes in Z with increased pressure at a given temperature. Temperature is constant, so choices C and D are eliminated. At very low pressures, gases behave ideally ($Z = 1$) regardless of temperature. As pressure is increased on real gases at low temperature, the molecules are moving so slowly that their attractive forces dominate yielding a value of PV lower than ideal and resulting in a $Z < 1$. Continuing to increase pressure will eventually cause the molecules to get close enough that they experience repulsive forces yielding a value of PV greater than ideal and resulting in a $Z > 1$.

3. **D** Looking at Equation 1, a value of $Z = 1$ results in the Ideal Gas Law, implying that a compressibility factor equal to this represents an ideal gas. Choice D shows a gas with a constant value of $Z = 1$.

4. **A** The passage states that the van der Waals equation corrects for real pressures and volumes. Looking at Equation 2, a is associated with the pressure term, while b is associated with the volume term. At high pressures and low temperatures, real gas molecules experience attractive forces and the gas is more compressible. The real gas pressure is therefore lower than ideal pressure and requires an additive correction: $P_{ideal} = P_{real} + \dfrac{an^2}{V^2}$. At high pressures, real gas molecular volume becomes significant and the gas is less compressible. The real gas volume is therefore higher than ideal volume and requires a subtractive correction: $V_{ideal} = V_{real} - nb$.

5. **C** Both real and ideal gases possess the same molecular mass, eliminating choices B and D. A decrease in repulsion would result in an increase in volume, eliminating choice A. The van der Waals equation corrects for the decrease in measured pressure in real gases due to intermolecular forces (and decreased momentum) and the increase in volume due to the gas occupying volume, making choice C the correct answer.

6. **C** Compressibility of $Z = 0.8$ is relatively close to the ideal value of $Z = 1$. Molecules which best exhibit ideal gas behavior have low molecular weights and weak intermolecular forces. Ammonia and water undergo hydrogen bonding, a strong intermolecular force, eliminating choices B and D. Bromine, which is non-polar like methane, is nonetheless heavier than methane, eliminating choice A and leaving choice C as the best answer.

7. **A** At the critical point, the attractive forces of the gas (causing condensation) cannot overcome the kinetic energy of the gas (temperature) resulting in a failure to condense making Item I true and eliminating choice D. Changes in volume will not impact the critical temperature as it is a property dependent upon intermolecular attractions, eliminating Item II and choice. Finally, ideal gases do not condense because they are assumed to have no intermolecular attraction. Therefore, they cannot have a critical temperature making Item III false and eliminating choice C.

SOLUTIONS TO PRACTICE PASSAGE 5

1. **C** According to salt solubility rules, mercury salts are insoluble except for nitrates (NO_3^-), perchlorates (ClO_4^-), and acetates (CH_3COO^-). Since the salt in Beaker 1 dissolved completely, it cannot be choice D. From the passage, Solution 1 has a concentration of 2 M, a temperature of 298 K, and produces an osmotic pressure of 147 atm. Given the value for R, solve for the van't Hoff factor:

$$\Pi = MiRT$$

$$i = \Pi/MRT$$

$$i = (147 \text{ atm})/(2\ M)(0.0821 \text{L·atm/K·mol})(298\text{K})$$

$$i \approx (150)/(2)(0.08)(300) \approx 3$$

Since, the van't Hoff factor is 3, the salt in Solution 1 must dissociate into three ions. Choices A and B dissociate into two ions, and choice C dissociates into three ions.

2. **B** $Hg(NO_3)_2$ undergoes the following equilibrium:

$$Hg(NO_3)_2 \rightleftharpoons Hg^{2+} + 2NO_3^-$$

Since choices C and D are both soluble, they will effectively add NO_3^- and Hg^{2+} ions into the solution (along with Ag^+ and ClO_4^- ions). According to Le Chatelier's principle, adding products would drive the equilibrium in the reverse direction toward the reactants, decreasing dissociation. According to salt solubility rules, $HgCl_2$ is insoluble and would therefore act as a spectator compound. Therefore, choice A would not shift the equilibrium significantly. Choice B is correct because Cl^- ions from NaCl would react with Hg^{2+} ions from $Hg(NO_3)_2$ causing $HgCl_2$ to precipitate out of solution. Since Hg^{2+} is a product of the original equilibrium and is being removed, Le Chatelier's principle predicts that this equilibrium will shift further to the right, increasing dissociation.

3. **B** Since each molecule of Hg_2CO_3 dissociates into 2 moles of Hg^+ and 1 mole of CO_3^-, x moles of Hg_2CO_3 would yield $2x$ moles of Hg^+ and x moles of CO_3^-. Substitute these variables into the K_{sp} expression to solve for the saturated Hg^+ concentration.

$$Hg_2(CO_3)(s) \rightleftharpoons 2Hg^+(aq) + CO_3^-(aq)$$

$$x \rightleftharpoons 2x + x$$

$$K_{sp} = [2Hg^+]^2[CO_3] = (2x)^2(x) = 4x^3 = 3.6 \times 10^{-17}$$

$$x^3 = 9 \times 10^{-18}$$

$$x \approx 2 \times 10^{-6}$$

$$[Hg^+] = 2x \approx 4 \times 10^{-6}$$

4. **A** Both the boiling point elevation ($\Delta T = k_b im$) and freezing point depression ($\Delta T = -k_f im$) are directly proportional to the molality, m, of the solution where $m = \dfrac{\text{moles solute}}{\text{kg solvent}}$. Because D_2O has a density of 1.1 g/cm³, 1 L of D_2O has greater mass than 1 L of H_2O. This decreases the value of m and therefore decreases the change in freezing point and boiling point temperatures making choice D incorrect and choice A correct. Vapor pressure depression ($\Delta P_A = -X_B P_A^\circ$) and osmotic pressure ($\Pi = MiRT$) are not dependent on mass of the solvent and are negligibly affected.

5. **D** The Lewis dot structure of XeF_4 reveals that Xe has four single bonds to each F and two lone pairs. Therefore, these molecules have octahedral geometry and a square planar shape eliminating choices A (Xe is sp^3d^2 hybridized) and C (Hg has a filled d shell and Xe has a filled p shell). Using the definition of formal charge $FC = V - B/2 - L$, xenon's formal charge is calculated to be zero ruling out choice B. According to the rules for assigning oxidation numbers, F has a -1 oxidation state; since the molecule has an overall neutral charge, the central atom must have a $+4$ oxidation state. Thus, choice D is correct.

6. **A** According to phase solubility rules, the solubility of gases in liquids increases with decreasing temperature. The phase solubility rules also state that solubility of gases in liquids increases with increasing pressure, eliminating choice B. Decreasing the volume of the water would decrease the total amount of mercury vapor dissolved in the water and would not affect the solubility of mercury in water, eliminating choice C. Finally, choice D is incorrect because the question is asking about a thermodynamic property rather than a kinetic property. The rate of mercury addition will have no effect on the solubility of mercury in solution.

7. **C** Since all mercury salts are insoluble besides nitrates, perchlorates, and acetates, a Hg cation will react with any other anion present and create a precipitate. Thus the Cl^- anions from $CaCl_2$ will react with Hg^{2+} cations from $Hg(ClO_4)_2$ to form the precipitate $HgCl_2$. Choice A is incorrect because Hg^{2+} cations will be consumed by Cl^- and according to Le Chatelier's principle, the $Hg(ClO_4)_2$ equilibrium will be shifted toward the ionic products. Choice B is incorrect because according to salt solubility rules all perchlorates are soluble. Choice D is incorrect because Cl^- anions will get consumed by reacting with the Hg^{2+} rather than forming Cl_2.

SOLUTIONS TO PRACTICE PASSAGE 6

1. **A** The passage states that bimolecular reactions occur between two molecules; therefore answer choices B and C can be eliminated. Bimolecular reactions produce one activated complex, as stated in paragraph 1, therefore D can be eliminated, making answer choice A correct.

2. **B**   The passage has experimental data and the rate expression can be determined for the bimolecular Reaction 1, so the rate constant can be determined, eliminating choice D. The overall rate order for any bimolecular reaction is 2, so the rate equation for Reaction 1 is: rate = k[Cl][Br_2]. Using Figure 1, the initial concentration of Br_2 is $1 \times 10^{-9}\,M$ and the initial concentration of Cl is $0.5 \times 10^{-9}\,M$. Since the initial rate tangent line passes through the origin, any point (such as $x = 0.02$, $y = 0.8$) along it can be used to solve for the slope and obtain the initial rate of the reaction:

$$\text{rate}_{\text{initial}} = \frac{\Delta \text{ concentration}}{\Delta \text{ time}} = \frac{0.8 \times 10^{-9}\,M}{2.0 \times 10^{-2}\,\text{s}} = 4 \times 10^{-8}\,M \cdot \text{s}^{-1}$$

Solve the rate equation for k:

$$k = \frac{\text{rate}_{\text{initial}}}{[\text{Cl}]_{\text{initial}}[\text{Br}_2]_{\text{initial}}}$$

$$k = \frac{4 \times 10^{-8}\,M \cdot \text{s}^{-1}}{(0.5 \times 10^{-9}\,M)(1.0 \times 10^{-9}\,M)} = 8 \times 10^{10}\,M^{-1}\text{s}^{-1}$$

Therefore, choice A can be eliminated because it is the wrong value, and choice C can be eliminated because it has the wrong units, leaving B as the correct answer.

3. **C** H_2O is a product of Step 7, making choice C correct. BrO_3^- is used in Step 1 and never seen again so it is a reactant and choice A can be eliminated. $HBrO_2$ gets produced in Step 3 and then used up in Step 4 making it an intermediate and eliminating choice B. HOBr is produced in Steps 3 and 5, and then completely used up in Step 6 so it is also an intermediate and choice D is eliminated.

4. **B**   This is a two-by-two question, and is best answered using process of elimination. Equations 1 and 2 can be used to answer this question. In Equation 2, $Z \propto \sqrt{T}$ so increasing T by a factor of 4 would increase Z by a factor of 2. This eliminates choices C and D. If Z is increased it causes k_T to increase by Equation 1. Also, since k_T is proportional to $e^{-1/T}$ in that same equation, increased temperature directly increases k_T independent of Z. Therefore, choice A is eliminated, and B is correct.

5. **B**   This question is best answered using process of elimination. Although intermediates can be detected, an activated complex is theoretical and cannot be detected, eliminating choice A. As indicated by Equations 1 and 2, the rate constant is independent of reactant concentrations, eliminating choice C. Although stoichiometry cannot necessarily be used to determine the rate law of an overall reaction, for a bimolecular reaction the reaction order is 2 by definition and is indicated by the stoichiometry, eliminating answer choice D. The passage states the steric factor depends on reactants colliding with the correct orientation. In complex reactions, the reactants have a lower probability of colliding with correct orientation so the steric factor will be lower, making choice B the best answer.

6. **D**   Although the reaction mechanism is outlined in the passage, it does not state which is the slow step of the reaction. It is therefore impossible to determine the order of the reaction with respect to BrO_3^- or the effect of a change of concentration on the rate of the reaction.

7. **C** Since the passage states that this reaction is a bimolecular reaction, the rate equation can be determined, eliminating answer choice D. Bimolecular reactions are second order by definition as the rate depends on the initial concentrations of both participants in the reaction. Cl_2 does not appear in the reaction at all, so choice A can be eliminated. Both ClBr and Br are products, so choice B can be eliminated, leaving choice C as the correct answer.

SOLUTIONS TO PRACTICE PASSAGE 8

1. **C** Looking at Figure 1, as more carbon dioxide is absorbed in ocean water the pH decreases, causing the pOH to increase (eliminate A). An increase in CO_2 concentration will not cause the K_a to change, since temperature is the only variable capable of causing such an effect (eliminate B). Choice D is incorrect because Figure 1 shows that as CO_2 concentration in seawater increases, CO_3^{2-} ion concentration decreases. Consequently, the equilibrium in Reaction #4 will shift to the right, resulting in increased calcium ion concentration. For the same reason, more calcium carbonate dissolves and the hardness of the shells would be expected to decrease.

2. **D** The passage states that mollusks prefer regions with high CO_3^{2-} ion concentration so they can maintain the calcium carbonate in their exoskeletons. CO_2 absorption leads to ocean acidification and decreased CO_3^{2-} ion concentration according to Figure 1. Shallow water is closer to the air-ocean interface where this effect is most likely to occur (eliminate A). The passage states that CO_3^{2-} ion concentration is relatively saturated in shallow water implying that at depth there is less available. In addition, deeper water is more likely to be colder, and this increases the solubility (i.e., breakdown) of calcium carbonate. Therefore, choice B is eliminated. Gases are more soluble in liquids as temperature decreases. Therefore, colder waters are more susceptible to ocean acidification and drops in CO_3^{2-} ion concentration (eliminate C). Calcium carbonate is unique because its solubility decreases with increased temperature. Therefore, warmer water temperatures may mitigate exoskeleton breakdown in the short term, making choice D the best answer.

3. **C** Plateaus indicate the buffer region when a weak acid is titrated with a strong base. These regions are the half equivalence points where pH equals pK_a. The pK_a values for the two acid dissociation reactions are between 3 and 4 (3.6) and between 10 and 11 (10.2) for Reactions #2 and #3 respectively.

4. **D** The general theme of this passage is that as carbon dioxide levels increase, water acidity increases and CO_3^{2-} ion concentration decreases. Thus, if carbon dioxide is removed, the acidity decreases (eliminate A and B) and the CO_3^{2-} ion concentration increases. Since this is the case, the equilibrium shown in Reaction #4 will shift to the left indicating that calcium carbonate will precipitate out of solution.

5. **B** Since a precipitate forms, the solution above it must be saturated. Given the stoichiometry of the solubility equilibrium: $CaCO_3(s) \rightleftharpoons Ca^{2+}(aq) + CO_3^{2-}(aq)$, X moles of calcium carbonate will dissociate into X moles of calcium ions and X moles of carbonate ions. Writing out the K_{sp} expression for this reaction and substituting, we get:

$$K_{sp} = [Ca^{2+}(aq)][CO_3^{2-}(aq)] = [X][X]$$

$$K_{sp} = X^2$$

$$8.7 \times 10^{-9} = X^2$$

$X = 9 \times 10^{-5}$ M, which corresponds to 9×10^{-5} moles in the 1 L solution given.

SOLUTIONS TO PRACTICE PASSAGE 9

1. **D**   The rapid expansion of gas that is insulated from the environment best approximates an adiabatic process, where no heat is exchanged between system and surroundings. All of the internal change of the system is in the form of work. During snowmaking, pressure decreases (eliminates C), the volume of water vapor increases (eliminates B), and the temperature rapidly decreases (eliminates A).

2. **A**   Wet bulb temperature can never exceed the dry bulb temperature. According to the passage, the wet bulb temperature results from the evaporation of water from a cloth surrounding the thermometer bulb. Provided the surrounding air is not saturated with moisture, the water on the cloth vaporizes, expands, and cools in an adiabatic process (no heat is added to make this happen). This cooling decreases the temperature reading of the thermometer. Wet bulb temperature is equal to dry bulb temperature at 100% relative humidity because no evaporation will take place. At anything less than 100% relative humidity, wet bulb temperature will be less than dry bulb temperature, eliminating B. The dew point is the temperature at which no more water can vaporize because the air is saturated at 100% humidity. At this point, both the wet and dry bulb readings are equal to the dew point, eliminating C. As temperature increases past the dew point, relative humidity decreases provided the moisture content of the air remains the same, and both wet and dry bulb readings exceed the dew point, eliminating D.

3. **B**   Deposition is a change from vapor to solid phase, so energy is released to the surroundings in an exothermic process. Therefore, the answer must be negative and choices A and C are eliminated. The enthalpy change of deposition is calculated by reversing the signs of the enthalpies of vaporization (gas to liquid) and fusion (liquid to solid) and adding them together. The values at 0°C from Table 1 are used because they are closest to snowmaking conditions. Therefore, $H_{dep} = -[H_{vap} + H_{fus}] = -[45 \text{ kJ mol}^{-1} + 6 \text{ kJ mol}^{-1}] = -51 \text{ kJ mol}^{-1}$.

4. **B**   As relative humidity increases, there is less of a gradient for evaporation to occur. Therefore, the water on the cloth of a wet bulb thermometer is less likely to evaporate resulting in less cooling. Differences between wet and dry bulb temperature readings increase with decreasing relative humidity, eliminating A. According to Figure 1, as relative humidity increases the range of possible snowmaking temperatures decreases. Heat of vaporization is a constant dependent on temperature and will not change with increasing humidity.

5.   **A**   Throttling during snowmaking approximates an adiabatic process, where no heat is exchanged between system and surroundings ($q = 0$). According to the first law of thermodynamics, $U = q + w$. For the adiabatic process of snowmaking:

$$U = q + w$$

$$U = 0 + w$$

$$U = w$$

As the water vapor expands and cools, its temperature and internal energy decrease and work is done by the gas on the surroundings (both U and w are negative quantities). Since q is 0 and both U and w are equivalent negative values, only choice A is possible.

6.   **C**   The initial vaporization of water from the cloth in a wet bulb thermometer is an adiabatic process. No heat is supplied to make this happen. As the water vaporizes it expands and does work on the environment. Therefore it loses internal energy (eliminates B) and cools both the cloth and the thermometer bulb. The temperature reading, a measure of average kinetic energy, falls as a result (eliminates A). Heat is not exchanged in an adiabatic process. The cloth cools not because it releases heat but because its internal energy decreases as the water vaporizes, expands, and does work on the surroundings (eliminates D).

7.   **A**   As stated in other solutions, wet bulb temperature will equal dry bulb temperature at 100% humidity and be less than dry bulb temperature at any lower relative humidity. Choices C and D both represent possible snowmaking conditions according to Figure 1 because at 100% humidity wet and dry bulb temperatures are the same. These points on the graph fall within the possible snowmaking region. Since choices A and B both have 50% relative humidity, choice A is the best answer because it is warmer than B. A wet bulb temperature of 0°C at 50% relative humidity is less than the dry bulb temperature (actually about 3°C in this case) which is the most likely to exceed limits for possible snowmaking.

SOLUTIONS TO PRACTICE PASSAGE 10

1.   **A**   Part of the energy requirement for hydrolysis comes from the surroundings, so the free energy that must be supplied by the battery must be less than the change in enthalpy for the overall reaction. This eliminates C and D. Gibb's Energy is determined by the formula $\Delta G = \Delta H - T\Delta S$. Substituting values for enthalpy, temperature, and entropy from the passage gives:

$$\Delta G = (286 \text{ kJ}) - (298 \text{ K})(0.16 \text{ kJ/K})$$
$$\Delta G \approx (286 \text{ kJ}) - (300 \text{ K})(0.16 \text{ kJ/K})$$
$$\Delta G \approx 286 \text{ kJ} - 48 \text{ kJ} \approx 238 \text{ kJ}$$

2. **C** Given the overall reaction for hydrolysis in the passage, the half reactions are as follows:

$$2H^+(aq) + 2e^- \rightarrow H_2(g) \text{ (reduction at cathode)}$$

$$H_2O(l) \rightarrow \frac{1}{2}O_2(g) + 2H^+(aq) + 2e^- \text{ (oxidation at anode)}$$

At the cathode, positive charge decreases and pH increases as protons are consumed (eliminates A). At the anode, positive charge increases and pH decreases as protons are generated (eliminates B and D).

3. **A** Choices C and D can be eliminated right away since positive potentials only occur for spontaneous reactions (which we do not have here since an external battery is required to drive the reaction). The problem can be solved using two different sets of half reactions from Table 1 whose addition will give the reaction for hydrolysis in the passage. In the first option the reduction reaction of oxygen gas to hydroxide is reversed (changing the sign) and the stoichiometry is divided by 2 (no effect on the magnitude of potential):

$$\text{CATHODE: } 2H^+(aq) + 2e^- \rightarrow H_2(g) \ E^\circ = 0.00$$

$$\text{ANODE: } H_2O(l) \rightarrow \frac{1}{2}O_2(g) + 2H^+(aq) + 2e^- \ E^\circ = -1.23$$

$$\text{NET: } H_2O(l) \rightarrow H_2(g) + \frac{1}{2}O_2(g) \ E^\circ = -1.23$$

In the second option the reduction of oxygen gas to hydroxide is again reversed (changing the sign) and the stoichiometry is divided by 2 (no effect on the magnitude of potential):

$$\text{CATHODE: } 2H_2O(l) + 2e^- \rightarrow H_2(g) + 2OH^-(aq) \ E^\circ = -0.83$$

$$\text{ANODE: } 2OH^-(aq) \rightarrow \frac{1}{2}O_2(g) + H_2O(l) + 2e^- \ E^\circ = -0.40$$

$$\text{NET: } H_2O(l) \rightarrow H_2(g) + \frac{1}{2}O_2(g) \ E^\circ = -1.23$$

4. **B** When $E_{cell} = 0$, the reaction is at equilibrium (eliminates A). At equilibrium, $Q = K_{eq}$ and the Nernst equation can be solved as follows:

$$E_{cell} = E_{cell}^\circ - \frac{RT}{zF} \ln Q$$

$$0 = E_{cell}^\circ - \frac{RT}{zF} \ln K_{eq}$$

$$\ln K_{eq} = \frac{E_{cell}^\circ zF}{RT}$$

$E^\circ_{cell} = -1.23$ V is a constant (eliminates D), and the only factors that are changing are K_{eq} and T:

$$\ln K_{eq} \propto \frac{-1.23}{T}$$

Because the standard cell potential is negative, as T increases from 298 to 400 K, ln K_{eq} also increases. Therefore, K_{eq} must increase. This makes sense because we expect K_{eq} to increase with increasing temperature for an endothermic reaction. Since the environment is contributing more energy at higher temperatures, the battery does not have to contribute as much free energy (eliminates C).

5.   C   Given the half reactions in hydrolysis, a negative charge accumulates in the fluid around the cathode, and a positive charge accumulates in the fluid around the anode:

$$2H^+(aq) + 2e^- \rightarrow H_2(g) \text{ (reduction at cathode)}$$

$$H_2O(l) \rightarrow \frac{1}{2}O_2(g) + 2H^+(aq) + 2e^- \text{ (oxidation at anode)}$$

This immediately hinders the flow of electrons and is the reason why the hydrolysis of pure water is very slow. Adding an electrolyte is like adding a salt bridge in that it neutralizes the charge build up. Like all cells, the salt bridge cation migrates to the cathode and the salt bridge anion migrates to the anode. Adding an electrolyte increases conductivity (eliminates D) and increases the rate of hydrolysis (eliminates A and B). The fact that $Na^+(aq)$ is less likely to be reduced than $H^+(aq)$ is beneficial for producing hydrogen and oxygen gas. Finally, $Cl^-(aq)$ has a lower oxidation potential than hydroxide and oxygen gas will preferentially be produced at the anode.

6.   D   Oxidation always occurs at the anode and reduction always occurs at the cathode of all cells. Oxygen gas is produced from the oxidation of water (or hydroxide ion) at the anode. This eliminates Item I, so A and C are also eliminated. Therefore, Item II must be correct. Since oxidation is loss of electrons and always occurs at the anode, Item II is true for all cells. Finally, electrolysis is not spontaneous, so electrons are forced towards a charge they would not go spontaneously. Therefore, the cathode is negative and the anode is positive in electrolytic cells. Item III is also correct and D is the answer.

7.   D   Adding an electrolyte minimizes charge build up and increases conductivity in electrolysis. However, it is important that the electrolyte is not preferentially oxidized or reduced instead of water. Therefore, the cation should be less likely to be reduced than hydronium (eliminates B) and the anion should be less likely to be oxidized (more likely to be reduced) than hydroxide (D is correct). The important comparisons are between the two cations in solution competing for reduction (eliminates A) or between the two anions in solution competing for oxidation (eliminates C).

Chapter 17
Biology on the MCAT

Biology is by far the most information-dense section on the MCAT. MCAT Biology topics span seven different semester-length courses (biochemistry, molecular biology, cell biology, microbiology, genetics, anatomy, and physiology). Further, the application of this material is potentially vast; passages can discuss anything from the details of some biochemical pathway to the complexities of genetic studies, to the nuances of an unusual disease. Fortunately, biology is the subject that MCAT students typically find the most interesting, and the one they have the most background in. People who want to go to medical school have an inherent interest in biology; thus this subject, although vast, seems more manageable than all the others on the MCAT.

Biology makes up about 70 to 80 percent of the questions in the Biological Sciences section of the test (the others are organic chemistry). A typical MCAT will have 5 to 6 Biology passages and about 8 to 9 Biology FSQs. Let's take a look at the passages.

TACKLING A PASSAGE

Generally speaking, time is not an issue in the BS section of the MCAT. Because students have a stronger background in biology than in other subjects, the passages seem more understandable; in fact, readers sometimes find themselves getting caught up and interested in the passage. Often, students report having about 5 to 10 minutes "left over" after completing the section. This means that an additional minute or so can potentially be spent on each passage, thinking and understanding.

Passage Types as They Apply to Biology

Information/Situation Presentation

This is the most common type of Biology passage on the MCAT. These passages generally appear as one of two variants: either a basic concept with additional levels of detail included (for example, all the detail you ever wanted to know about the electron transport chain), or a novel concept with ties to basic information (for example, a rare demyelinating disease). Either way, Biology passages are notorious for testing concepts in unusual contexts. The key to dealing with these passages is to, first, not become anxious about all the stuff you might not know, and second, figure out how the basics you do know apply to the new situation. For example, you might be presented with a passage that introduces hormones you never heard of, or novel drugs to combat diseases you didn't know existed. First, don't panic. Second, look for how these new things fit into familiar categories: for example, "peptide vs. steroid," or "sympathetic antagonist." Then answer the questions with these basics in mind.

That said, you have to know your basics. This will increase your confidence in answering freestanding questions, as well as increase the speed with which to find the information in the passage. The astute MCAT student will never waste time staring at a question thinking, "Should I know this?" Instead, because she has a solid understanding of the necessary core knowledge, she'll say, "No, I am NOT expected to know this, and I am going to look for it in the passage."

Experiment/Research Presentation

This is the second most common type of Biology passage. It typically presents the details behind an experiment along with data tables, graphs, and figures. Often these are the most difficult passages to deal with because they require an understanding of the reasoning behind the experiment, the logic to each step, and the ability to analyze the results and form conclusions.

Persuasive Reasoning

This is the least common passage type in Biology. It typically describes some biological phenomenon, and then offers one or more theories to explain it. Questions in Persuasive Reasoning passages ask you to determine support for one of the theories, or present new evidence and ask which theory is now contradicted.

One last thought about Biology passages in general: Because the array of topics is so vast, Biology passages often pull questions from multiple areas of biology into a single, general topic. Consider, for example, a passage on renal function. Question topics could include basics about the kidney, transmembrane transport, autonomic control, blood pressure, hormones, biochemical energy needs, or a genetics question about a rare kidney disease.

READING A BIOLOGY PASSAGE

Although tempting, try not to get bogged down reading all the little details in a passage. Again, because most premeds have an inherent interest in biology and the mechanisms behind disease, it's very easy to get lost in the science behind the passages. In spite of having that "extra" time, you don't want to use it all up reading what isn't necessary. Each passage type requires a slightly different style of reading.

Information/Situation Presentation passages require the least reading. These should be skimmed to get an idea of the location of information within the passage. These passages include a fair amount of detail that you might not need, so save the reading of these details until a question comes up about them. Then go back and read for the finer nuances.

Experiment/Research Presentation passages require the most reading. You are practically guaranteed to get questions that ask you about the details of the experiment, why a particular step was carried out, why the results are what they are, or how the result might change if a particular variable is altered. It's worth spending a little more time reading to understand the experiment. However, because there will be a fair number of questions unrelated to the experiment, you might consider answering these first, then going back for the experiment details.

Persuasive Argument passages are somewhere in the middle. You can skim them for location of information, but you also want to spend a little time reading the details of and thinking about the arguments presented. It is extremely likely that you will be asked a question about them.

Advanced Reading Skills

To improve your ability to read and glean information from a passage, you need to practice. Be critical when you read the content; watch for vague areas or holes in the passage that aren't explained clearly. Remember that information about new topics will be woven throughout the passage; you may need to piece together information from several paragraphs and a figure to get the whole picture.

After you've read, highlighted, and mapped a passage (more on this in a bit) stop and ask yourself the following questions:

- What was this passage about? What was the conclusion or main point?
- Was there a paragraph that was mostly background?
- Were there paragraphs or figures that seemed useless?
- What information was found in each paragraph? Why was that paragraph there?
- Are there any holes in the story?
- What extra information could I have pulled out of the passage? What inferences or conclusions could I make?
- If something unique was explained or mentioned, what might be its purpose?
- What am I *not* being told?
- Can I summarize the purpose and/or results of the experiment in a few sentences?
- Were there any comparisons in the passage?

This takes a while at first, but eventually becomes second nature and you will start doing it as you are reading the passage. If you have a study group you are working with, consider doing this as an exercise with your study partners. Take turns asking and answering the questions above. Having to explain something to someone else so not only solidifies your own knowledge, but helps you see where you might be weak.

MAPPING A BIOLOGY PASSAGE

Mapping a Biology passage is a combination of highlighting and scratch paper notes that can help you organize and understand the passage information.

Resist the temptation to highlight everything! (Everyone has done this: You're reading a biology textbook with a highlighter, and then look back and realize that the whole page is yellow!) Restrict your highlighting to a few things:

- the main theme of a paragraph.
- an unusual or unfamiliar term that is defined specifically for that passage (e.g., something that is italicized).
- statements that either support the main theme or contradict the main theme.
- list topics: sometimes lists appear in paragraph form within a passage. Highlight the general topic of the list.

Scratch paper should be organized. Make sure the passage number appears at the top of your scratch paper notes. For each paragraph, note "P1," "P2," etc., on the scratch paper, and jot down a few notes about that paragraph. Try to translate biology jargon into your own words using everyday language (this is particularly useful for experiments). Also, make sure to note down simple relationships (e.g., the relationship between two variables).

Pay attention to equations, figures, and the like to see what type of information they deal with. Don't spend a lot of time analyzing at this point, but do jot down on your scratch paper "Fig 1" and a brief summary of the data. Also, if you've discovered a list in the passage, note its topic and location down on your scratch paper.

Let's take a look at how we might highlight and map a passage from Practice Test 1. Below is passage 4, on eye physiology.

The wall of the human eye is composed of three layers of tissue, an outer layer of tough connective tissue, a middle layer of darkly pigmented vascular tissue, and an inner layer of neural tissue. The outer layer is subdivided into the sclera, the white portion, and the cornea, the clear portion. The inner layer is more commonly known as the *retina* and contains several types of cells.

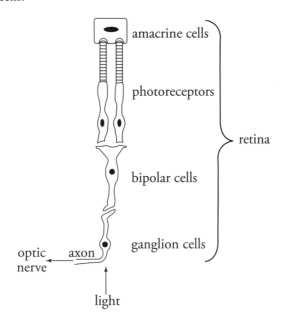

Figure 1 Retina Structure

The photoreceptors of the retina include rods and cones which respond to light under different circumstances. Rods are more sensitive to light but cannot distinguish color; cones are less sensitive to light overall, but can respond to different wavelengths. Response to light involves visual pigments, which in all cases consist of a light-absorbing molecule called *retinal* (derived from vitamin A) bound to a protein called *opsin*. The type of opsin in the visual pigment determines the wavelength specificity of the retinal. The specific visual pigment in rod cells is called *rhodopsin*.

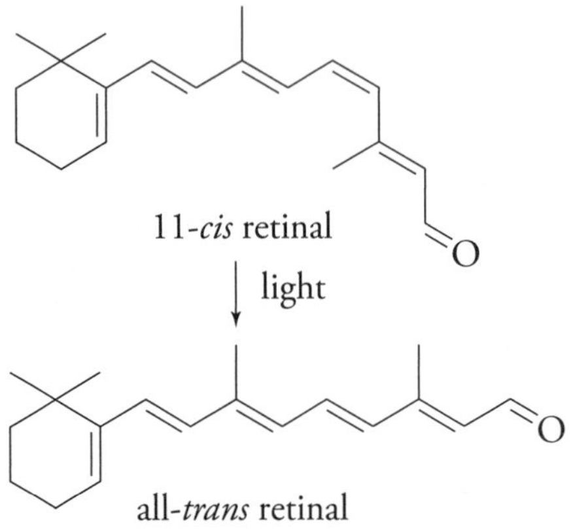

11-*cis* retinal

light

all-*trans* retinal

Figure 2 The Two Forms of Retinal

In the absence of light, Na^+ channels in the membranes of rod cells are kept open by cGMP. The conformational change in retinal upon light absorption causes changes in opsin as well; this triggers a pathway by which phosphodiesterase (PDE) is activated. Active PDE converts cGMP to GMP, causing it to dissociate from the Na^+ channel and the channel to close. Until retinal regains its bent shape (helped by enzymes), the rod is unable to respond further to light.

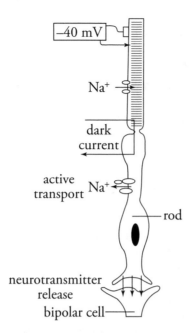

Figure 3   Rod Cell in Darkness

Visual defects can be caused by abnormal visual pigments or by misshapen eyeballs; for example, myopia (nearsightedness) is due to an eyeball that is too long, causing light rays from distant objects to focus in front of the retina so the image appears blurry.

Analysis and Passage Map

This passage is an Information Presentation passage and starts out with a paragraph about the structure of the eye and its layers. This is primarily a background paragraph and can be skimmed quickly, with a few words highlighted. Figure 1 shows the detail of the retina.

The second paragraph goes into more detail about the photoreceptors, and specifically compares the functions of rods and cones. There are few more italicized terms; this paragraph is presenting information that is beyond what you are expected to know about the eye for the MCAT. Figure 2 shows the conversion between the two forms of retinal.

The third paragraph presents details about rod cells, and in particular points out a unique feature of rod cells: that their Na^+ channels are typically open in light. On stimulation by light, they close. This is unusual behavior in the nervous system, since it is the opposite of what typically occurs. Figure 3 confirms this, as the cell in darkness appears to be resting at -40 mV, 30 mV more positive than typical neurons rest at.

The final paragraph is a brief description of visual defects. Like paragraph 1, it only needs to be skimmed briefly. Here's what your passage map might look like:

P1 – 3 layers of eyeball, Fig 1 retina detail
P2 – photoreceptors
  rods no color, more sensitive
  cones less sensitive, respond to different colors
  details on vis pigments. Fig 2 convert retinal
P3 – rod function. WEIRD Na⁺ channels open in dark, close in light.
  depol in light, hyperpol in dark
P4 – visual defects

Let's take a look at another passage from Practice Test 1. Below is passage 2, an Experiment/Research Presentation passage.

The development of sexual characteristics depends upon various factors, the most important of which are hormonal control, environmental stimuli, and the genetic makeup of the individual. The hormones that contribute to the development include the steroid hormones estrogen, progesterone, and testosterone, as well as the pituitary hormones FSH (follicle-stimulating hormone) and LH (luteinizing hormone).

To study the mechanism by which estrogen exerts its effects, a researcher performed the following experiments using cell culture assays.

Experiment 1:

Human embryonic placental mesenchyme (HEPM) cells were grown for 48 hours in Dulbecco's Modified Eagle Medium (DMEM), with media change every 12 hours. Upon confluent growth, cells were exposed to a 10 mg per mL solution of green fluorescent-labeled estrogen for 1 hour. Cells were rinsed with DMEM and observed under confocal fluorescent microscopy.

Experiment 2:

HEPM cells were grown to confluence as in Experiment 1. Cells were exposed to Pesticide A for 1 hour, followed by the 10 mg/mL solution of labeled estrogen, rinsed as in Experiment 1, and observed under confocal fluorescent microscopy.

Experiment 3:

Experiment 1 was repeated with Chinese Hamster Ovary (CHO) cells instead of HEPM cells.

Experiment 4:

CHO cells injected with cytoplasmic extracts of HEPM cells were grown to confluence, exposed to the 10 mg/mL solution of labeled estrogen for 1 hour, and observed under confocal fluorescent microscopy.

The results of these experiments are given in Table 1.

Table 1 Detection of Estrogen
(+ indicates presence of estrogen)

Experiment	Media	Cytoplasm	Nucleus
1	+	+	+
2	+	+	+
3	+	+	+
4	+	+	+

After observing the cells in each experiment, the researcher bathed the cells in a solution containing 10 mg/mL of a red fluorescent probe that binds specifically to the estrogen receptor only when its active site is occupied. After 1 hour, the cells were rinsed with DMEM and observed under confocal fluorescent microscopy. The results are presented in Table 2.

The researcher also repeated Experiment 2 using Pesticide B, an estrogen analog, instead of Pesticide A. Results from other researchers had shown that Pesticide B binds to the active site of the cytosolic estrogen receptor (with an affinity 10,000 times greater than that of estrogen) and causes increased transcription of mRNA.

Table 2 Observed Fluorescence and Estrogen Effects
(G = green, R = red)

Experiment	Media	Cytoplasm	Nucleus	Estrogen effects observed?
1	G only	G and R	G and R	Yes
2	G only	G only	G only	No
3	G only	G only	G only	No
4	G only	G and R	G and R	Yes

Based on these results, the researcher determined that estrogen had no effect when not bound to a cytosolic, estrogen-specific receptor.

Analysis and Passage Map

This passage starts out with a very general background paragraph. Not much to do here, but it does tell us that estrogen is going to be the hormone of focus.

The next few paragraphs are short descriptions of four different experiments. These should be read to understand not only what's happening in each experiment but also what the differences in the experiments are. Note this on your scratch paper.

Table 1 shows the results of the four experiments. It should jump out at you that estrogen is found everywhere; in other words, it is not restricted from any area of the cell.

After Table 1, the passage describes two modifications to the experiments. As with the original experiments, it's worth taking a little time to read and understand what's going on. The first big difference is that the researchers aren't just looking for the presence of estrogen, but also want to know when it's bound to it's receptor. The second big difference is the testing of an estrogen analog, Pesticide B.

Table 2 shows the results of when estrogen is bound and when it isn't. These results could be combined with the experiment description results on your map:

P1 – hormones that contribute to development, estrogen
E1 – HEPM cells exposed to estrogen, green + red = estrogen effects
E2 – Pesticide A, green only, must inhibit binding of estrogen to recept.
E3 – CHO cells, green only, no recept.
E4 – CHO cells + HEPM cytoplasm, green + red, recept is in cytoplasm
Table 1 – estrogen is not restricted from anywhere in the cell
Further exp'ts – red probe for bound active site, and Pesticide B (estrogen analog w/higher affinity)

One last thought about passages: remember that, as with all sections on the MCAT, you can do the passages in the order *you* want to. There are no extra points for taking the test in order. Generally, passages will fall into one of three main subject groups:

* non-physiology
* physiology
* Organic Chemistry

Figure out which group you are most comfortable with, and do those passages first.

TACKLING THE QUESTIONS

Questions in the Biology section mimic the three typical questions of the science sections in general: Memory, Explicit, and Implicit.

Question Types as They Apply to Biology

Memory Questions

Memory questions are exactly what they sound like: They test your knowledge of some specific fact or concept. While Memory questions are typically found as freestanding questions, they can also be tucked into a passage. These questions, aside from requiring memorization, do not generally cause problems for students because they are similar to the types of questions that appear on a typical college biology exam. Below is an example of a freestanding Memory question from Practice Test 1:

Regarding embryogenesis, which of the following sequence of events is in correct order?

A) Implantation—cleavage—gastrulation—neurulation—blastulation

B) Blastulation—implantation—cleavage—neurulation—gastrulation

C) Implantation—blastulation—gastrulation—cleavage—neurulation

D) Cleavage—blastulation—implantation—gastrulation—neurulation

Here's another example. This question is a Memory question from Passage 7 in Practice Test 1:

The genital organs of the *guevedoche* that develop at puberty are derivatives of the mesodermal germ layer. Which of the following is/are also derivatives of the mesodermal germ layer?

I. Skeletal muscle
II. Liver
III. Kidney

A) I only
B) II only
C) I and III only
D) II and III only

Note that this question includes an additional, unnecessary sentence at the beginning, but it is a Memory question all the same. You don't need to know anything about the *guevedoche* to answer the question, and the information in that first sentence does not help you in any way.

There is no specific "trick" to answering Memory questions; either you know the answer or you don't .

It's usually a good idea to tackle all freestanding questions in the section first, since they are typically Memory questions and don't require a lot of thought or analysis.

The correct answer to the embryogenesis question above is D, and the correct answer to the germ layer question is C.

If you find that you are missing a fair number of Memory questions, it is a sure sign that you don't know the content well enough. Go back and review.

Explicit Questions

True, pure Explicit questions are rare in the Biology section. A purely Explicit question can be answered only with information in the passage. Below is an example of a pure Explicit question taken from the eye passage above:

The middle layer of the eyeball wall most likely contains:

A) bipolar cells.
B) photoreceptors.
C) blood vessels.
D) collagen fibers.

Referring back to the map for this passage, it indicates that information about the layers of the eyeball are in paragraph 1. It states that the middle layer is a "darkly pigmented vascular layer," meaning that it contains blood vessels. The correct answer is C.

However, more often in the biology section, Explicit questions are more of a blend of Explicit and Memory; they require not only retrieval of passage information, but also recall of some relevant fact. They usually do not require a lot of analysis or connections. Here's an example of the more common type of Explicit question:

Pesticide A most likely functions as:

A) an agonist.
B) an inhibitor.
C) a lipase.
D) a receptor.

To answer this question, you first need to retrieve information from the passage about the effects of Pesticide A. From Table 2 we know that it prevents estrogen from binding to its receptor (and we noted this on our passage map). You also need to remember the definitions of the terms in the answer choices (agonists cause similar effects, inhibitors prevent effects, lipases break down lipids, and receptors bind ligands to cause effects). Based on our known definitions, choices A and D can be eliminated, and while Pesticide A could be functioning as a lipase that breaks down estrogen, "inhibitor" is a more accurate term (choice B is better than choice C and is the correct answer).

A final subgroup in the Explicit question category are graph interpretation questions. These fall into one of two types; one, those that ask you to take graphical information from the passage and convert it to a text answer, or those that take text from the passage and ask you to convert it to a graph. On the following page is an example of the latter type:

Which of the following graphs would best illustrate the binding of estrogen (E) to its receptor in the presence of its analog, Pesticide B?

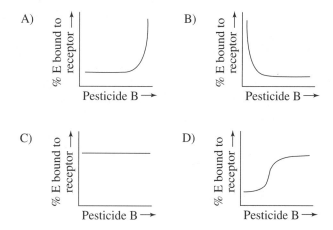

From our passage map, we know that information about Pesticide B is found near the end of the passage, where it describes "further experiments." The passage states that Pesticide B functions as an estrogen analog that binds to the estrogen receptor with a much higher affinity than does estrogen. In other words, if Pesticide B is around, the receptor will preferentially bind it, and not estrogen. So as the concentration of Pesticide B rises, the amount of estrogen bound to the receptor should fall. This is shown in choice B.

If you find that you are missing Explicit questions, practice your passage mapping. Make sure you aren't missing the critical items in the passage that lead you to the right answer. Slow down a little; take an extra 15 to 30 seconds per passage to read or think about it more carefully.

Implicit Questions

Implicit questions require the most thought. These require recall not only of biology information but also information gleaned from the passage, and a more in-depth analysis of how the two relate. Implicit questions require more analysis and connections to be made than Explicit questions. Often they take the form "If… then…." Below is an example of a classic Implicit question, taken from the Experiment passage shown above.

If Experiment 2 were repeated, but this time exposing the cells first to Pesticide A and then to Pesticide B before exposing them to the green fluorescent-labeled estrogen and the red fluorescent probe, which of the following statements will most likely be true?

A) Pesticide A and Pesticide B bind to the same site on the estrogen receptor.
B) Estrogen effects would be observed.
C) Only green fluorescence would be observed.
D) Both green and red fluorescence would be observed.

To answer this question, conclusions have to be drawn from the experiments described in the passage, and new conclusions have to be predicted based on the new circumstance. Many many more connections need to be made than when answering an Explicit question. From the passage, we need to figure out that Pesticide A is an inhibitor. We also have to figure out that it does not bind at the active site of the receptor (data from Table 2). We have to know what green fluorescence and red fluorescence imply. We have to draw on the information provided about Pesticide B to know that it is an analog and that it binds to the active site of the estrogen receptor. We have to combine all of this together and come to a logical conclusion: Since Pesticide A is an inhibitor, it would prevent the binding of Pesticide B and thus prevent estrogen effects (choice B can be eliminated). If Pesticide B cannot bind, we would only see green fluorescence (choice D can be eliminated and choice C is probably correct). Since Pesticide A by itself does not produce red fluorescence, it must not be binding at the active site, which is where Pesticide B binds, (choice A can be eliminated and choice C is definitely correct).

Here's another example of an Implicit question, drawn from the same passage:

When the researcher performed Experiment 2 using Pesticide B instead of Pesticide A, which of the following fluorescence and estrogen effects did the researcher most likely observe?

A) *Media*: green and red
   Cytoplasm: green and red
   Nucleus: green and red
   Estrogen effects: no

B) *Media*: green only
   Cytoplasm: green and red
   Nucleus: green and red
   Estrogen effects: no

C) *Media*: green only
   Cytoplasm: green and red
   Nucleus: green and red
   Estrogen effects: yes

D) *Media*: green only
   Cytoplasm: green and red
   Nucleus: green only
   Estrogen effects: no

To answer this question we again must combine passage information with logical inference and working memory. Since red fluorescence indicates binding of the receptor, and since the receptor is never in the media, there can never be red fluorescence in the media (choice A can be eliminated). We know from the passage that Pesticide B binds at the active site of the receptor, and we know that the receptor is found in the cytoplasm. We also know from the passage that Pesticide B causes increased mRNA transcription, and we know from memory that to induce mRNA transcription, the receptor must move into the nucleus. Thus, red fluorescence must be observed in the nucleus as well (choice D can be eliminated). Since Pesticide B is defined as an "estrogen analog," and since we know from memory that analogs cause similar effects, it is likely that estrogen effects will be observed. The fact that increased mRNA transcription occurs supports this idea (choice B can be eliminated and choice C is correct). Again, many more connections need to be made to answer Implicit question; process of elimination is typically the best approach.

If you find that you are missing a lot of Implicit questions, make sure first of all that you are using POE aggressively. Second, go back and review the explanations for the correct answer, and figure out where your logic went awry. Did you miss an important fact in the passage? Did you forget the relevant Biology content? Did you follow the logical train of thought to the right answer? Once you figure out where you made your mistake, you will know how to correct it.

SUMMARY OF THE APPROACH TO BIOLOGY

1. Remember that content in Biology is vast, so don't panic if something seems completely unfamiliar. Understand the basic content well, find the basics in the unfamiliar topic, and apply them to the questions.
2. Take the section in the order you want to. Start with freestanding questions, since those are typically Memory and easier.
3. To tackle the passages, determine your strongest subtopic (non-physiology, physiology, or O-Chem) and do those passages first.
4. Know how to read and map the passage. Don't get bogged down in the interesting subject and science. Remember that Experiment/Research Presentation passages require the most reading, thought, and analysis, so if these are difficult for you, save them until the end.
5. Remember that time is usually not an issue on the BS section, so feel free to slow down a little, or go back and review questions that require more thought.
6. Translate complex biology terminology and descriptions into simple everyday language. For example, "In the absence of light, Na^+ channels in the membranes of rod cells are kept open by cGMP. The conformational change in retinal upon light absorption causes changes in opsin as well; this triggers a pathway by which phosphodiesterase (PDE) is activated. Active PDE converts cGMP to GMP, causing it to dissociate from the Na^+ channel and the channel to close," should become "Na^+ channels are open in the dark and closed in the light."
7. **Practice.** The more passages you do, the better you'll get.

MCAT BIOLOGY TOPIC LIST[1]

Biochemistry
A. Enzyme Structure and Function
 1. substrates and specificity
 2. activation energy
 3. reaction coordinate graph
 4. enzyme regulation (phosphorylation, feedback inhibition, allosteric regulation)
 5. competitive/noncompetitive inhibition

B. Cellular Metabolism
 1. glycolysis
 2. PDC/Krebs cycle
 3. electron transport chain/oxidative phosphorylation
 4. fatty acid and protein metabolism

Molecular Biology
A. DNA Structure, Function, and Replication
 1. double helix, deoxyribose, phosphate, bases
 2. base pairing
 3. role in Central Dogma
 4. competitive/noncompetitive inhibition
 5. comparisons between eukaryotes and prokaryotes (DNA structure and replication)
 6. eukaryotic chromosomes (chromosomal proteins, centromeres, telomeres)
 7. mechanism of replication and enzymes involved
 8. semiconservative
 9. types of mutations (missense, nonsense, silent, frameshift)

B. Transcription
 1. Central Dogma (DNA → RNA → protein)
 2. genetic code (degenerate, start and stop codons)
 3. mechanism of transcription, comparison to replication
 4. regulation of transcription (promoters, DNA binding proteins, transcription factors)
 5. eukaryotic mRNA (mRNA processing including capping, tailing, splicing, location, enzymes involved)
 6. prokaryotic mRNA (no processing, location, enzymes involved)

C. Translation
 1. ribosome structure (prokaryotic and eukaryotic)
 2. roles of mRNA, tRNA, and ribosome in protein synthesis
 3. codon-anticodon relationship
 4. energy requirements

D. Lab Techniques
 1. restriction enzymes and plasmids
 2. blotting and hybridization (Southern, northern, western)
 3. gene cloning
 4. PCR

[1] Adapted from *The Official Guide to the MCAT Exam*, 2009 ed., © 2009 Association of American Medical Colleges

Microbiology

A. Viruses
1. definition
2. structure, including enveloped and non-enveloped
3. relative size compared to prokaryotes and eukaryotes
4. genome
5. life cycles (lytic, lysogenic, productive, retroviral)

B. Bacteria
1. structure
2. genome and plasmids
3. classification by shape (cocci, bacilli, spirilli)
4. classification as eubacteria or archaebacteria
5. classification as aerobes or anaerobes
6. cell wall, flagella
7. binary fission for population growth
8. methods of acquiring genetic diversity (conjugation, transduction, transformation)
9. acquisition of antibiotic resistance

C. Fungi
1. general structure
2. life cycle

Cell Biology

A. Generalized Eukaryotic Cells
1. structure and function of all organelles (nucleus, nucleolus, mitochondria, rough ER, smooth ER, Golgi apparatus, lysosomes)
2. secretory pathway (transmembrane and secreted proteins)
3. plasma membrane structure and general function
4. exo- and endocytosis
5. osmosis/diffusion, passive and active transport, membrane potential
6. receptors and cell signaling pathways (second messengers, G-proteins)
7. cytoskeleton filaments, cilia and flagella, centrioles, MTOC
8. cell junctions (desmosomes, tight junctions, gap junctions)
9. cell cycle and mitosis, including G_0
10. apoptosis
11. cancer

Genetics and Evolution

A. Genetics
1. genes and alleles
2. genotype, phenotype, homozygous, heterozygous
3. classical dominance, incomplete dominance, codominance
4. recessiveness
5. penetrance and expressivity
6. Punnett squares, testcross
7. pedigree analysis
8. rules of probability (multiplication, addition)
9. Mendel's rules (segregation of alleles, independent assortment)
10. meiosis, and comparison of meiosis to mitosis
11. linkage and recombination
12. sex-linked genes, mitochondrial inheritance
13. mutations and chromosomal rearrangements
14. Hardy-Weinberg (equations, conditions)

B. Evolution
1. natural selection and fitness
2. speciation, adaptation, competition
3. inbreeding
4. convergent/divergent evolution, parallel evolution
5. genetic drift
6. symbiotic relationships (parasitism, mutualism, commensalism)
7. general origin of life

C. Taxonomy
1. defining characteristics of kingdoms
2. chordate features
3. vertebrate classes

Anatomy and Physiology

A. Nervous System
1. neuron structure, including myelin and myelinating cells
2. resting potential, action potential
3. propagation of action potential, saltatory conduction
4. synapses, electrical and chemical
5. summation (excitation, inhibition), frequency of firing
6. overall system function (sensory input, integration, motor output)
7. organization of nervous system
8. CNS roles (brain and spinal cord)
9. PNS (somatic and autonomic, sympathetic and parasympathetic)
10. reflexes
11. classification of sensory receptors
12. general hearing (ear structure, general mechanism)
13. general vision (eye structure, photoreceptors)

B. Endocrine System
1. function
2. endocrine glands and products
3. types of hormones and transport
4. specificity of hormones and their actions
5. control (feedback)

C. Cardiovascular System
1. function
2. heart structure/function, pulmonary and systemic circulation
3. blood vessel structure, function, pressures, flow (arteries, veins, capillaries)
4. blood pressure (systolic, diastolic, regulation)
5. cardiac action potential, pacemaker role in heart
6. blood composition and clotting mechanisms
7. gas transport (O_2 and CO_2)
8. hemoglobin and O_2 affinity

D. Lymphatic System
1. function
2. source and composition of lymph
3. lymph nodes

E. Immune System
1. innate immunity and inflammation
2. antigen, antibody function, antibody structure
3. cells and functions (B cells, T cells, phagocytes)
4. mechanism of stimulation, antigen presentation (MHC I, MHC II)

F. Digestive System
1. alimentary canal structure and function (mouth, esophagus, stomach, small intestine, large intestine)
2. saliva, peristalsis, sphincters
3. hormones and enzymes
4. liver functions, bile
5. gallbladder function
6. pancreas, endocrine and exocrine function

G. Excretory System
1. other organs (ureter, bladder, urethra)
2. kidney and nephron structure
3. formation of urine, functions of parts of nephron (PCT, loop of Henle, DCT, collecting duct)
4. urine concentration, role of hormones
5. role of kidney in homeostasis (blood pressure regulation, osmoregulation, acid-base balance)

H. Muscular System
1. functions (movement, protection)
2. characteristics of skeletal, cardiac, and smooth muscle
3. structure of striated vs nonstriated muscle
4. sarcomere structure and sliding filament theory
5. role of calcium, troponin, tropomyosin
6. nervous control of voluntary muscle

I. Skeletal System
    1. functions (support, protection, mineral storage)
    2. connective tissue, general structure/function
    3. bone and joint structures
    4. cartilage, ligaments, tendons
    5. osteoblast/osteoclast functions
    6. hormones that regulate calcium

J. Respiratory System
    1. general functions (gas exchange, pH regulation)
    2. structures and functions of the conduction zone and respiratory zone
    3. mechanism of ventilation, structure of diaphragm, rib cage
    4. lung elasticity, surface tension

K. Skin
    1. functions (homeostasis, thermoregulation)
    2. thermoregulation
    3. structure (layers, cell types, tissue types)
    4. epithelial cells

L. Reproductive Systems
    1. male and female structures and functions
    2. spermatogenesis and oogenesis
    3. menstrual cycle and hormones
    4. fertilization

M. Development
    1. embryonic stage (cleavage, implantation, blastulation, gastrulation, neurulation)
    2. fate of primary germ layers
    3. fetal stage (major landmarks)
    4. labor, lactation
    5. determination/differentiation, cell communication
    6. programmed cell death

Chapter 18
Biology
Practice Section

FREESTANDING QUESTIONS

1. *Staphylococcus epidermidis* is a common cause of wound infections among hospital patients. *S. epidermidis* are facultative anaerobes that usually inhabit the skin and mucus membranes. Which of the following is true about cellular respiration in *S. epidermidis*?

   A) *S. epidermidis* can produce NADH but not $FADH_2$.
   B) *S. epidermidis* can produce NADH only in the matrix of the mitochondria.
   C) *S. epidermidis* can produce both NADH and $FADH_2$ in the cytoplasm.
   D) *S. epidermidis* can produce $FADH_2$ via fermentation.

2. Rank these mutations in order from most serious to least serious.

   I. A point mutation in the DNA of a gene
   II. An insertion of five base pairs in a non-gene coding region of the DNA
   III. A single base pair deletion in an mRNA
   IV. A point mutation in the first base of the anti-codon of a tRNA molecule

   A) II, IV, I, III
   B) I, III, IV, II
   C) I, IV, II, III
   D) III, III, IV, I

3. A researcher incorporates a constitutive viral promoter before the cyclin D1 gene. Cyclin D1 competes with CKI-p16 to activate a cyclin-dependent kinase (CDK) and helps drives the cell into the S phase of the cell cycle. Which of the following would be the most likely effect of this modification?

   A) Increased binding of CKI-p16 to allosteric CDK site
   B) Decreased helicase activity
   C) Phosphorylation and inhibition of retinoblastoma (*Rb*) activity
   D) Decreased time in the G_2 phase

4. What inheritance pattern is mostly likely demonstrated below?

   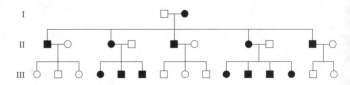

   A) Autosomal dominant
   B) X-linked dominant
   C) Mitochondrial inheritance
   D) X-linked recessive

5. A patient's chart indicates that she is experiencing elevated blood glucose, increased protein catabolism, and an enlarged adrenal gland. What is the likely cause of these conditions?

   A) Elevated glucagon levels
   B) Elevated ACTH levels
   C) Elevated growth hormone levels
   D) Elevated cortisol levels

6. A researcher conducts an *in vitro* experiment with a neuron where calcium leak channels are added to the plasma membrane. What effect would this have on the neuron?

   A) Decrease in neurotransmitter release
   B) Decrease in resting membrane potential
   C) Increase in resting membrane potential
   D) No effect because resting membrane potential is dictated by sodium and potassium.

7. Which of the following statements regarding the cardiac conduction system is NOT true?

A) The cardiac conduction system is not neural, but is composed of specialized cardiac myocytes that lack significant contractile machinery and are capable of efficient signal transmission.

B) The atrial and ventricular muscle cells are electrically connected via gap junctions so that all the cardiac myocytes act as a functional syncytium.

C) A slight delay of impulse transmission at the AV node allows the atrial to finish their contraction prior to ventricular systole.

D) Baseline parasympathetic input to the SA node during normal, everyday situations reduces its intrinsic firing rate.

8. Lupus is an autoimmune disorder that targets the skin and the kidneys. Pregnant women are easier to diagnose with lupus than non-pregnant women. What is the most likely explanation for this?

A) Their immune system is weakened because of the pregnancy.

B) The autoreactive antibodies can cross the placenta and attack the fetus.

C) Increased fat deposition leads to a greater likelihood of autoreactivity.

D) The lupus virus will attack the fetus.

9. Orlistat, a poorly-absorbed derivative of lipstatin, is prescribed to treat obesity. Which of the following is the most likely mechanism for orlistat?

A) Blocks transport of fatty acids from intestinal epithelia directly into the blood

B) Inhibits pancreatic lipase

C) Blocks absorption of macromolecules in the colon

D) Decreases appetite by blocking the secretions of chief cells

10. Lasix is a diuretic which inhibits the active transport activity of the Na^+-K^+-$2Cl^-$ symporter in the thick ascending limb of the loop of Henle. Which of the following explains why Lasix can be used to treat hypertension?

A) The resulting high ion concentration in the blood causes the body to retain more water.

B) The resulting high ion concentration in the filtrate causes the body to excrete more water.

C) The resulting low ion concentration in the filtrate causes the body to excrete more water.

D) The resulting low ion concentration in the blood causes the body to retain more water.

11. Body plethysmography is a method of obtaining very sensitive lung measurements. A patient is placed in an airtight chamber, often referred to as a "body box," with a mouthpiece in place. At the end of a normal expiration, a shutter on the mouthpiece is closed and the patient attempts to inhale against the closed mouthpiece. What happens to the airway pressure, lung volume, box pressure, and box volume?

A) ↑ airway pressure, ↓ lung volume, ↑ box pressure, ↓ box volume

B) ↑ airway pressure, ↑ lung volume, ↓ box pressure, ↑ box volume

C) ↓ airway pressure, ↑ lung volume, ↑ box pressure, ↓ box volume

D) ↓ airway pressure, ↓ lung volume, ↑ box pressure, ↑ box volume

12. The placenta serves which of the following functions?

I. Transfer of oxygenated blood from mother to fetus
II. Transfer of carbon dioxide from fetus to mother
III. Transfer of nutrients from mother to fetus

A) II only
B) I and III
C) II and III
D) I, II and III

PRACTICE PASSAGE 1

Hyperhomocysteinemia is a condition characterized by a markedly elevated plasma concentration of homocysteine, which damages endothelial cells and is associated with an increased risk of occlusive vascular disease, thrombosis, and stroke. Although the precise mechanism by which elevated levels of homocysteine damage the vasculature has yet to be definitively proven, experimental studies suggest that homocysteine damages and inhibits the formation of collagen, elastin, and proteoglycans, the structural components that constitute arteries.

Deficiencies in the metabolism of homocysteine, an intermediate in the production of the amino acid methionine, arise from either a genetic defect in one of the enzymes that metabolizes homocysteine or from nutritional deficiencies of the vitamins involved in homocysteine metabolism.

Homocysteine is an amino acid that differs from cysteine by an extra methylene group before the thiol group. The metabolism of homocysteine involves two intersecting pathways: *remethylation* and *transsulfuration*. In the remethylation pathway, homocysteine is converted into methionine by the addition of a methyl group onto its sulfur atom. The methyl group is donated by methyl-tetrahydrofolate in a vitamin B12-dependent reaction. In the transsulfuration pathway, homocysteine irreversibly combines with serine to form cystathionine in a reaction catalyzed by cystathionine β-synthase.

One mechanism, obtained from experimental evidence, suggests that the coordination of these two pathways is regulated by S-adenosyl-methionine. S-adenosyl-methionine acts as an allosteric inhibitor of methylenetetrahydrofolate reductase (MTHFR) and an activator of cystathionine β-synthase.

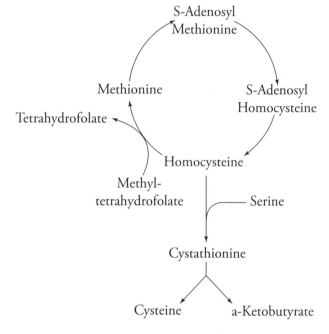

Figure 1 Homocysteine metabolism

1. An individual whose diet lacks sufficient quantities of vitamin B12 would exhibit a decrease in the activity of the enzyme that converts methyl-tetrahydrofolate into tetrahydrofolate. This would result in which of the following?

A) Increased activity of methylenetetrahydrofolate reductase
B) Increased levels of methionine
C) Decreased activity of cystathionine β-synthase
D) Increased levels of cysteine

2. A comparison of the plasma levels of homocysteine before and after the ingestion of a large dose of the amino acid methionine is referred to as the methionine load test. In normal individuals, there would be a small rise in the levels of homocysteine that would then return back to baseline levels within a few hours. Administration of the methionine load test would result in which of the following?

A) Decreased activity of cystathionine β-synthase
B) Increased activity of cystathionine β-synthase
C) Decreased quantity of methylenetetrahydrofolate reductase (MTHFR)
D) Increased quantity of methylenetetrahydrofolate reductase (MTHFR)

3. Cystathionine β-synthase deficiency is a condition in which homocysteine transsulfuration is defective thereby diverting homocysteine towards the remethylation pathway. Although the rate of methionine synthesis initially increases, which reduces the levels of homocysteine, eventually homocysteine levels accumulate resulting in hyperhomocysteinemia. Which of the following best explains why this occurs?

A) Depleted levels of methyl-tetrahydrofolate
B) Accumulation of methionine
C) Inhibition of methylenetetrahydrofolate reductase
D) Inhibition of cystathionine β-synthase

4. Atherosclerosis is a disease that is often the result of an inflammatory process in which the endothelial lining of the arteries become damaged. Elevated levels of homocysteine in the plasma also damage the endothelial lining of arteries. Both of these conditions would result in which of the following?

A) An increased likelihood of developing a heart attack
B) A decreased likelihood of developing coronary artery disease (CAD)
C) A decreased likelihood of developing a stroke
D) An increased likelihood of developing multiple sclerosis

5. A patient presents with elevated levels of homocysteine. In order to distinguish between a nutritional deficiency (lack of B12 in the diet) and a homozygous cystathionine β-synthase defect, a clinician decides to administer a methionine load test. Upon ingestion of a large dose of methionine, there is a transient increase in the plasma levels of homocysteine. Based on this result, the clinician concludes that this rise in plasma homocysteine levels is due to insufficient dietary intake of vitamin B12. All of the following would support the clinician's conclusion EXCEPT:

A) the patient's plasma cysteine levels remain constant through the trial period and for several days afterward.
B) a substantial supplement of vitamin B12 was co-administered with the large dose of methionine.
C) the patient exhibited a delayed increase in α-ketobutyrate levels.
D) the patient's levels of S-adenosyl-homocysteine exhibited a transient increase.

6. If a methionine load test with radioactive labeled ^{35}S was administered to a patient, which of the following would NOT exhibit radioactivity?

A) Homocysteine
B) Methionine
C) Cystathionine
D) α-Ketobutyrate

7. Vasodilation is a widening of blood vessels due to the relaxation of smooth muscles within the vessels walls. This endothelium-dependent activity results from the relaxing action of nitric oxide on the blood vessel wall. Experimental evidence suggests that homocysteine interferes with this action by acting as a prooxidant that produces H_2O_2, which inactivates nitric oxide. Which of the following would support this finding?

A) Homocysteine was found to decrease the activity of glutathione peroxidase, an anti-oxidative enzyme.
B) Endothelial nitric oxide synthase (eNOS), which synthesizes nitric oxide, was shown to have no change in activity.
C) Homocysteine interferes with the gene expression of endothelial nitric oxide synthase (eNOS) by reducing the amount of its transcription.
D) The endothelium lining of the blood vessel wall no longer responds to nitric oxide.

PRACTICE PASSAGE 2

The hepatitis B virus (HBV) is a member of the hepadnavirus family and is found worldwide as a cause of chronic liver disease and hepatocellular cancer. The fully infectious virus, also referred to as the *Dane particle*, has a partially double stranded DNA genome attached at one end to a viral polymerase. It is contained in an icosahedral nucleocapsid core tucked in an outer lipid envelope containing multiple membrane surface proteins.

The virion carries four genes denoted by *C, X, P,* and *S*. Gene *C* encodes the core protein used to form the viral structure. Gene *P* encodes the polymerase. Gene *S* encodes the surface antigen which is used to recognize and enter liver cells. It has three in-frame start codons referred to as pre-*S*1, pre-*S*2, and *S*. Gene *X* has an unknown function. Presence of the surface antigen indicates that an individual is capable of transmitting the disease.

The immune response to HBV is complex and can cause confusion for the clinician. Upon viral entry to the body by blood or mucosal contact, the first antigen recognized is the surface antigen (HBsAg) which can trigger a humoral response (production of anti-sAg). As hepatocyte infection occurs, viral replication leads to the eventual production of the corresponding antibody (anti-core). IgM is the transient first-line antibody, replaced by IgG for lasting defense (as in long-term exposure or vaccination). A third antigen, referred to as the e antigen (HBeAg), is a splice variant of the core antigen. It serves as a marker of active replication and infectivity and, like other antigens, provokes a humoral response (anti-eAg). Typically, acute HBV is cleared from the body within 6 months from infection. As a defense to host immunity, hepatitis B produces non-infectious spherical and filamentous bodies lacking core and genetic components. They are composed only of lipid and protein and mimic the outermost layer of the Dane particle. These are produced in excess and can reach concentrations of up to 10^{13} particles/mL (300 mg/mL) which is far in excess of corresponding antibody concentrations.

In long term HBV infection, failure of an effective humoral response against HBsAg results in ongoing, often asymptomatic infection. However, these individuals remain capable of transmitting the disease and are known as "chronic carriers."

An interesting phenomenon occurs with a related (-)RNA virus, hepatitis D (HDV). It is missing the HBV equivalent of gene *S*. By itself, HDV is harmless, but when paired with HBV, sharing of the surface antigen occurs and a superinfection results, with much more extensive disease than with HBV alone.

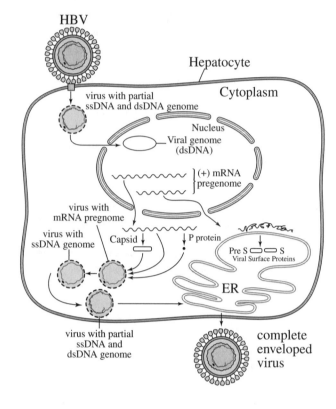

Figure 1 Hepatitis B life cycle

1. If a filamentous body were isolated from an infected individual and injected into an uninfected healthy individual what antibodies would be formed?

A) Anti-core IgM
B) Anti-eAg IgG
C) Anti-sAg IgM
D) Anti-sAg IgG

2. Which of the following would be detected in the blood of a person chronically infected with hepatitis B?

A) Anti-core IgG, anti-sAg
B) HBsAg, anti-core IgM, anti-core IgG
C) HBsAg, anti-core IgG,
D) HBsAg, anti-core IgG, anti-sAg

3. Which of the following would be the result of hepatocyte infection with a Dane particle lacking both gene *P* and a viral polymerase?

A) Viral DNA in the nucleus, viral mRNA in the cytoplasm, spherical bodies in the blood, undetectable levels of Dane particles in the blood.
B) Viral DNA in the nucleus, viral mRNA in the cytoplasm, high levels of Dane particles in both the cytoplasm and blood.
C) No detectable viral DNA, mRNA or Dane particles in either the cytoplasm or blood.
D) Viral DNA in the nucleus, no viral mRNA in the cytoplasm, no Dane particles in the cytoplasm or blood.

4. Gene therapy has been proposed as a possible treatment for chronic hepatitis B infection. Which of the following methods would be the best approach?

A) Insertion of additional genes into the host genome that encode anti-core IgM and IgG
B) Retroviral insertion of a nucleotide sequence to disrupt the viral genome integrated in the host genome
C) Insertion of proteases that degrade viral proteins
D) Retroviral insertion of a nucleotide sequence into the host genome that codes for (-)RNA

5. Would HDV be expected to carry a viral polymerase?

A) No; it encodes a polymerase translated as an early gene.
B) No; it is able to rely on host enzymes for replication.
C) Yes; its replication relies on an RNA dependent RNA polymerase.
D) Yes; it evolved from HBV and has a similar genome.

6. Which of the following mutations would most likely lead to a virus incapable of infecting liver cells?

A) Missense mutation in pre-*S*2
B) Nonsense mutation late in *S*
C) Single base pair insertion in pre-*S*1
D) Three nucleotide deletion early in *S*

PRACTICE PASSAGE 3

The eukaryotic cell cycle and its control mechanisms are highly conserved through evolution. The cell cycle is divided into 5 main phases: G_1, S, G_2, M and the optional senescence phase G_0. The most vital checkpoint pathways function at the G_1/S transition and the G_2/M transition. Fission yeast are non-pathogenic, and use many of the same general biochemical pathways that mammals do, thus the fission yeast *Schizosaccharomyces pombe* is a model organism commonly used to study the cell cycle and checkpoint pathways.

The nuclear genome of fission yeast has been completely sequenced. The *S. pombe* genome contains 12.5 megabases of DNA, divided into 3 chromosomes. There are a little over 5000 protein-coding genes and the average length of a gene is 1400 base pairs. Approximately 400 replication origins have been found and current predictions state that 94% of the genome is transcribed, although there is extensive variation in different stages and conditions. The mitochondrial genome of *S. pombe* has also been sequenced; it is 20 kilobases in length and codes for 11 genes.

Cell cycle progression is controlled by cyclin-dependent kinases (CDKs) and their cyclin binding partners. Protein levels of the cyclins rise and fall with the cell cycle due to periodic transcription and regulated protein degradation. Fission yeast have only one CDK, called Cdc2, which can bind to one of 7 different cyclin partners, depending on the cell cycle phase. Cdc13 is the only cyclin that controls the G_2/M transition; activation of the Cdc2-Cdc13 complex triggers the cell to enter the M-phase.

Cdc2 is expressed throughout the cell cycle, but the activity levels of Cdc2 are low in G_1, moderate in S-phase and G_2, and high during mitosis. The activity of Cdc2 is regulated by cyclin binding and via phosphorylation; Cdc2 can be phosphorylated on its fifteenth amino acid, which is a tyrosine (Y15).

Cdc13 protein levels start to rise through G_2. Cdc13 associates with Cdc2 and this complex is moved to the nucleus. One of two kinases (either Mik1 or Wee1) phosphorylate Y15 on Cdc2 and keep it inactive. Once proper cellular checkpoints have been passed, the cell is ready to proceed to M-phase: Wee1 and Mik1 are inactivated, and Cdc25 is transported to the nucleus by a transporter protein called Sal3. Cdc25 is a phosphatase and has the opposite function as Wee1 and Mik1. Many of the cellular checkpoint pathways function to control Wee1 and Cdc25 and this is how they regulate progression through the cell cycle. Once dephosphorylated on Y15, Cdc2 is active and phosphorylates many proteins in the cell to cause entry into mitosis.

1. A fission yeast mutant is isolated in the lab and examined under the microscope. The cells are much smaller than wild type control cells. This mutant most likely has a:

A) mutation in the promoter of Wee1 that causes decreased transcription.
B) silent mutation in Cdc13.
C) mutation in the promoter of Sal3 that causes transcription silencing.
D) nonsense mutation in Cdc25.

2. Which of the following are determinants of the G_2/M checkpoint?

I. Ensure that genomic replication is complete
II. Take inventory of nucleotide levels
III. Check for mutations or DNA instability

A) II only
B) I and II
C) I and III
D) I, II and III

3. *S. pombe* are easy to culture in the laboratory; they can be grown on agar plates, or in liquid culture and they have a relatively short doubling time. *S. pombe* have:

A) a cell wall made of peptidoglycan and a 70S ribosome.
B) a cell wall made of chitin and a 80S ribosome.
C) a cell wall made of cellulose and a 80S ribosome.
D) no cell wall and a 80S ribosome.

4. Many different enzymes are used as regulators of other enzymes in various cell pathways, including metabolic pathways, biosynthesis, energy production, and the cell cycle. A phosphatase is:

A) an enzyme that reverses the action of a kinase and removes phosphate groups.
B) an enzyme that adds phosphate groups to molecules, using ATP as the phosphate source.
C) an enzyme that removes phosphate groups from only proteins.
D) a protein that increases the activation energy of a reaction, increasing the reaction rate.

5. The regulation of CDKs includes:

A) post-translational modification and allosteric regulation.
B) allosteric regulation and proteolytic cleavage.
C) proteolytic cleavage and protein associations.
D) protein associations and post-translational modification.

6. A researcher discovered a yeast with a mutation in the Sal3 promoter that causes its constitutive activation. Cells with this mutation would be:

A) larger than wild type cells and spend more time in G_2.
B) smaller than wild type cells and spend more time in G_2.
C) larger than wild type cells and spend less time in G_2.
D) smaller than wild type cells and spend less time in G_2.

7. A pharmaceutical company is trying to develop drugs to treat onychomycosis, fungal infections of the nails. The best drug to pursue would be:

A) one that promotes and increases chitin synthesis.
B) one that inhibits redox reactions in the electron transport chain.
C) one that decreases production of ergosterol, a plasma membrane component.
D) one that limits associations between the 40S and 60S ribosome.

PRACTICE PASSAGE 4

Melanocytes are cells that produce melanin, the pigment responsible for eye color and other pigmentation. They have unique organelles called *melanosomes*, which are similar to lysosomes and are responsible for the synthesis of the pigment melanin from toxic precursor compounds such phenols and quinones. There are two major forms of melanin: *eumelanin* which is brown to black in color, and pheomelanin which is yellow to red in color. The regulation of the production of eumelanin versus pheomelanin involves a G-protein coupled receptor (melanocortin 1 receptor or MC1R) expressed on the surface of melanocytes. If a melanocyte stimulating hormone (MSH) ligand binds the receptor, the cells produces eumelanin; if an agouti signaling protein (ASIP) ligand binds the receptor, the cell produces pheomelanin.

Tyrosinase (encoded by the gene TYR) is an enzyme that functions in the melanin biosynthetic pathway. Oculocutaneous albinism II protein (or OCA2) is a melanosomal transmembrane protein that also functions in the melanin production pathway. Recent work has shown that there are 58 alleles of OCA2, due to SNPs (single nucleotide polymorphisms) in regulatory sequences, introns and exons. For example, in humans with blue eyes (which are typically recessive to brown eyes), the OCA2 protein tends to have arginine at amino acid 305 (305R) and glutamine at amino acid 419 (419Q); in humans with brown eyes, the OCA2 protein tends to have tryptophan at amino acid 305 (305W) and arginine at amino acid 419 (419R). OCA2 is one of the major determinants of blue or brown eye color, but these same signaling and biosynthetic pathways also control other aspects of human pigmentation.

It was initially thought that eye color was determined by the number of melanocytes, but this has since been shown to be untrue. Most people have approximately the same number of melanocytes. The wide variety in pigmentation is due to differences in the number of the melanosomes and the relative proportion of the two melanin molecules eumelanin and pheomelanin.

Fluorescence *in situ* hybridization (FISH) is a powerful molecular genetic laboratory technique, where fluorescently labeled probes are hybridized to fixed chromosome clusters. These chromosomes can come from tissues, tumors, or cells. Most FISH is carried out on metaphase chromosomes because subsequent data interpretation is significantly more difficult on interphase nuclei. Using this technique, researchers have determined that in humans, the OCA2 gene is located on the long arm of chromosome 15.

Biologists have also studied the evolution of pigmentation.

Computational biologists line up gene or protein sequences from different organisms and compare them to determine the sequences that are most closely related. Using this type of analysis, researchers generate gene or protein phylogenetic trees, which show how certain genes evolved over time. When this analysis was done for the protein sequence of OCA2, a highly conserved protein, the phylogenetic tree in Figure 1 was generated. It was found that OCA2 varied in length between 650 amino acids in fission yeast and 838 amino acids in humans. Vertices indicate divergence of protein evolution and the presence of a common ancestor protein

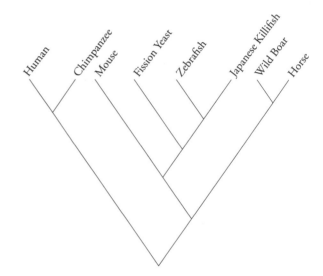

Figure 1 The phylogenetic tree based on comparison of OCA2 protein sequences in eight organisms

1. Eye color, skin color and hair color in humans are examples of:

A) monogenism, where the trait is determined by a single gene with dominant and recessive alleles.

B) codominance, where two alleles of a single gene are expressed simultaneously.

C) polygenism, where the trait is determined by several genes with several alleles.

D) incomplete dominance, where alleles of one gene blend together to give intermediate phenotypes.

2. The OCA2 gene overlaps with another gene called HERC2, which has two alleles: the wild type allele, and a recessive allele A1 which has been linked to a genetic predisposition to Crohn's disease. A woman with a $OCA2^{305R}$:$HERC2^{wt}$ chromosome and a $OCA2^{305W}$:$HERC2^{A1}$ chromosome mates with a homozygous $OCA2^{305R/305R}$:$HERC2^{A1/A1}$ man. Their children will most likely be:

A) 25% normal with blue eyes, 25% normal with brown eyes, 25% blue eyed with a risk of Crohn's disease and 25% brown eyed with a risk of Crohn's disease.
B) 50% normal with blue eyes and 50% brown eyed with a risk of Crohn's disease.
C) 50% blue eyed with a risk of Crohn's disease and 50% normal with brown eyes.
D) 100% blue eyed with a risk of Crohn's disease.

3. Based on Figure 1, which of the following is least supported?

A) The OCA2 proteins in the eight species studies would be considered homologous.
B) The OCA2 protein is conserved across eukaryotes.
C) Zebrafish and Japanese killifish have a OCA2 common ancestor protein which is more related that that between horse and human.
D) Humans and chimpanzees are more closely related than fission yeast and the wild boar.

4. Parents with blue eyes can have children with:

A) only blue eyes because this trait is recessive.
B) blue or green eyes because both of these are recessive to darker colored eyes.
C) any number of eye colors, including brown eyes, since the genetic basis of this trait it so complex.
D) any number of eye colors, due to Mendel's law of independent assortment and recombination.

5. A FISH probe should be made of:

A) an antibody that binds to a DNA epitope, covalently linked to a fluorescent segment of DNA.
B) a segment of double stranded DNA which is complementary to the gene being studied, covalently linked to a fluorescent protein.
C) a segment of single stranded DNA which is complementary to the gene being studied, covalently linked to a fluorochrome.
D) a single stranded piece of RNA ionically linked to a fluorescent segment of DNA.

6. Melanocytes are located in the:

A) epidermis, hair follicles, choroid and iris.
B) dermis, hair follicles, choroid and iris.
C) sebaceous glands, hypodermis and retina.
D) dermis, hypodermis, hair follicles, iris and vitreous humor.

7. A man is homozygous for an allele of MC1R that preferentially binds MSH ($MC1R^{PM/PM}$) and also has the wild type form of agouti signaling protein ($ASIP^{wt/wt}$). His mate has two normal alleles of melanocortin 1 receptor ($MC1R^{wt/wt}$) and has an allele of agouti signaling protein that demonstrates a very high affinity for MC1R ($ASIP^{HA/HA}$). The skin color of their child will most likely be:

A) the same as the father's due to its $MC1R^{PM/wt}$:$ASIP^{wt/wt}$ genotype.
B) the same as the mother's due to its $MC1R^{wt/wt}$:$ASIP^{wt/HA}$ genotype.
C) darker than the father's but lighter than the mother's due to its $MC1R^{PM/wt}$:$ASIP^{wt/HA}$ genotype.
D) lighter than the father's but darker than the mother's due to its $MC1R^{PM/wt}$:$ASIP^{wt/HA}$ genotype.

PRACTICE PASSAGE 5

The amyloid precursor protein (APP) is an integral transmembrane glycoprotein which is highly expressed in the brain and plays an important role in neuronal function. The cleaving of APP by β- and γ-secretases generate amyloid β-peptide (Aβ), causing the formation of extracellular neuritic plaques characteristic of Alzheimer's disease (AD). The rate of Aβ production is believed to be a key determinant of the onset and progression of AD.

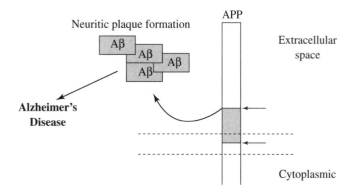

Figure 1 APP processing by β- and γ- secretases and generation of Aβ

Several recent findings support the idea that the intracellular transport and subcellular localization of APP are crucial determinants of APP processing and Aβ generation. APP can be internalized from the cell membrane to the endosomes and back to the cell membrane (recycling pathway). Endosomal APP can also be targeted to the lysosomes for degradation (degradative pathway). Endosomes are intracellular compartments where the sequential action of β- and γ-secretases generate Aβ. On the other hand, cleavage of APP by α-secretase, which prevents the production of Aβ, occurs in the late compartments of the secretory pathway, such as the Golgi.

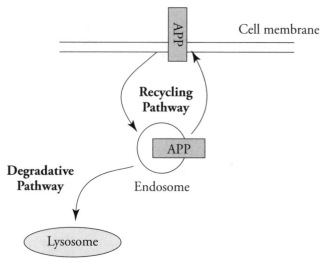

Figure 2 Intracellular transport and localization of APP

Numb is an evolutionarily conserved protein that is involved in neuronal maturation, differentiation, and survival. Numb can associate with vesicles and endosomes, functioning as an endocytic adapter protein. Humans produce two alternatively spliced variants of Numb that differ in length; the long Numb (L-Numb) and the short Numb (S-Numb). Previous work has demonstrated an interaction between APP and both Numb isoforms in brain lysates and in cell culture. Considering that Numb is an endocytic adapter protein, it was investigated whether expression of the Numb isoforms influences the trafficking and processing of **APP**.

Experiment 1

Each of the human Numb isoforms was overexpressed in neuronal cells by transfection. Both the amount of total cellular APP protein and the amount of Aβ peptide released into the medium were measured. Untransfected neural cells that express moderate levels of both Numb isoforms were used as controls.

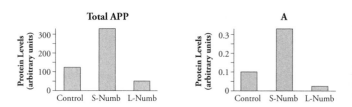

Figure 3 Effects of Numb isoforms on APP and Aβ levels in neural cells

Experiment 2

To determine whether the Numb isoforms affect the transport of APP to different intracellular compartments, neural cells transfected with S-Numb or L-Numb were treated with an inhibitor of the recycling pathway (monensin), or an inhibitor of the lysosome (chloroquine) for 6 hours. Monensin does not affect the internalization of proteins from the cell surface and chloroquine does not interfere with the recycling pathway.

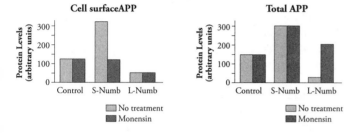

Figure 4 Effects of Monensin and Chloroquine treatment in neural cells transfected with the Numb isoforms

1. The investigators transfected neuronal cells plated in small culture dishes and 48 hours later measured the levels of Aβ protein. Which of the following procedures should be implemented to measure the levels of Aβ?

A) Place the culture dishes under a microscope and directly count the amount of Aβ.
B) Harvest the cells, break down the cell membrane, and measure the levels of cellular Aβ using a specific antibody.
C) Harvest the cells, break down the cell membrane, and measure the levels of cellular Aβ using PCR.
D) Harvest the condition media from the dishes and use an ELISA (Enzyme-Linked Immunosorbent Assay) coated with anti-Aβ peptide to measure the levels of Aβ released.

2. Alzheimer's disease begins with episodic memory loss, which worsens over time, accompanied by noticeable defects in learning and behavior. Light microscopy in postmortem brain sections of Alzheimer's patients will reveal neuritic plaques and damaged neural networks at all of the following brain areas, EXCEPT the:

A) frontal lobe.
B) hippocampus.
C) hypothalamus.
D) cortex.

3. According to the information in the passage, which of the following conclusions can be drawn regarding the trafficking of APP in neural cells?

I. Expression of the L-Numb isoform can reduce APP protein levels by facilitating the lysosomal degradation of APP.
II. Expression of the S-Numb isoform facilitates the trafficking of APP along the recycling pathway.
III. In untransfected neural cells both Numb isoforms participate in the regulation of APP levels.

A) I only
B) II only
C) I and II only
D) I, II and III

4. According to the information provided in the passage, all of the following strategies can be effective in reducing the levels of Aβ in untransfected (control) neural cells, EXCEPT:

A) inhibition of γ-secretase.
B) activation of α-secretase.
C) induction of L-Numb mRNA.
D) inhibition of the lysosome.

5. Which of the following independent clinical findings would most strengthen the investigators' results?

A) Postmortem analysis of brains from Alzheimer's disease patients showed reduced levels of total Numb mRNA.
B) Postmortem analysis of brains from Alzheimer's disease patients have endosomes that stain positive for Numb.
C) Alzheimer's patients show defects in the alternative splicing machinery and the γ-secretase activity.
D) Brains from transgenic mice that exclusively express the L-Numb isoform showed reduced formation of neuritic plaques compared to controls.

6. Aβ peptides can negatively regulate various steps of acetylcholine (ACh) synthesis, release, and signaling. Which of the following would be the best target for pharmacological intervention?

A) A drug that inhibits postsynaptic ACh receptors
B) A drug that blocks voltage-gated Na^+ channels
C) An allosteric inhibitor of acetylcholinesterase
D) A drug that inhibits choline reuptake by cholinergic neurons

PRACTICE PASSAGE 6

HCl secretion by gastric parietal cells contributes to digestion by establishing an optimal pH for proteolytic enzyme function. H^+ and Cl^- ions are released into the lumen of the stomach in response to distinct triggers at the basolateral membrane of parietal cells. Receptors specific for histamine, ACh, and gastrin initiate second messenger cascades, which ultimately converge to potentiate acid secretion. This input leads to increased levels of the H^+/K^+-ATPase as well as accelerated H^+/K^+ exchange at luminal membranes. Figure 1 shows the direct effects of histamine, ACh, and gastrin on parietal cells. Gastrin also has an indirect effect on parietal cells by stimulating nearby mast cells to secrete histamine. Parietal cells rely heavily on oxidative phosphorylation to sustain H^+/K^+-ATPase function and one of the steepest ion gradients in the human body.

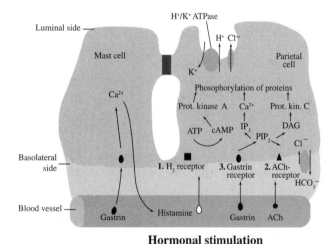

Hormonal stimulation

Figure 1 Stimulation of acid secretion

A necessary balance exists between acid production and the protection of intestinal cells against its potentially destructive effects. The presence of excessive acid or an increased susceptibility to acid results in defects in intestinal mucosa. Mucosal erosions, the hallmark of peptic ulcer disease (PUD), typically cause nausea, pain, and bleeding. PUD may be complicated when the ulcer invades through the muscular layers of the intestinal organ, leading to perforation or penetration into adjacent organs. Most cases of PUD are linked to chronic non-steroidal anti-inflammatory drug (NSAID) use, or to infection with *Helicobacter pylori*, a bacterium that invades and causes chronic inflammation in gastric and duodenal cells. NSAIDs decrease the production of inflammatory mediators, but also decrease the production of other molecules (including prostaglandin E) that protect the intestinal lining from acid.

Rarer causes of PUD are conditions that increase circulating levels of histamine or gastrin. Zollinger-Ellison syndrome (ZES), for example, is caused by a gastrin-secreting tumor in the stomach. Patients with ZES have very high levels of gastrin and often develop multiple ulcers. The majority of ZES patients also suffers from malabsorptive diarrhea as a result of acid-mediated precipitation of bile salts, inactivation of pancreatic enzymes, and destruction of intestinal mucosal surfaces. About 25% of gastrin-secreting tumors form as part of a multiple endocrine neoplasia syndrome type 1 (MEN-1), in which patients also develop hypersecreting tumors of the parathyroid glands and pituitary gland.

Treatments for PUD include anti-histamine drugs (e.g., cimetidine, ranitidine), proton pump inhibitors (e.g., omeprazole, esomeprazole), which bind directly to luminal portions of H^+/K^+-ATPase proteins, and, when appropriate, antibiotics. In refractory or very complicated cases, surgery may be indicated. Aside from resecting affected portions of stomach or bowel, surgeons may elect to perform a bilateral vagotomy, in which terminal branches of the right and left vagus nerves are severed in an attempt to minimize acid secretion.

1. Which of the following regarding neural innervation of parietal cells is true?

A) The vagus nerve provides parasympathetic innervation, which decreases intracellular calcium.

B) The vagus nerve provides parasympathetic innervation, which increases intracellular calcium.

C) The vagus nerve provides sympathetic innervation, which decreases intracellular calcium.

D) The vagus nerve provides sympathetic innervation, which increases intracellular calcium.

2. After a patient undergoes a bilateral vagotomy for a perforated duodenal ulcer, which of the following recommendations should be made regarding follow-up treatment with omeprazole or another drug in the same class?

A) It should not be prescribed because this drug class increases HCl secretion.
B) It need not be prescribed because bilateral vagotomy effectively eliminates HCl secretion.
C) It should be prescribed because this drug directly inhibits second messenger proteins involved in HCl production.
D) It should be prescribed because there are multiple ways of activating second messenger proteins involved in HCl production.

3. Which of the following conditions is LEAST likely to be associated with increased HCl secretion from parietal cells?

A) Zollinger-Ellison syndrome
B) Systemic mastocytosis (increased number and infiltration of mast cells into tissues)
C) Basophilic leukemia (clonal expansion of basophils)
D) Multiple myeloma (clonal expansion of plasma cells)

4. Misoprostol is a synthetic analog of prostaglandin E. Which of the following is true regarding the use of misoprostol in a patient with PUD?

A) Misoprostol inhibits cAMP and calcium release mechanisms, and promotes ulcer healing.
B) Misoprostol promotes cAMP and calcium release mechanisms, and promotes ulcer healing.
C) Misoprostol inhibits cAMP and calcium release mechanisms, and prevents ulcer healing.
D) Misoprostol promotes cAMP and calcium release mechanisms, and prevents ulcer healing.

5. Which of the following is likely to be observed in a patient with MEN-1?

  I.   Decreased parietal acid secretion
  II. Hypercalcemia
  III. Hypocalcemia

A) I and II
B) I and III
C) II only
D) III only

6. Which of the following contributes to the diarrhea experienced by ZES patients?

A) Precipitation of bile salts hinders protein breakdown and amino acid absorption.
B) Increased HCl in the stomach and small intestine breaks down lipases and amylases.
C) Gastrin-releasing cells replace insulin-releasing cells.
D) Vagotomy in these patients leads to increased water reabsorption by colonic mucosal cells.

7. Which of the following is NOT true regarding parietal cells?

A) They do not rely on mitochondrial enzymes for ATP production.
B) They play a role in Vitamin B12 metabolism.
C) They are regulated via neural, paracrine, and endocrine mechanisms.
D) They play a role in protein digestion in the stomach.

PRACTICE PASSAGE 7

John Freke of Saint Bartholomew's Hospital in 1736 described a disease where large swellings of fused bone were felt on the back of a 14 year old patient. These swellings had been growing for three years and had formed a "fixed bony pair of bodice" on the patient's torso. Until recently, the cause of fibrodysplasia ossificans progressiva (FOP) remained a mystery, but recent research has greatly expanded the understanding of the pathophysiology behind this disease.

FOP is characterized by two clinical features: malformations of the great toes and progressive heterotropic ossification (HO). Extensive HO begins in the first decade of life and occurs with significant pain at sites of tissue damage and inflammation. Heterotropic bone replaces skeletal muscle and connective tissue, but spares the diaphragm, tongue, and extraocular muscles. HO progresses throughout the patient's lifetime, often resulting in impaired mobility and life-threatening complications.

Recently, the gene responsible for FOP has been identified as an activin receptor IA (ACVR1); a missense mutation in its activation domain results in the disease. ACVR1 functions as a bone morphogenetic protein (BMP) receptor and remains constitutively activated upon mutation; this results in overactive osteogenesis.

Signal transduction inhibitors (STIs) for ACVR1 are an area of significant research in the treatment of FOP. The ATP-binding site on the BMP receptor can be exploited to ensure specificity of STIs in FOP treatment and avoid cross reacting with similar BMP receptors. Because STIs are not yet available, current treatment focuses on supportive therapy and managing inflammation.

1. A pathologist examines a biopsied tissue sample under high resolution and observes numerous red, mononucleated, striated cells. The tissue is organized and contains a white infiltrate of unknown identity. Based on this sample, is this patient suffering from FOP and how does the pathologist know?

A) Yes, the infiltrate is due to mature bone matrix deposition.
B) Yes, the infiltrate is collagen.
C) No, skeletal muscle would not be an effective location to detect ossification.
D) Unknown, this biopsy does not provide sufficient information with regard to FOP.

2. Researchers conduct a broad search of medical records and found a few families in which multiple affected individuals are present in successive generations. Which inheritance pattern would be expected in this family, and what is a possible reason for this pattern?

A) Dominant; a single locus mutation results in increased osteogenesis.
B) Dominant; but the mutation shows varied expressivity .
C) Recessive; the disease is likely underreported due to its minor clinical presentation.
D) Recessive; this is a rare disease likely due to the haploinsufficicy of the ACVR1 mutation.

3. Which of the following is a potential molecular mechanism by which a patient could develop fibrodysplasia ossificans progressiva?

A) Extensive DNA intercalation
B) Site-specific DNA acetylation
C) A DNA transition mutation
D) A silent mutation

4. Which of the following is NOT involved in bone remodeling?

A) Osteoclasts
B) Collagen deposition
C) Fibrinogen
D) Sex hormones

5. A patient with fibrodysplasia ossificans progressiva presents at the doctor's office. Which of the following physical exam findings would you expect to find in this patient?

A) Tongue deviates to one side when the patient is instructed to stick it out
B) Nystagmus (rapid involuntary oscillations of the eye)
C) Severe dyspnea (labored respiration)
D) Nuchal rigidity (neck stiffness)

6. According to the passage, which of the following is the most effective treatment for FOP?

A) Surgery to remove the overgrown bone
B) Sonification of overgrown bone to aid in bone particle removal
C) Systemic glucocorticoids
D) Oral calcitonin

7. In the development of an STI for the treatment of FOB, a researcher discovers an increase in muscular intracellular calcium in an animal model that results in increased muscular tone. Which of the following is the LEAST likely cause?

A) The STI acts as a receptor antagonist on the motor endplate.
B) The STI inhibits acetylcholinesterase.
C) The STI decreases the sarcoplasmic reticulum membrane integrity.
D) The STI inhibits the Ca^{2+}-ATPase.

PRACTICE PASSAGE 8

Since the end of the 1800s, the mineral *asbestos* has been used in industrial applications that require resistance to high levels of heat, in addition to the ability to withstand chemical or electrical damage. Its strength and flexibility come from its thin, fibrous structure. The exploitation of these properties extends as far back as ancient Greece, although its use was not nearly as widespread as it has been over the last 150 years.

The fibers can be inhaled into the lungs, where they are neither broken down nor cleared. The attempt to clear them causes inflammation, scarring, and fibrosis of the lungs, which leads to shortness of breath, coughing, chest pain, and decreased tolerance for physical activity. This combination of symptoms is referred to as *asbestosis*. The continued presence of the fibers in the lungs can act as a carcinogen, particularly to the cells in the pleural membranes surrounding the lungs. *Mesothelioma* is a type of cancer typically caused by exposure to asbestos; nearly 50% of exposed individuals develop mesothelioma. Fibers phagocytosed by cells interfere with chromatin, causing chromosomal anomalies which can lead to tumor suppressor gene deletion. The cancer manifests as malignant cell growth within the flat, cuboidal cells composing these tissue layers. The risk of mesothelioma is nine times greater in asbestos-exposed individuals than in the general population, and can be as high as 50 times greater in asbestos-exposed individuals who also smoke.

Symptoms of mesothelioma can be diffuse, such as shortness of breath, weight loss, and painful breathing and coughing. The impact on lungs is pronounced, particularly due to the formation of pleural effusions. These accumulations of fluid between the membranes create increasing pressure on the lungs that can make breathing difficult. Surgical treatment has been found to be of limited benefit; the standard of care relies heavily on chemotherapy and in many cases, radiation. Due to the contiguous nature of the tissues with other parts of the body, metastasis is common.

Ubiquitous placement of asbestos into insulating and fireproofing materials over the last several decades has lead to extensive efforts at abatement, particularly in public buildings such as schools. The danger of even limited exposure has been highlighted most dramatically by World War II shipbuilders who worked with large amounts of asbestos. This leads to contentious debates about the relative safety of leaving asbestos-containing materials in place versus the risk implicit in removing them.

1. In a patient presenting with a mesothelioma-induced pleural effusion, which of the following would be expected to be increased?

    I.   Pleural pressure
    II. Respiratory rate
    III. Heart rate

A) I
B) I and II
C) II and III
D) I, II and III

2. Mesothelioma can also be found in the peritoneum, the membrane surrounding the organs of the gut. Which of the following is the LEAST likely way for this area of the body to be exposed to asbestos?

A) Movement of asbestos fibers from the lung to the GI tract via the mucociliary escalator
B) Handling brake pads containing asbestos fibers
C) Passage of asbestos fibers into the lymphatic system from which they then come in contact with the peritoneum
D) Performing asbestos abatement without the use of a full-face respirator

3. Chest X-rays are a routine part of the diagnostic procedure for mesothelioma. Which of the following would be an expected finding in the chest X-ray of a patient with mesothelioma?

A) Increased levels of SMRP (soluble mesothelin-related proteins) in the serum
B) Fractures of the ribs due to lack of hydroxyapatite deposition
C) Decreased residual volume
D) Thickening of the pleural membranes

4. Exposure to asbestos may trigger scarring of the lungs, causing pleural fibrosis (development of fibrous tissue in the pleura), a subsequent loss of lung elasticity, and a reduction in total lung capacity. These are the hallmarks of restrictive lung disease. Shortness of breath in asbestosis would be MOST similar to shortness of breath due to:

A) intense cardiovascular exercise.
B) a low oxygen environment.
C) inflamed airways during an asthma attack.
D) diaphragm paralysis from a spinal cord injury.

5. A patient receives a liver lobe transplant from a donor with mesothelioma. Should the recipient patient worry about an increased risk of cancer?

A) Yes, because mesothelioma metastasizes, so cancerous cells could be in the liver.
B) Yes, because cancerous cells would already be present in the liver.
C) No, because the pleural membranes are not being donated.
D) No, because cancer cannot be spread via organ donation.

6. What would be the impact on the intercostal and abdominal muscles in a patient with mesothelioma?

A) The intercostals would engage more and the abdominals would be used less to facilitate breathing, especially when experiencing a pleural effusion.
B) The intercostals would engage more and the abdominals would engage more to facilitate breathing, especially when experiencing a pleural effusion.
C) The intercostals would be used less and the abdominals would be used less to facilitate breathing, especially when experiencing a pleural effusion.
D) The intercostals would be used less and the abdominals would engage more to facilitate breathing, especially when experiencing a pleural effusion.

7. Which of the following would be the LEAST helpful for a patient with asbestosis?

A) Regular diagnostic chest X-rays
B) Chemotherapy
C) Smoking cessation
D) Oxygen therapy

PRACTICE PASSAGE 9

Gastrulation is a key developmental process and involves the formation of the three primary germ layers. It requires large amounts of cell migration and a process known as epithelial-mesenchymal transition (EMT). This is particularly essential for the formation of the mesoderm, the middle germ layer.

An EMT can be easily studied in the lab because epithelial and mesenchymal cells are very different. When grown in the lab, epithelial cells form layers and grow closely together in clusters. The cells typically have a cobblestone appearance and are closely joined to their neighboring cells. Importantly, these cells also have polarity, with an apical surface and a basolateral surface. Mesenchymal cells look different: they do not form an organized cell layer, have no polarity, contact their neighbors only focally, and are spindle shaped. Mesenchymal cells are precursor cells that develop into connective tissue, blood vessels, and lymphatic tissue.

Epithelial and mesenchymal cells also express different and mutually exclusive protein markers. Mesenchymal cells express vimentin as an intermediate filament, N-cadherin as an adhesion protein, and make fibronectin which is exported to the extracellular matrix. In contrast, epithelial cells express cytokeratins as intermediate filament proteins and E-cadherin in adherens cell junctions.

Gastrulation starts in a region of the embryo known as the "Organizer." Over the last 20 years, it has been found that the Organizer region expresses several transcription factors at high levels. One of these is a protein called Goosecoid, which is coded for by the Gsc gene. Goosecoid is an EMT-promoting transcription factor that plays a major role in gastrulation. This was first shown in the frog embryo, in a series of experiments:

Experiment 1

Frog embryos were isolated at the 32-cell stage, where each of the cells is called a blastomere. The Gsc transcript (generated from cDNA) was injected into a blastomere on the ventral side to cause over-expression of the Gsc protein. This caused the formation of an abnormal blastopore lip on the ventral side of the embryo. Normally, one blastopore lip forms (on the dorsal side), and this is where mesoderm formation and gastrulation cell movements originate.

Experiment 2

Frog embryos were isolated at the 32-cell stage and Gsc was over-expressed in a dorsal blastomere, similar to in Experiment 1. Normally, the blastopore lip has two cell populations (Figure 1): *marginal zone cells*, which involute and contribute to elongation of the body axis, and *deep zone cells*, which crawl forward to form the leading edge of the mesoderm. Overexpression of Gsc in a dorsal blastomere changes marginal zone cells to deep zone cells; overall, these embryos have more migratory cells.

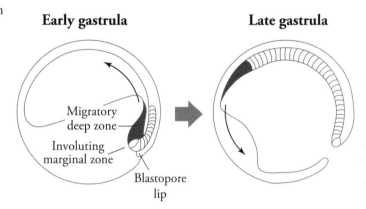

Figure 1 Early and late gastrulation in the frog embryo

1. The Goosecoid protein would contain which of the following?

A) Nuclear localization signal and disulfide bonds
B) Nuclear localization signal and DNA binding motifs
C) Signal sequence and disulfide bonds
D) Signal sequence and DNA binding motifs

2. Which of the following is true about the embryo used in the experiments?

A) The embryo would have to be post-gastrulation and the molecule injected into the blastomeres would have to be single stranded RNA either with or without introns.
B) The embryo would have to be pre-gastrulation and the molecule injected into the blastomeres would have to be single stranded RNA without introns.
C) The embryo would have to be post-gastrulation and the molecule injected into the blastomeres would have to be single stranded DNA generated from RNA.
D) The embryo would have to be pre-gastrulation and the molecule injected into the blastomeres would have to be double stranded DNA without introns.

3. A cell that expresses cytokeratins, E-cadherin and vimentin could be best classified as:

A) epithelial.
B) mesodermal.
C) mesenchymal.
D) undergoing EMT.

4. Why do the experiments in the passage support a role for Gsc in EMT?

A) The formation of a second blastopore lip would require cell proliferation, which is consistent with the role of Gsc as a transcription factor.
B) Changes from crawling migratory cells to involuting marginal zone cells would require changes in cellular transcription.
C) In both experiments, Gsc overexpression induced increased cell movement and changes in the early steps of mesoderm formation.
D) Gsc overexpression caused changes in the blastopore lip (including the number of lips and their architecture), where formation of the inner germ layer starts.

5. Which of the following is most similar to EMT?

A) Cancer metastasis, where a tumor-initiating cell leaves the bulk tumor, migrates and settles in a new niche
B) The nephron, where epithelial cells are surrounded by interstitium
C) Neutrophils and macrophages squeezing out of capillary clefts
D) Peristalsis of the gastrointestinal tract and the resulting migration of food undergoing digestion

6. Which of the following would be most affected in an organism with abnormal EMT?

A) Brain and vasculature
B) Respiratory and gastrointestinal systems
C) Epidermis and dermis
D) Lymphatic system and urogenital organs

7. Vimentin most likely functions in which of the following?

A) Cytokinesis
B) Structural support of the cell
C) Intracellular transport
D) Mitotic spindle formation

Chapter 19
Biology Practice
Section Solutions

SOLUTIONS TO FREESTANDING QUESTIONS

1. **C** According to the question stem, *S. epidermidis* are facultative anaerobes. Facultative an-aerobes synthesize ATP via aerobic respiration if oxygen is present, but revert to anaerobic respiration (fermentation) if oxygen is not present. NADH and $FADH_2$ are both produced during the Krebs cycle (choice A can be eliminated). *S. epidermidis* are prokaryotes, so they do not have membrane-bound organelles such as mitochondria (choice B can be eliminated). The Krebs cycle takes place in the cytoplasm of prokaryotes and produces both NADH and $FADH_2$ (choice C is correct). Fermentation regenerates NAD^+ by oxidizing NADH; it does not produce $FADH_2$ (choice D can be eliminated).

2. **C** A mutation within the gene coding region of the DNA is the worst type of mutation be-cause it will be conserved throughout all progeny of that cell, and every time that gene is transcribed and translated that mistake will show (Item I is the most serious; choices A and D can be eliminated). Note that neither of the remaining answer choices have Item II as the next most serious mutation, so we only need to evaluation Items III and IV. A single base deletion in an mRNA molecule (Item III) would cause a frameshift and would cause the gene product to be useless, however, since mRNAs are transient within the cytoplasm, this effect would be temporary. If there is a mistake in the anti-codon of a tRNA (Item IV) it will likely place the wrong amino acid every time that codon comes up in any gene. There is some redundancy among anticodons of tRNA molecules, but very little with the first base, so this will definitely lead to errors in the protein products of all genes (Item IV is more serious that Item III, and choice B can be eliminated). Note that Item I is still more serious, because tRNAs are also somewhat transient; an error in DNA is always more serious than an error in RNA. Item II is the least serious. An insertion of five bases in a non-gene coding segment of the DNA would theoretically have no effect since no gene product is made from these regions of the DNA. Sometimes, however, these regions are used for gene regulation; without any more information as to the use of this particular non-gene coding region, we cannot really make any determination as to its seriousness.

3. **C** This question is best tackled by process of elimination, since you are not expected to know the fine details of these particular proteins. Introduction of the constitutive promoter would increase transcription and translation of the cyclin D1 gene, leading to increased levels of this protein. If cyclin D1 competes with CKI-p16, and there is now more cyclin D1, then there should be *decreased* binding of CKI-p16 to the allosteric site (choice A is wrong). Fur-ther, if the cyclin D1-activated CDK drives the cell into the S phase, there would be an increase in DNA replication and increased helicase activity (choice B is wrong). Since it is a kinase that is activated, phosphorylation of something is likely, and *Rb* is a tumor suppres-sor protein that inhibits cell cycle progression. Inhibition of *Rb* could be the mechanism by which the CDK drives entry into the S phase (choice C is correct). The question text only describes an effect on S-phase entry, there is no reason to assume that the G_2 phase would be affected. Each cell cycle checkpoint relies upon a different set of signals and modification of one of those signals would not necessarily have an impact on the duration of the other phases (choice D is wrong).

4. **C** This is most likely mitochondrial inheritance. Only females pass along the disease, and every child of an affected female is affected. If this were autosomal dominant inheritance, only about 50% of the progeny from the affected Generation II females would be affected, not the 100% as shown in the pedigree. Also, about 50% of the progeny from affected Generation II males would be affected, not the 0% shown (choice A is wrong). An X-linked

dominant disorder would show in all females and half their male progeny, as well as all daughters of affected males (choice B is wrong). An X-linked recessive disorder would not be passed from mother to daughter if the father was unaffected (choice D is wrong).

5. **B**   ACTH stimulates the adrenal gland, and as such would cause an increase in its size. Additionally, ACTH promotes the release of cortisol, and the subsequent rise in cortisol levels explains the elevated blood glucose and increased protein catabolism. Note, however, that elevated cortisol by itself cannot explain the increased adrenal size (choice D is wrong). Although elevated glucagon levels would lead to elevated blood glucose, it would not explain the other two symptoms (choice A is wrong), and elevated growth hormone levels would result in increased protein synthesis, not catabolism (choice C is wrong).

6. **C**   The resting membrane potential is due to concentration gradients of ions across the plasma membrane and the membrane permeability of these ions. Calcium concentrations are low within the cell; by increasing calcium permeability (via calcium leak channels), calcium would flow into the cell and the entry of this positive ion would cause the resting membrane potential to increase (choice C is correct and choice B is wrong. Sodium and potassium are the two most important ions dictating resting membrane potential in neurons under normal conditions; however increased calcium permeability is not a normal condition. Permeability of all ions must be considered when determining resting membrane potential (choice D is wrong) An increase in intracellular calcium would result in an increase in neurotransmitter release, not a decrease (choice A is not correct).

7. **B**   The atrial and ventricular myocytes are separated by a band of connective tissue and the valves of the heart, and are not electrically connected. This is one of the primary reasons for the existence of the conduction system at all; to provide a pathway for the impulse to travel to the ventricles (choice B is false and is the correct answer choice). The conduction system is not neurally derived; all the autorhythmic cells of the conduction system, including the SA and AV nodes are specialized cardiac muscle cells (choice A is true and can be eliminated). The impulse originates at the SA node, but is delayed at the AV node to give time for the atria to finish their contraction prior to ventricular contraction (choice C is true and can be eliminated). Baseline parasympathetic input, called "vagal tone," brings the intrinsic rate of firing of the SA node from about 100 beats/minute to about 80 beats/minute (choice D is true and can be eliminated).

8. **B**   Autoreactive antibodies produced by the mother can cross the placenta and will attack the fetus, providing a host of new symptoms (congenital heart block, neonatal lupus rash, hepatitis) which may allow for an easier diagnosis. Note that it is not necessary to determine this in order to get the question right; a process-of-elimination approach to this question would be very effective. Lupus is caused by an overactive immune system attacking self tissues. Thus, weakening the immune system would, if anything, reduce the severity of the disease, and make it more difficult to diagnose (choice A is false). There is no reason to assume that increased fat deposition would increase the likelihood of autoreactivity. If that were true, there would be a higher frequency of autoimmune disorders in obese individuals. Further, there is no guarantee that pregnant women necessarily have increased fat deposition. There are plenty of very thin pregnant women (choice C is false). Lupus is not caused by infection by a "lupus virus"; it is an autoimmune disorder (choice D is false).

9. **B** Pancreatic lipase is responsible for fat digestion; inhibiting its action would prevent the effective digestion and subsequent absorption of fats. Fatty acids are not absorbed directly into the bloodstream from the intestinal lumen; they must be processed into triglycerides before being absorbed. Furthermore, they are not technically "transported"; because they are hydrophobic they can simply diffuse across the cell membranes (choice A is wrong). There is no absorption of macromolecules in the colon, only water and ions, and in any case, macromolecules are digested to monomers before being absorbed anywhere (choice C is wrong). Chief cells secrete pepsinogen, the precursor to pepsin, a protease. Pepsinogen has no effect on appetite, so the suppression of its secretion will have no effect either (choice D is wrong). Note that knowledge of lipstatin or orlistat is unnecessary to answer this question successfully; the answer choice can be determined by process of elimination.

10. **B** The thick ascending limb of the loop of Henle pumps ions out of the filtrate into the renal medulla. If Lasix inhibits the Na^+-K^+-$2Cl^-$ symporter, then those ions will remain in the filtrate (choice A is wrong), and ion concentration in the filtrate will be higher than normal (choice C is wrong). If the filtrate is more concentrated, it will tend to hold on to water in the collecting duct, and less water will be reabsorbed into the blood. This leads to an increase in water excretion, which lowers blood pressure (choice B is correct). Note that a low blood ion concentration would not lead to a retention of water; ion concentration needs to be high to retain water (choice D is wrong).

11. **C** Boyle's law states that pressure × volume is constant (at a constant temperature). Therefore, as the patient tries to inhale, the rib cage expands, pressure inside the airways decreases (choices A and B can be eliminated), and the lung volume increases (choice D can be eliminated and choice C is correct). Note also, that since the box is airtight, as the rib cage expands, the box pressure is increased, and the box volume would decrease.

12. **C** Since a fetus cannot eat or breathe for itself, the placenta supplies the developing fetus with oxygen and nutrients, while allowing waste to be eliminated. Item I is false: While the mother transfers oxygen to the fetus via the placenta, no actual blood is transferred (choices B and D can be eliminated). Note that both of the remaining answer choices include Item II, thus Item II must be true and we can focus on Item III. Item III is true: The mother transfers nutrients via the placenta to the fetus (choice A can be eliminated and choice C is correct). Note that Item II is in fact true: Waste products, including carbon dioxide, are transferred from the fetus to the mother via the placenta.

SOLUTIONS TO PRACTICE PASSAGE 1

1. **D** Methylenetetrahydrofolate reductase (MTHFR) is the enzyme that requires vitamin B12 in order to convert homocysteine to methionine. A lack of vitamin B12 would result in a decrease in the activity of MTHFR (choice A is wrong). And since the activity of MTHFR is diminished due to lack of vitamin B12, the levels of methionine would correspondingly decrease (choice B is wrong). This would lead to an accumulation of homocysteine (produced from methionine in the diet) which would then be diverted towards the transsulfuration pathway, resulting in an increase in the activity of cystathionine β-synthase (choice C is wrong) and increased levels of cysteine (choice D is correct).

2. **B** An increase in methionine levels, due to the methionine load test, would lead to an increase in S-adenosyl-homocysteine levels that would subsequently lead to an increase in homocysteine levels. This increase in homocysteine levels would be metabolized through either the remethylation pathway or the transsulfuration pathway. According to the last paragraph of the passage, "S-adenosyl-methionine acts as an allosteric inhibitor of methylenetetrahydrofolate reductase (MTHFR) and an activator of cystathionine β-synthase." The increased levels of S-adenosyl-methionine would enhance, not inhibit, the activity of cystathionine β-synthase (choice B is correct and A is wrong). Additionally, since S-adenosyl-methionine acts as an allosteric inhibitor of MTHFR, the activity of MTHFR would decrease. Based on the information provided in the passage, it cannot be inferred as to how the quantity of MTHFR would change with regard to any changes in the amounts of methionine, S-adenosyl-methionine, or homocysteine (choice C and choice D are both wrong).

3. **C** Since the transsulfuration pathway is non-functional, the metabolism of homocysteine is diverted towards the remethylation pathway. Initially, methylenetetrahydrofolate reductase (MTHFR) would have an increase in activity as there is more homocysteine to metabolize, but this would also result in an increase in S-adenosyl-methionine levels. According to the last paragraph of the passage, "S-adenosyl-methionine acts as an allosteric inhibitor of methylenetetrahydrofolate reductase (MTHFR)...". The allosteric inhibition of MTHFR combined with a lack of functional cystathionine β-synthase would result in an eventual increase in homocysteine levels (choice C is correct). Theoretically, S-adenosyl-methionine would also inhibit cystathionine β-synthase, but since this enzyme is non-functional or absent altogether, inhibition would have no effect (choice D is wrong). Since MTHFR is inhibited, methionine would not accumulate (choice B is wrong), and if anything, there would be an increase in methyl-tetrahydrofolate, not a decrease (since it is not being used by the inhibited MTHFR, choice A is wrong).

4. **A** The passage states that increased levels of homocysteine damages endothelial cells and is associated with an increased risk of occlusive vascular disease, thrombosis, and stroke (choice C is wrong). An occlusion, or blockage, of coronary arteries would increase the likelihood of developing a heart attack (choice A is correct). Moreover, endothelial cell damage would increase, rather than decrease, the likelihood of developing coronary artery disease and stroke (choice B is wrong). The word "sclerosis" in atherosclerosis and multiple sclerosis is simply a red herring. There is no mention of multiple sclerosis within the passage nor can this be inferred based on the information given in the passage (choice D is wrong).

5. **A** An increase in methionine ingestion would be expected to cause an increase in homocysteine levels, as well as the intermediates S-adenosyl methionine and S-adenosyl homocysteine. However, if there is no defect in cystathionine β-synthase, the excess homocysteine would be diverted into the transsulfuration pathway and the rise would be transient (as would the rise in intermediates—choice D supports the conclusion and can be eliminated). There would follow a rise in cysteine and α-ketobutyrate (choice C supports the conclusion and can be eliminated). However if the patient's cysteine levels remain constant (or if the rise in homocysteine levels was not transient), it would suggest that the defect lies with cystathionine β-synthase and is not due to a nutritional deficiency (choice A does not support the conclusion and is the correct answer choice). Administration of vitamin B12 with the methionine load is necessary to temporarily eliminate the nutritional insufficiency and thereby facilitate the metabolism of homocysteine via the remethylation pathway. If B12 was not

administered, homocysteine levels would remain elevated and it would not be possible to distinguish between nutritional insufficiency and a cystathionine β-synthase defect (choice B supports the conclusion and can be eliminated).

6.   **D**   As the question stem states, methionine has a sulfur atom that is radioactively labeled (choice B is wrong). Tracking this sulfur atom is made difficult as none of the molecular structures of the answer choices are provided. Nonetheless, there are two things that are needed in order to solve this question. The first is to recognize that the name of the pathway provides a clue to its biochemical activity. The *remethylation* pathway involves adding a methyl group onto homocysteine, that was removed when proceeding through the cycle. In other words, the radioactive sulfur atom found in the methionine would also be found in homocysteine (choice A is wrong). The second bit of information needed is that the amino acid cysteine contains a sulfur atom. This information can be extracted from the passage as it mentions that cysteine contains a sulfur atom (a thiol group), as well as from outside knowledge in that two cysteine amino acids (reduced form) can form a disulfide bridge to become cystine (oxidized form). Since both homocysteine and cysteine contain a sulfur atom, it can be inferred that homocysteine contributed the sulfur atom to cystathionine, which then contributed the sulfur atom to cysteine (choice C is wrong). By the process of elimination, α-ketobutyrate, would not contain a sulfur atom and hence would not be radioactive (choice D is correct).

7.   **A**   According to the question stem, homocysteine produces H_2O_2 that inactivates nitric oxide. Glutathione peroxidase is an enzyme with anti-oxidative activities; it converts H_2O_2 into H_2O. If homocysteine is able to inhibit glutathione peroxidase, the levels of H_2O_2 would increase, and nitric oxide would be inactivated (choice A is correct). The activity of endothelial nitric oxide synthase (eNOS) neither supports nor refutes the finding that H_2O_2 produced by homocysteine inactivates nitric oxide (choice B is wrong). A decrease in the transcription of eNOS would result in a decreased amount of the enzyme responsible for the production of nitric oxide. The reduction in nitric oxide levels would contribute to a reduction in vasodilation, and have the same end result as inactivating nitric oxide. However, this does not support the finding that homocysteine acts to produce H_2O_2 (choice C is wrong). Lastly, the response (or lack of response) of the endothelium lining to nitric oxide tells you nothing about the mechanism by which homocysteine may exert its effect (choice D is wrong).

SOLUTIONS TO PRACTICE PASSAGE 2

1.   **C**   A filamentous body is defined in the passage as the outermost coat of the hepatitis B virus. It is basically the lipid envelope of the virus with the normal surface antigen proteins interspersed, but without any genetic material or core protein. Injecting a filamentous body into a healthy uninfected person would cause the immune system to recognize the surface antigen (HBsAg) and create a humoral (antibody) response against it (choices A and B are wrong). The immune system always responds to new antigens by making IgM subtype antibodies first. After a period of time it produces IgG subtypes which give lasting immunity and memory against recurring infection (choice C is correct and choice D is wrong).

2. **C** The passage states that chronic infection involves the "failure of an effective humoral immune response against HBsAg," i.e., the absence of anti-sAg (choices A and D are wrong). The passage also states that IgM type antibodies are the first response, and that over time these are replaced with IgG; thus in chronic infection, only anti-core IgG would be present (choice B can be eliminated and choice C is correct).

3. **A** A good approach to questions on the MCAT is to ask whether this is a something you already know or if it must be solved using information in the passage. Since the MCAT tests general concepts, you are not expected to know how specific viruses replicate. Thus, this is information you need to pull from the passage. Figure 1 shows the purpose of the viral polymerase. It shows HBV with a partially double stranded DNA genome sending its DNA into the host nucleus. In the nucleus the viral DNA is converted to (+) mRNA which is shown being sent to the cytoplasm and acted upon by P protein (the viral polymerase) before being packaged into a capsid for production of a new virus. It is subtle, but the P protein must be acting as an RNA-dependent DNA polymerase since it is converting (+) mRNA into DNA (the new HBV genome). Normal human cells do not contain any polymerase that acts on RNA to make DNA so this must be specific to the virus. (Note that this is similar to a retrovirus, but HBV is not a retrovirus because its genome is not integrated into the host genome; further, retroviruses have RNA genomes.) Thus, a virus lacking the *P* gene and viral polymerase would be able to infect cells and move its DNA genome into the nucleus, and mRNA could be produced from the viral genome (using the host RNA polymerase II which makes mRNA from DNA), so viral mRNA would be detected in the cytoplasm (choices C and D are wrong). Figure 1 also shows that spherical bodies (which do not contain any viral genetic material) can be made in the absence of viral polymerase. However, Dane particles (another name for infectious hepatitis B virus) would not be made because the virus without any viral polymerase could not replicate its genome (choice A is correct and choice B is wrong).

4. **D** Gene therapy involves the insertion of new gene sequences to help (permanently) counter the negative effects of some disease or condition. Thus the insertion of proteases (presumably only into infected cells; this type of specificity is difficult) does not qualify as gene therapy (proteases are enzymes), and would at best be a temporary help (choice C is wrong). The best way to counter the HBV would be to insert a nucleotide sequence that codes for the (−)RNA. This would allow the host to create (−)RNA complementary to the (+) mRNA of the virus. The (−)RNA would bind the (+) mRNA and prevent viral replication. This could keep the viral levels low and make the person less infectious since double-stranded mRNA cannot be translated by ribosomes (choice D is correct). HBV is not a retrovirus and therefore does not integrate its genome into the host genome (choice B is wrong). Insertion of additional antibody genes would be marginally helpful at best, and would do nothing to decrease or stop viral replication (choice D is better than choice A).

5. **C** HDV is a (−)RNA virus. It must somehow make an RNA genome using an RNA template (choice C is correct). There is no enzyme in the human host cell that normally reads RNA to make RNA (choice B is wrong). Since HDV is a (−)RNA virus, a (+) mRNA version must be created before translation can occur, and the creation of (+) mRNA requires the RNA dependent RNA polymerase, so the virus must carry this enzyme with it (choice A is wrong). The passage does not mention anywhere that HDV evolved directly from HBV and there is no reason to assume this (choice D is not supported and is wrong).

6. **C** A single-base pair insertion would cause a reading frame shift. This would be devastating for the *S* gene in HBV because it has three start codons, all in-frame. Not only would the start codons be affected, but even if another start codon existed in the new reading frame, the amino acid sequence of the protein would be completely altered. Since the *S* gene encodes the surface antigen required for entry into liver cells, a virus with this mutation would likely be incapable of infection (choice C is correct). A missense mutation causes the substitution of one amino acid for another. Since pre-*S2* is a start codon, this could be bad, but the passage states that the *S* gene has three in-frame start codons, so it is likely that one of the other two start codons could be used, translation would start, and protein structure would be unaffected (choice A is wrong). A nonsense mutation replaces an amino acid codon with a stop codon. This leads to a truncated protein, but if it is late in the *S* gene, it may still have some activity (choice C is better than choice B). A three-nucleotide deletion in the *S* gene would result in the loss of one amino acid (which in some cases could affect the three-dimensional structure of the resulting protein) but this is not as devastating an effect as is a reading frame shift (choice C is better than choice D).

SOLUTIONS TO PRACTICE PASSAGE 3

1. **A** The passage states that Wee1 inhibits the activity of Cdc2. This would keep the cell in G_2 and prevent mitosis. Decreased expression of Wee1 would cause the cells to pass through G_2 and enter mitosis early; they would therefore be smaller than wild type cells (choice A is correct). Sal3 and Cdc25 promote Cdc2 activation and therefore help push the cell through G_2 and into M-phase. Decreased Sal3 levels would cause the cell to stay in G_2 phase longer, resulting in larger or elongated cells (choice C is incorrect), and a nonsense mutation in Cdc25 would cause the same phenotype (choice D is incorrect). A silent mutation by its very definition has no effect (choice B is incorrect).

2. **C** Before the cell divides, it must check the integrity of the genome it is passing to the daughter cells. This includes making sure DNA replication is complete (Item I is true, choice A can be eliminated) and mutations have been repaired (Item III is true, choice B can be eliminated). Item II is false: Checking the levels of nucleotides in the cell is part of the G_1/S checkpoint (the other major checkpoint pathway mentioned in the passage), since these building blocks are required for DNA replication (choice D can be eliminated and choice C is correct).

3. **B** Yeast are fungi, are eukaryotic, and have a cell wall (choice D is wrong). The fungal cell wall is made of chitin (choice B is correct). The bacterial cell wall is made of peptidoglycan (choice A is wrong), and the plant cell wall is made of cellulose (choice C is wrong). Note that prokaryotes have a 70S ribosome and eukaryotes have an 80S ribosome, since yeast are eukaryotic, their ribosome is 80S.

4. **A** The passage states that Cdc25 is a phosphatase and has the opposite effect as the kinases Wee1 and Mik1. Since kinases add a phosphate group to molecules (such as proteins, lipids, carbohydrates or nucleic acids) using ATP as the source of the phosphate, a phosphatase must therefore remove phosphate groups (choice A is correct and choice B is wrong). There

is no information in the passage to support the fact that phosphatases work EXCLUSIVELY on proteins (choice C is too specific and can be eliminated). Choice D is a false statement and mixes up concepts in reaction kinetics: enzymes function to *decrease* activation energy, this increases the reaction rate (choice D is wrong).

5. **D** The passage states that the activity of Cdc2, a CDK, is regulated by cyclin binding (cyclins are proteins, choices A and B can be eliminated) and phosphorylation, a type of post-translational modification (choice C can be eliminated). There is no information in the passage on allosteric regulation of Cdc2 or proteolytic cleavage.

6. **D** This is a two-by-two question because you need to decide if the cell will be smaller or larger, and if they spend more or less time in G_2. Luckily, two of the answer options are relatively easy to eliminate: options B and C are impossible; a cell cannot spend more time in a growth phase and be smaller than wild type cells, and vice versa (choices B and C are wrong). If a fission yeast cell over-expresses Sal3, it will be pushed through G_2 and will enter M-phase early. Less time in G_2 means the cells will be smaller (choice D is correct and choice A is wrong).

7. **C** This is a tricky question that requires POE. Fungi have a cell wall made of chitin, so promoting chitin synthesis would not harm the fungus. In fact, many antifungal drugs target and decrease chitin biosynthesis (choice A can be eliminated). Inhibiting the electron transport chain or inhibiting eukaryotic translation (by preventing ribosome association) would also harm the patient (choices B and D can be eliminated). This leaves choice C as the best answer; ergosterol is a steroid that fungi use in their plasma membrane, similar to how animals use cholesterol. Since animals do not use ergosterol, the patient would be fine and the fungi would be harmed. This is the basis for many anti-fungal remedies. Note that you did not need to be familiar with ergosterol, but only needed to be able to eliminate the other three answer choices.

SOLUTIONS TO PRACTICE PASSAGE 4

1. **C** The passage discusses many proteins and genes that control pigmentation in humans (MC1R, MSH, ASIP, TYR and OCA2) and mentions that OCA2 alone has 58 alleles that have so far been documented. This information best matches choice C, since several genes are involved in pigmentation phenotypes. All other answer choices indicate that only a single gene is involved (choices A, B, and D are wrong). Note that while simplistic genetics examples many times use eye color to demonstrate monogenism, based on information in the passage, this is an oversimplification (choice A is wrong). Be careful not to bring "outside knowledge" in to answer a question; rely more heavily on what the passage tells you.

2. **B** Based on information in the passage, alleles of OCA2 are one of the major determinants of eye color. The woman in the question stem will have brown eyes because she is heterozygous for OCA2 and has an allele that is associated with blue eyes (305R) and an allele associated with brown eyes (305W). Because the question stem says that the OCA2 gene and the HERC2 gene overlap, they must be linked (they are 0 map units apart). This means that

crossing over will not occur between these two genes and they will be inherited as a unit. The father in this question is acting like a testcross; that is, he is homozygous recessive for both genes. Therefore, the offspring produced will either get the OCA2^{305R}:HERC2^{wt} chromosome or the OCA2^{305W}:HERC2^{A1} chromosome from the mother and a OCA2^{305R}:HERC2^{A1} chromosome from the father. The children will be 50% OCA2$^{305R/305R}$:HERC2$^{wt/A1}$ (blue eyed with no increased risk of Crohn's disease; note that the A1 allele of HERC2 is recessive to the wild type allele) and 50% OCA2$^{305W/305R}$:HERC2$^{A1/A1}$ (brown eyes with an increased risk of Crohn's disease). This matches answer choice B. Note than choice A is what would occur if the two genes were not linked.

3. D   Homologous proteins or genes are those that have evolved from a common ancestor. This matches the information in Figure 1, since the OCA2 protein in all organisms on the figure originated with the ancestor protein represented by the point at the bottom (choice A is supported and can be eliminated). The eight organisms on the figure are all eukaryotes and from diverse families (fungi, mammals, fish, choice B is supported and can be eliminated). Remember that yeast are fungi and therefore eukaryotic. OCA2 in Zebrafish and Japanese killifish share a common ancestor which is not far away in evolutionary terms (i.e., is not very far down the diagram). In contrast, the common ancestor protein between human and horse OCA2 protein is the point at the bottom of the diagram; this is farther away in evolutionary terms (choice C is supported and can be eliminated). While choice D may be true based on logic and background information on evolution, it is not supported by Figure 1; this phylogenetic tree contains information on how the OCA2 proteins are evolutionarily related, NOT how organisms are related (choice D is the least supported and the correct answer choice).

4. C   While the passage states that brown eyes are typically dominant over blue eyes, it also emphasizes that human eye color (and pigmentation in general) is genetically very complex and due to the interactions of dozens of different genes. This would support the statement that "any number of eye colors" is possible (choices A and B can be eliminated). Note that this is similar to Question 1, where the simplistic classical view of eye color inheritance and genetics is not actually correct. Genetic complexity (multiple gene products interacting with multiple other gene products) is a better explanation than Mendel's law of independent assortment and recombination, which are mechanisms used to generate random combinations of alleles in gametes (choice C is better than choice D). Note that while it is rare, blue-eyed parents CAN have brown-eyed children.

5. C   The passage states that during FISH, fluorescently labeled probes are hybridized to chromosome clusters. This is similar to how probes are used in Southern and northern blots. The probe must be single stranded DNA or RNA if it is going to hybridize or bind to the chromosomes (which are denatured first, also similar to in Southern or northern blotting), and should be covalently linked to the fluorescent molecule. An antibody is not typically used to bind DNA, and in any case, there is no easy way to generate a "fluorescent segment of DNA." It is much easier to use fluorescent molecules or dyes (choices A and D are wrong). A double-stranded probe will not bind the chromosomes because it will be complementary to itself (choice B is wrong). Don't let the word "fluorochrome" confuse you; "chrome" has to do with color or pigments and a "fluorochrome" is a fluorescent molecule or dye. Even without this information, process of elimination can be used to find the best answer.

6. **A** This is a free-standing question. Melanocytes are located in the epidermis but not the dermis (which is composed of connective tissue, choices B and D are wrong) or the hypodermis (which is primarily made of adipose tissue, choice C is wrong). In the epidermis they control skin color. Melanocytes in hair follicles control hair color. Both the choroid and the iris in the eye contain melanocytes, but other structures in the eye, such as a the retina and the vitreous humor, do not.

7. **D** This is a difficult question to work through. If the father's MC1R proteins preferentially bind MSH, his melanocytes will make lots of eumelanin, which the passage says is a dark pigment. Note that he will also have wild type levels of ASIP, but if it is binding to the MC1R receptor with less frequency or affinity (because his receptors preferentially bind MSH), it will have less effect. It is the ratio of ASIP vs. MSH binding that is going to determine the phenotype. The mother's form of ASIP binds MC1R with a high affinity, meaning her melanocytes will make lots of pheomelanin, which the passage says is a light pigment. Therefore, the father's skin will be darker than the mother's skin (choice C is not possible). The genotype of all their children will be MC1R$^{PM/wt}$: ASIP$^{wt/HA}$ since both parents are homozygous (choices A and B can be eliminated). This leaves choice D as the best answer. The child will express some MC1R that preferentially binds MSH and some wild type MC1R receptor. The child will also express some wild type ASIP and some ASIP that has a high affinity for its receptor. Overall, this will result in the melanocytes of the child producing a more even ratio of eumelanin and pheomelanin; this means the skin color of the child will most likely be intermediate between the dark color of its father and the lighter color of its mother (choice D is correct).

SOLUTIONS TO PRACTICE PASSAGE 5

1. **D** Aβ peptide is released into the extracellular space (Figure 1 and Experiment 1) so it should be found in the condition media of the culture dishes. ELISA is the preferred method for secreted proteins found in the media, blood or extracellular space, therefore the harvested media can be used with an ELISA coated with anti-Aβ to measure the levels of Aβ. Because the protein is secreted, any answer that suggests the measurement of cellular Aβ should be eliminated (choices B and C are wrong). Further, it is impossible to visualize and measure any protein or peptide with a microscope (choice A is wrong).

2. **C** Any brain area related to memory, learning, and/or behavior should be eliminated. The frontal lobe is critical in reasoning, planning, attention, and movement, and is consistent with the AD symptoms described (choice A would show plaques and damage and can be eliminated). Note also that the frontal lobe is part of the cortex; because there cannot be two right answers, choice D can also be eliminated. The hippocampus is critical in long-term storage of associative and episodic memories and the retrieval of face-name associations; this consistent with the AD symptoms described (choice B would show plaques and damage and can be eliminated). The hypothalamus is the only choice that is not associated with memory, learning or behavior control; rather, it controls basic functions and homeostasis of the body (temperature regulation, osmotic regulation, hormone release, etc., choice C would not show plaques and damage and is the correct answer choice).

3. **D** Item I is true: According to Figure 4, chloroquine (lysosomal inhibition) restores the total APP levels in L-Numb cells, suggesting that L-Numb isoform facilitates lysosomal degradation of APP (choice B can be eliminated). Item II is true: Monensin (recycling pathway inhibitor) reduces cell surface APP levels in S-Numb cells, suggesting that S-Numb isoform facilitates APP trafficking along the recycling pathway, from the endosome to cell surface and back (choice A can be eliminated). Item III is true: The passage states (Experiment 1) that untransfected neural cells express both Numb isoforms at moderate levels, so it is likely that the balance between the opposing functions of Numb isoforms maintain APP levels (choice C can be eliminated).

4. **D** The question refers specifically to Aβ levels in untransfected (control) neural cells, so any mechanism or condition that would normally reduce Aβ levels in cells can be eliminated. Since γ-secretase is necessary to generate Aβ, inhibiting γ-secretase should reduce Aβ levels in any cell (choice A can be eliminated). The passage states in paragraph two that cleavage of APP by α-secretase prevents the generation of Aβ (choice B would reduce Aβ levels and can be eliminated). Induction of L-Numb mRNA will increase L-Numb protein; from Figure 3 it can be seen that this would reduces Aβ levels (choice C can be eliminated). However, Figure 4 shows that control neural cells treated with a lysosomal inhibitor do not show changes in APP levels; it can be assumed that there would be no reduction in Aβ levels either (choice D would not reduce Aβ and is the correct answer choice).

5. **D** Since the investigators were specifically looking at the role that Numb isoforms might play in APP trafficking, the correct answer should include data that address the role of the Numb isoforms, rather than general statements on Numb. The only answer choice that does this is choice D. L-Numb reduces Aβ which has been shown to cause neuritic plaque formation (first paragraph). Therefore, reduced neuritic plaque formation in mice that selectively express L-Numb would specifically support the investigators' data (choice D is correct). Reduced levels of Numb mRNA is a general observation that does not provide any information on the specific functions of the Numb isoforms in the brain (choice A is wrong). Numb is found in the endosomes of all cells, regardless of their disease state (see the third paragraph, choice B is wrong). General defects in the splicing machinery could potentially affect hundreds of protein isoforms (not just Numb); further, the activity of γ-secretase is unrelated to Numb function (choice C is wrong).

6. **C** Since the Aβ peptides negatively regulate ACh synthesis, release, and signaling, any kind of pharmacological intervention should be targeted at increasing ACh or its activity. An inhibitor of acetylcholinesterase (AChE) would prolong the life of ACh in the synaptic cleft, thus increasing its effect on the postsynaptic cell. Drugs that inhibit postsynaptic ACh receptors would be a poor choice because they would inhibit ACh signaling (choice A is wrong). Blocking voltage-gated Na⁺ channels would have severe consequences throughout the body, as virtually all nervous system and muscular activity would be inhibited (choice B is wrong). Inhibition of choline reuptake by cholinergic neurons would reduce or prevent ACh synthesis (choice D is wrong).

SOLUTIONS TO PRACTICE PASSAGE 6

1. **B** This is a two-by-two question since you need to make two decisions to find the best answer. The parasympathetic (not sympathetic) autonomic nervous system promotes the "rest and digest" functions of the body by increasing digestive hormone secretion and acid production (choice C and D can be eliminated). According to the figure, both acetylcholine and gastrin promote the release of IP_3 and increased intracellular calcium levels (choice B is correct and choice A is wrong).

2. **D** While bilateral vagotomy decreases vagal (parasympathetic) input to parietal cells and decreases acid secretion, there are at least two other mechanisms by which the H^+/K^+-ATPase may be stimulated (see Figure 1). Gastrin and histamine both bind to receptors on parietal cells and activate second messenger cascades that lead to acid secretion (choice D is correct and choice B is wrong). Omeprazole is a proton pump inhibitor and acts to decrease acid secretion, not increase it (choice A is wrong). The passage states that proton pump inhibitors bind to luminal portions of the H^+/K^+-ATPase; thus they do not access the interior of parietal cells and cannot directly interact with second messenger proteins (choice C is wrong).

3. **D** ZES is associated with increased gastrin, which binds to parietal cells and increases HCl secretion (choice A can be eliminated). Histamine also binds to parietal cells and promotes acid secretion. Both mast cells and basophils release histamine and would therefore promote increased acid levels (choices B and C can be eliminated). Plasma cells make antibodies, and there is no information in the passage suggesting that antibodies stimulate acid secretion (choice D is least likely to lead to increased HCl and is the correct answer choice).

4. **A** This is another two-by-two question. The passage states that prostaglandin E helps protect the intestinal lining from acid. Thus misoprostol, a prostaglandin E analog, would be expected to do the same thing. Protecting the intestinal lining from acid would promote ulcer healing (choice C and D are wrong). From the figure, the cAMP and calcium release mechanisms are involved in promoting acid secretion; to have a protective effect, misoprostol would have to inhibit these signal cascades (choice A is correct and choice B is wrong).

5. **C** Item I is false: The passage states that patients with MEN-1 may develop gastrin-secreting tumors. This would increase parietal acid secretion (choices A and B can be eliminated). Note that Items II and III are opposites, so only one of them can be true. Item II is true: MEN-1 patients also develop hypersecreting parathyroid tumors. Increased parathyroid hormone would increase calcium levels (Item III is false, choice D can be eliminated, and choice C is correct).

6. **B** The passage states that increased acid causes bile salt precipitation and degradation of pancreatic enzymes. Bile salt precipitation would hinder fat emulsification and digestion, not protein digestion (choice A is wrong). The pancreatic enzymes include lipases and amylases, which aid in the digestion of fats and carbohydrates, respectively. If the fats and carbohydrates are not digested, they will pass into the large intestine where their presence would act osmotically to prevent the reabsorption of water. When water is not reabsorbed from the large intestine, diarrhea is the result (choice B is correct). There is no reason to assume that gastrin-secreting cells would replace insulin-releasing cells, and in any case, this would not contribute to diarrhea (choice C is wrong). Not all ZES patients undergo vagotomy, and even if they did, increase water reabsorption would reduce the likelihood of diarrhea (choice D is wrong).

7. **A** The passage states that parietal cells rely on oxidative phosphorylation for ATP production. Therefore, these cells contain large numbers of mitochondria (choice A is false and the correct answer choice). Parietal cells also secrete gastric intrinsic factor, which binds Vitamin B12; this increases the absorption of Vitamin B12 in the ileum (choice B is true and can be eliminated). Vagal input constitutes "neural input," histamine release from neighboring mast cells constitutes "paracrine input," and gastrin released into the blood stream from the stomach, pancreas, and small bowel constitutes "endocrine input" (choice C is true and can be eliminated). Acid release from the parietal cells allows the activation of pepsinogen, which aids in protein digestion in the stomach (choice D is true and can be eliminated).

SOLUTIONS TO PRACTICE PASSAGE 7

1. **D** This biopsy is of cardiac muscle (mononucleated, striated cells) and would not undergo heterotropic ossification (HO); therefore, we cannot conclude whether this patient is suffering from FOP (choice D is correct, and choices A and B are wrong). Skeletal muscle can undergo HO and would be a logical tissue in which to detect ossification (choice C is wrong).

2. **A** Affected individuals present in successive generations is a characteristic of a dominant allele inheritance pattern (choices C and D are wrong). Dominant disorders require that only a single allele have the mutation, and osteogenesis (bone formation) is a characteristic of this disease (choice A is correct). "Varied expressivity" means that there is a large variation in phenotypes of affected individuals. There is no information given regarding the specific phenotypes of the affected individuals, and in any case, this would not explain the observed inheritance pattern (choice B is wrong).

3. **C** The passage states that the gene responsible for FOP has a missense mutation in it activation domain. A DNA transition (exchange of a purine for a purine or a pyrimidine for a pyrimidine) could result in a missense mutation and subsequent disease (choice C is correct). Extensive DNA intercalation would likely lead massive mutations and cell death (choice A is not correct), and acetylation changes gene expression but does not result in a missense mutation (choice B is not correct). A silent mutation results from a mutation in the DNA where the amino acid sequence remains the same and would not result in disease (choice D is not correct).

4. **C** Osteoclasts are directly involved in bone remodeling by reabsorbing bone (choice A is involved and can be eliminated). Osteoblasts are responsible for replacing bone with bone matrix constituents, including collagen (choice B is involved and can be eliminated). Sex hormones (particularly estrogen) depress the activity of osteoclasts, and when present at normal physiological levels help to maintain bone mass. When levels fall (e.g., menopause), osteoclast activity increases, and bone density falls due to the disruption to normal remodeling (choice D is involved and can be eliminated). Fibrinogen, however, is a blood protein involved in clotting. It is not involved in bone remodeling (choice C is not involved and is the correct answer choice).

5. D According to the passage, FOP spares the diaphragm, tongue, and extraocular muscles, meaning we would expect normal physical exam findings in these areas (choices A, B, and C are not potential areas of ossification and are less likely to result in abnormal findings). Nuchal rigidity (neck stiffness) could occur due to ossification of the skeletal muscle in the neck (choice D is correct).

6. C According to the passage, current treatment for FOP focuses on supportive therapy and management of inflammation. Glucocorticoids reduce inflammation and could help decrease the degree of heterotropic ossification in the patient (choice C is a viable treatment). Both surgical removal of bone and sonification would likely result in trauma which may worsen the condition (choices A and B are not viable treatments). Oral calcitonin, a polypeptide, would be digested in the stomach and would not have significant therapeutic benefit; more importantly, calcitonin helps stimulate osteoblasts and bone formation which is clearly not the best option is FOP (choice D is wrong).

7. A If the STI acted as an antagonist (inhibitor) at the motor endplate, fewer ligand-gated ion channels would open and the cell may fail to depolarize sufficiently to result in the opening of voltage-gated calcium channels. This would result in decreased cytosolic calcium (choice A is least likely to explain an increase in intracellular calcium and increased muscular tone). Acetylcholinesterase (AChE) is responsible for the destruction of acetylcholine at the neuromuscular junction. Inhibiting AChE would result in increased levels of ACh, increased muscular stimulation, and increased intracellular calcium levels (choice B is a possible cause and can be eliminated)). Since calcium is stored in the sarcoplasmic reticulum (SR), disruption of the SR membrane integrity could result in an increase in intracellular calcium (choice C is a possible cause and can be eliminated). The Ca^{2+}-ATPase is responsible for removing calcium from the cytosol and returning it to the sarcoplasmic reticulum. Its inhibition would result in increased intracellular calcium (choice D is a possible cause and can be eliminated).

SOLUTIONS TO PRACTICE PASSAGE 8

1. D As this is a Roman numeral question, be sure to use POE as each statement is evaluated. Item I is true: As fluid fills the pleural space, the pressure would become more positive (choice C can be eliminated). Item II is true: The increased pressure on the lungs makes expansion, and thus breathing, difficult. The patient will need to breathe more frequently in order to move the same amount of air (choice A can be eliminated). Item III is true: An increased heart rate will; accompany the increase in respiratory rate in order to increase the amount of blood moving through the lungs. This would hopefully improve oxygenation (choice B can be eliminated and choice D is correct).

2. B If asbestos is already in the lungs, fibers could be coughed up and then swallowed (choice A is possible and can be eliminated). The lymphatic system could provide a direct connection between the lungs and the peritoneum by which the fibers could travel (choice C is possible and can be eliminated). The process of removing asbestos causes fibers to become highly airborne; without the use of appropriate protective equipment, asbestos could be swallowed

or inhaled (choice D is possible and can be eliminated). Handling brake pads containing asbestos is the least risky of the options; the fibers are not likely to be airborne, thus minimizing both respiratory and peritoneal exposure (choice B is the best answer).

3. **D**   An increased thickness in the pleural membranes would be expected due to the malignant cell growth that characterizes mesothelioma as a cancer (choice D is the best answer). There is no reason to assume a lack of hydroxyapatite deposition (choice B is wrong). Choices A and C describes things that cannot be measured via chest X-ray; serum protein levels are measured by blood-tests (choice A is wrong) and residual volume is measured by spirometry as part of a test for lung function (choice C is wrong).

4. **D**   The key words in the question text are "reduction in total lung capacity" and "loss of elasticity." Although exercise and a low oxygen environment can result in shortness of breath, there is no reduction in total lung capacity and the lungs remain compliant (elastic; choices A and B can be eliminated). Asthma is more properly described as an obstructive disease, in which air flow is reduced due to narrowed bronchial tubes. Again, there is no loss of elasticity or reduction in total lung capacity (choice C can be eliminated). However, diaphragm paralysis would result in a significant reduction of the ability of the lungs to expand. Although intercostal muscles can attempt to compensate for the loss of diaphragmatic function, they cannot produce the size-changes in the chest cavity that the diaphragm can. Thus, lung expansion would be reduced and total lung capacity would fall. Medically this is classified as a "neuromuscular restrictive lung disorder (choice D is correct).

5. **A**   Since cancer cells could be transferred during the organ transplant, and immunosuppression necessarily accompanies the receipt of a donated organ, the answer to the question is "yes" (choices C and D can be eliminated). The remaining answer options differ in tone; choice B is more absolute than choice A. It cannot be assumed that cancer cells are definitely present in the liver, but it is possible due to the likely metastasis as well as the close proximity of the liver to the pleural membranes (choice A is better than choice B).

6. **B**   This is a two-by-two question, one in which two decisions and POE will lead to the correct answer. In patients with mesothelioma, and particularly those experiencing a pleural effusion, breathing becomes more labored and difficult. This is true for both inspiration and expiration. The need to work harder to inhale will create greater work for the intercostal muscles (choices C and D can be eliminated), while the need to work harder to exhale will necessitate the use of the abdominal muscles (choice A can be eliminated and choice B is correct).

7. **B**   Since asbestosis has an increased risk of progression to cancer, regular diagnostic chest X-rays would be warranted to detect early changes that might suggest carcinoma (choice A would be helpful and can be eliminated). The passages states that asbestosis patients who smoke have an even greater risk of progression to cancer than those who do not, thus smoking cessation would be helpful (note that this would be helpful for anyone, not just asbestosis patients; choice C can be eliminated). The symptoms of asbestosis include shortness of breath, which can reduce oxygen delivery to the blood, so oxygen therapy could help increase oxygen saturation (choice D would be helpful and can be eliminated). However, chemotherapy is not indicated in asbestosis, only in mesothelioma, and not all cases of asbestosis progress to cancer (choice B would be the least helpful and is the correct answer).

SOLUTIONS TO PRACTICE PASSAGE 9

1. **B**   This is a two-by-two question, where two decisions need to be made to find the correct answer. Since Goosecoid is a transcription factor, it must be localized in the nucleus. Nuclear proteins contain a nuclear localization sign, not a signal sequence, which targets proteins to the secretory pathway (choices C and D can be eliminated). Since it is a transcription factor, Goosecoid binds DNA and must therefore have DNA binding motifs (choice B is correct and choice A is wrong).

2. **B**   Since the experiments are studying gastrulation, the injections must be done on a pre-gastrulation embryo, not a post-gastrulation embryo, where the process under study is already over (choices A and C can be eliminated). The passage says that the Gsc *transcript* is injected, which means the molecule must be RNA (choice D can be eliminated and choice B is correct).

3. **D**   The passages states that cytokeratins and E-cadherin are markers of epithelial cells, while vimentin is a marker of mesenchymal cells. Since these cells are expressing both, they must be undergoing an EMT (that is, they are in the process of changing from epithelial cells to mesenchymal cells; choice D is correct and choices A and C are wrong). No information is given in the passage on mesodermal cells (choice B is wrong).

4. **C**   This is a tricky question and POE of the answer choices is the best strategy. Gastrulation in general requires a lot of cell proliferation since the embryo is growing and becoming more complex. However, there is no information in the passage to indicate that Gsc affects cell proliferation, nor that proliferation requires EMT (choice A is not supported). While choice B is a true statement, it is the opposite from what was observed in the second experiment, where involuting marginal zone cells changed to crawling migratory cells and (choice B is not supported). The formation of a second blastopore lip would require cell migration and EMT, since these are two requirements for gastrulation and mesoderm formation. The switch from relatively stationary but involuting cells (marginal zone cells) to the crawling deep zone cells would also require cell migration and EMT. Note that the passage hints that epithelial cells are relatively stationary and connected to each other, whereas mesenchymal cells are more mobile due to their minimal cell adhesions (choice C is correct). Choice D is only partially correct: the first part of the sentence is fine, but the blastopore lip is where mesoderm formation starts, not formation of the inner germ layer (i.e., endoderm, choice D is wrong).

5. **A**   The passage says that EMT is a change in cell identity, morphology, and migration. Cancer cells leaving the bulk tumor and migrating often involve an EMT, as these cells must change from relatively stationary epithelial cells to more migratory mesenchymal cells (choice A is correct). Although the nephron contains epithelial cells and interstitium (a derivative of mesenchymal cells), it does not switch between the two (choice B is wrong). While choices C and D both describe migration (of cells or of food), they do not describe a change in cell identity and morphology (choices C and D are wrong).

6. **D**   The passage states that EMT is especially essential for formation of the mesoderm. Both the lymphatic system and the urogenital organs are derived from the mesoderm layer and as such, would be affected the most in an organism with abnormal EMT (choice D is correct). The brain is derived from ectoderm (choice A is wrong), the respiratory and gastrointestinal systems are derived from endoderm (choice B is wrong), and the epidermis is derived from ectoderm (choice C is wrong).

7. **B**   The passage describes vimentin as an intermediate filament. Intermediate filaments have structural roles in the cell (choice B is correct). Cytokinesis (the pinching of a dividing parent cell into two daughter cells) involves a ring of actin (microfilaments, choice A is wrong). Intracellular transport and the formation of the mitotic spindle involve microtubules, not intermediate filaments (choices C and D are wrong).

Chapter 20
Organic Chemistry
on the MCAT

Organic chemistry is the least prevalent subject tested on the MCAT, and comprises about 20–25 percent of the Biological Sciences section. These questions are typically distributed between three to five free-standing questions and either one longer passage (with six or seven questions) or two very short passages (usually with four questions each). Though it represents comparatively few questions, you cannot ignore Organic Chemistry, focus solely on Biology, and expect to push into the 11–15 range for your Biological Sciences score. In addition, the O-Chem topics covered span two college semesters' worth of material. Luckily, the questions can all be categorized into a few big picture topics, which we will discuss in detail later. For now, let's talk about what you can expect from O-Chem passages.

TACKLING A PASSAGE

In general, some sort of biologically important compound or reaction provides the context for O-Chem passages. The text of the passage might contain biologically related concepts or facts, but a sure sign that you're reading an O-Chem passage and not a Biology passage will be chemical structures, usually lots of them.

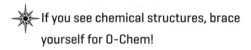
If you see chemical structures, brace yourself for O-Chem!

Your approach to reading and mapping an O-Chem passage should be a bit different than your approach for all other subjects. The reason? There is hardly ever information within the text of an O-Chem passage that will be useful or needed to answer passage-based questions. The most important information in these passages will be in the form of chemical structures from synthetic or mechanistic schemes, or experimental data from a table, graph, or figure. Often, complicated syntheses and mechanisms can be intimidating because of all the detail presented, and they can slow you down considerably if you pay too much attention to this information during your first run through the passage. Be sure to read the titles of figures or schemes to get a sense of the big picture being presented, then jump into answering the questions quickly.

O-CHEM PASSAGE TYPES

The main science passage types mentioned previously, when considered in the context of O-Chem, look something like this:

Information and/or Situation Presentation

These are the most common types of O-Chem passages, and generally present:

- A multistep synthetic scheme, a novel reaction, or atypical outcomes of reactions you might already be familiar with. Questions associated with these passages might ask you to analyze or classify the steps of the process described, or use common laboratory techniques to analyze intermediate compounds in the synthesis. You might need to justify the exceptions to the rules as described.

- A class of biologically important molecules. Questions associated with these passages could ask you to analyze the molecules with a common laboratory technique, or simply ask about their structure or their relationship to each other. You might also need to predict the reactivity of the molecules if treated with a given reagent.

- A biochemical process or mechanism. Questions here often test your understanding of the stability of intermediates and ask you to explain why the reaction occurs in the manner described. Given a new reactant, you might need to use the mechanistic steps to predict the product of a reaction.

Experiment/Research Presentation

This type of passage presents the details of an experiment or a mechanistic study, and often includes spectroscopy data (IR or NMR) in the form of lists or tables. Questions ask you to interpret data and identify the likely pathway of reaction. You might also need to identify compounds, or simply choose the appropriate technique to achieve the desired purification or product identification.

Persuasive Reasoning

This is the least common type of O-Chem passage, but can appear as a comparison of two mechanisms that attempt to explain the outcome of a reaction. Questions ask you to evaluate the arguments presented and will likely relate to the stability of intermediates.

READING AN O-CHEM PASSAGE

You should never really *read* much of the text of an O-Chem passage, but rather, just skim through the text. Remember that most of the important information you'll use from an O-Chem passage will be in the form of the structures and data presented. O-Chem passage-based questions are often essentially free-standing questions. They require only reference to a structure given in the passage in order to answer. However, as you're skimming the passage, you won't know which structures, reaction steps, or data will be the useful bits, AND you won't be able to mark or highlight structures in any way using your on-screen tools. That means that when skimming, you should get a general sense of the importance of each figure or table by reading titles and headings, but not get bogged down in

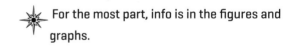

For the most part, info is in the figures and graphs.

the details of the figures in any way. You want to know where to go to examine the details when a question refers you to a particular synthetic step or structure along the pathway, something the MCAT is amazingly kind enough to do in most cases.

While you're reading, be on the lookout for new *italicized* terms in the text to highlight, or unexpected outcomes of experiments and exceptions to rules. The MCAT will ask you to apply the science fundamentals you've studied to novel situations, so look for and highlight anything that might be out of the ordinary.

MAPPING AN O-CHEM PASSAGE

It will often be the case that the text of a passage will reproduce information presented in a more visually useful manner, such as a flowchart, reaction scheme, or mechanism. Try to focus on the structures, and resist the urge to make a lot of yellow marks in the text.

Since you cannot highlight any structures in the passage (this is unfortunate, since structures are the place you'll get most of your necessary information), remember to use your scratch paper to make note of anything related to a reaction scheme or mechanism, especially if it's taken you some time to come to your conclusion. Keep your scratch paper organized so it will be a useful tool if you need to refer to it while checking back over your answers toward the end of the section. Label each new passage with a number on your paper, and give it an identifying title that summarizes the main point of the passage.

If you reach an important conclusion while answering questions, be sure to make note of it on your scratch paper too. For example, if a passage asks you to analyze a mechanistic study, and you determine that the first reaction described proceeds through the S_N2 mechanism, jot down "Rxn 1 = S_N2" under the passage number and title. Other questions may require this information in order to proceed, and a brief note beats wasted time reconfirming your conclusion while trying to answer a subsequent question. Your O-Chem passage map will begin to develop as you answer your questions, but before jumping into answering them, you will likely have very little to jot down.

The passage below is an example of an Information Presentation passage (of the second type described above). Note the minimal highlighting. The shaded were seemingly important upon a first pass to identify what the passage was about and to predict the types of questions with which it might be associated. You'll find upon review of the questions, however, that nothing but structures was necessary to answer any of the passage-based questions.

The small milkweed bug, *Lygaeus kalmii*, produces and emits a number of C_5-C_8 alkenals. Some of these small, fragrant, organic molecules are used to attract conspecific males or females for mating; thus, they act as sex pheromones. Others of the molecules are strongly malodorous and are used for defense.

Collaborating scientists in Brazil, the Netherlands, and Maryland have recently developed a method of noninvasive sampling and identification of these small organic molecules from live insects. This method involves the use of gas chromatography and mass spectrometry for the separation and identification of the components of the mixture of molecules involved in the sex- and defense-pheromone response in *L. kalmii*. Several of the molecules identified in this manner are shown in Figure 1.

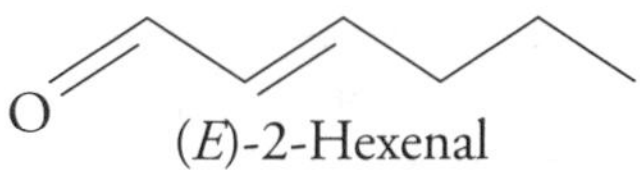

(E)-2-Hexenal

(E,E)-2,4-Octadienal

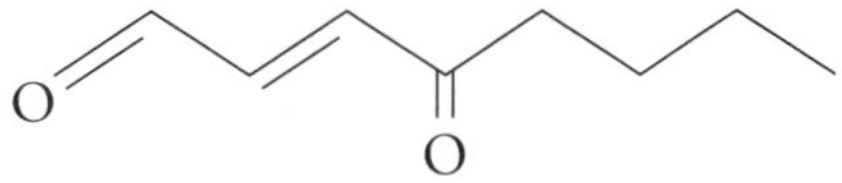

4-Oxo-(E)-2-Octenal

Figure 1 Molecules Identified Using Gas Chromatography and Mass Spectrometry

In addition to its mass spectrum, Molecule A, shown below, was also identified by its ^{1}H NMR spectrum:

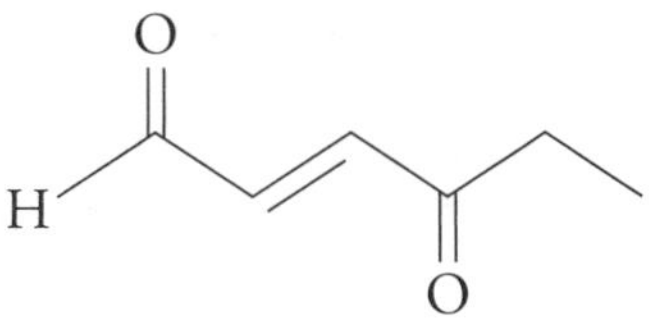

Molecule A

Remember not to get bogged down in spectroscopic data before a question specifically asks you to analyze it. Here is an example of a passage map for the passage above. This is what you might jot down on your scratch paper:

P1 – alkenals
P2 – separation and identification of alkenals
P3 – NMR data

The passage below is another example of an Information Presentation passage (of the third type described above). While the passage has much more text to wade through, only one small piece of it proves to be important in an Explicit question (addressed in detail later). Highlighted items are related to the main point of each paragraph, include new definitions, or provide examples of phenomena. The figures presented are more complex than those in the first passage, and the questions related to them are likely to be more involved as well.

Dyes are ionizable, aromatic compounds that absorb visible light due to the presence of a highly conjugated system of p orbitals. The observed color is one that is complementary to the wavelength of light absorbed by the molecule (complementary color pairs are red/green, orange/blue, and yellow/violet). Dyes bind to the materials to be colored, such as fabrics or paper, through inter- and intramolecular interactions, including hydrogen bonds, ionic interactions, covalent bonds, and coordinate covalent bonds. The stronger the interaction between dye molecule and fiber, the more permanent the color will be. When a dye covalently bonds to a fiber, it becomes a part of the fabric itself and cannot be washed away.

Two of the most common dye types are mordant dyes and direct dyes. A mordant is a polyvalent metal ion (usually Al^{3+} or Fe^{3+}) that forms a coordination complex with certain dyes. Mordants chelate to the fabric as well as the dye molecule, thereby improving their colorfastness. Mordant dyes are primarily used on protein-based fibers such as wool, silk, angora, and cashmere since the mordant can bind to the constituent amino acids of these fibers. Direct dyes are typically charged molecules, and interact with the material to be dyed through ionic forces or hydrogen bonding. As such they tend to bleed more than mordant dyes. Direct dyes are more commonly used on cellulose fibers such as cotton, linen, or hemp.

Azo dyes, a subclass of direct dyes, may be used in a dyeing technique in which an insoluble azo compound is produced directly onto or within a fiber. This is achieved by treating the fiber first with a diazonium component, followed by a coupling component. With suitable adjustment of dye bath conditions the two components react to produce the required insoluble azo dye. The coupling reagent used in the final step is typically a molecule containing either a phenolic hydroxyl group or an arylamine. The synthesis of methyl orange, an azo dye, is shown in Figure 1.

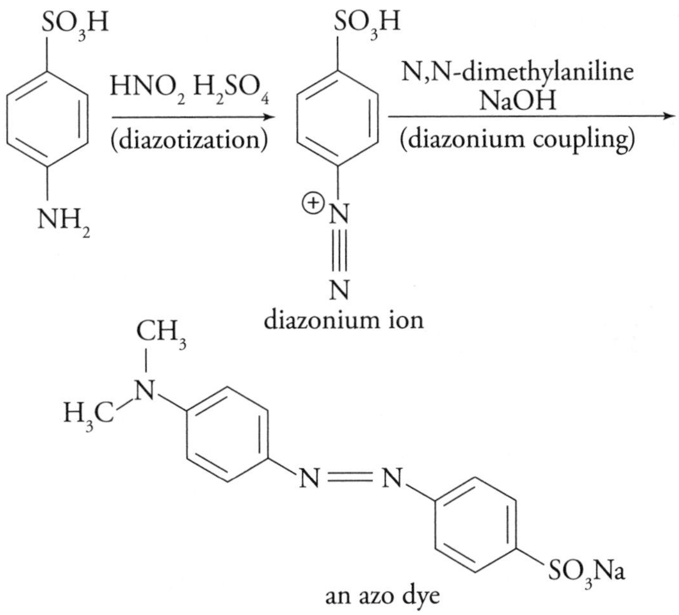

Figure 1 Synthesis of methyl orange

Figure 2 below represents the mechanism of the diazonium coupling reaction in the synthesis of methyl orange.

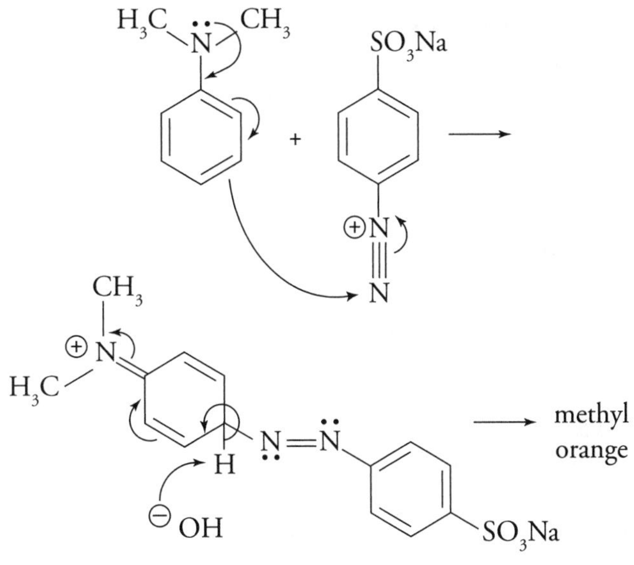

Figure 2 Mechanism of diazonium coupling

This is what you might jot down on your scratch paper for the passage above:

P1 – what dyes are and how they work
P2 – Definitions: mordant dye vs. direct dyes, fiber types dyed
P3 – Structure requirements for diazocoupling

TACKLING THE QUESTIONS

It's always best to answer all the freestanding questions in the Biological Sciences section before beginning to read the passages. By starting with some Memory questions, you can jump start your brain, earn some quick points, and ensure you've answered some of the easiest questions on the test before time runs out.

The Organic Chemistry passage-based questions are some of the most straightforward ones on the entire exam and, as a result, some of the quickest ones to answer. It may be a wise strategy to consider doing the O-Chem passages before the Biology ones to help bank up some extra time to spend on the wordier, more involved Biology passages.

However, you should also consider starting with the subject (Biology or O-Chem) you feel the most comfortable with, saving your more difficult subject for last. Whatever subject you choose, do all of the passages in one subject first before switching. In addition, do the passages within a subject in the order with which you feel most comfortable, leaving the topic you struggle with most, or the passage that appears to be the most difficult, for last. Within the passages themselves, tackle the easier questions first, leaving the most time consuming ones for last.

O-CHEM QUESTION TYPES

Memory Questions

These questions can be answered directly from prior knowledge and represent about 35 percent of the total number of questions. You can often recognize this question type by the length of the answer choices; one- or two-word answer choices are a good indication that you have the answer to these questions in your head already. Freestanding questions are commonly Memory questions since there is no passage to refer to. In addition, O-Chem passages often have "hidden" FSQs associated with them. This is another good reason to get to the questions quickly, rather than getting stuck reading details within the passage text.

Here's an example of not only a "hidden" FSQ but also a Memory question from the passage above on alkenals:

> If a chemist were to react (*E,E*)-2-4-octadienal with NaBH$_4$ in ethanol and monitor the reaction by TLC, the spot corresponding to the product would be expected to have an R_f value that is:
>
> A) less than that of the starting material.
> B) equal to that of the starting material.
> C) greater than that of the starting material.
> D) greater than 1.

While the passage shows the structure of the molecule described in the question, the suffix of the name is really all that is required to answer this question. By knowing that a reducing agent like NaBH$_4$ can be used to convert an aldehyde into an alcohol, and that alcohols are more polar than carbonyl compounds, giving them lower R_f values, you can deduce the correct answer (choice A) with no reference to the passage at all. Additionally, there is NO information in the passage, beyond the structure of the molecule, that could prove useful in answering this question.

Here is a true freestanding question that is also a Memory question:

> Which of the following acetylating conditions will convert diethylamine into an amide at the fastest rate?
>
> A) Acetic acid / HCl
> B) Acetic anhydride
> C) Acetyl chloride
> D) Ethyl acetate

Your first step to attacking this question should be to consider what type of reaction is described. The conversion of an amine to an amide is a nucleophilic addition-elimination, where the amine acts as the nucleophile. Therefore, you're looking for the answer choice with the best electrophile, thereby increasing the reaction rate. Knowing the relative reactivities of carboxylic acids derivatives (amide < ester < anhydride < acid halide) allows you to eliminate choices B and D. In order to choose between the remaining answers that include a carboxylic acid and an acid derivative, rely on your fundamentals. Ask yourself: How would an amine be expected to behave under each set of conditions? When you consider that amines are not only nucleophilic but also basic, you can deduce that they will be protonated by both the HCl and the acetic acid to yield a non-nucleophilic conjugate acid under the conditions of answer choice A. The nucleophilic addition reaction is therefore faster with the acid chloride derivative, making answer choice C correct.

Explicit Questions

These questions have answers that are explicitly stated in the passage. To answer them correctly, for example, may just require finding a definition, reading a graph, or making a simple connection. Explicit questions represent about 15 percent of the total number of questions, and are much more common in other sections of the test that rely more on reading comprehension. Since chemical structures are the most common source of referenced information in an O-Chem passage, Explicit questions in this section might ask you to identify the number of chiral centers in a given molecule, or to identify whether a particular functional group is present or not.

Here's an example of an Explicit question from the azo dye passage:

> Mordant dyes are used in biological assays in addition to the textile industry. Which of the following biologically important molecules is most likely to be labeled by a mordant dye?
>
> A) Glycogen
> B) Chromatin
> C) Cholesterol
> D) Starch

You should recognize the term "mordant" as a new term you highlighted while reading the passage, so go back to the text to retrieve the important information. The passage states that mordants generally bind to protein-based fibers. Without this information, you might be able to eliminate choices A and D (glycogen and starch) since they are both carbohydrates, and as such, are not likely to be the answer. With the passage information at your disposal, however, this becomes a bit of a Memory question, and you need only determine which of your answer choices contain proteins. Cholesterol, a lipid, can be eliminated in addition to the two carbohydrates, leaving choice B as the correct answer (note that chromatin contains both proteins and DNA).

Implicit Questions

These questions require you to apply knowledge to a new situation or make a more complex connection; the answer is typically implied by the information in the passage. Answer choices are generally longer, and may come in two parts, where the second half provides an explanation for the first. As mentioned before, the relevant information in the passage is often a molecular structure, but the analysis required to answer the question is more involved than for Explicit questions that rely on structures. Implicit style questions make up about 50 percent of the total number of O-Chem questions.

Here's an example of an Implicit question from the azo dye passage:

> The diazonium coupling reaction in Figure 2 is faster than most electrophilic substitutions of benzene. Which of the following statements best explains this fact?
>
> A)   The diazonium ion is an electron withdrawing substituent, making its benzene ring a better electrophile than benzene.
> B)   The diazonium ion is a good nucleophile.
> C)   The dimethylamino group is an electron donating substituent, making its benzene ring a better electrophile than benzene.
> D)   The dimethylamino group is an electron donating substituent, making its benzene ring a better nucleophile than benzene.

Since these answer choices are relatively long (and most have a second clause), try to use POE to eliminate choices based on obvious false statements in the first part of the answer. Remember, if any part of an answer choice is false, the entire statement can be eliminated. The first half of all the choices makes a statement about the inductive effects of substituents, or, in the case of answer choice B, the nucleophilicity of a compound. Refer to the structures in Figure 2. You should note that the diazonium ion is positively charged and therefore electron deficient. Since nucleophiles are by definition electron rich, choice B can be eliminated. The first halves of the remaining answer choices are all valid statements, since a positively charged substituent will pull electron density toward it, while an amine with a lone pair of electrons on the nitrogen will push electron density toward the ring. This question requires a more critical approach to distinguish between answer choices.

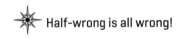 Half-wrong is all wrong!

You should identify this as an Implicit question since it asks you to compare a new reaction to one you might already be familiar with. Consider, then, what you already know about the electrophilic aromatic substitution (EAS) reactions of benzene. Since benzene has six pi electrons and is electron rich, it should behave as a nucleophile in EAS reactions. This fundamental piece of information about the reactivity of benzene allows you to eliminate choices A and C. It does not matter whether the indicated substituents in Figure 2 make benzene a better or worse electrophile, since in the context of this reaction benzene behaves as a nucleophile. The remaining answer (choice D) is not only internally consistent but also answers the question.

Content Categories

O-Chem questions can be further classified from a content perspective into five main categories. Instead of trying to memorize a lot of detailed information, try to generalize as much as possible, and focus on the fundamentals of structure and stability when approaching questions. Remember that the MCAT is more likely to ask you to apply fundamental concepts to novel situations rather than ask you to recall an exception to a rule and regurgitate trivia. Just about every O-Chem question can be put into one of the following five categories:

Structure

Questions are generally about functional groups, stereochemistry, isomers, electron density (nucleophiles vs. electrophiles), and nomenclature.

Stability

This generally refers to stability of products or reaction intermediates. These questions often ask about inductive effects, resonance, steric strain, torsional strain, ring strain, etc.

Reaction types

Questions might ask you to simply classify a given reaction (more of a memory question), or you may need to use knowledge about how a reaction proceeds in order to answer a more complex question about intermediates or products (generally Implicit questions).

Laboratory practices

These questions may ask you to identify an appropriate separation technique (extraction, chromatography, distillation, etc.) for a given mixture of compounds, or ask you to interpret/predict the results of a separation procedure. You might also be asked to choose an appropriate spectroscopic technique (IR, NMR, mass spec, UV-vis, etc.) to identify a compound, or interpret spectroscopic data.

Predict the product

Given a starting material and reaction conditions, choose the major product of the reaction. This will only be a one step synthesis; no multi-step processes will be presented.

MCAT ORGANIC CHEMISTRY TOPIC LIST[1]

Structure

- Nomenclature
- Bonding
    1. Structural formulas
    2. Sigma and pi bonds, effect on bond length, energies, and rigidity
    3. Hybrid orbitals
    4. VSEPR theory
    5. Hydrogen bonding
- A. Stereochemistry
    1. Isomers
    2. Polarization of light, specific rotation
    3. Absolute and relative configuration (R and S, E and Z)
    4. Racemic mixtures, separation of enantiomers

Stability

- A. Delocalized electrons and resonance
- B. Induction
- C. Ring strain in cyclic compounds
- D. Steric strain
- E. Acidity of classes of oxygen-containing compounds
- F. Effect of chain branching

Reaction Types

- A. Combustions of hydrocarbons
- B. Free radical halogenations of hydrocarbons
    1. stability of free radicals
    2. chain reaction mechanism
    3. inhibition

- C. Nucleophilic Substitutions (S_N1 and S_N2) of alcohols and alkyl halides
    1. nucleophiles
    2. electrophiles
    3. leaving groups
    4. mechanisms
    5. stereochemistry
    6. reaction rates/rate laws

- D. Elimination reactions (E1 and E2) of alcohols and alkyl halides
    1. bases
        a. weak vs. strong
        b. small vs. bulky
    2. mechanisms
    3. stereochemistry
    4. reaction rates/rate laws

- E. Reactivity and reactions of aldehydes and ketones
    1. keto–enol tautomerism
        a. 1,3-dicarbonyl compounds, internal hydrogen bonding
    2. acidity of α hydrogens
    3. oxidations to carboxylic acids
    4. Wittig reaction to alkenes
    5. Nucleophilic additions
        a. alcohol formation
            I. from hydride reduction
            II. from organometallic reagents (Grignard reagents)
        b. acetal, hemiacetal formation
        c. imine, enamine formation
        d. aldol condensation
        e. Michael addition of α,β-unsaturated carbonyl compounds
        f. Wolff-Kishner reaction

---

[1] Adapted from *The Official Guide to the MCAT Exam*, 2009 ed., © 2009 Association of American Medical Colleges

F.   Reactivity and reactions of carboxylic acids
1.   physical properties, solubility, and hydrogen bonding
2.   reduction to alcohols
3.   decarboxylation (β-keto acids)
G.   Reactivity and reactions of carboxylic acid derivatives (acid chlorides, anhydrides, amides, esters)
1.   relative reactivity of acid derivatives
2.   Hofmann rearrangement and elimination reactions
3.   addition-elimination reactions
a.   preparation of acid derivatives
b.   interconversions of acid derivatives
c.   esterification/transesterification
d.   hydrolysis of fats and glycerides (saponification)
e.   formation and hydrolysis of amides

Laboratory Techniques

A.   Absorption Spectroscopy
1.   IR
2.   UV-vis
B.   Mass Spectrometry
1. ^{1}H NMR Spectroscopy
C.   Separations and Purifications
1.   extractions
2.   distillation
3.   chromatography (gas-liquid, paper, thin-layer)
D.   Recrystallization

Biological Molecules

A.   Carbohydrates
1.   nomenclature, classification
2.   absolute configurations
3.   epimers, anomers, cyclic structures
4.   reactions
B.   Proteins
1.   absolute configurations
2.   amino acid classification (acid/base, hydrophobic/hydrophilic)
3.   primary, secondary structure
4.   reactions
C.   Lipids
1.   structure (free fatty acids, triglycerides, phospholipids, terpenes, steroids)
D.   Nucleic acids

Chapter 21
Organic Chemistry
Practice Section

FREESTANDING QUESTIONS

1. Which of the following answer choices lists two pairs of diastereomers?

| I | II | III | IV |

A) I, III and II, IV
B) I, II and II, III
C) I, III and I, IV
D) II, IV and III, IV

2. Cyclobutanone derivates are known to be photochemically active, undergoing reactions such as shown below.

The primary driving force for this photochemical reaction is which of the following?

A) The formation of strong C—O σ-bonds
B) The formation of the stable, neutral transition state
C) The elimination of ring-strain
D) The ability of the five-membered cyclic product to stabilize itself in a chair conformation

3. "Ionic liquids" are pairs of organic cations and anions that are liquid at room temperature. When used as solvents they greatly aid many types of reactions. Which of the following choices best describes the reactions which would be significantly aided by being carried out in an ionic liquid?

  I. S_N2
  II. S_N1
  III. Radcal substitution

A) I and II only
B) II only
C) III only
D) I, II and III

4. A scientist discovered the following reaction and measured its rate.

She found that the rate of the reaction was 6×10^{-2} M/s when [A] = 0.30 M, and [HBr] = 3 M. What is the rate constant, k, for the reaction?

A) 2.0×10^{-1} s^{-1}
B) 2.0×10^{-1} $s^{-1}M^{-1}$
C) 6.6×10^{-2} s^{-1}
D) 6.6×10^{-2} $s^{-1}M^{-1}$

5. Which of the following fatty acids has the highest melting point?

A) (3E, 5E)-octa-3,5-dienoic acid
B) (3E, 5E)-deca-3,5-dienoic acid
C) (3Z, 5Z)-octa-3,5-dienoic acid
D) (3Z, 5Z)-deca-3,5-dienoic acid

6. The following reaction was monitored by thin layer chromatography. How does the R_f value of the product compare to the R_f value of the reactant?

A) The product has a higher R_f value because it is less polar.
B) The reactant has higher R_f value because it is less polar.
C) The reactant has a higher R_f value because it is more polar.
D) The product has a higher R_f value because it is more polar.

7. Which of the following statements is NOT true regarding the following molecule?

A) This compound is meso and is therefore optically inactive.
B) The ^{13}C NMR displays four signals.
C) Compared to a cyclohexanol, this compound would have a greater R_f value on a thin layer chromatography plate.
D) The compound has two distinct mirror planes of symmetry.

8. The IR stretching frequency of a bond is a measure of bond strength, with stronger bonds requiring more energy to cause stretching. The IR stretching frequency of a ketone is found to do which of the following when placed in acidic solution?

A) Disappear
B) Remain constant
C) Increase
D) Decrease

9. Infrared spectroscopy could be used to discern which two molecules from each other?

   I.   An amine and an imine
   II. An alcohol and a carboxylic acid
   III. Glucose and fructose

A) II only
B) I and II only
C) I and III only
D) I, II, III

10. A dipeptide is synthesized with the sequence Asp-Glu. The aspartic acid residue has an observed pK_a of 2.10 for its side chain. In free glutamic acid, the side chain has an expected pK_a of 2.15. However, in this dipeptide, it is likely that the observed pK_a of the glutamic acid side chain will be:

A) higher due to a favorable ionic interaction between the deprotonated side chains.
B) lower due to a favorable ionic interaction between the deprotonated side chains.
C) higher due to an unfavorable ionic interaction between the deprotonated side chains.
D) lower due to an unfavorable ionic interaction between the deprotonated side chains.

11. In the dipeptide shown below, all of the labeled dihedral angles may freely rotate EXCEPT:

A) ω
B) ψ
C) χ
D) ϕ

12. Which of the following would increase the rate of the reaction shown below?

   I.   Addition of acid
   II. Addition of base
   III. Increased concentration of EtOH

A) I
B) I and II
C) I and III
D) I, II, and III

PRACTICE PASSAGE 1

The di-π-methane rearrangement (Figure 1) is a photochemical reaction that produces ene-substituted cyclopropanes from 1,4-dienes. The rearrangement formally amounts to a 1,2-shift of one of the two alkenes, coupled to bond formation between the terminal carbons of the non-migrating allylic system.

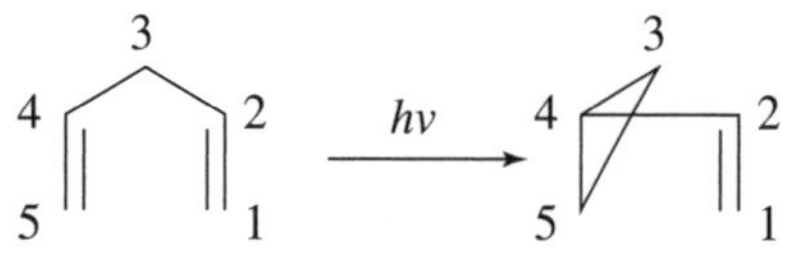

Figure 1   Di-π-methane rearrangement

A similar transformation, called the oxa-di-π-methane rearrangement, can occur when one of the carbon-carbon double bonds is replaced by a carbonyl. This rearrangement was used to convert bicyclo[2.2.2]oct-2-ene-5-one (Compound 1) into tricyclo[3.3.0.0^{2,8}]octan-3-one (Compound 2) by irradiating a 1% acetone solution of Compound 1 with ultraviolet light (Figure 2).

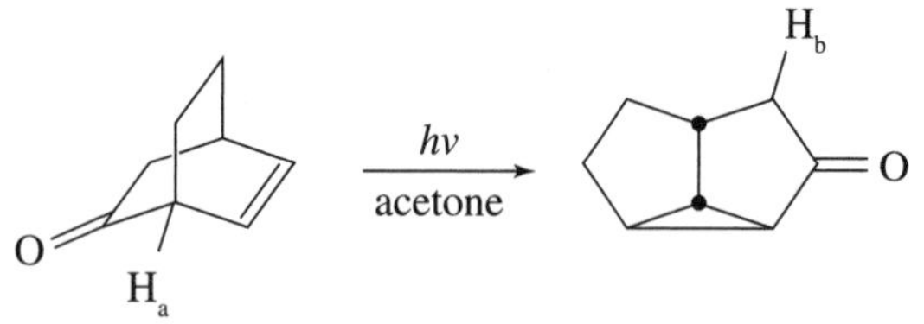

Compound 1   **Compound 2**

Figure 2   Oxa-di-π-methane rearrangement of bicyclic enone (Compound 1)

The mechanism by which both reactions occur involves radical intermediates, as shown in Figure 3.

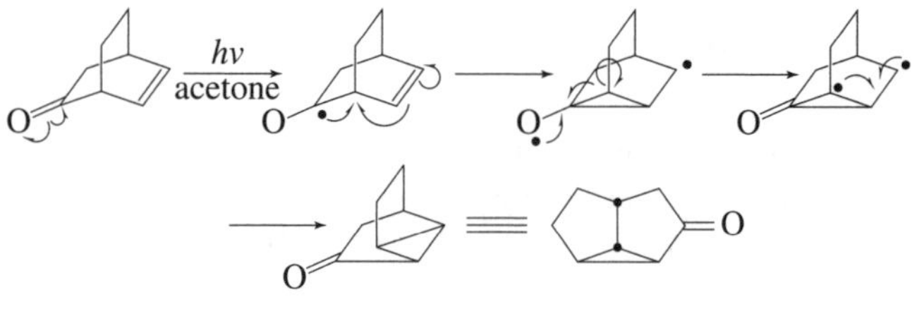

Figure 3   Mechanism of the oxa-di-π-methane rearrangement

If the irradiation described above is conducted at higher concentrations, or in other solvents, the chances of a Norrish type I cleavage (Step 1, Figure 4) increase. Norrish type I cleavage can be followed by a different radical rearrangement (Step 2, Figure 4) that competes with the oxa-di-π-methane rearrangement, forming predominantly Compound 3.

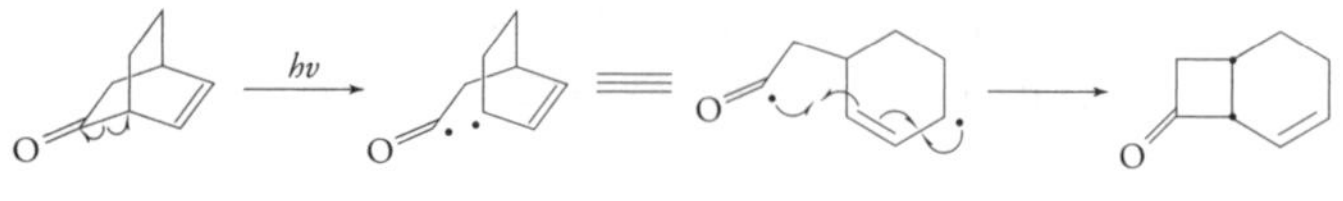

Compound 3

Figure 4   Norrish type I cleavage and rearrangement

1. What are the absolute configurations of C-1 and C-4 in Compound 1, respectively?

A) *R, S*
B) *R, R*
C) *S, S*
D) *S, R*

2. The reaction in Figure 2 can be best classified as:

A) an oxidation, because the reactant gains electrons during the rearrangement.
B) a reduction, because a carbon-carbon double bond was hydrogenated.
C) neither an oxidation nor a reduction, because the reactant and product have the same number of degrees of unsaturation.
D) an elimination, because a π bond was broken.

3. Is Compound 1 or Compound 2 more acidic at the indicated H atoms in Figure 2?

A) Compound 1, because the enolate formed upon removing H$_a$ has more resonance structures due to the conjugation with the alkene.
B) Compound 1, because the enolate formed upon removing H$_a$ is more substituted.
C) Compound 2, because H$_b$ is less sterically hindered, allowing for easier removal by a base.
D) Compound 2, because the negative charge formed upon removing H$_a$ cannot be resonance stabilized due to the nonplanar nature of the enolate.

4. What is the relationship between Compounds 1 and 3?

A) Geometric isomers
B) Structural isomers
C) Enantiomers
D) Diastereomers

5. The product of the rearrangement shown in Figure 3 can be most easily distinguished from the starting material using which of the following techniques?

A) Infrared spectroscopy
B) Mass spectroscopy
C) UV-vis spectroscopy
D) Gas chromatography

6. How many degrees of unsaturation are in Compound 2?

A) 1
B) 2
C) 3
D) 4

7. If (*E*)-4-methylhexa-1,4-diene undergoes a di-π-methane rearrangement, which of the following could be the product?

A)

B)

C)

D)

PRACTICE PASSAGE 2

In an internal combustion engine, fuel and air are mixed under pressure and ignited. The resulting combustion produces a flame that should evenly consume the fuel-air mixture in the piston. As a result of this smooth burning, the engine will run efficiently and provide the maximum power output. However, some hydrocarbons are prone to self-ignition under pressure resulting in noticeable pulses and noises in the engine, commonly referred to as "knocking," which decrease efficiency. The octane rating of a compound is an indication of how well it resists this compression detonation.

Isooctane (2,2,4-trimethylpentane) burns very smoothly and was assigned an octane rating of 100, as the standard against which other compounds are measured. n-Heptane on the other hand, tends to self-detonate easily and is assigned an octane rating of 0. Each hydrocarbon has its own anti-knock capabilities dependent on the size and structure of the molecule. Table 1 below shows several hydrocarbons and their corresponding octane ratings.

Table 1   Octane Ratings of Various Hydrocarbons

Name	Structure	Formula	Octane
n-heptane	$CH_3(CH_2)_5CH_3$	C_7H_{16}	0
2-methylheptane	$CH_3(CH_2)_4CH(CH_3)_2$	C_8H_{18}	23
n-hexane	$CH_3(CH_2)_4CH_3$	C_6H_{14}	25
2-methylhexane	$CH_3(CH_2)_3CH(CH_3)_2$	C_7H_{16}	45
n-pentane	$CH_3(CH_2)_3CH_3$	C_5H_{12}	62
methylcyclohexane	$C_6H_{11}CH_3$	C_7H_{14}	75
2, 4-dimethylpentane	$(CH_3)_2CHCH_2CH(CH_3)_2$	C_7H_{16}	83
2-methylbutane	$CH_3CH_2CH(CH_3)_2$	C_5H_{12}	93
cyclohexane	C_6H_{12}	C_6H_{12}	97
2, 2, 4-trmethylpentane	$(CH_3)_2CHCH_2C(CH_3)_3$	C_8H_{18}	100
benzene	C_6H_6	C_6H_6	101
toluene	$C_6H_6CH_3$	C_7H_8	112

Gasoline is a mixture of hydrocarbons containing on average between five and twelve carbons per molecule. However, not all hydrocarbons from crude oil of that size can be included in the mixture that makes it to the gas pump due to knocking. Out of the many fractions of crude oil separated during distillation, the two used to increase the octane of the gas mix are the short chain naphtha fractions (C5-C9) and the longer chain gas oil fractions (C12-C18). The components are refined via *catalytic reforming* and *catalytic cracking*, respectively.

The feed mixture for the reforming process is comprised of roughly 45-70% saturated paraffins, 20-25% naphthenes (cyclic hydrocarbons), 4-14% aromatics, and 0-2% olefins. As the name implies, the starting compounds are *reformed*, such that their structure is changed to improve the octane rating. For example, n-pentane can be isomerized to 2-methylbutane, and n-hexane can be dehydrocyclized to produce benzene. The final reformate is enriched with up to 60-75% high octane aromatics while the naphthene and paraffin percentages are dramatically decreased.

Catalytic cracking takes the gas oil fraction and breaks the molecules into smaller straight chain or branched compounds with a more desirable octane profile. During this process, a C—C single bond is cleaved but no hydrogen is added to or removed from the compound to produce the products.

1. To minimize the health hazards of gasoline, the carcinogenic benzene produced during reforming is often alkylated to form new, substituted aromatic compounds. In such a reaction, benzene would be expected to behave as a(n):

A) Lewis acid.
B) Brønsted acid.
C) nucleophile.
D) oxidizing agent.

2. According to information in the passage, how many signals should the ^{13}C NMR spectrum of isooctane have?

A) 4
B) 5
C) 7
D) 8

3. Which of the following features generally increase(s) the octane rating of a hydrocarbon?

    I. Tertiary carbons
    II. High molecular weight
    III. Degrees of unsaturation

A) I only
B) I and III only
C) II and III only
D) I, II, and III

4. If 3,5-diethyloctane is subjected to cracking conditions, which pair of molecules below are possible products of the reaction?

A)

B)

C)

D)

5. "Grassoline" is the name given to gasoline produced from cellulosic biomass. Cellulose is hydrolyzed to simple sugars, which are then converted into hydroxymethylfurfural (shown below), before finally becoming hydrocarbons. Which of the following describes the conversion of glucose into HMF?

A) Oxidation
B) Dehydration
C) Isomerization
D) Hydrogenation

6. Based on information in Table 1, which of the following should be true for isomeric hydrocarbons?

A) Octane and boiling point increase due to increased branching in the molecule.
B) Octane and boiling point decrease due to increased branching in the molecule.
C) Octane increases and boiling point decreases due to decreased branching in the molecule.
D) Octane decreases and boiling point increases due to decreased branching in the molecule.

7. Which of the following compounds in Table 1 has the largest degree of unsaturation?

A) *n*-pentane
B) Methylcyclohexane
C) Toluene
D) 2,2,4-trimethylpentane

PRACTICE PASSAGE 3

Selectively exploiting compounds with more than one reactive site is of interest to researchers wishing to build large molecular frameworks from simple core molecules. Studies have recently been carried out on the substitution chemistry of vinyl epoxides, since these compounds can be substituted with nucleophiles at either an epoxide carbon, in standard S_N2 fashion, or at the vinyl end the molecule through a related mechanism known as S_N2' (Scheme 1).

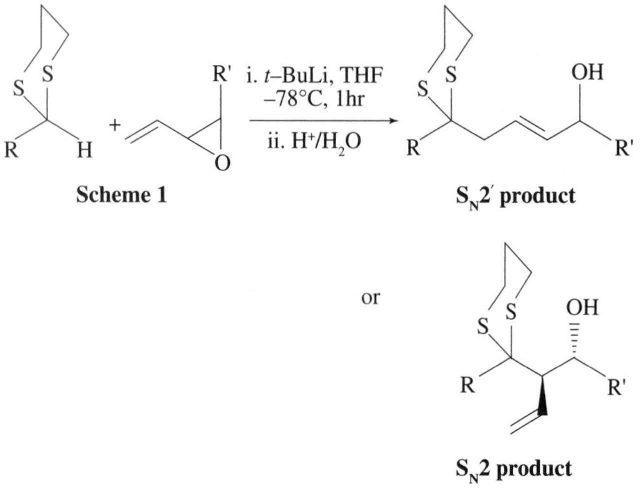

Scheme 1

S_N2' **product**

or

S_N2 **product**

Scheme 1

In this reaction a lithiated dithiane is formed by deprotonation of the initial dithiane using the very strong base *tert*-butyllithium. The new organolithium compound attacks the vinyl epoxide forming the final substitution products. It was found that the site of attack, and thus the final product, was controlled by the steric bulk of the dithiane near the deprotonated carbon. The table below details these results.

R	Ratio S_N2:S_N2'
H	100:0
phenyl	100:0
i-propyl	0:100
Si-(*i*-propyl)$_3$	0:100

1. A dithiane bearing which of the following R groups is *most* likely to give solely the S_N2' product?

A) Methyl
B) *t*-Butyl
C) Cyclohexyl
D) *n*-Propyl

2. If these reactions were run at room temperature instead of –78°C which of the following might you expect from the product distribution?

A) The S_N2 mechanism would become more dominant.
B) The S_N2' mechanism would become more dominant.
C) An equal mixture of the two mechanisms would be seen for all dithianes.
D) There would be no change in product distribution.

3. *tert*-Butyllithium is extremely pyrophoric and dangerous to handle. What might be a complication in substituting *n*-butyllithium for *tert*-butyllithium?

A) *n*-Butyllithium isn't sufficiently basic to deprotonate the dithiane.
B) *n*-Butyllithium is unstable and undergoes dimerization reactions resulting in the formation of *n*-octane.
C) *n*-Butyllithium can deprotonate the vinyl epoxide leading to premature epoxide opening.
D) *n*-Butyllithium can act as a nucleophile and open the epoxide via substitution.

4. Another reaction, under the same conditions as shown in Scheme 1 and utilizing $-SiH(CH_3)_2$ as the R group, went entirely though the S_N2 pathway despite having similar substitution to the case where R is *i*-propyl. Which of the following could explain these results?

A) The lower electronegativity of Si, compared to C, creates a strong nucleophile which favors the S_N2 mechanism.
B) The larger size of Si, compared to C, maintains a larger distance between the anionic carbon and the steric bulk of the methyl groups.
C) The hydrogen on the Si atom is acidic enough to hydrogen bond to the oxygen atom of the epoxide, aligning the anion for S_N2 attack on the epoxide carbons.
D) The larger size of the Si atom, compared to the C, provides steric shielding to the anionic carbon, favoring the S_N2 pathway.

5. The lack of ether products found in the reaction mixture indicates which of the following?

A) Oxyanions cannot open epoxides.
B) Nucleophilic attack by the lithiated dithiane is the fast step in the reaction.
C) Deprotonation of the dithiane is the fast step in the reaction.
D) Ethers are unstable to *tert*-butyllithium.

6. The reaction shown below is known as a 1,4-Brook rearrangement. It involves swapping an organosilicon moiety with a hydrogen atom of an alcohol group four atoms away.

In trials of the reaction in Scheme 1 with four silicon-containing R groups only one of the following showed the Brook rearrangement product. Which was it?

A) $-SiH(CH_3)_2$
B) $-Si(i\text{-propyl})_3$
C) $-Si(t\text{-butyl})(i\text{-propyl})_2$
D) $-Si(i\text{-propyl})(CH_3)_2$

PRACTICE PASSAGE 4

Scientists have long been interested in understanding the reactivity of organic compounds during a chemical reaction. In order to gain insight into the reactivity of organic nucleophiles, studies have been performed on the addition of different classes of α-substituted benzyl anions, derived from compounds such as Compound 1 (below), to electrophiles such as quinone methides (Compound 2 below, $\lambda_{max} = 393$ nm) and benzylhydrylium ions (Compound 3 below, $\lambda_{max} = 621$ nm). These types of electrophiles were chosen because the reaction rates could be easily monitored by UV-vis spectrometry.

$R_1 = SO_2CF_3, NO_2$
$X = H, CH_3, CN, NO_2$

1

2

1. KO*t*Bu
   DMSO
   ─────────→ PRODUCT
2. H⁺

AND

$R_1 = SO_2CF_3, NO_2$
$X = H, CH_3, CN, NO_2$

1

3

1. KO*t*Bu
   DMSO
   ─────────→ PRODUCT
2. H⁺

Recently, scientists wanted to compare the nucleophilicity of α-CN-substituted benzyl anions derived from Compounds 4a-d (shown below) to that of α-SO_2CF_3- and α-NO_2-substituted benzyl anions. (The respective pK_a values of Compounds 4a-d in DMSO are 16.0, 18.1, 23.0, and 12.3.)

4a

4b

4c

4d

The conjugate addition of Compound 4c to Compound 5 to form Compound 6 served as the baseline reaction for this study:

4c

5

1. KO*t*Bu
   DMSO
   ─────────→ **6**
2. H⁺

(Adapted from *J. Org. Chem.* 2009, 74, 75–81.)

1. What is the role of KOtBu in these reactions?

A) Brønsted base
B) Brønsted acid
C) Leaving group
D) Electrophile

2. In the ^{1}H NMR spectrum for the compound below, what are the splitting patterns of H^a and H^b?

A) H^a = singlet, H^b = singlet
B) H^a = doublet, H^b = singlet
C) H^a = doublet, H^b = doublet
D) H^a = doublet, H^b = doublet of doublets

3. According to the passage, which compound would have the strongest conjugate base?

A) 4a
B) 4b
C) 4c
D) 4d

4. Why was UV-vis spectroscopy a useful method for determining the rates of the addition reactions?

A) Because the electrophiles do not have extended conjugation and do not absorb in the visible wavelength range.
B) Because the electrophiles do not have extended conjugation and absorb in the visible wavelength range.
C) Because the electrophiles have extended conjugation and do not absorb in the visible wavelength range.
D) Because the electrophiles have extended conjugation and absorb in the visible wavelength range.

5. What is the most stable structure for compound 6?

A)

B)

C)

D)

6. Which of the following statements is/are true concerning Compounds 4a-4d based on their pK_a values?

  I. CN is electron withdrawing and helps to stabilize nucleophile formation of 4a through resonance.
  II. CF$_3$ is electron withdrawing and helps to stabilize nucleophile formation of 4b through induction.
  III. NO$_2$ is electron donating and helps to stabilize nucleophile formation of 4d through resonance.

A) I only
B) I and II only
C) II and III only
D) I, II, and III

PRACTICE PASSAGE 5

Carbon-carbon π bonds are relatively weak (~270 kJ/mol) and are electron rich unless substituted with electron-withdrawing groups. As such, electrophiles often easily react with alkenes and alkynes, though the mechanism of electrophilic addition differs somewhat depending on reagent.

Halogenation reactions stereoselectively convert alkenes into alkyl halides with predictable stereochemistry, owing to the way that Br_2 adds to opposite sides of the double bond (termed *anti*-addition). Alkynes may form alkenyl halides or tetra-substituted alkyl halides (Figure 1). Because an alkyne has two π bonds, it is susceptible to a second addition if two equivalents of the halogen are used, as shown with 3-hexyne below.

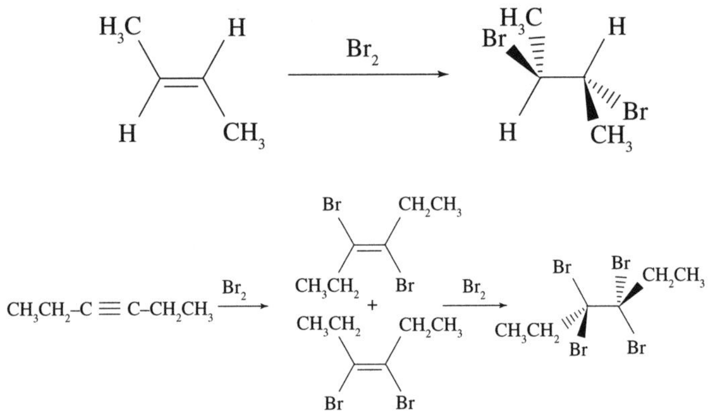

Figure 1   Halogenation of unsaturated hydrocarbons

Hydration of alkenes via hydroboration-oxidation results in the regioselective formation of the least substituted, or *anti-Markovnikov* alcohol (Figure 2).

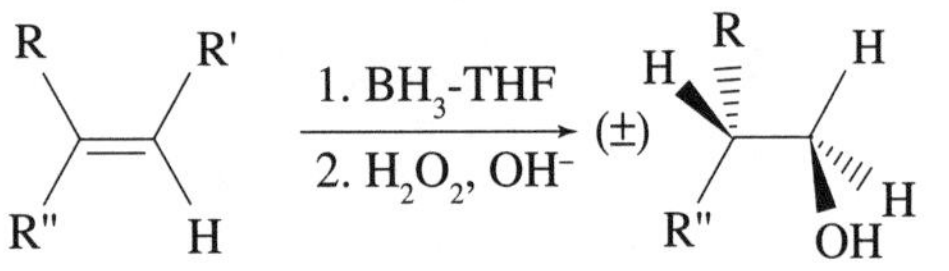

Figure 2   Anti-Markovnikov hydration

The reaction is proposed to take place through a four-center transition state, with each borane molecule able to react with a total of three alkenes (Figure 3). Finally, the organoborane is oxidized by hydrogen peroxide in the presence of base to form the alcohol.

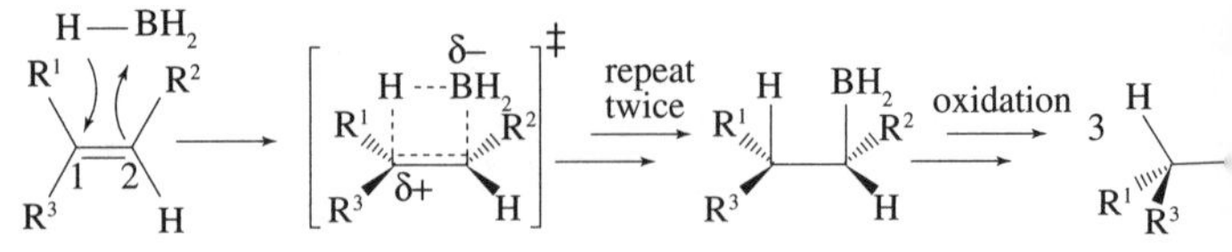

Figure 3   Hydroboration-oxidation reaction detail

Bulkier borane reagents are used to prevent the addition of a second equivalent of boron to the alkene π bond formed upon the initial addition of borane to the alkyne. Once oxidized, the enol product will rearrange to yield an aldehyde, the anti-Markovnikov addition product.

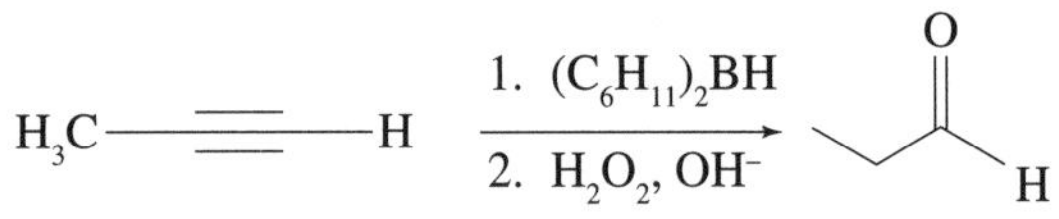

Figure 4   Hydroboration-oxidation of 1-propyne

1. Which of the following explains the regiochemical outcome of hydroboration-oxidation described in the Figure 3?

    I.   The transition state that leads to Markovnikov addition is more sterically hindered.
    II. The concerted process requires that the substituents add to the same face of the double bond.
    III. The partial charge on carbon in the transition state is more stable on C1 than C2.

    A) I only
    B) II only
    C) I and II only
    D) I and III only

2. Which of the following can be an intermediate formed during the reaction shown in Figure 4?

A) HO   H

B) H   H
          OH

C) H   OH
         H

D) H$_2$B   OH
          H

3. The addition of the second equivalent of Br$_2$ to an alkyne is much slower than the addition of the first addition of Br$_2$ to an alkene, even though the reactions take place at sp^2 hybridized carbons in both cases. What is the best explanation for this observation?

A) The first equivalent of added Br$_2$ sterically hinders the second addition reaction.
B) The (E)-dibromoalkene is less nucleophilic than the unsubstituted alkene.
C) The addition of the second equivalent of Br$_2$ is less exothermic than the addition of the first.
D) The dibromide is more stable than the tetrabromide.

4. Which of the following would be part of the ^{1}H NMR spectrum of the product of the alkyne dibromination in Figure 1?

A) Two 3 H triplets
B) Two 2 H quartets
C) One 6 H triplet
D) One 4 H triplet

5. If the product in Figure 4 is refluxed in D$_2$O, what is the maximum number of deuterium atoms that could be incorporated into the structure?

A) 1
B) 2
C) 3
D) 5

6. What is the most likely product formed when 2-pentyne is hydrated using the conditions described in Figure 4?

A)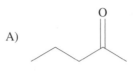

B)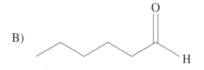

C)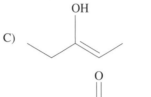

D)

7. Which of the following best describes the product of the halogenation of *trans*-2-butene in Figure 1?

A) Chiral
B) Racemic
C) *Syn*
D) Meso

PRACTICE PASSAGE 6

According to the World Health Organization (WHO), depression is a serious mental health problem that affects over 120 million people worldwide. About 15% of the adult US population will suffer from depression at least once in their lifetime.

The birth of selective serotonin reuptake inhibitors (SSRIs) began in 1970 with the discovery of fluoxetine, a highly selective SSRI, which is marketed as Prozac™. Relative to other depression therapies on the market at the time, Prozac made history because its superior safety profile rocketed it to annual sales of over $3 billion.

The original synthetic route to fluoxetine is described in Figure 1.

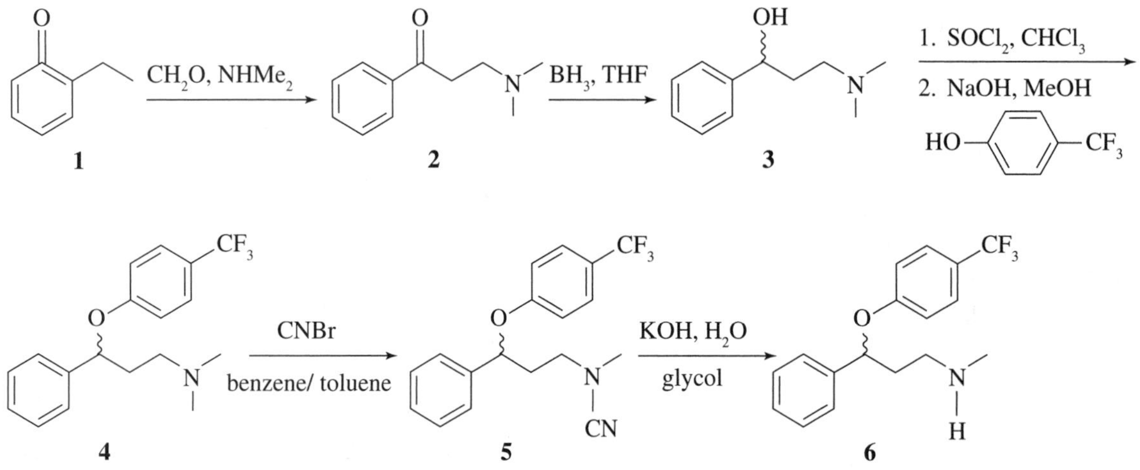

Figure 1 The original commercial synthesis of fluoxetine (Prozac™).

Both fluoxetine enantiomers have similar activity *in vitro*, However, the (*S*)-enantiomer is the dominant therapeutic drug because it is eliminated more slowly *in vivo*, which prolongs the duration of its effects.

1. The first step in the synthesis of fluoxetine is the Mannich reaction of acetophenone (1). What electrophilic intermediate is formed when formaldehyde and dimethylamine are combined?

A)

B)

C)

D)

2. Which of the two fluoxetine enantiomers is thermodynamically more stable?

A) (S) since it is eliminated more slowly.
B) (S) since it is more active *in vitro*.
C) (R) since it has a shorter duration of action.
D) Neither, they are thermodynamically equivalent.

3. In the first step of the transformation from Compound 3 to Compound 4, the OH group is converted to a Cl. What is the most likely mechanism for the second step that produces Compound 4?

A) S_N1, because a racemic mixture is formed.
B) S_N1, because a strong base is used.
C) S_N2, because a strong nucleophile is used.
D) S_N2, because a stable carbocation can be formed.

4. An alternative way to synthesize Compound 2 is the 1,4-addition of dimethylamine to which of the following ketones?

A)

B)

C)

D)

5. In the transformation of Compound 2 to Compound 3, what is an alternative reagent to BH_3?

A) BF_3
B) PCC
C) $NaCNBH_3$
D) O_3, H_2O_2

6. In the transformation from Compound 4 to Compound 5, CNBr is used to remove a methyl group from the tertiary nitrogen. The central carbon of CNBr is most likely acting as a:

A) Lewis base
B) Leaving group
C) Nucleophile
D) Electrophile

PRACTICE PASSAGE 7

Gelsemine (Figure 1) has been widely studied due to its complex structure that includes a total of six rings, and scientists have made many attempts to synthesize the molecule in a stereoselective way.

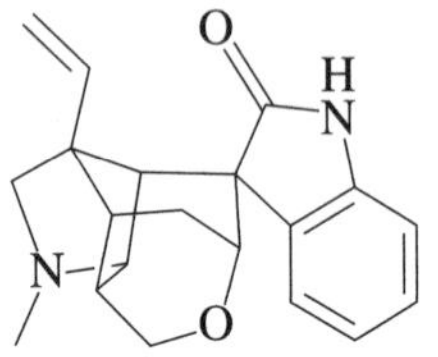

Figure 1   Gelsemine

Part of one synthesis is shown in Figure 2, and shows the successful addition of the fourth and fifth rings of the compound.

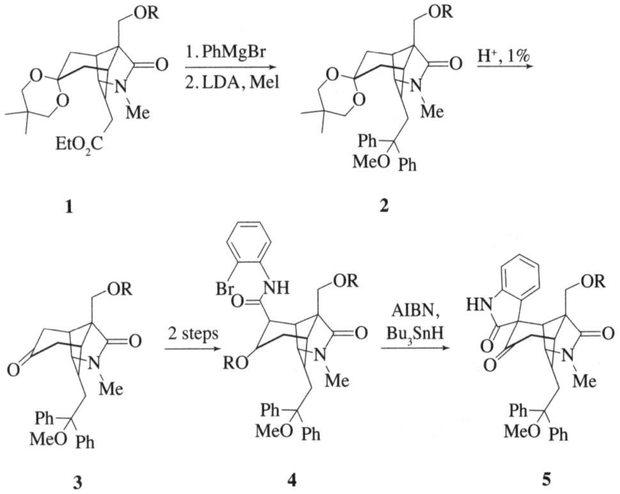

Figure 2   Partial synthesis of gelsemine

Two key steps along the synthetic route to tetracyclic Compound 1 are shown below in Figure 3.

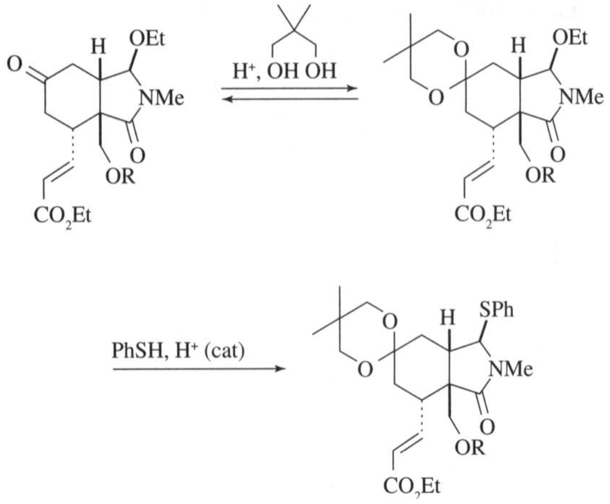

Figure 3   Early steps of gelsemine synthesis

1. Why is the ketone in Compound 3 protected during the first two steps of the synthesis?

A) The hemiacetal prevents the less reactive ketone from being deprotonated.
B) The acetal prevents Grignard addition to the ketone.
C) The acetal, being equatorial, provides extra stability.
D) The hemiacetal prevents the ketone from forming a tertiary alcohol during the Grignard addition.

2. Compound 4 is treated with a radical initiator to form a phenyl radical, which leads to the formation of Compound 5. Why does the radical form at this site?

A) Homolytic cleavage of the C—Br bond forms a resonance-stabilized phenyl radical.
B) Homolytic cleavage of the C—Br bond forms a stable, secondary radical.
C) Homolytic cleavage of the C—Br bond forms a radical that is stabilized by the nearby nitrogen.
D) Heterolytic cleavage of a C—H bond forms a stable carbanion.

3. Why is no Grignard addition to the carbonyl of the amide observed in Step 1 of Figure 1?

A) The carbonyl carbon in the amide is more electrophilic than that of the ester, but the leaving group ($-NR_2$) is not as stable.
B) The carbonyl carbon in the amide is less electrophilic than that of the ester.
C) The carbonyl carbon of the ester is less electrophilic than that of the amide, but its leaving group ($-OEt$) is less stable.
D) Addition to the ester results in a release of steric strain.

4. When Compound 5 is treated with excess H^+, what process occurs to yield which new, stable product?

A) Loss of methanol to give a trisubstituted alkene
B) Loss of OR to give a tetrasubstituted alkene
C) Formation of an enol from the ketone
D) Formation of enols from both amides

5. While performing the first step of the synthesis shown in Figure 2, it was noted that one change in the reaction conditions greatly improved the yield. Which of the following could be that change?

A) Addition of more H^+
B) Removal of water
C) Addition of base
D) Cooling the reaction

6. Why does the second step of Figure 2 yield only one product, and not a mixture of diastereomers?

A) S_N2 reactions have only one possible stereochemical outcome.
B) Addition of the nucleophile from the same side of the molecule as the OR group is less sterically hindered.
C) An internal hydrogen bond between the sulfur atom and the hydrogen at the ring juncture makes this the most stable diastereomer.
D) The product shown is resonance stabilized.

7. How many chiral centers does gelsemine have?

A) 5
B) 6
C) 7
D) 8

PRACTICE PASSAGE 8

Gas chromatography (GC) is a technique used to separate organic materials based on differences in volatility. In a GC, a heat source is applied to vaporize the analyte after injection. In order for a substance to be effectively separated using GC, it must be vaporized without decomposing. The gaseous analyte is then carried through a column by a mobile phase consisting of an inert gas, such as Ne or N_2. As the analyte passes through the column, it goes through multiple condensation-evaporation cycles as it adsorbs onto the liquid or solid stationary phase. Substances with greater volatility will spend less time adsorbed, and pass through the column with faster retention times.

Although GC is an effective separation technique, it cannot distinguish between two molecules with the same retention time. However, combining a GC with a mass spectrometer (MS) in a GC-MS apparatus allows each peak that elutes from the GC to be identified by mass, which in turn provides additional information as to its chemical identity. Mass spectrometry is a powerful technique that accurately can detect substances across a wide range of molecular weights, from small organic compounds to protein complexes.

In the mass spectrometer, analyte molecules (M) are chemically ionized in the presence of a reagent gas, such as methane, and a stream of electrons. An example of chemical ionization is Reaction 1. The ionized molecules are then separated and detected, and produce a peak corresponding to their mass/charge ratio (*m/z*).

$$\text{Step (a): } CH_4 + e^- \rightarrow CH_4^+ + 2e^-$$

$$\text{Step (b): } CH_4^+ + CH_4 \rightarrow CH_5^+ + CH_3$$

$$\text{Step (c): } M + CH_5^+ \rightarrow CH_4 + [M + H]^+$$

Reaction 1

Portable GC-MS machines are often used as part of security screening features at airports to detect the presence of prohibited substances such as narcotics and explosives. One explosive that is targeted for detection by GC-MS is tetryl, a compound used to make detonators and explosive booster charges. When a sample of tetryl is fed into a GC-MS, it produces peaks corresponding to the chemicals TNT, RDX, and N-methylpicramide, the structures of which are shown in Figure 1.

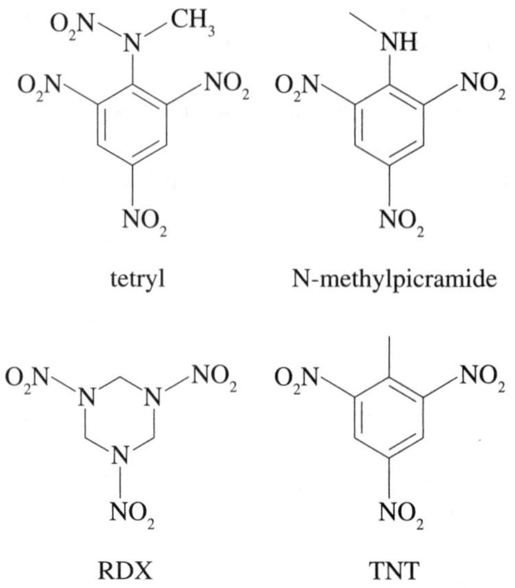

tetryl   N-methylpicramide

RDX   TNT

Figure 1

1. What is the IUPAC name for TNT?

A) 1,3,5-trinitro-2-methylbenzene
B) 2-methyl-1,3,5-trinitrobenzene
C) 2,4,6-trinitrotoluene
D) 1,3,5-trinitrotoluene

2. In what order would you expect the components of tetryl to elute from the GC column?

A) RDX > TNT > N-methylpicramide
B) N-methylpicramide > TNT > RDX
C) N-methylpicramide > RDX > TNT
D) RDX > N-methylpicramide > TNT

3. Which of the following best explains why GC-MS analysis of tetryl does not produce a peak corresponding to tetryl?

A) Tetryl is too large to be analyzed by mass spectrometry.
B) Tetryl is too polar and adsorbs too tightly to the stationary phase inside the GC column.
C) The tetryl coelutes with the RDX and therefore its signal cannot be detected.
D) Since tetryl is a highly reactive compound, the heat of vaporization at the GC injection site causes the tetryl to degrade into more stable components.

4. What would be the result of increasing the temperature at which the GC is run?

A) Poorer separation and faster elution times
B) Poor separation and slower elution times
C) Better separation and faster elution times
D) Better separation and slower elution times

5. If a molecule M is chemically ionized as shown in Reaction 1 using CD_4 rather than CH_4, the resulting mass spectrometry peak for M will have a value that is:

A) the same as that of the M ionized in CH_4.
B) one less than that of M ionized in CH_4.
C) one more than that of M ionized in CH_4.
D) two more than that of M ionized in CH_4.

6. During the chemical ionization step of mass spectrometry as shown in Reaction 1, M may be broken into different ionized fragments depending on the acidity of the reagent gas used in Step (c). For example, when a strong acid is used as the reagent gas, RDX produces fragments with m/z values of 75 and 49. Which of the following reagent gases is the least likely to produce these fragments?

A) CH_4
B) H_2
C) NH_3
D) CH_3CH_3

PRACTICE PASSAGE 9

Bile is a greenish fluid produced in the liver that helps dispose of the liver's waste products and aids in the digestion of fats. It is stored in the gallbladder and emptied into the small intestine via the common bile duct when needed. The principle components of bile are bile acids, cholesterol, and bilirubin. The liver enzymatically converts cholesterol (1) into one of two primary bile acids, cholic acid (2) or chenodeoxycholic acid (3).

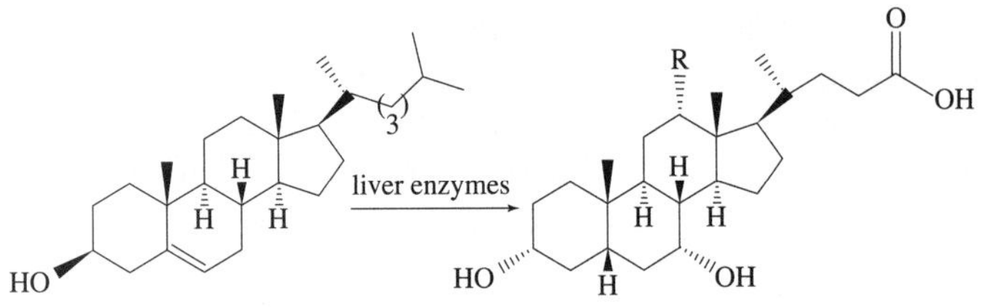

cholesterol (1)

cholic acid (2): R = OH
chenodeoxycholic acid (3): R = H

These acids are then coupled with glycine, an amino acid, or taurine, one of the few known naturally occurring sulfonic acids. Taurocholic acid (4) is readily converted into its salt in the duodenum upon mixing with pancreatic secretions containing lipase and bicarbonate.

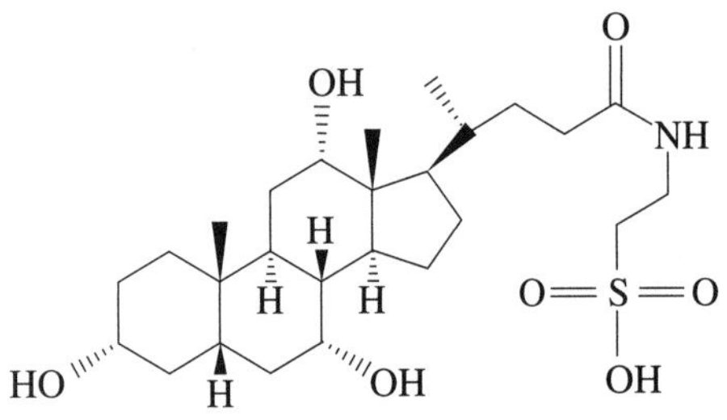

taurocholic acid (4)

Bile acids are amphipathic. It is this property that allows them to emulsify fat globules into microscopic micelles, increasing fat surface area and aiding digestion by lipase.

Bacteria in the colon convert Compounds 2 and 3 into their respective secondary bile acids 5 and 6, shown below. Bile salts are not passively absorbed in the small intestine, but secondary bile acids are actively absorbed in the colon where the pH is less basic. Up to 95% of the bile acids produced by the liver are reabsorbed and can be used in the digestive process up to twenty times.

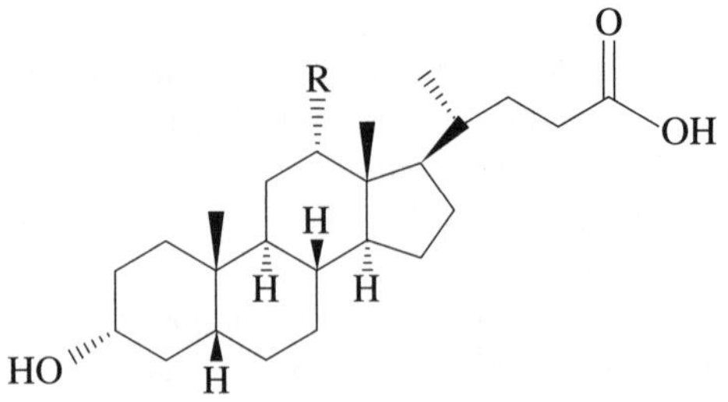

lithocholic acid (5): R = H
deoxycholic acid (6): R = OH

1. Which of following transformations do liver enzymes employ to produce primary bile acids?

A) Elimination
B) Saponification
C) Oxidation
D) Dehydration

2. Rank compounds 1-4 by increasing solubility in water.

A) 3 < 1 < 2 < 4
B) 1 < 3 < 4 < 2
C) 4 < 2 < 3 < 1
D) 1 < 3 < 2 < 4

3. Which of the following contributes to the fact that the small intestine cannot passively absorb bile salts?

   I.   Taurine and glycine have low pK_a values.
  II.   Bile salts are hydrophobic.
 III.   Pancreatic secretions increase intestinal pH.

A) I only
B) I and II only
C) I and III only
D) II and III only

4. How many chiral centers does cholesterol have?

A) 7
B) 8
C) 9
D) 10

5. Lipase works to hydrolyze which of the following functional groups?

A) Amide
B) Ester
C) Ether
D) Hemiacetal

6. Taurine is a derivative of the amino acid cysteine, shown above. Which of the following reactions is a necessary part of the biochemical conversion of cysteine to taurine in the body?

A) Decarboxylation of the carboxyl group
B) Protonation of the basic amine
C) Reduction of the thiol group
D) Conversion of the primary amine to an imine

Chapter 22
Organic Chemistry
Practice Section
Solutions

Solutions to Freestanding Questions

1. **B**   Stereoisomers in which all stereocenters are inverted are enantiomers, while stereoisomers with at least one, but not all, inverted chiral centers are diastereomers. Molecules I and III are an enantiomeric pair (eliminate choices A and C); Molecules II and IV are enantiomers as well (eliminate choice D). All other pairs of molecules are diastereomers.

2. **C**   Four-membered rings are very strained, especially those with sp^2 hybridized carbons. As such the expansion to the much more favorable five-membered ring is the primary driving force. Choice A is incorrect because while it is true in general that two σ–bonds are better energetically than one double bond, if this were the driving force we could expect this type of reaction to happen with rings of any size, which it does not. Choice B is incorrect because the transition state is the highest energy portion of the reaction coordinate, and as such is inherently unstable. Choice D is incorrect because cyclohexane rings stabilize themselves in the chair conformation, not cyclopentane-type rings.

3. **B**   Ionic liquids would aid any reaction that has a charged intermediate or transition state, as they would be able to arrange constitutive ions to counterbalance the charges. Neither Item I nor Item III has a charged intermediate. S_N2 reactions are hindered by protic solvents because of their partially-charged nature and would therefore be hindered by ionic liquids. Radical substitution reactions are charge-neutral throughout, and wouldn't be aided by excess ionic charge in their vicinity.

4. **A**   From the resultant stereochemistry and the reaction conditions (tertiary center, protic solvent), we can determine that the reaction type is S_N1. From there we know that the rate law for this S_N1 reaction would be: rate = k[A], or $0.06 = k(0.3)$. Doing the algebra we find that $k = 0.2$. Since the reaction is first order the units on k are s^{-1}. The units s$^{-1}M^{-1}$ are for a second order reaction, eliminating both choices B and D. Answer choice D would be correct for an S_N2 reaction with the same concentrations and rate.

5. **A**   Although hemiacetal formation is catalyzed by both acid and base, conversion of the hemiacetal to the acetal requires a catalytic amount of acid to protonate the hemiacetal OH group so it can leave as water. The presence of base would prevent this from occurring, and slow acetal formation. Therefore, choices B and D can be eliminated, and Item I is true; it catalyzes both hemiacetal and acetal formation. Although hemiacetal formation occurs through nucleophilic addition, a bimolecular mechanism that involves both the carbonyl compound and the nucleophile (in this case, EtOH), the rate limiting step of this reaction is the conversion of the hemiacetal to the acetal. This conversion is an S_N1 reaction, which requires formation of a high-energy carbocation intermediate. Therefore, the kinetics of the rate limiting step are independent of the concentration of EtOH, and increasing its concentration would not increase the rate of the reaction.

6. **A**   Even though you may not understand the reaction, if you recognize this as a two-by-two question, you can eliminate choices C and D by knowing that R_f values are higher for less polar molecules and lower for more polar molecules. In this reaction, the starting alcohol undergoes an intramolecular ring closure to produce an ether that is less polar than the alcohol, so the product would have a higher R_f value (eliminate choice B).

7. **A**   This compound is not optically active (achiral), but it is because it does not possess any chiral centers, not because it is meso. All of the other statements are true.

8.   **D**   The carbonyl group in a ketone doesn't disappear in acidic solution, so neither will its stretching frequency (eliminate choice A). When protonated we can expect the following resonance structures:

With more single bond character we can expect the C=O signal to shift slightly toward C—O, and therefore to lower frequencies (eliminate choices B and C).

9.   **D**   Infrared spectroscopy identifies functional groups. Since all Roman numeral items refer to molecules with different functional groups, choice D is the best answer. Item I refers to a molecule with a C—N bond (amine) and a molecule with a C=N bond (imine) which will generate different resonances. Since Item I is true, choice A can be eliminated. Item II compares an alcohol with an –OH group to a carboxyl group (–COOH). While this compound will have an –OH signal in its spectrum, it will also have a peak for the carbonyl making it distinguishable from the alcohol. Since Item II is true, choice C can be eliminated. Item III is also true because glucose is an aldose (contains an aldehyde) while fructose is a ketose (contains a ketone). While these structures are very similar, the ketone stretch will be slightly different from the aldehyde stretch, making the molecules distinguishable.

10.   **C**   This problem can be approached as a two-by-two. First, consider that when aspartic acid and glutamic acid are deprotonated, they go from having neutral side chains to having a negative charge. Repulsion between these two negative charges creates an unfavorable ionic interaction (eliminate choices A and B). If the side chain of glutamic acid has a higher observed pK_a, the repulsion can be avoided somewhat since the group will be deprotonated only at higher pH, and therefore a narrower range of conditions (eliminate choice D).

11.   **A**   Since the peptide bond has partial double bond character, it cannot freely rotate. The peptide bond is labeled as ω, making choice A the correct answer. The rest of the labeled dihedral angles are all single bonds, and therefore can freely rotate.

12.   **B**   In general, larger molecules have higher melting points due to increased London dispersion forces. Eliminate choices A and C since they have eight carbons (octa), while the molecules in choices B and D have ten carbons (deca). The remaining difference between B and D is the presence of *E* or *Z* double bonds. *Z* double bonds introduce kinks in the fatty acid chain, making it more difficult for the molecules to pack together, therefore reducing their melting point. This eliminates choice D.

Solutions to Practice Passage 1

1. **B**   The first thing to realize is that C-1 is the tertiary carbon at the back of the molecule while C-4 is the tertiary carbon at the front of the molecule. The name of Compound 1 given in the passage should help to elucidate this since the ketone is indicated to be at C-5 while the double bond is in the second position. Assigning priorities for C-1 gives the following:

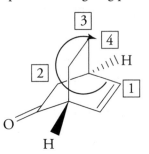

The first point of difference is the alkene at the right of the molecule, which gets first priority, then due to the presence of the carbonyl, the left side of the molecule is the second priority group. The top bridge of the two CH$_2$ groups is priority three, while the H is priority four. Since the H is already in the back of the molecule, connecting groups 1 to 2 to 3 forms a clockwise arc; therefore the stereocenter is the *R* configuration (eliminate choices C and D). For C-4, priorities should be assigned as follows:

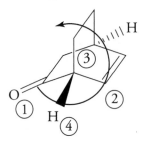

The carbonyl carbon is first priority, followed by the alkene, then the alkane. While groups 1 to 2 to 3 trace a counterclockwise arc indicating an *S* configuration, since the fourth group is in the front, switch the assignment to again give an *R* stereocenter (eliminate choice A).

2. **C**   Choice A can be eliminated since loss of electrons (not a gain) is oxidation, and no electrons are gained during the reaction anyway. While a C=C double bond does disappear during the reaction, it is due to a reorganization of electrons to form a new ring, not because H$_2$ has been added to the π bond (eliminate choice B). Elimination reactions generally end with the formation of a π bond, not the removal of one (eliminate D). In organic chemistry, oxidation states can often be tied to the number of degrees of unsaturation in the molecule. In this instance, a π bond is replaced by a new ring, so the oxidation level of the molecule is unchanged.

3. **D**   The strength of an acid is determined by the stability of its conjugate base, so compare the enolates formed in each case to determine which is more stable. Just because a proton can be removed faster does not mean it produces the most stable enolate. Remember that kinetics and thermodynamics tell us different things about molecules, and eliminate choice C. Choices A and B both suggest that Compound 1 has a more stable enolate that forms

because of more resonance structures that help to stabilize charge, and the fact that more substituted double bonds are more stable. However, they both depend on the fact that the negative charge produced upon deprotonation of H_a can exist in a p orbital parallel to the π systems of the carbonyl and alkene. Because of the bridging carbons in the bicyclic molecule, the orbital cannot exist with the correct orientation, and therefore does not provide the resonance stabilization expected (eliminate choices A and B).

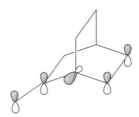

4. **B** Compounds 1 and 3 have the same molecular formulas, but their constituent atoms are connected differently, making them structural or constitutional isomers. Stereoisomers like geometric isomers, enantiomers, and diastereomers require the same connectivity of atoms but different orientations in space, and therefore choices A, C, and D can be eliminated.

5. **A** The starting material has a carbon-carbon double bond as well as a carbon-oxygen double bond. These molecules can be easily distinguished from each other since infrared spectroscopy is used specifically to identify functional groups. The spectrum of the product would be missing the C=C stretch at 1650 cm^{-1}. Mass spectroscopy would distinguish molecules that had different molecular weights, but isomers are not distinguishable in this way (eliminate choice B). UV-vis spectroscopy is used to identify conjugated π systems, but neither the starting material nor the product contains more than isolated double bonds (eliminate choice C). While gas chromatography would indicate the presence of two compounds, since they are both ketones, they are likely to have very little difference in their polarities and boiling points. Even though they might be separable by this method, it's not easy to predict their relative boiling points in order to distinguish between them (eliminate choice D).

6. **D** Degrees of unsaturation can be counted quickly when given the structure of a molecule since all rings and π bonds count as one degree of unsaturation each. Compound 2 has a total of three rings and one π bond, giving it four degrees of unsaturation. If using the formula: degrees of unsaturation = $((2n + 2) - x)/2$, where $n = 8$ (# of carbons) and $x = 10$ (# of hydrogens), then $((2 × 8) + 2 - 10) = 8$, and $8/2 = 4$.

7. **C** According to Figure 1, the di-π-methane rearrangement forms a cyclopropane ring with a double bond next to the ring. None of the three atoms in the ring are a part of the double bond, however, so choice D can be eliminated. In addition, since this is simply a rearrangement and no atoms are lost from the starting material while forming the product, by counting the carbons in (E)-4-methylhexa-1,4-diene, shown below (seven), and comparing to the remaining products, you can eliminate choice B since it only has six carbons.

Finally, by sketching out the diene in question and forming the new connections as described in Figure 1, two possible products can be formed depending on which double bond appears to do the 1,2-shift:

These structures indicate that the cyclopropane ring in the product should either have three substituents or one; choice A can be eliminated. Choice C is identical to the product shown from the first reaction above.

Solutions to Practice Passage 2

1. **C**   Benzene is electron rich with three C=C π-bonds. As such, the only behavior of the listed choices which makes sense is nucleophilic. In fact, aromatics like benzene, when treated with very strong electrophiles or other severe conditions (such as reformation), will act nucleophilically, adding substituents. Hydrogen is then eliminated from the ring restoring aromaticity. Choice A can be eliminated since Lewis acids are electron pair acceptors and electron deficient. Benzene is highly unlikely to donate a proton since the carbanion conjugate base would be highly unstable due to carbon's low electronegativity (eliminate choice B). With no highly electronegative atoms in the molecule, benzene cannot behave as an oxidizing agent (eliminate choice D).

2. **B**   The passage states that isooctane has the IUPAC name 2,2,4-trimethylpentane. The non-equivalent carbons are labeled in the structure below. Note that while the quaternary carbon has no hydrogen attached, it will still show up in the carbon spectrum. Be careful of choice A as a trap answer since there will be four signals in the 1H NMR spectrum.

3. **B**   This question asks about three variables that have the potential to impact octane rating, so in order to determine what effect each has, choose pairs or a series of molecules that only differ by one of these variables at a time. For example, by comparing only the straight chain alkanes, we can see that the higher the molecular weight, the lower the octane rating. Since Item II is false, eliminate choices C and D. Based on the remaining choices, Item I must be true. (Tertiary carbons indicate branching in a molecule, and between pairs of isomeric compounds with the *same* molecular weight such as *n*-heptane and 2-methylhexane, the more highly branched one has a higher octane.) Finally, rings and π-bonds are degrees of unsaturation, and aromatic compounds like benzene and toluene have both. When compared to the other 6 and 7 carbon hydrocarbons, respectively, aromatic compounds have a much higher octane rating (as the passage text suggests), while showing minimal changes in molecular weight. Similarly, comparing *n*-hexane and cyclohexane shows an increased rating, so even one unit of unsaturation appears to increase octane rating (eliminate choice A).

4. **A** The passage states that cracking is a process used to break large molecules into smaller ones by breaking a C—C bond, but with no change in the amount of hydrogen. The molecule in question, 3,5-diethyloctane (shown below) has a formula of $C_{12}H_{26}$ as a saturated compound.

The only pair of molecules that could be products of the reaction must therefore have a total of 12 carbons and 26 hydrogens. While choices B, C, and D look like possible fragments achieved from breaking the indicated bonds on the molecule below, since the carbons that were once connected must have their valences satisfied, one product must be an alkene if the other is an alkane, making choices B, C, and D incorrect.

5. **B** The formula for any carbohydrate is $C_nH_{2n}O_n$, or in the case of glucose, the building block of cellulose, $C_6H_{12}O_6$. The formula of HMF is $C_6H_6O_3$, so the reaction shows a net loss of six hydrogens and three oxygens, or three water molecules. This is therefore a dehydration reaction, a type of elimination.

In an oxidation, we'd expect more oxygen in the molecule, not less (eliminate choice A). An isomerism is incorrect since the molecules do not have the same molecular formulas (eliminate choice C). Hydrogenation would add H_2 to the molecule, but in this case H (and O) are removed (eliminate choice D).

6. **D** According to Table 1, when comparing isomeric compounds the more highly branched one will have a higher octane rating (eliminate choices B and C). The relationship between branching and boiling point, however, is an inverse one. As branching in a molecule increases, London dispersion forces between molecules weaken due to decreased surface area between molecules. Weaker intermolecular forces mean lower boiling points (eliminate choice A).

7. **C** A saturated hydrocarbon is one with a maximum number of hydrogen atoms in the molecule, and a formula of C_nH_{2n+2}. Both *n*-pentane and 2,2,4-trimethylpentane fit this formula, so choices A and D can be eliminated. Methyl*cyclo*hexane has one ring, giving it one unit of saturation. Toluene, with seven Cs, should have 2(7) + 2 = 16 hydrogens if saturated. Since it's aromatic, however, it has three double bonds and a ring, for a total of four degrees of saturation and only 8 hydrogens (eliminate choice B).

Solutions to Practice Passage 3

1. **B** It is apparent that large, bulky R groups favor the S_N2' pathway. Thus, choices A and D can be eliminated as they are smaller than the other two choices. A *t*-butyl group is larger near the carbon where chemistry is happening than is the cyclohexyl group, and because the ring structure prohibits rotation, it is in fact less sterically bulky than the *i*-propyl group at the carbon of interest. Choice B is the best option because it represents the largest steric bulk.

2. **A** Since the S_N2 mechanism is favored in reactions with small, unhindered dithianes, it gives the *thermodynamic* product (the product of lowest final energy). The S_N2' mechanism gives the *kinetic* product since the bulk of the dithiane prohibits the formation of the thermo-dynamic product. The reaction is run under cold conditions to utilize the large activation energy required to react bulky dithianes at the epoxide carbons and thus promote the for-mation of the kinetic product. With warmer temperatures there might be enough ambient energy to facilitate the S_N2 mechanism even with the bulky dithianes.

3. **D** Organometallic compounds, such as lithiated compounds or Grignard reagents, are very good nucleophiles. The use of *t*-butyllithium prevents nucleophilic chemistry thanks to the bulk of the *t*-butyl group around the anionic carbon. *n*-Butyllithium is just about as strong a base as *t*-butyllithium, so choice A can be eliminated. For this same reason choice C can be eliminated, because if deprotonation of the epoxide is an issue with *n*-butyllithium it would have been a problem with *t*-butyllithium. Two anions cannot undergo dimerization reactions, so choice B is eliminated.

4. **B** Silicon has a larger radius than does carbon. Thus, groups bound to the silicon atom will be, on average, at a greater distance to the anionic carbon than groups bound to a carbon. The silicon atom provides a "spacer" of sorts, between the carbon of interest and the steric bulk. Choice A is incorrect because it is the bulk of the nucleophile that plays the deciding role, and, one silicon bearing reagent in the table is shown to go through only the S_N2' pathway. Choice C is incorrect because hydrogen is more electronegative than silicon, and as such all H atoms bound to silicon are hydritic, not acidic. Choice D is incorrect because, as the pas-sage indicates, steric bulk near the carbanion favors S_N2'.

5. **C** Carbanions are better nucleophiles than oxyanions, so as long as the fast step is deproton-ation of the dithiane, the only substitution present should be attack of the lithiated dithiane on the epoxide. If the attack by the lithiated dithiane is faster than the deprotonation of the dithiane, one might expect a buildup of oxyanion in solution (prior to the acidification step). We know that oxyanions *can* and *do* attack epoxides (choice A is incorrect) so any buildup of oxyanion in the absence of the better carbanion nucleophile would surely produce ethers. Choice D is incorrect due to the fact that if ethers were unstable to *t*-butyllithium the reac-tion could not be run in THF, nor could the ether-like epoxide ring survive.

6. **A** The 1,4-Brook rearrangement can only take place when the organosilicon group is three carbons away from the hydroxyl. This necessitates the S_N2 mechanism, which means that we seek the smallest of the four choices. The smallest is choice A.

Solutions to Practice Passage 4

1. **A**   KOtBu is a Brønsted base and is used to form the benzyl anions for these reactions. Choice B can be eliminated because a Brønsted acid is a proton donor, but KOtBu has no protons to donate. Choice C can be eliminated because leaving groups are a part of a larger molecule in either substitutions or eliminations, while the reagent in this case is added to the reaction mix. Choice D can be eliminated because an electrophile is an electron pair acceptor and KOtBu is an electron pair donor.

2. **D**   According to the structure below, H^a is coupled to only H^b, which makes the splitting pattern for H^a a doublet according to the $n + 1$ rule. This allows us to eliminate choice A. Since H^b splits H^a, the converse must also be true. Therefore we can eliminate all answer choices where H^b is a singlet, in this case choice B. Since H^b is coupled to H^a and also H^c, a hydrogen not explicitly drawn in the question, the $n + 1$ rule predicts that the splitting pattern for H^b should be a doublet of doublets because H^b has two different neighboring hydrogens that both split the H^b signal, though not equally (so a triplet is not seen). Choice C is a trap answer if H^c was not recognized as being important.

3. **C**   The passage provides pK_a data for these four compounds. Remember that pK_a is a measure of acid strength; the greater the pK_a, the weaker the acid. Also remember that the weaker an acid is, the stronger its conjugate base will be. Therefore, of the four compounds, the weakest acid is 4c since it has the greatest pK_a value; it will have the strongest conjugate base.

4. **D**   UV-vis spectroscopy is useful to identify conjugated π systems (those with extended systems of alternating single and double bonds) that absorb light in the visible wavelength range (380-780 nm). Choices A and B can be eliminated because the passage shows that the electrophiles have conjugated systems. Choice C is incorrect because the passage indicates that the lmax for both electrophiles is within the visible wavelength range.

5. **B**   The passage indicates that the reaction is a conjugate addition, which means that the nucleophile adds to the end of an electrophilic conjugated π system (one that contains a carbonyl). This knowledge allows us to quickly eliminate choices A (which shows addition to the unfunctionalized benzene ring, a nucleophile) and D (which shows addition directly to the carbonyl carbon). It might appear that choice C would be the best choice since conjugate addition often refers to addition to the β-carbon of an α,β-unsaturated carbonyl compound. However, the conjugation in the electrophile actually extends to the delta (δ) carbon (α-β-γ-δ), and the nucleophile will add there instead. Choice B is the most stable product due to the formation of an aromatic ring upon addition.

6. **B** Item I is true. The CN group is electron withdrawing and stabilizes the benzyl anion by delocalizing charge across several atoms via π bond interactions (the definition of resonance). The more resonance structures a molecule has the more stable it is. This extra stability helps lower the pK_a of the compound (eliminate choice C).

Item II is also true. CF_3 is an electron-withdrawing group because fluorine is the most electronegative atom. The fluorine atoms pull electron density directly through the sigma bonds of the molecule (the definition of induction) and stabilize formation of the nucleophile, lowering the pK_a compared to 4c, the unsubstituted compound. Therefore, we can eliminate choice A. Item III is false. NO_2 is electron withdrawing (not donating), though it does stabilize nucleophile formation through resonance, and has similar resonance structures to the CN substituted compound.

Solutions to Practice Passage 5

1. **D** Since the OH group replaces the BH_2 group in the oxidation step of the reaction, the regioselectivity is determined in the first step of the mechanism. Since the BH_2 (or BRH or BR_2) groups are larger than the H, the four-center transition state is more stable if the bulkier groups add to the least substituted carbon of the double bond (labeled C2 in Figure 2). Since Item I is true, eliminate choice B. While it's true that the four-membered ring transition state forces the addition of the H and BR_2 groups to occur in a *syn* fashion, this determines stereochemistry, not which carbon of the double bond gets the larger group, and therefore has no connection to regiochemistry (eliminate choice C). Since the positive charge shown in the transition state is on the more substituted carbon of the double bond, and the more substituted a carbocation is the more stable it is, Item III is also a true statement (eliminate choice A).

2. **C** The passage states that the addition of water to alkynes occurs with anti-Markovnikov regiochemistry, so the OH group should add to the less substituted (terminal) carbon of the triple bond (eliminate choice A). Since the OH group replaces the BH_2 group during the oxidation step, these substituents should not be present on the same intermediate (eliminate choice D). Figures 2 and 3 show that the H and OH of the water equivalent add to the same face of the π bond (in a *syn* fashion), so should end up on the same side of the double bond in the intermediate enol that is formed (eliminate choice B). The correct enol intermediate (choice C) tautomerizes to form the more stable aldehyde product.

3. **B** The passage states that π bonds are nucleophilic unless they are substituted with electron-withdrawing groups. Bromine is relatively electronegative and pulls electron density away from the double bond in the alkenyl dibromide, thereby decreasing the rate of the addition of the nucleophilic π electrons to the second equivalent of Br_2. While Br is a large atom, the two Br atoms in the intermediate alkene are bonded to sp^2 hybridized, trigonal planar carbons of the double bond and have a minimal impact on the sterics of the reaction (eliminate choice A). Since the question asks about the rate of the addition reaction, both choices C and D can be eliminated since they attempt to justify the outcome using thermodynamic concepts.

4. **C** Choices A and B imply that the two ethyl groups in the molecule are different, thereby giving a total of four types of nonequivalent Hs in the molecule. However, the final product is symmetrical making both ethyl groups in the molecule identical (eliminate choice A and B). Therefore, there should be a total of two signals in the ^1H NMR spectrum, one for the CH_2 groups and one for the CH_3 groups. According to the $n + 1$ rule, the splitting pattern of the methylene signal should be split into four lines by the three neighboring Hs on the methyl group (eliminate choice D), and the methyl group signal should be split into three lines by the two neighboring Hs on the methylene group.

5. **B** The aldehyde in Figure 4 has two PD: α-hydrogens that can be exchanged with the deuterium isotope from the D_2O solvent. Only the Hs adjacent to the carbonyl are acidic and can do this exchange, so the β-hydrogens and the aldehyde hydrogen will remain as H (eliminate choices C and D). Since there are two α-hydrogens, both will eventually be replaced (eliminate choice A).

6. **A** As previously discussed, when water adds to the π bond of an alkyne an enol will be formed. While the enol in choice C is a possible intermediate along the hydration pathway of 2-pentyne, we know the keto form is more stable, and the passage indicates in Figure 4 that the carbonyl is the major product (eliminate choice C). The passage also states that terminal alkynes selectively produce aldehydes due to anti-Markovnikov addition of water to the triple bond. However, the two carbon atoms of an internal triple bond are equally substituted, so unless the alkyne is symmetrical, two possible ketone products will form instead of an aldehyde as the OH must add to a secondary carbon (eliminate choices B and D—note also that choice D only has four carbons).

7. **D** The product of the reaction has chiral centers and an internal mirror plane, making it a meso compound (see below). Meso compounds are not optically active, and are therefore not chiral (eliminate choice A). A racemic mixture cannot form in this instance since a meso compound is its own mirror image (eliminate choice B). The bromine atoms add in an *anti* fashion for this reaction, not a *syn* one, so choice C can be eliminated.

Solutions to Practice Passage 6

1. **C** The likely pathway for this reaction is for the nucleophilic N of the amine to attack the electrophilic C of the carbonyl in formaldehyde. In order for choice B to form, the nucleophilic nitrogen would be required to attack the nucleophilic oxygen. Since the question asks for an electrophilic intermediate, choice A should be eliminated since both the N and O atoms have lone electron pairs, and as such are reasonable nucleophiles instead. Choice D can be eliminated because it does not have the correct number of carbon atoms. Choice C is the best option since it has a positive charge making it a great electrophile, and shows a new C–N bond has formed.

2. **D** Since the fluoxetine compounds are enantiomers, they have the same thermodynamic energy state. Their different behavior *in vivo* is not due to thermodynamics, but to the chiral environment of a biological organism. Choices A, B and C can be eliminated because they make a connection between *in vivo* behavior and thermodynamics, which is false.

3. **C** In this reaction the chlorine atom is being substituted with the conjugate base of trifluoromethyl phenol. Since the nucleophilic atom is an O with a negative charge, this strong nucleophile is likely to attack the 2° C and kick out the good leaving group in a concerted mechanism. While both the starting material and products show a mixture of configurations at the site of substitution, this is because the reduction in Step 2 is not stereospecific. Since the starting Compound 3 was not chiral, we cannot know for sure that the stereocenter is racemized in Step 3, so choice A is not a conclusive answer. Choice B can be eliminated since in the presence of a strong base an elimination reaction (E2) is the likely

pathway, and if substitution occurs instead, OH⁻ is the stronger base, so we'd expect to see an alcohol as Product 4. Choice D can be eliminated since S_N2 reactions do not go through carbocation intermediates, even though should one form next to the benzene ring it would be very stable.

4. **C** The 1,4-addition of dimethylamine to the ketone shown in choice C will lead to Compound 2. A 1,4-addition requires a C=C in conjugation with a carbonyl, therefore choice B can be eliminated. Choice A can do a 1,4-addition, but the product will have an extra methyl group at the α position. Choice D can be eliminated because the product will have an extra methoxy group at the β-position.

5. **C** BH_3 is being used as a reducing agent since the product has fewer bonds to oxygen than the reactant. Choices B and D can be eliminated because they are common oxidizing agents, while choice A is a good Lewis acid, though not a redox reagent. Choice C can be recognized as a reducing agent since it still has several H atoms attached to an electropositive element (boron).

6. **D** The central carbon of CNBr is extremely electron deficient due to the electron withdrawing capacity of the adjacent nitrogen and bromine. This makes carbon have a partial positive charge and therefore act as an electrophile. Since the CN bond of the reagent gets attached in the product, the Br that has disappeared is the leaving group, so eliminate choice B. Choices A and C can be eliminated since they are the same and can't both be correct.

Solutions to Practice Passage 7

1. **B** Hemiacetals and acetals have the general formulas shown below; this shows that the functional group in the molecule is an acetal (eliminate choices A and D).

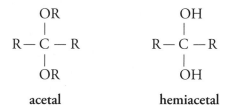

The acetal has two bonds to the six-membered ring, one of which is axial and the other equatorial (eliminate choice C). Ketones are more reactive than esters; therefore, if the ketone had been present during the Grignard addition, the Grignard reagent would have added there instead.

2. **C** Radicals are formed by homolytic bond cleavage (eliminate choice D). A phenyl radical is similar to a vinyl radical in that the unpaired electron is on a carbon of a double bond, which is unstable and cannot be stabilized by resonance (eliminate choices A and B). The radical must therefore be stabilized by the neighboring nitrogen to permit this otherwise unstable species to form (choice C is correct).

3. **B** Addition to the amide might result in a release of strain from breaking the ring; however, there is no such strain present in the ester (eliminate choice D). When comparing the possible leaving groups (−NR$_2$ or −OR), −OR is the better leaving group. Since oxygen is more electronegative than nitrogen, it can better stabilize a negative charge (eliminate choice C). Amides are less electrophilic at the carbonyl carbon for much the same reason—the two oxygen atoms surrounding the carbonyl carbon in an ester inductively withdraw more electron density from the carbon. In an amide, the less electronegative nitrogen is less inductively withdrawing, resulting in a smaller partial positive charge at the carbonyl carbon (choice A can be eliminated).

4. **A** Elimination of the OR group is not possible since there is no β hydrogen available for abstraction, so eliminate choice B. The enol form of a ketone is the less stable tautomer, so eliminate choice C. Neither amide is capable of forming an enol as neither has α protons (eliminate choice D). Loss of methanol, however, would give a stable, trisubstituted alkene.

5. **B** Knowing that this is an equilibrium reaction, using Le Chatelier's principle will help predict conditions that will favor the product. The formation of an acetal yields water as a product. Removal of a product forces an equilibrium reaction to the right, thereby increasing the yield. H$^+$ is a catalyst for the reaction; catalysts do not affect the equilibrium position of a reaction (eliminate choice A). Adding base would slow the reaction by neutralizing the catalyst, but again, would not affect the position of the equilibrium (eliminate choice C). Not knowing whether the reaction is exothermic or endothermic, it cannot be determined what effect cooling the reaction would have (eliminate choice D).

6. **B** Because the H and CH$_2$OR groups are on the top side of the ring system, that means the five and six membered rings are fused in a *cis* fashion. This leaves the bottom side of the five membered ring highly hindered sterically, as shown in the 3-D image of the molecule below.

If a nucleophile approached from the same side as the OR group (the opposite side of the ring system) there is much less steric hindrance. While it is true that S$_N$2 reactions have a predictable stereochemical outcome, they proceed with an inversion of stereochemistry. In this case, stereochemistry is maintained, so an S$_N$2 reaction could not have produced this diastereomer (eliminate choice A). Hydrogen bonds are formed between a hydrogen attached to F, O or N and a lone pair on F, O or N. There is therefore no possibility of a hydrogen bond to a sulfur atom (eliminate choice C). Resonance stabilization requires a π bond; the sulfur atom is attached through only a σ bond (eliminate choice D).

7. **C** Carbons with four different substituents are chiral. The chiral centers of gelsemine are marked in the structure below.

Solutions to Practice Passage 8

1. **B** Although toluene is the common name for a benzene ring with a single methyl group, it is not part of IUPAC nomenclature, and therefore choices C and D may be eliminated. For molecules with multiple substituents, the name should list the substituents in alphabetical order. Therefore, the methyl group should be listed before the nitro groups, and choice B is a better answer than choice A.

2. **A** The passage states that GC separates molecules based on their volatility, and that molecules with greater volatility are eluted faster. In general, molecules with stronger intermolecular forces are less volatile. It is easiest to compare intermolecular forces among molecules with the greatest structural similarities. Among these three molecules, TNT and N-methylpicramide are the most similar, since they are both benzene derivatives and differ only by a secondary amine present on N-methylpicramide but not on TNT. Since this amine is capable of hydrogen bonding and is more polar than the methyl group on TNT, N-methylpicramide is likely to have greater intermolecular forces than TNT, and therefore be less volatile. This means that TNT should elute before N-methylpicramide. The only answer choice in which this is true is A.

3. **D** The passage states that in order for a molecule to be effectively separated via GC, it must not decompose upon heating. By definition, explosives are highly unstable materials that are often triggered by exposure to heat, therefore it is extremely likely that upon heating they will decompose, making choice D the best answer. Tetryl cannot hydrogen bond, as N-methylpicramide can, therefore if N-methylpicramide is not too polar to be eluted from the GC column, it is unlikely that tetryl is (eliminate choice B). Tetryl is also not significantly larger than the other compounds, and is certainly not at the upper limit of the molecular weights that can be detected by mass spectrometry, which can be used to detect much larger molecules such as proteins, as mentioned in the passage (eliminate choice A). The passage also points out that one of the advantages of GC-MS over traditional GC is that if molecules coelute, they can still be distinguished based on differences in mass. Since RDX and tetryl have different molecular weights, even if they were coeluted from the GC they could still be individually detected via MS (eliminate choice C).

4. **A** The passage states molecules that are more volatile will elute from the GC column faster. As temperature is increased, the analyte molecules on the column spend more time in the gas phase. This allows them to be carried further by the mobile phase, and results in faster elution times. This eliminates choices B and D. However, as the molecules spend more time in the gas phase, they go through fewer evaporation/condensation cycles. This results in less separation between molecules with different volatilities, since there are fewer opportunities for each gas to partition between the liquid and gas phases. Therefore, choice A is the best answer.

5. **C** As shown in Reaction 1, M is ionized as it picks up an H^+ from the reagent gas, CH_4, to become $[M + H]^+$. If CD_4 were used instead of CH_4^+, M would pick up a D^+ rather than an H^+, and become $[M + D]^+$. Since H has an atomic weight of 1 and D (deuterium) has an atomic weight of 2, $[M + D]^+$ should have an *m/z* that is one higher than $[M + H]^+$.

6. **C** The gases as listed are actually the conjugate bases of the reagent gases in their acidic form. As shown in Reaction 1, these gases gain an H^+ in Step b) and then act as acids in Step c) to donate an H^+ to the analyte molecule, M. All of the gases listed are very unstable in their protonated form, making them very strong acids, with the exception of C, NH_3, whose conjugate is a weak acid, NH_4^+. Therefore, NH_3 is the least likely to result in the fragmentation pattern characteristic of a strong acid reagent gas. Another way to view this problem is by using a "one of these things is not like the other," strategy, since NH_3 is the only base on the list. This is valid, since the conjugate of a strong acid has no basic properties, whereas the conjugate of a weak acid is a weak base.

Solutions to Practice Passage 9

1. **C** While the liver makes more than one change to the structure of cholesterol to create a bile acid, the biggest change is the incorporation of a new carboxylic acid group, which contains three new bonds to oxygen atoms. More oxygen in the molecule constitutes an oxidation. In an elimination, we'd expect to see the creation of more π bonds in the molecule, so choice A can be discounted. Dehydration is the removal of water from a molecule, and is a type of elimination reaction, so choice D can also be ignored. Saponification is another way to describe the basic hydrolysis of ester bonds, typically in a triglyceride. This makes choice B incorrect.

2. **D** Attack this ranking problem by looking for an extreme and eliminating answer choices as you go. The least soluble compound in water would have the fewest polar functional groups. In this case cholesterol has only one OH group, so eliminate choices A and C. By looking at the other extreme of the remaining two choices, Compound 2 has three OH groups and a COOH group to help dissolve it in water, while Compound 4 has the additional sulfonic acid group because of the addition of the taurine adduct. This extra functional group makes choice D the best answer.

3. **C**   Salts are charged, making them water soluble or hydrophilic; Item II is false (choices B and D can be eliminated). By looking at the remaining choices, Item I must be true, so focus on Item III to answer the question quickly. The passage states that pancreatic secretions contain bicarbonate, a base, which raises the pH of the small intestine. High pH means a high concentration of OH^- is present to deprotonate the bile acid, yielding its charged conjugate base. Since Item III is a true statement, choice C is the best answer. To address Item I, the pK_a of the carboxyl group of an amino acid like glycine is about 2 (and the sulfonic acid of taurine is even more acidic), while the pH of the small intestine is greater than 7. When the pK_a of a functional group is smaller than the environmental pH, the group will exist in its deprotonated or charged form. This confirms Item I as true.

4. **B**   Chiral centers are carbons with four different substituents attached, so these carbons must have sp^3 hybridization. Good places to look in a complicated ring system like a steroid are at all the ring junctures. The chiral centers in cholesterol are indicated in the structure below.

5. **B**   According to the passage, lipase is an enzyme that breaks down fats, or triglycerides, which contain three ester functional groups. Amides are the functional groups present in proteins so eliminate choice A, hemiacetals are present in sugars (eliminate choice D), and ethers are not largely important functional groups in any biologically important molecules (eliminate choice C).

6. **A**   Compare the structure of cysteine given in the question to the structure of taurine, which can be deduced from the structure of taurocholic acid given in the passage.

cysteine   taurine

The amino group is still present in taurine and has been coupled to the carboxyl group of the bile acid to form a new amide bond (eliminate choices B and D). The thiol group in cysteine cannot be reduced anymore, but has instead been highly oxidized with the addition of five bonds to oxygen in order to form taurine (eliminate choice C). By process of elimination, decarboxylation must have taken place. The COOH group of the amino acid has been lost since no carbonyl group is present in the new substituent of Compound 4 in the passage.

NOTES